TWIN CITIES GUIDE

Sixth Edition, 1982

Compiled and Edited by Laurie A. Morse

db

DORN BOOKS
A Division of Dorn Communications, Inc.
Edina, Minn.

Published by Dorn Books,
a division of Dorn Communications, Inc.,
7101 York Av. S., Edina, Minn. 55435

Printed in the United States of America
at Viking Press, Inc., Eden Prairie, Minn.

ISBN 0-934070-07-5

Book design: Mark Wilken
Cover photograph and design: Mark Wilken

Photo credits: Minnesota Dept. of Transportation Communication Office, page 10; Minneapolis Convention & Tourism Commission, pages 13, 40; Olof Kallstrom, page 19; Forest J. Sorenson, page 28; Jim Majerus, pages 51, 283, 301, 322; Sally French, Metropolitan Council, pages 61, 278; Joe Twohy, White Bear Press, page 79; General Mills, Inc., page 109; Tom Foley, University of Minnesota, page 141; Hyatt Regency Hotel, page 148; L'hotel Sofitel, page 152; Thoen Photography, Naegele Restaurants, page 169; Radisson Hotels, page 176; Leamington Hotel, page 185; George Heinrich, Children's Theatre Company, page 213; M. Andrew, Minnesota Dance Theatre, page 226; St. Paul Chamber Orchestra, page 231; Minneapolis Institute of Arts, page 238; St. Paul Area Chamber of Commerce, page 255; Minnesota Zoo, page 266; South St. Paul Rodeo, page 275; Minnesota Kicks, page 310; Minnesota Twins, page 312; Sally Fefrecoren, Ridgedale Center, page 326; Gabbert & Beck, page 332; Saari & Forrai, page 352; Don Getsug, page 388; United Way of Minneapolis, pages 394, 403.

Table of Contents

Maps and Diagrams

EMERGENCY TELEPHONE NUMBERS

	Minneapolis Area	St. Paul Area
Ambulance	348-2345	224-7371
Alcohol Detoxification Center	347-6111	298-5951
Battered Women	827-2841	227-8284
Child Abuse	348-3552	291-6795
Crisis Center	347-3161	347-3161
Fire	348-2345	224-7371
First Call for Help (24-hour information)	340-7431	340-7431
Gas Emergency	372-5050	221-4411
Highway Emergency	541-9411	425-3246
Poison Center	347-3141	221-2113
Police	348-2345	291-1234
Suicide Prevention	347-2222	347-2222

For emergency numbers of suburban communities, check the inside front cover of your telephone directory. Police, fire, and ambulance emergency numbers are different in each city. Immediate response by the correct agency requires that you call the department that serves the city you live in.

TRAVELER'S INFORMATION

Minneapolis Chamber of Commerce	348-4330
St. Paul Chamber of Commerce	222-5561
Minnesota Department of Tourism	296-5029
Minnesota International Center	373-3200
Interpreters Network	1 (800) 255-3050
Road Conditions	296-3076
Highway Emergency (Eastern Metro)	425-3246
(Western Metro)	541-9411

GENERAL INFORMATION

Arts Resource and Information Center	870-3131
First Call for Help	340-7431
Happenings Line	224-9665
Library Reference Service	(Minneapolis) 830-4933
	(St. Paul) 292-6307
Outdoor Line (20-cent charge)	1-976-4444
Pollen Count	633-6698
Road Condition Report	296-3076
Sports (20-cent charge)	1-976-1313
Star Watch	376-5587
Tel-Law	222-5297
Tel-Med	721-7575
Time and Temperature	874-8700
Weather (20-cent charge)	1-976-1212
Zip Code Information	827-7733

CITIZEN COMPLAINT AND INFORMATION NUMBERS

	Minneapolis Area	St. Paul Area
Air Quality	663-6698	663-6698
Airport Noise	726-9411	726-9411
Animal Complaints	348-4250	292-6600
Consumer Fraud	296-2331	296-2331
Discrimination	296-5663	298-4288
Dutch Elm Reports	822-2126	488-7291
Minneapolis Mayor's Office	348-2100	———
Mosquito Control	645-3051	645-3051
Parking Tickets	348-2040	298-5212
St. Paul City Complaint Office	———	298-4747
Snow-Emergency Information	348-2487	298-4321
Snowplowing	348-2471	292-6600
Senior Citizen Services	296-2770	291-8323
State Income Tax Information	296-3781	296-3781

INTRODUCTION

The *Twin Cities Guide* is designed to present a maximum amount of information to help you enjoy life in the Twin Cities, whether you are here for a weekend or for a lifetime. The information included in this book represents as rich a variety of attractions and establishments as possible. No matter what your age, your interests, or your budget, there are things in the *Twin Cities Guide* for you.

The Twin Cities metropolitan area is changing rapidly—shops come and go, new restaurants open, programs are added or expanded. Even favorite establishments with long histories and lofty reputations occasionally change locations, revise menus, or shift their manner of service or decor. Keeping track of these changes has been our job over the course of six editions. We hope you find the new information useful.

Guidebooks are generally designed with visitors and newcomers in mind, providing basic information on attractions and entertainment. The *Twin Cities Guide* does all that. New residents will find information on such basics as registering to vote and getting a driver's license, as well as descriptions of our residential neighborhoods and suburbs, particularly helpful. Visitors will find this book serves a variety of their needs, too, supplying information on everything from restaurants and shopping spots to how to find one's way through our skyway systems. This *Guide,* however, goes beyond the basics. In a large sense, it is written for the Twin Citian who *loves* the Twin Cities. *Twin Cities Guide* explores Minneapolis, St. Paul, and the surrounding suburbs, pointing out attractions and opportunities many residents haven't had the chance to discover on their own.

This book is not limited to listings of restaurants and stores. It contains descriptions of neighborhoods, community services, recreational opportunities, historic sites, annual events, and much more. It is, we believe, the most comprehensive source of information on Twin Cities arts organizations available. To make the guide even more useful, we've included sources where readers can obtain additional information on a great number of topics, either by mail or by phone. Arts and sports enthusiasts will appreciate the addition this year of seating diagrams for major Twin Cities theaters, arenas, and auditoriums. The addition of locator symbols should make geographic placement of the listings easier for readers.

The *Twin Cities Guide* is designed to be kept and used for reference throughout the year. This edition's compact, handier-to-use format lends itself to being stored in glove compartments and handbags for spur-of-the-moment ideas on where to shop and dine, or where to go for an afternoon outing. A second copy next to the telephone at your home or office is a must.

We hope you enjoy this book, and we'd enjoy hearing from you. Please mail your comments or suggestions—including those for new listings or deletions in our next edition—to: *Twin Cities Guide,* Dorn Communications, Inc., 7101 York Av. S., Edina, MN 55435.

HOW TO USE THIS BOOK

Material in this edition of the *Twin Cities Guide* was compiled during the spring and summer of 1981. Every attempt has been made to insure accurate, up-to-date information. However, because shops, restaurants, and other establishments change their policies and hours frequently, readers are advised to call ahead before making final plans. We should also point out that a listing is not necessarily a recommendation, although we have tried to list attractions with reputations for quality, uniqueness, and popularity, while including establishments appealing to a wide variety of tastes.

To get the most out of the *Twin Cities Guide,* we suggest that you use it in conjunction with a detailed street map of the metropolitan area. For easy geographic reference, a numerical locator symbol has been included with the address of most listings in the book. Each locator number corresponds to a section of the metropolitan area, which we have divided into 12 parts. A map of these sections and their corresponding numbers can be found on pages 8-9. The *Guide* is fully indexed to provide quick access to its thousands of listings.

ACKNOWLEDGMENTS

We wish to thank all the public and private agencies and individual businesses that provided information and assistance. Special thanks to the Metropolitan Council, the Minneapolis Planning Department, the St. Paul Planning Division, the Arts Resource and Information Center, and the Minneapolis and St. Paul public libraries.

Your steadfast help has made this book possible.
—*The Editors*

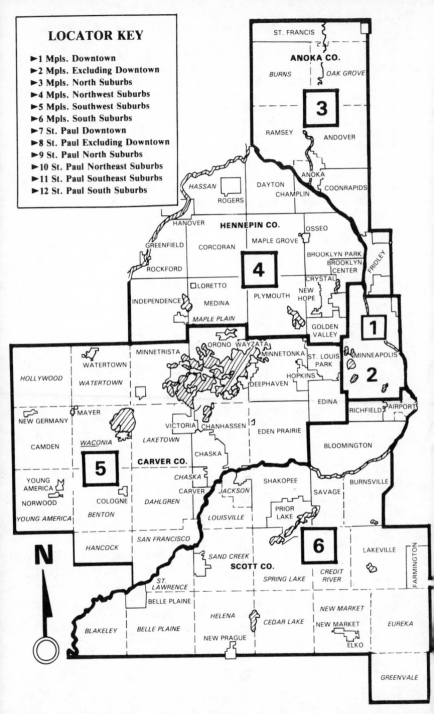

LOCATOR KEY

▶1 Mpls. Downtown
▶2 Mpls. Excluding Downtown
▶3 Mpls. North Suburbs
▶4 Mpls. Northwest Suburbs
▶5 Mpls. Southwest Suburbs
▶6 Mpls. South Suburbs
▶7 St. Paul Downtown
▶8 St. Paul Excluding Downtown
▶9 St. Paul North Suburbs
▶10 St. Paul Northeast Suburbs
▶11 St. Paul Southeast Suburbs
▶12 St. Paul South Suburbs

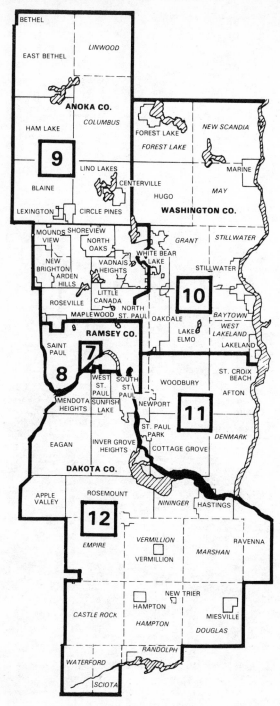

BETHEL

EAST BETHEL

LINWOOD

ANOKA CO.

COLUMBUS

HAM LAKE

9

BLAINE

LINO LAKES

LEXINGTON

CIRCLE PINES

CENTERVILLE

HUGO

FOREST LAKE

FOREST LAKE

NEW SCANDIA

MARINE

MAY

WASHINGTON CO.

MOUNDS VIEW

SHOREVIEW

NORTH OAKS

WHITE BEAR LAKE

GRANT

STILLWATER

NEW BRIGHTON

VADNAIS HEIGHTS

ARDEN HILLS

LITTLE CANADA

ROSEVILLE

MAPLEWOOD

NORTH ST. PAUL

OAKDALE

STILLWATER

BAYTOWN

WEST LAKELAND

LAKE ELMO

RAMSEY CO.

10

SAINT PAUL

7

8

WEST ST. PAUL

SOUTH ST. PAUL

MENDOTA HEIGHTS

SUNFISH LAKE

NEWPORT

WOODBURY

LAKELAND

ST. CROIX BEACH

AFTON

11

EAGAN

INVER GROVE HEIGHTS

ST. PAUL PARK

COTTAGE GROVE

DENMARK

DAKOTA CO.

APPLE VALLEY

ROSEMOUNT

NININGER

HASTINGS

12

EMPIRE

VERMILLION

VERMILLION

MARSHAN

RAVENNA

CASTLE ROCK

HAMPTON

NEW TRIER

HAMPTON

MIESVILLE

DOUGLAS

RANDOLPH

WATERFORD

SCIOTA

9

Into downtown Minneapolis from the south.

Chapter One

THE BASICS

DEFINING THE METRO AREA

The state of Minnesota has designated a Twin Cities planning region of seven counties: Anoka, Carver, Dakota, Hennepin, Ramsey, Scott, and Washington. For most purposes this is considered to be the metropolitan area, although the federal government adds two counties in Minnesota and one in Wisconsin to form the Standard Metropolitan Statistical Area for Minneapolis-St. Paul. With just over two million people, the 10-county Twin Cities area ranked 16th among the nation's metropolitan areas in population according to the 1980 census.

Located south and east of the center of Minnesota, the seven-county metropolitan area measures 65 miles from northern Anoka County to southern Dakota County, and 60 miles from the Washington County-Wisconsin border to western Carver County. At the heart of the region is what urban planners call the "contiguous urban area"—Minneapolis, St. Paul, and adjacent suburbs. But much outlying countryside lies within the seven-county area, and the Metropolitan Council, the main regional planning agency, has designated 14 small towns as "freestanding growth areas"* within the region.

The Metropolitan Council has estimated the population of the seven-county area at 1,985,705, roughly half the total for the state of Minnesota, as of April 1, 1980. Some 641,181 people, one third of the area's total, live in Minneapolis or St. Paul. The council expects modest population gains to replace steady losses by the two central cities during the remainder of this century, but even then Minneapolis and St. Paul will have considerably fewer residents than they did at their peaks—Minneapolis, 521,718 in the 1950 census; St. Paul, 313,411 in the 1960 census. Growth in the region will be concentrated along the outer edges of the already developed suburban ring, according to council projections.

---

*Anoka, Belle Plaine, Chaska, Farmington, Forest Lake, Hastings, Jordan, Lakeville, New Prague, Prior Lake, Rosemount, Shakopee, Stillwater, and Waconia.

THE PEOPLE

Contrary to popular belief, Twin Citians represent a wide variety of religions and national backgrounds. The reason this variety isn't generally recognized is that except for the Catholic and Lutheran religions and Scandinavian, German, and Irish nationalities, the number in each group is relatively small.

According to 1980 census figures, the almost two-million people in the seven-county area included 49,964 blacks, 21,866 Hispanics, 15,665 American Indians, and 39,005 classified by the census as "other," mostly Asian-Americans. It is widely believed, however, that the census undercounted blacks and other minorities. The number of Asian-Americans in the Twin Cities has increased considerably in the past couple of years with the resettlement of southeast Asian refugees.

ORIGINS

Minneapolis and St. Paul grew up side-by-side as river towns on what was considered America's western frontier in the mid-19th century. St. Paul is the older of the two cities, having been a more immediate offspring of the Fort Snelling military outpost. Minneapolis was a product of the development of St. Anthony Falls as a milling center, and it eventually

Populations of metro-area counties as of April 1, 1980

Anoka	195,998
Carver	37,046
Dakota	194,111
Hennepin	941,411
Ramsey	459,784
Scott	43,784
Washington	113,571
Seven-county total	1,985,705
Chisago	25,717
St. Croix (Wis.)	43,872
Wright	58,962
Ten-county total	2,114,256

SOURCE: Metropolitan Council

Population for the seven-county area and for Minneapolis and St. Paul

	Population April 1, 1980	Projected population 1990	Projected population 2000
Seven-county area	1,985,705	2,261,000	2,471,000
Minneapolis	370,951	375,000	380,000
St. Paul	270,230	270,000	275,000

SOURCE: Metropolitan Council

surpassed St. Paul in population. St. Paul was established as the capital when Minnesota attained statehood in 1858. It retains its role as the state's government center.

The site that was to become the Twin Cities was first seen by a European in 1680, a full two years before Sir Isaac Newton outlined his law of gravity, and a year before William Penn and his Quaker followers set out to found Pennsylvania. Father Louis Hennepin, a Flemish friar who had been traveling with French explorers, was captured by Indians and led to a camp on Mille Lacs Lake in central Minnesota. En route, he witnessed the cascade of the Mississippi near where Minneapolis is today, and named it St. Anthony Falls. Hennepin was eventually rescued, and French explorers soon claimed the falls and the surrounding countryside for the glory of France.

White settlement of the area didn't begin until almost 150 years later, when Fort St. Anthony (later renamed Fort Snelling) was built at the confluence of the Minnesota and Mississippi rivers. The site of the fort had been purchased from the Indians in 1805, when Zebulon Pike was exploring the Louisiana Purchase for the U.S. government.

Early civilian settlers around the fort were mostly French Catholic traders. One of these, a colorful bootlegger named Pierre "Pig's Eye" Parrant, settled on the site of what was to become the city of St. Paul. The settlement was called Pig's Eye until it was officially incorporated in 1849 and renamed St. Paul in honor of the Chapel of St. Paul, a log church Father Lucian Galtier had built there in 1841.

Minneapolis began as the village of St. Anthony, a milling center on the Mississippi's east bank

Downtown Minneapolis and one of its several skyways.

near St. Anthony Falls. Flour- and lumber-milling operations eventually spilled over to the west bank of the river, and a local newspaper held a contest to name the west-bank settlement. The winning entry, submitted by St. Anthony schoolteacher Charles Hoag, was Minneapolis, a combination of the Sioux word for water and the Greek word for city. In 1853 Minneapolis was officially incorporated, and the village of St. Anthony became part of the new city.

THE WEATHER

Weather isn't just a topic of idle conversation to many Twin Citians—it's an obsession. The area's climatic extremes and frequent changes in weather, and such stultifying controversies as whether it's the heat or the humidity, give people plenty to talk about while steering clear of politics and religion.

Natives who cherish Minnesota's variety of meteorological phenomena refer to "the theater of seasons." Newcomers arriving between Thanksgiving and Easter might call it "the theater of the absurd." The average daily high temperature in January is 21.2 °F, the low 3.2 °F.* The words "above" and "below" (zero) are regular parts of winter weather reports.

Folk wisdom credits the area's climate with keeping out "unde-

---

*The National Weather Service official who provided this information added that it could be misleading because "we very seldom see any so-called average weather" in the Twin Cities.

sirables" through natural selection. Actually, almost anyone can get through a Minnesota winter. Those determined to take advantage of the season's unique recreational opportunities—skiing, skating, snowmobiling—rather than passively ride it out seem to enjoy it most. A February trip to Hawaii also can help.

If less is said about the area's summers than its winters, maybe it's because the natives want to keep the former for themselves. The average daily high during July, the warmest month, is 82.4 °F, and the late sunsets allow golfing, tennis-playing, and fishing well into summer evenings. The average daily low during July is 61.4 °F. Although actual temperatures vary considerably from these norms, temperatures drop enough most summer nights to provide "good sleeping weather" with scant need for air conditioning.

Heating degree days and wind chill are helpful measures of different aspects of cold. Heating degree days indicate both relative building heating requirements and cumulative cold. Wind chill indicates how cold the combination of wind and temperature feels to exposed skin.

To hear a 24-hour weather information tape, call (1) 976-1212. (There's a 20-cent charge.)

To hear a free four-minute tape describing current astronomical phenomena, call Minnesota Starwatch, 376-5587. The tape is updated every two weeks.

Severe Weather

The Twin Cities is situated in an

area that is vulnerable to thunderstorms, hail, and occasional tornados during the spring and summer months. When tornados occur, they generally touch down in the outlying sections of the seven-county area, skirting the more heavily populated urban centers.

Twin Cities Weather Statistics

All-time high temperature:
108 °F set July 14, 1936

All-time low temperature:
−34 °F set Jan. 22, 1936, tied Jan. 19, 1970

Average annual precipitation:
25.94 inches (liquid)

Average snowfall per season:
46.3 inches

Average date of first freeze:
Oct. 13

Average date of last freeze:
April 29

Earliest freeze:
Sept. 3, 1974

Latest freeze:
May 24, 1925

Average temperatures by month (°F):
Jan., 12.2; Feb., 16.5; March, 28.3; April, 45.1; May, 57; June, 66.9; July, 71.9; Aug., 70.2; Sept., 60; Oct., 50; Nov., 32.4; Dec., 18.6

SOURCE: National Weather Service

The cities of Minneapolis and St. Paul have been struck by tornados five times in the last 100 years—most recently on June 14, 1981. That tornado cut a diagonal path through the cities, felling trees and causing significant damage in portions of Edina, south Minneapolis, and the Roseville area on the north edge of St. Paul. Two fatalities resulted from that storm.

Civil defense sirens are sounded if a tornado has been *sighted* in the metropolitan region. If you hear these sirens, *take cover immediately*. Don't pause to close windows, pack food, or bring in the wash. Go directly to the basement of your home or place of business, or to an area on a lower floor away from windows. If you are caught outdoors during a tornado, take cover in a ditch or other low-lying area.

If threatening weather is expected, local radio and television stations issue frequent weather bulletins. These bulletins may include a severe thunderstorm or tornado *watch*. A *watch* means that conditions are right for these storms to occur. A tornado *warning* is issued when a funnel cloud has been sighted in the region. If a tornado *warning* is issued, you should take cover and remain there until the media report that an all-clear signal has been given.

Weatherball Watching

Digital time and temperature displays are common on commercial buildings around the country, and the Twin Cities has its share. However, old-timers in the area remember when the Northwestern Weatherball was the only visual weather indicator in town. North-western National Bank has incorporated 16 weatherballs into signs on the offices of its affiliates. These balls, usually visible at quite a distance, change color to indicate forecast changes in the weather. The color code is as follows: red—warm weather predicted; white—cold weather predicted; green—no change. If the weatherball is blinking, rain or snow is expected.

COST OF LIVING

According to the U.S. Bureau of Labor Statistics, the cost of living for a family of four in the Twin Cities was slightly less than the national average in 1980. In a survey of living costs in 24 American cities, Minneapolis-St. Paul ranked 17th, along with Houston and Kansas City. Minnesota State Planning Agency figures for 1978 (the latest available) show that median incomes in most of our metropolitan counties were slightly above the national median for that year.

Median income of two-parent families, by county, 1978	
Anoka	$22,259
Carver	19,722
Dakota	23,302
Hennepin	22,609
Ramsey	21,262
Scott	21,275
Washington	23,255
SOURCE: State Planning Agency	

PAYING THE PIPER

Sales Tax

The Minnesota sales tax was boosted from four to five percent in July 1981. This means that consumers now pay five cents in tax for every dollar spent on goods in the state. Heating fuel, clothing, shelter expenses (such as rent), and food to be cooked at home are exempt from the sales tax. Restaurant meals and hotel or motel expenses are taxable.

State Income Tax

Minnesota ranks among the top 10 states in the nation in terms of personal income taxes. For detailed information about the state income tax, call 296-3781.

Minnesota Homestead Property Tax Credit

Owner-occupied single-family homes in Minnesota are entitled to a property tax credit commonly referred to as a "homestead" credit. This credit can reduce your local property taxes by as much as 60 percent. To apply for the homestead credit, new home-owners must bring their deed or contract for deed to their city offices as soon after closing as possible and fill out a homestead form. Homeowners renew their homestead status by signing and returning the homestead form their city tax office mails to them once a year, in January. For complete information on the homestead credit, call your city property tax department, or contact a knowledgeable realtor.

REGISTERING TO VOTE

If you're a U.S. citizen at least 18 years old and have lived in Minnesota at least 20 days prior to an election, you're eligible to vote. Register at City Hall in Minneapolis or St. Paul, or at any Hennepin County Government Service Center up to 20 days before an election, or at the polls the day of the election. Bring identification showing your address or a registered neighbor to vouch for your residency. Re-registration is required every time you move.

REGISTERING YOUR CAR

If you own a motor vehicle, it must be registered within 60 days of your moving to Minnesota. Bring the title or, if there's a lien on the vehicle, the previous registration, and evidence you've obtained Minnesota no-fault insurance* to the Hennepin or Ramsey county courthouse or any Hennepin County Government Service Center. A binder from your insurance agent and the name of the company and date the policy was applied for will do.

The time of year you must register your car is determined alphabetically by your last name. If it's less than a year ahead, you will pay a pro-rated fraction of the annual registration fee for the initial registration.

Annual fees range from $12 to more than $200, depending on the value of the vehicle. Minnesota law does not require the inspection of motor vehicles.

GETTING A DRIVER'S LICENSE

You also must obtain a Minnesota driver's license within 60 days of moving into the state. This involves taking only a written test if you already hold a license from another state that requires a road test. License testing stations are listed in the telephone directory under "Minnesota State Offices—License Information." The minimum age for obtaining a license is 16 for those who have had approved driver's training, 18 for those who have not.

A basic driver's license costs $10 and must be renewed every four years and whenever the holder moves. Retesting is not required unless your license has been revoked. Licenses can be renewed at the Hennepin and Ramsey county courthouses, Hennepin County Government Service Centers, and Driver's License Testing stations and substations.

GETTING A LIBRARY CARD

Library cards are issued without charge by both the Minneapolis

---

*Under the state's partial no-fault system, each motorist is required to have the following minimum coverages: personal injury—$20,000 medical and rehabilitation expenses, and $10,000 nonmedical expenses; liability—$25,000 per person, $50,000 per accident, and $10,000 property damage; uninsured motorist—$25,000 per person and $50,000 per accident.

and St. Paul public libraries. To get one, just stop in the main library downtown, 300 Nicollet Mall in Minneapolis, 90 W. Fourth St. in St. Paul, or any of the 14 Minneapolis community libraries or 10 St. Paul branch libraries, and fill out a simple form. Minneapolis library cards are valid until the holder moves; St. Paul library cards must be renewed every two years.

Cards issued by the Minneapolis and St. Paul public libraries and most suburban libraries are honored at other libraries throughout the seven-county area participating in MELSA, the Metropolitan Library Service Agency.

The Minneapolis public libraries have a total of some 1.5 million books; the St. Paul libraries, more than one million. Neither figure includes periodicals, recordings, films, and other materials.

Hours of operation of community and branch libraries in Minneapolis and St. Paul vary, so it's best to call ahead. The Minneapolis central library is open 9 a.m. to 9 p.m. Monday through Thursday, and 9 a.m. to 5:30 p.m. Friday and Saturday from Labor Day through Memorial Day. The library is closed Saturdays during the summer. The St. Paul central library is open 9 a.m. to 9 p.m. Monday and Thursday, and 9 a.m. to 5:30 p.m. Tuesday, Wednesday, Friday, and Saturday. Closed Saturday during the summer.

DOG LICENSES

Dogs in both Minneapolis and St. Paul must be licensed, vaccinated, and kept in a fenced-in area or on a leash. Owners in both cities are required to clean up feces left by their animals on public property.

Licenses in Minneapolis are valid from January to January, and cost $3 for a spayed or neutered animal, $6 for others. This fee is expected to be raised to $6 and $10 in January 1982. Licenses may be obtained by visiting or writing City Hall. Licenses in St. Paul are valid from March to March, and may be obtained at City Hall or the dog pound at 1285 W. Jessamine Av. Applications are available at most St. Paul fire stations. St. Paul dog licenses cost $3, 50 cents for senior citizens.

Owners of dogs cited for running at large can be fined $25 in Minneapolis, $25-$100 in St. Paul.

The licensed dog populations of the cities are approximately 12,000 in Minneapolis, 7,000 in St. Paul.

TELEPHONE SERVICE

Minneapolis, St. Paul, and most of their suburbs are served by the Northwestern Bell Telephone Co. It wasn't always that way; the cities once had two telephone companies, and people in the Midway area had separate phones for Minneapolis and St. Paul.

To start telephone service, visit the nearest Phone Center Store listed in your telephone directory if your home has modular jacks; if not, call or visit the nearest Northwestern Bell business office listed in your directory. For customers with modular jacks, service generally becomes effective in about 48 hours, but during peak periods of late May through September it may take a week.

At this writing, the basic monthly charge for a single residential telephone line is $9.44 in Minneapolis and St. Paul, and slightly more than that in the surrounding suburban areas. The monthly rental fee for the least expensive (black, rotary dial) telephone is $1.50, making the total monthly charge for basic service and equipment $10.94. These rates are expected to increase in early 1982. A one-time service connection fee is charged to customers starting new phone service or changing the address of their present service. This fee begins at $27.75 (for people who pick up or move their own telephones and connect them themselves) and increases rapidly for service calls. These charges are expected to more than double if a pending rate increase is approved.

Twin Cities area telephone customers enjoy the third largest toll-free calling area in the country, behind only Los Angeles and Atlanta. A map of the 2,663-square-mile area appears in your directory. As of June 1981, 791,685 Twin Cities area telephone customers could reach one another without charge.

Under an experimental program that was expected to be renewed for this year, Twin Cities area telephone customers no longer have had unlimited use of local directory assistance (411). In return for giving up this privilege, they've been getting a 53-cent credit on each month's bill and five free local directory assistance

There's no place like home in the Twin Cities.

calls per month. Additional local directory assistance calls cost 20 cents each.

Other phone facts:

The Twin Cities area does *not* have a 911 emergency call system, but plans for one are in the works. Emergency numbers are listed in your directory.

Dial "1" before the area code and number when direct-dialing long-distance calls.

The Minneapolis white and yellow pages, the St. Paul directory, and directories for other Minnesota communities are available free at Phone Center Stores.

ELECTRIC SERVICE

If you've just moved to the Twin Cities area from the East Coast, where a lot of electricity is generated by burning costly oil, be prepared for a pleasant surprise when you open your first electric bill. But if nuclear power makes you uneasy, the money you'll be saving might not be worth it. Northern States Power Co. (NSP), which serves Minneapolis, St. Paul, and most suburbs, has nuclear power plants at nearby Monticello and Prairie Island. These plants were expected to generate 41 percent of the utility's power last year. Nationally, only about 11 percent of all power generated is nuclear.

Prior to a rate increase NSP filed last year, the typical 550-kilowatt-hour-per-month user paid $30.63 for that electricity during the summer, slightly less during the winter. The increase, if granted in full by state regulators, would increase the typical month-

ly summer bill to $33.97.

To start electric service in your home, call the nearest NSP division office or customer business office listed in your telephone directory.

For information about a wide variety of energy-related matters, call "Ask NSP" at 330-6000.

NATURAL GAS SERVICE

Natural gas service is provided in Minneapolis and most of its suburbs by the Minnesota Gas Co., better known as Minnegasco. Gas service is provided in St. Paul and most of its suburbs by Northern States Power Co. (NSP). Neither supplier has a moratorium on accepting new customers. Those moving into houses or apartments with metered gas service, or into new homes needing such service, should call their nearest Minnegasco or NSP office listed in the telephone directory.

As this was written, Minnegasco's residential customers were paying a minimum monthly bill of $3.50 for 300 cubic feet of gas or less used, 35.3 cents for the next 3,700 cubic feet, and 30.7 cents for each additional 100 cubic feet consumed over 4,000. NSP customers were paying 37.17 cents per 100 cubic feet regardless of how much they used, plus a $2 customer charge per month and adjustments for gas NSP purchased outside of normal channels. If gas is used for heating, there is no sales tax on the bills for November through April.

Minnegasco estimates its average heating customer was paying

$610 per year for gas, and an NSP customer would pay a similar amount. However, the supplier of gas to both Minnegasco and NSP has filed for a rate increase, and, if any part of it is approved, Twin Cities customers will be paying significantly more for gas.

WATER AND SEWAGE

Both Minneapolis and St. Paul have municipal water utilities, and the procedure for starting service is the same for both. Call 348-2433 in Minneapolis and 298-4267 in St. Paul to get a final reading for the former occupant of your home and to start the billing in your name. Virtually all apartment buildings have centralized billing with landlords paying for all water used.

The cost of water in Minneapolis is 65 cents per 100 cubic feet, plus 65 cents per 100 cubic feet for sewage. In St. Paul, the rates are 55 cents per 100 cubic feet for water plus a quarterly use fee of $2.80, and 84 cents per 100 cubic feet for sewage. However, in both cities the sewage bill for the year is based on winter water consumption, which is usually less, because much of the additional water used during the summer is not returned to the sewers.

Minneapolis, the City of Lakes, gets its drinking water from the Mississippi River. The intake and treatment plant are at 43rd Av. and Marshall St. N.E. in the suburb of Fridley. St. Paul gets its water from a chain of lakes north of the city and from the Mississippi. The treatment plant is at 1900 Rice St. Sewage from both cities is treated at the Metropolitan Waste Control Commission's major plant at Pig's Eye, southeast of downtown St. Paul.

DOCTORS, DENTISTS, HMOs

Choosing a doctor is never easy, but for people in the Twin Cities there's an additional element that makes the task even more difficult. An alternative to the traditional doctor-patient relationship, HMOs—health maintenance organizations—provide comprehensive medical services for some 350,000 people, 18 percent of the area's population.

Basically, an HMO is a private corporation that delivers medical care through an organized group of providers, either with clinics of its own or through contracted professionals in private practice. Members, their employers or both pre-pay for HMO services, which include everything from routine medical and dental checkups to hospitalization.

One advantage of HMOs is less paperwork and lower costs because the same organization is both insurer and provider. HMOs also tend to emphasize preventive services because they cost patients nothing extra and the HMO has financial incentives to reduce more costly treatment and hospitalization. The major disadvantage is that patients must use only the clinics or providers associated with their HMO.

Young families with a greater need for primary medical care may benefit from joining an HMO. People who have developed a close relationship with a particular doctor, those who need specialized care, and the elderly, who tend to be hospitalized relatively often, might do better under traditional insurance plans.

HMO membership is generally offered as an employee benefit. Only two of the seven Twin Cities HMOs offer individual memberships. Some employers offer a choice of HMO membership or health insurance, and some offer a choice among two or more HMOs.

Twin Cities HMOs:

Group Health Plan Inc.,* 2500 Como Av., St. Paul, 641-3100.

HMO Minnesota, 3535 Blue Cross Rd., St. Paul, 456-8433.

MedCenter Health Plan, 4951 Excelsior Blvd., St. Louis Park, 927-3185.

Nicollet-Eitel Health Plan, 7901 Xerxes Av. S, Minneapolis, 888-3350.

Physicians Health Plan, 510 Marquette Av., Suite 500, Minneapolis, 340-7800.

Coordinated Health Care, 258 University Av., St. Paul, 221-2091.

Share Health Plan,* 7920 Cedar Av., Minneapolis, 854-2377.

BANKS AND SAVINGS-AND-LOANS

For many years, "branch banking" was considered an obscene expression by rural-dominated Minnesota legislatures attuned to small-town bankers who feared

---

*HMOs offering individual membership.

being taken over by giants from the Twin Cities. Well, some rural banks have been taken over by bank holding companies based in the Twin Cities, and the legislature now allows *limited* branch banking. There are restrictions, however, and they could affect which financial institution gets your business.

Since 1977, Minnesota banks have been allowed two "detached facilities" within 25 miles of their main bank. In 1980, these branches were given the right to offer all services available at the main bank. In addition, a limited number of banking functions can be offered at electronic terminals, which are unrestricted in number and location.

The Twin Cities has two major bank holding corporations. First Bank System and Northwest Bancorporation. Although the banks owned by these corporations present common advertising images, they operate as separate banks. However, you might be able to use the electronic terminal at another bank in the same system as your own to withdraw cash from your checking account, to transfer money between checking and savings, or to make loan payments. If being able to bank at more than one location is important to you, ask about detached facilities and electronic terminals before deciding which bank to do business with.

Several Twin Cities financial institutions, mostly savings-and-loan associations, participate in a "Passcard" system that allows account holders to deposit and withdraw money at numerous stores throughout the area. Savings-and-loan associations are not affected by Minnesota's restrictions on branch banking. Banks, savings-and-loans, Minnesota's one mutual savings bank (the Farmers & Mechanics Savings Bank of Minneapolis), and credit unions offer a bewildering array of accounts, other services, and premiums. There are too many, and they change too often, to be listed here.

GLOSSARY OF TWIN CITIES TERMS

"If you want to know the subject, you have to know the vocabulary." That advice from a teacher we had in junior high school applies to cities and their people as well as to earth science. Much of what's unusual or important to know about the Twin Cities and Twin Citians can be summed up in a few words. Here they are:

AAtrex, et al.—TV commercials for products like AAtrex, Treflan, and (our favorite) Bigfoot Lorsban are aimed at farmers. The products are herbicides and insecticides (weed and bug killers). Welcome to the Midwest.

Aquatennial—Ten days of water sports and other festivities held in Minneapolis each July. The Mill City's summer answer to St. Paul's venerable Winter Carnival, held in late January.

Beer, 3.2—There are two kinds of beer in Minnesota: strong, which you get at a cocktail lounge or liquor store, and 3.2, which you get at a grocery store, restaurant with a beer and wine license, or 3.2 bar. The number is the per-

centage of alcohol in the beer.

Bites per minute—What Metropolitan Mosquito Control District officials use to measure the effectiveness of their spraying programs.

CDC—Short for Control Data Corp., a large Twin Cities-based computer firm.

City Center—A major new shopping, office, and hotel development under construction in the heart of downtown Minneapolis. It is expected to be completed in 1983.

Clean Indoor Air Act—This controversial Minnesota law forbids smoking in public buildings except in designated smoking areas. Restaurants are required to have separate sections reserved for smokers and non-smokers.

Come with—Minnesotans often drop the object of the preposition.

The Crosstown—County Hwy. 62, an east-west commuting route that runs along the southern edge of Minneapolis, from the Mississippi River to suburban Minnetonka.

DFL—The letters stand for Democratic-Farmer-Labor, the name of the Democratic Party in Minnesota. The Farmer-Labor Coalition was a separate, progressive group whose merger with the Democrats in the 1940s was engineered by Hubert Humphrey.

The Dales—These are some major suburban shopping centers: Brookdale, Ridgedale, Rosedale, and Southdale. They have inspired take-offs such as Dinkydale, a one-building shopping arcade in the Dinkytown business district near the University of Minnesota's Minneapolis campus.

The Dome—A publicly financed and therefore controversial domed stadium is being built in downtown Minneapolis. This spring (1982) it will replace Metropolitan Stadium in Bloomington, where the Twins, Kicks, and Vikings have played since their respective inceptions.

East Bank, West Bank—Although the Mississippi River is part of the border between Minneapolis and St. Paul, parts of both cities are found on both sides of the river. East Bank and West Bank generally refer to parts of the University of Minnesota's Minneapolis campus and surrounding areas.

Edina—This upper-middle-class southwest Minneapolis suburb represents the American Dream, Twin Cities style.

Elevators—In addition to those in buildings, the Twin Cities has numerous grain elevators—concrete monoliths in which wheat and corn are stored.

Fridley—The opposite of Edina in image, this suburb is an extension of blue-collar "Nordeast" Minneapolis.

Frogtown—No one knows for sure whether St. Paul's Thomas-Dale neighborhood got its nickname from the original animal inhabitants of its once-swampy land or from the French-Canadian heritage of its early human settlers.

Geese—Those large, hungry birds that frequent Lake of the Isles, often in great numbers.

Hennepin Av.—Once the heart of downtown Minneapolis, Hennepin Av. has become the 42nd St. of the Upper Midwest, a tawdry strip of bars, fast-food outlets, and movie theaters cruised by pimps, prostitutes, street preachers, and lots of people with nothing to do. City officials hope recent renovations and redevelopment in progress along Hennepin will improve the avenue without quite sanitizing it.

Heron rookeries—Located near Pig's Eye Lake close to downtown St. Paul. Some environmentalists feel the nesting area will be endangered by plans to expand river barge operations in the area.

Hook echo—An image on weather radar that indicates a tornado may be present—a term often heard during summer storm reports.

Humidity—Along with the heat, humidity is a favorite topic of summer conversation and controversy; as in, "It's not the heat, it's the humidity...."

Independent-Republicans—Minnesota Republicans recently adopted this name in hope of appealing to the state's many independent voters.

Ish—An expression of disgust.

Kenwood—This neighborhood of large older homes near Lake of the Isles is the inner-city Minneapolis version of Edina: a fashionable place to live. Crocus Hill is the St. Paul equivalent.

The lake—Where most Twin Citians are when they're not at the office. (See *Up north.*)

Loop—The downtowns of both Minneapolis and St. Paul sometimes are referred to, Chicago-style, as the Loop.

Lutefisk—A traditional Scandinavian dish, lutefisk is cod that has been soaked in lye (it's rinsed thoroughly before being eaten).

The Mall—Nicollet Mall is the main shopping street of downtown Minneapolis. It's closed to private cars.

The Met—Metropolitan Stadium and the adjacent Metropolitan Sports Center in Bloomington both are referred to as the Met. Soon, the Met will refer only to the Sports Center, since the 25-year-old ballpark has been condemned to demolition.

Mill City—Minneapolis got the nickname because of the lumber- and then grain-milling that was a mainstay of the economy in the 19th and early 20th centuries. Relatively little milling is done in Minneapolis today.

Minnesota state bird—Unofficially, the mosquito. Officially, the loon.

Nordeast—This section of Minneapolis east of the Mississippi River is known for its Eastern European ethnic heritage, the pride of its residents, and its many fine restaurants. The East Side of St. Paul has a similar character.

Old Federal Courts Building—Old names die hard. Now called the Landmark Center, this building has been renovated and houses several St. Paul arts organizations. Located in downtown St. Paul at 75 W. Fifth St.

Outstate—Everything in Minnesota that's not in the Twin Cities metropolitan area is outstate.

Pig's Eye—The original name of St. Paul was taken from that of the city's first white settler—Pierre "Pig's Eye" Parrant. Pig's Eye Lake is east of downtown St. Paul along the Mississippi River.

Plug-in—This is the short electrical cord dangling from the front of some cars. It's attached to a heater, which keeps the engine warm when it's plugged in on cold mornings.

Pop—Soda, to you Easterners.

Quality of life—Studies have shown that the Twin Cities area has good parks and schools and lots of culture and is therefore a good place to live, despite the severe winters and high taxes. This is known as quality of life.

Ramp—A tiered parking garage.

The Range—The Mesabi Iron Range of northeastern Minnesota is a center for the mining of taconite, a form of low-grade iron ore. The Range is known for colorful characters such as Jim Klobuchar and Steve Cannon (See *A Brief Who's Who*), Bob Dylan (born Zimmerman), and former Gov. Rudy Perpich.

Seven Corners—The intersection of Washington and Cedar Avs. on the West Bank in Minneapolis produces an improbable seven corners, due to disruption of the city's grid pattern by the Mississippi River. Seven Corners is a center of theater and nightlife on the West Bank.

Skyways—These second-story-level enclosed pedestrian bridges connect many of the buildings in downtown Minneapolis and St. Paul.

Slush—What snow and ice become while they melt.

Snowmobiles—Owners say these motorized winter recreational vehicles are fun and useful for rescue work and emergency transportation. Critics say they're noisy, wasteful of energy, and possibly damaging to the environment.

The Star-Journal—Like most cities, Minneapolis has seen several daily newspapers die. The *Journal* was absorbed into *The Minneapolis Star* many years ago, but some old-timers prefer to keep it alive.

The Strip—There are many commercial strip highways in the Twin Cities suburbs, but I-494 in Bloomington is The Strip.

Svenskarnasdag—Minnesota has adopted the custom of celebrating Midsummer Day from Sweden. It's the closest Saturday to June 24 in Sweden, the following Sunday in Minnesota.

Tennys—Back east, they're called sneakers.

Theater of seasons—The variety of weather in the Twin Cities is so great, it's bound to keep you entertained.

Town Square—A major new shopping, office, and hotel complex in downtown St. Paul; it includes a four-story, glass-enclosed public park.

Trumpeter swans—Once native to Minnesota, these birds are the world's largest waterfowl. Efforts are underway to restore the swans to Twin Cities-area habitats.

Uff da!—This all-purpose Scandinavian expression is used whenever things don't work out quite as well as planned. It's roughly equivalent to the Yiddish *oy vey!*

Up north—Up north, where the lakes are, is where Twin Citians head in droves for summer weekends and vacations.

Uptown—Fashionable older business districts in Minneapolis (at Hennepin Av. and Lake St.) and St. Paul (at Grand and Lexington Avs.) are both known as Uptown.

Volvo station wagon—This is what families in Edina and Kenwood are supposed to drive.

Wind chill—Wind makes cold feel even colder. The wind chill index tells you exactly how cold a particular combination of wind and temperature feels on your skin.

A BRIEF WHO'S WHO

It's an adage among journalists that names make news, and these Twin Citians have done just that, nationally as well as locally:

Loni Anderson—This former Miss Roseville stars in television's *WKRP in Cincinnati.*

Charlie Boone and Roger Erickson—WCCO-AM talk-show hosts famous for their "worst jokes."

Rudy Boschwitz—Now a U.S. Senator, Boschwitz became well-known by appearing in television commercials for his successful Plywood Minnesota business.

Anthony Bouza—The former New York City cop is now the outspoken and controversial Minneapolis police chief.

Herb Brooks—This St. Paul native coached the 1980 U.S. Olympic hockey team to an upset victory over the Soviet Union. He had been coach of the outstanding University of Minnesota hockey team, and now coaches the professional New York Rangers.

Warren Burger—The chief justice of the U.S. Supreme Court is a St. Paul native and graduate of what is now the William Mitchell College of Law. Burger and Harry Blackmun (of Rochester) are the high court's "Minnesota Twins."

Steve Cannon—Drivin' home with Cannon and his friends (Ma

Linger, Morgan Mundane, and Backlash LaRue) on WCCO-AM is a Twin Cities commuting tradition.

Curt Carlson—His Carlson Companies make up one of the area's largest and most visible privately held corporations. Carlson owns, among other things, the Radisson hotels, and is behind a planned $300-million office and residential development in Minnetonka and Plymouth.

Barbara Flanagan—*The Minneapolis Star*'s crusading columnist for urban beautification, historic preservation, and sidewalk cafes (yes, in Minnesota).

Bud Grant—The crew-cut, steely eyed coach of the Minnesota Vikings; he stars in his own television show during the football season.

Calvin Griffith—The relative parsimony of the controversial owner of the Minnesota Twins has caused the departure of Rod Carew and other stars to higher-paying teams. In 1982, he'll be counting on the new domed stadium to rejuvenate flagging local interest in big-league baseball.

Judith Guest—The author of *Ordinary People*. She lives and works in Edina.

Richard Guindon—Former *Minneapolis Tribune* "social cartoonist" used to poke fun at the people, institutions, and weather of the Twin Cities. He recently defected to Detroit, where he pens his nationally syndicated cartoons.

Sid Hartman—This *Minneapolis Tribune* sports columnist also names a "Sports Hero" every day on WCCO-AM.

Walter Heller—A University of Minnesota economics professor and former presidential advisor, Heller is still quoted frequently by the national media.

Garrison Keillor—This noted autoharpist stars in the *Prairie Home Companion* program on Minnesota Public Radio, broadcast live each Saturday from downtown St. Paul.

Linda Kelsey—The *Lou Grant Show*'s Billie Newman is a St. Paul native.

George Latimer—The bearded, plain-talking, Democratic mayor of St. Paul may well be the most popular politician now active in these parts. His Minneapolis counterpart, Don Fraser, also a popular local Democrat, is up for re-election in November 1981.

Bob Lurtsema—"Benchwarmer Bob" has been far more successful as a spokesman for Twin City Federal Savings and Loan than he was as a lineman for the Minnesota Vikings.

Stan Mayslack—This former professional wrestler dishes up some of the world's largest roast-beef sandwiches in his Nordeast Minneapolis bar. Be sure to hold your plate with both hands.

Ron Meshbesher—If there's a spectacular criminal case in the news, he'll probably be arguing for the defense—and winning.

Pat Miles—Co-anchor of WCCO-TV's local news, Ms. Miles has quickly become one of the hottest media personalities in town.

Walter Mondale—Former Vice President who makes his Minnesota home in Afton, on the St. Croix River, when he isn't working at his law practice in Washington.

Dave Moore—The Twin Cities' version of Walter Cronkite gives the news on Channel 4.

The Pillsburys—The Lake Minnetonka milling family has been very active in state government and Independent-Republican politics.

Charles Schulz—The creator of the *Peanuts* comic strip is a St. Paul native who now lives in California.

Eric Sevareid—The retired CBS news commentator caused quite a stir when he advocated an end to mandatory ROTC at the University of Minnesota in the 1930s.

Gerry Spiess—A White Bear Lake schoolteacher who has gained international recognition by sailing his 10-foot home-made sailboat, *Yankee Girl*, on marathon solo ocean voyages. At this writing, Spiess was crossing the Pacific, en route from Long Beach, Calif., to Sydney, Australia.

Oliver Towne—Pen name for Gareth Hiebert, *St. Paul Dispatch* columnist.

The State Capitol complex near downtown St. Paul.

Chapter Two

GETTING AROUND, GETTING AWAY

Despite recent improvements in local bus service, the automobile remains the dominant means of transportation in the Twin Cities. A wide-ranging—though still incomplete—freeway system makes traveling by car almost anywhere in the metropolitan area quick and easy, except possibly during the rush hour and in extreme weather.

The basic source of information for Minnesota motorists is the state driver's manual, available at all license exam stations and substations (listed in the telephone directory under "Minnesota State Offices—License Information"), the Hennepin and Ramsey county courthouses, and Hennepin County government service centers.

Maps of Minneapolis and St. Paul are available at service stations, in stores, and for a slight charge at the chambers of commerce, 15 S. Fifth St., Minneapolis 55402 (348-4330), and 701 N. Central Tower, 445 Minnesota St., St. Paul 55102 (222-5561). State highway maps are available free from the Minnesota Tourist Information Center, 408 Cedar St., St. Paul 55101 (296-5029). For information on the condition of Minnesota highways, call 296-3076.

NAVIGATING BY CAR

Somewhere between the order of midtown Manhattan and the sprawl of Los Angeles lies the Twin Cities.

These are the main rules—and exceptions—to keep in mind when navigating the Twin Cities by car:

Minneapolis

Minneapolis is divided into four parts: north, south, northeast, and southeast. Each has a different system of naming and numbering streets and avenues, but block numbers do conform to those of numbered streets and avenues throughout the city.

In north Minneapolis, both east-west and north-south thoroughfares are generally called avenues. West of Lyndale Av. N., the north-south avenues are named in alphabetical order toward the west: Aldrich, Bryant, Colfax.... East-west avenues are numbered consecutively south to north. East of Lyndale, north-south thoroughfares are streets. Exceptions are Washington Av. N., which runs north-south near the river; Broadway, which runs east-west before angling to the northwest; and Lowry Av., which runs east-west. Hwy. 55 (Olson Memorial Hwy.) runs east-west through the southern part of north Minneapolis.

The alphabetical avenues west of Lyndale continue into south Minneapolis. East-west thoroughfares are streets, which are numbered consecutively north to south. Nicollet Av. divides east and west. East of Nicollet, avenues are numbered consecutively west to east. Exceptions are a few named avenues east of Nicollet, such as Park, Portland, and Chicago; Hennepin Av., which runs

southwest from downtown; Hiawatha Av. (Hwy. 55), and a few parallel avenues, which run southeast from downtown. The major north-south highway in south Minneapolis is I-35W; east-west routes include I-94 and Hwy. 12 in the northern part of south Minneapolis and County Hwy. 62 (Crosstown Hwy.) on the city's southern edge.

North and south Minneapolis come together downtown, where streets run northwest to southeast and avenues run southwest to northeast to conform to an angle in the Mississippi River. Basically, streets and avenues downtown follow the pattern of those in south Minneapolis. However, streets as well as avenues are labeled north or south. Streets southeast of Hennepin Av. are

SKYWAYS

Minneapolis and St. Paul both have second-story, climate-controlled walkway systems called skyways downtown. The most visible portions of the skyway systems are the glass-enclosed bridges that connect the second stories of major downtown buildings, allowing pedestrians to cross from one block to another without going outside. The skyways also extend through downtown blocks by means of corridors that channel pedestrian traffic. These corridors have become secondary shopping streets, lined with specialty shops and restaurants, and open onto the sales floors of large department stores. Occasionally, skyway explorers will find a skylit garden or a fountain.

In Minneapolis, the IDS Center's Crystal Court is considered the hub of the skyway system. In St. Paul, the new Town Square serves the same purpose. To reach the skyways in either town, take an escalator to the second floor of a building in the system (see the skyway maps on 31, 33). Once you're in the skyways, color-coded maps at major intersections will help you. The skyway system is not always easily accessible to persons in wheelchairs, because steps have been used in some places to connect buildings with different floor heights.

MINNEAPOLIS SKYWAY SYSTEM

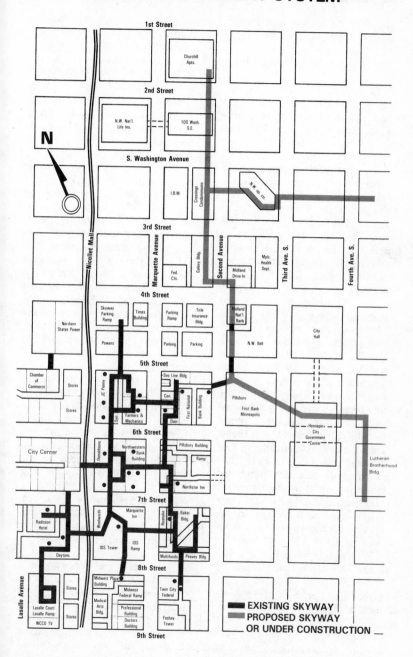

south; those northwest of Hennepin are north. Washington Av., a main downtown thoroughfare, lies between Second and Third Sts.

In northeast Minneapolis, it's the streets that run north-south and the avenues that run east-west. Streets are numbered consecutively east from the river through Seventh St. N.E. where the names of the presidents in order of service through Hoover take over. Exceptions are University Av. (Hwy. 47) between Third and Fourth Sts. N.E. and Central Av. (Hwy. 65) between Van Buren and Tyler Sts. N.E. E. Hennepin Av. forms the southern edge of northeast Minneapolis. The major highway in northeast Minneapolis is I-35W, which runs northeast from downtown.

In southeast Minneapolis between the University of Minnesota and St. Anthony Main and Central Av., streets run northwest to southeast, and avenues run northeast to southwest. Streets are numbered consecutively northeast from the river; avenues are numbered consecutively southeast from Central Av. North and east of the University, avenues run north-south and are numbered consecutively from west to east. Southeast of the University, there is no discernible pattern to the curving residential streets. Exceptions to the grid include Main St. S.E., which replaces First St. S.E. along the river, and University Av. S.E. (Hwy. 47), which replaces Third St. S.E. Major highways are I-35W and I-94.

St. Paul

Many Minneapolitans, not to mention newcomers and visitors, despair of ever finding their way around St. Paul. Except for a few downtown streets, there is no numerical or alphabetical pattern to the names of streets and avenues.

Major north-south thoroughfares (west to east) include: Cretin Av. (named for the first bishop of St. Paul), Cleveland Av., Snelling Av., Lexington Av., Dale St., Rice St., Edgerton St., Arcade St., White Bear Av., and McKnight Rd. Most are served by exits off I-94, which runs east-west through the city. Major east-west routes (north to south) include Larpenteur Av., Maryland Av., University Av., Marshall Av., Summit Av., and Ford Pkwy. W. Seventh St. (Old Fort Rd.) and Shepard Rd. run southwest from downtown along the Mississippi River. Warner Rd. runs east from downtown to Hwys. 10 and 61, which head southeast from the city.

In downtown St. Paul, major streets run northwest to southeast: St. Peter, Wabasha, Cedar, Minnesota, Robert, Jackson, Sibley, from southwest to northeast. Cross streets are numbered starting with Fourth St. from Kellogg Blvd., which runs along the river bluff.

The address numbering system in St. Paul can be disorienting, with addresses numerically close together actually blocks apart.

Suburbs and Freeways

Major streets and avenues extend from Minneapolis and St. Paul into adjacent suburbs. Street and avenue names and numbers in Minneapolis generally extend

ST. PAUL SKYWAY SYSTEM

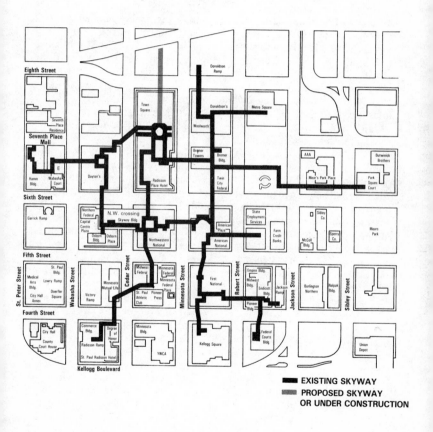

EXISTING SKYWAY

PROPOSED SKYWAY
OR UNDER CONSTRUCTION

33

from those of the adjacent part of the city. There are many exceptions, however, especially in the more distant suburbs.

In addition to I-35E, I-35W, and I-94, Twin Cities suburbs are served by an interstate beltway system consisting of I-494 to the south and I-694 to the north. Major north-south routes in the western suburbs are County Hwy. 18 and Hwy. 100. The major east-west route in the Minneapolis suburbs is Hwy. 12. Running east from Stillwater, Hwy. 36 becomes a major thoroughfare in the suburbs north of St. Paul.

There are no tolls on any Twin Cities area bridge or highway.

Major uncompleted freeway segments include I-35E southwest of downtown St. Paul, I-494 south of St. Paul, and I-94 northwest of downtown Minneapolis.

It is important when using the freeways, especially in the center cities, to watch the signs carefully for lane shifts, merges, and numerous other irregularities. Also, many interchanges have entrance and exit ramps in one direction only—so don't assume you can get back the way you came.

Snow Emergencies

Don't be alarmed if a snow emergency is declared—unless your vehicle is parked on a street that's scheduled to be cleared. All a snow emergency means is that enough of the white stuff has accumulated to justify bringing out the plows. It is illegal to park on streets scheduled to be plowed, and violators are likely to be tagged and/or towed away (en-forcement of snow emergency rules is very strict).

The basic rules are the same in Minneapolis and St. Paul: Once a snow emergency has been declared, marked snow emergency routes are plowed first (in Minneapolis, these also are designated by blue street signs). East-west residential streets are plowed on even-numbered days (remember, both east and even begin with *E*), north-south streets on odd-numbered days. In both cities, most east-west streets are designated with brown street signs, north-south streets with green signs.

In Minneapolis, a snow emergency lasts for 72 hours (three full days) and may be extended. Emergency routes are plowed from 9 p.m. to 8 the next morning. Residential streets are plowed from 8 a.m. to 8 p.m. Parking is prohibited during those times. The fine for violating snow emergency parking rules in Minneapolis is $25, plus towing and storage fees; in St. Paul the fine is $15.

In St. Paul, parking is prohibited on emergency routes until they are plowed *curb-to-curb*. Parking is prohibited on even- and odd-numbered days until east-west and north-south streets, respectively, have been plowed curb-to-curb.

It seems that every rule must have its exception, and for snow emergencies the exception is the Experimental Plowing Plan for southwest Minneapolis. If you live—or park—in the area bounded by France Av. S. on the west, W. 44th St. east to Lake Harriet and then W. 46th St. on the north, I-35W on the east and the Crosstown Hwy. (County Hwy. 62) on the south, a complicated set of special rules applies to you during snow emergencies. Call 348-2487 for details.

Snow emergencies are announced on the radio, on television, and in local newspapers. To confirm that an emergency has been declared, call 348-2487 in Minneapolis, 298-4321 in St. Paul.

Parking Violations

In Minneapolis fines for meter and overtime parking violations are $5. In St. Paul the fine for an expired-meter ticket is $6, all other parking violations $5.

COMMUTER SERVICES

MINNESOTA RIDESHARE, 333 Sibley St., Suite 109, St. Paul 55101.
297-3800

Minnesota Rideshare is a public agency designed to encourage carpooling, mass transit, and other energy-saving methods of commuting. For no charge, Rideshare will match your commuting needs with other commuters in your area and help you form a car pool. It also provides vans and assistance in forming van pools. If you are simply considering taking MTC buses to work, Rideshare will send you the appropriate route information. Most arrangements can be handled over the telephone. Rideshare office hours are M-F 8 a.m. to 5 p.m. An answering device takes telephone messages after office hours.

TRAVELING BY BUS

Public transportation in most of the seven-county area is provided by the Metropolitan Transit Commission (MTC), which operates more than 1,100 buses over some 125 routes. Service is concentrated in Minneapolis and St. Paul and on suburban routes to and from the downtowns. For route and schedule information, call 827-7733 from 6 to 1 a.m. weekdays, 7 a.m. to 11 p.m. weekends. For information by teletypewriter for the hearing- and speech-impaired, call 824-5202.

The MTC cooperates in Metro Mobility, which provides door-to-door service in Minneapolis, St. Paul, and some suburbs for those whose handicaps prevent them from using standard buses. For information, call 644-1119.

Bus schedules and system maps can be obtained at MTC information centers in the IDS Center Crystal Court, downtown Minneapolis, and on the street level of Town Square, downtown St. Paul. Maps may be ordered by mail from the MTC, 801 American Center Building, St. Paul 55101. Enclose 50 cents for the map and 18 cents for postage. Schedules are free, and may be ordered by mail from the MTC Transit Operating Division, 3118 Nicollet Av., Minneapolis 55408, or picked up at any of the 200 or so retailers and financial institutions that carry them.

As this is written, the basic bus fare is 60 cents. Add 10 cents for freeway express service; 15 cents for each additional zone crossed for zones two and three, and 10 cents for crossing into zone four.

The first zone consists of overlapping circles extending six miles each from downtown Minneapolis and downtown St. Paul. Subsequent zones about two miles wide surround the first zone. Transfers are free and should be requested when boarding.

Senior citizens ride for a flat 10 cents during non-peak times and for free if they qualify under income guidelines. Riders under 18 pay a base fare of 20 cents during non-peak times, plus express and zone charges. All rides within downtown Minneapolis are only 25 cents; within downtown St. Paul only 10 cents; and rides within the suburbs are only 60 cents, even if a zone line is crossed. The MTC offers special weekend family passes for $2, monthly passes, 10-trip tickets, and tokens. Visit the information centers or call 827-7733 for details.

Suburban Bus

MEDICINE LAKE BUS CO., 835 Decatur Av. N., Golden Valley 55427.
545-9417

No Sunday service. Serves Golden Valley, New Hope, Crystal, Medina, Maple Grove, and portions of Minneapolis.

METROPOLITAN TRANSIT COMMISSION, Transit Information Center.
827-7733

NORTH SUBURBAN LINES, 8600 N.E. Xylite, Blaine 55434.
784-7196

No Sunday service. Serves St. Paul and northern suburbs.

VALLEY TRANSIT, 7066 Stillwater Blvd. N., Oakdale 55119.

No Sunday service. Serves the Stillwater-Bayport area.

CALLING A CAB

If you want a cab, call for it. Taxis do not cruise in Minneapolis and St. Paul, although they can be found at cab stands in both cities. Cabs are usually readily available at the airport.

Cabs are licensed, and fares are set by the cities. Minneapolis licenses 248 cabs year-round, plus an additional 48 during the winter. St. Paul has about 100 licensed cabs. Fares as this is written are 95 cents for the first 1/11 mile and 20 cents for each additional 1/11 mile in Minneapolis. At these rates the first mile in Minneapolis costs $2.15; each additional mile, $1.10. In St. Paul, the fare is $1 for the first 1/8 mile, 10 cents for each additional 1/8 mile. Check the Yellow Pages under "Taxi Cabs" for cab companies operating in other areas.

HANDICAPPED ACCESSIBILITY

Federal and state laws now require that public facilities and programs be accessible to the handicapped. Unfortunately, some buildings antedating these laws limit the mobility of those in wheelchairs. Many of the skyways in downtown Minneapolis use steps to connect buildings with different floor heights and are therefore inaccessible. The St. Paul skyway system is partially accessible.

Any facility open to the public built after November 1976 must be wheelchair-accessible by state law. Federal law requires programs receiving federal funds to be accessible, but not every site at which a service is provided need be accessible. Call the facility or program in advance, or call the Minnesota Council for the Handicapped at 296-6785; the council keeps a list of accessible programs and facilities, and can help handicapped individuals and groups meet a variety of needs.

The Minnesota Department of Transportation sponsors a transportation service for handicapped persons called Metro Mobility. This service includes responsive bus services that use vehicles fitted for transporting wheelchairs; a shared-ride taxi service; and a network of non-profit transportation providers who offer services in the suburban metropolitan area. Metro Mobility's programs vary depending on where you live. Call 644-1119 for complete information.

AIR TRAVEL

The Minneapolis-St. Paul International Airport (Wold-Chamberlain Field) is just south of Minneapolis and St. Paul, and is reached by taking I-494 to the terminal entrance at the eastern edge of the airport. The airport is about 12 miles from downtown Minneapolis, about 10 miles from downtown St. Paul.

Airport Telephone Numbers

Emergency (medical crisis, airport police, lost-and-found, car-

starting service):	726-1177
Airport information:	726-5309
Traveler's Aid:	726-9435
Servicemen's Center:	726-9156
Airport Director's Office:	726-1717

Airport Taxi, Bus, and Limousine Service

Information on limousine and city bus service is available on the lower level of the airport terminal building. Taxi service is available just outside the terminal's baggage-claim area. Major hotels in the Twin Cities maintain free reservation telephones at the airport, located on the lower level of the terminal near the baggage-claim area.

Airport Parking

Short-term parking is available near the terminal entrance. Rates for short-term parking are 75 cents for the first half hour, 50 cents for each additional hour. There is no maximum charge in the short-term lot.

General parking includes the main terminal parking lot and the parking deck. Overflow parking is located just south of the terminal lot. Both general and overflow lots are served by free shuttle-bus service, and the rates for both are $1 for the first hour, 50 cents for each additional hour. The 24-hour maximum charge is $5.

Ramp parking is available close to the terminal. Ramp parking rates are $3 for the first hour, 75 cents for each additional hour. The maximum 24-hour charge is $13.

Airlines

The Minneapolis-St. Paul International Airport is served by the following airlines. Telephone numbers are for information and reservations.

Major Carriers

AIR WISCONSIN
726-5881

AMERICAN AIRLINES
339-6070

BRANIFF INTERNATIONAL
339-3131

CONTINENTAL AIRLINES
332-1471

EASTERN AIRLINES
339-9520

NORTHWEST AIRLINES
726-1234

OZARK AIRLINES
333-3421

REPUBLIC AIRLINES
726-7100

TEXAS INTERNATIONAL
341-2442

US AIR
338-5841

UNITED AIR LINES
339-3671

WESTERN AIR LINES
726-4141

**CHARTER AND
  INTERNATIONAL FLIGHTS**
726-5214

Commuter Airlines

BIG SKY
726-7100

LAKE LAND
(715) 234-4186

LAKE STATE
(800) 722-0554

MESABA
(800) 622-5782

MIDWEST AVIATION
(507) 532-3164

MISSISSIPPI VALLEY
(800) 356-9160

Secondary Airports

AIRLAKE AIRPORT, 215th St. W. and Hamburg Av., Lakeville. 469-4040 ►6

ANOKA COUNTY AIRPORT, 2289 County Rd. J, Blaine. ►9 786-9490

CRYSTAL FIELD, Bass Lake Rd. and Hwy. 52, Crystal. ►4 537-4096

FLYING CLOUD FIELD, 10110 Flying Cloud Dr., Eden Prairie. ►5 941-3545

LAKE ELMO AIRPORT, County Rd. 18 and 30th St. N., Lake Elmo. ►10 777-6300

ST. PAUL DOWNTOWN AIRPORT (HOLMAN FIELD), Airport Blvd., St. Paul. ►7 224-4306

RAIL

AMTRAK, Twin Cities Passenger Station, 730 Transfer Rd. (two blocks north of University Av.), St. Paul. ►8
644-1127

Call 339-2382 for general information and reservations. At this writing the Twin Cities are served by two trains a day. This service, however, could be reduced or cancelled at any time.

INTER-CITY BUS

MINNEAPOLIS PASSENGER DEPOT, 29 N. Ninth St., Minneapolis. ►1
371-3311

ST. PAUL PASSENGER DEPOT, Ninth and St. Peter Sts., St. Paul. ►7
222-0507

In both Minneapolis and St. Paul, call 371-3311 for fare and schedule information for Greyhound, Jefferson, and Zephyr Bus Lines. Call 338-8351 for fare and schedule information on Greyhound's Duluth service. Greyhound suburban stations are located at 12 Bridge Square, Anoka, 421-3443; 9601 Garfield Av. S., Bloomington, 888-8600; Prior Av. N. and Charles Av. (Midway), St. Paul, 645-8126; 2465 Fairview Av. N., Roseville, 636-4276; and 6919 Wayzata Blvd., St. Louis Park, 544-5692.

Distance in miles between the Twin Cities and major U.S. cities	
Atlanta	1,121
Baltimore	1,113
Boston	1,390
Buffalo	949
Chicago	410
Dallas	949
Denver	917
Des Moines	245
Detroit	685
Fargo	239
Kansas City	443
Las Vegas	1,659
Los Angeles	1,857
Miami	1,769
Milwaukee	337
New York	1,217
Rapid City	577
Philadelphia	1,195
Portland (Ore.)	1,724
St. Louis	630
San Francisco	1,979
Seattle	1,653
Washington, D.C.	1,090

Tending to the ducks and geese on Lake of the Isles.

Chapter Three

THE CITIES

MINNEAPOLIS (Hennepin County)

Minneapolis has two features that the national media continually marvel at: a vital downtown and an extensive, innovative park system. The park system is what *residents* tend to focus on—five major lakes and dozens of miles of parkway provide recreational space for residents from the entire region. Neighborhood parks, smaller lakes, and Mississippi riverfront recreational areas complete the park inventory. Set amid well-kept residential neighborhoods, Minneapolis parks are instantly accessible. Populated by joggers, cyclists, and leisurely strollers, and by skiers and skaters in the winter, the lakes and parkways give the city a country club atmosphere all year around.

Downtown Minneapolis is as well-planned as the city's park system, and has not encountered the urban decay that has plagued many Eastern cities. Minneapolis has managed to stem the flow of major tenants from downtown to the suburbs, and through an aggressive development campaign has maintained its reputation as a corporate headquarters city, as well as a cultural and retail center. The business community has played a major role in keeping the downtown vital, investing more than a half-billion dollars in downtown construction and renovation in the last 10 years.

The focal point downtown is the 51-story IDS Tower, a corporate office building that is also the center of downtown retail activity, forming the hub of the city's skyway system (enclosed pedestrian bridges connecting downtown buildings). The tower's Crystal Court opens onto the Nicollet Mall, an open-air pedestrian boulevard that was recently extended south to include the Holiday Inn and the new 23-story Hyatt Regency Hotel. When the City Center opens next year in the heart of the Nicollet Mall area, it will include more than 100 shops, a new Donaldsons department store, the International Multifoods Co. tower, and a luxury hotel. It is meant to be a major feature of a downtown profile that includes the new Pillsbury world headquarters, the Lutheran Brotherhood building, and 42 other new or restored buildings.

The main campus of the University of Minnesota is in Minneapolis, as

41

are the Guthrie Theater, Children's Theatre, the Institute of Arts, Walker Art Center, and the Minnesota Orchestra—all nationally recognized in their fields. The Hubert H. Humphrey Metrodome, scheduled to open in April, will make downtown Minneapolis a professional sports center, as home stadium for the Minnesota Vikings, Twins, and Kicks.

The population of Minneapolis has declined considerably since its peak of more than 550,000 in the mid-1950s. This has been due largely to a decline in family size and the movement of families to the suburbs. Sections of Minneapolis have concentrations of the remaining elderly and/or young people. Large parts of the city remain good places to raise children, and attracting and retaining families is a major goal of the city administration.

Minneapolis has experienced most of the problems faced by major cities around the country. But its economic strength, natural advantages, and strong leadership have kept it a vital, growing business center with exceptional attributes in the arts and recreation fields as well.

Minneapolis at a Glance

Population—
1970:	434,400
1980:	370,091
1990:	375,000

Area (in acres)—
Land:	36,279
Water:	1,351
Total:	37,630

Bus service: MTC

School district: 1 (Minneapolis)
Schools: 12 public high schools, 10 junior highs, 47 elementary; 13 private high schools, 31 elementary

Taxes on $68,000 home: $502
Rank 1 (high) to 90 (low)   11

City Hall phone: 348-3000 (city-county information)
Chamber phone: 370-9132

ST. PAUL (Ramsey County)

Of the Twin Cities, St. Paul has the image of being the staid older sister, content with its reputation for history and government, and leaving growth and innovation to Minneapolis. But that image is changing rapidly as St. Paul acquires a new look that is drawing more and more businesses and residents to its downtown.

Town Square opened last year in the center of downtown, featuring an attractive four-level indoor park, and serving as a much-needed focal point for the area. The complex includes a major hotel, retail stores, and two office towers. Other recent additions to downtown include the Minnesota Public Radio building, with an electronic news banner that adds flash to a once-gray area; an addition to the St. Paul Cos. headquarters; and several condominium buildings. The Adult Detention Center, perhaps the most unusual of the new downtown buildings, is built into a rock bluff overlooking the Mississippi River and is barely visible to pedestrians passing above it on Kellogg Blvd.

St. Paul is a national leader in historic preservation and the recycling of older buildings. The old Federal Courts Building has been restored and turned into Landmark Center, an elegant performance, gallery, and headquarters space for area arts organizations. Park Square Court, a specialty building, is another conversion, while Lowertown, an area of old warehouses, is being brought to life as an "urban village" with new housing and renovated commercial space. Most of the downtown buildings are linked by an extensive skyway system, making St. Paul, like Minneapolis, an efficient "winter city."

St. Paul's vitality is not limited to downtown. Energy Park, a residential, commercial, and office development whose focus will be energy technology, is scheduled for construction in the Midway community, near the site of the old Midway Stadium. Supported by the city, Control Data Corp., and the Wilder Foundation, Energy Park will be one of the most innovative mixed-use developments in the nation.

Other city neighborhoods are being refurbished. Historic Ramsey Hill, overlooking downtown, has been converted from a rundown section to a concentration of beautifully restored homes and apartments, many selling as high-priced condominiums. Summit Av., five miles of elms and mansions, runs past Ramsey Hill and other historic neighborhoods to the western edge of the city. Parallel to Summit is Grand Av., featuring a string of specialty stores, small shopping centers and restaurants.

St. Paul's cultural offerings include the St. Paul-Ramsey Arts & Science Council, the Chimera Theatre, the Minnesota Museum of Art, and the world-renowned St. Paul Chamber Orchestra. The new Science Museum of Minnesota, with its spectacular Omnitheater, has become one of downtown St. Paul's most popular attractions.

In addition to the University of Minnesota's St. Paul campus on its northern border, St. Paul is home to several highly regarded private colleges and professional schools, including Hamline University, Macalester College, and the Colleges of St. Thomas and St. Catherine.

St. Paul's neighborhoods vary in personality and housing opportunities, and the city's commitment to district planning insures that they will remain good places to raise families. Many areas have a friendly, small-town feel, and rents and home prices are often lower than in comparable parts of Minneapolis.

St. Paul at a Glance

Population—	
1970:	309,866
1980:	268,248
1990:	270,000
Area (in acres)—	
Land:	33,411
Water:	2,069
Total:	35,480
Bus service:	MTC
School district:	625 (St. Paul)
Schools:	Six public high schools, 4 junior highs, 38 elementary; 10 private high schools, 35 elementary
Taxes on $68,000 home:	$496
Rank 1 (high) to 90 (low):	14
City Hall phone:	298-4012 (city-county information)
Chamber phone:	222-5561

CITY NEIGHBORHOODS

Outside of the bustling and cosmopolitan atmosphere of the Twin Cities' downtowns, Minneapolis and St. Paul can be described as a series of residential villages held together by common interests and urban services. Spread over the more than 100-square-mile area that both cities cover is a mosaic of neighborhoods that have developed at different times for different reasons. Each has its own flavor and character, and residents of many of them cling fiercely to their neighborhood identity. Ask a city resident where he or she lives, and more likely than not the answer will be "Kenwood" or "St. Anthony," rather than a specific address.

For planning purposes the cities have grouped neighborhoods into communities. Each community usually has its own library, schools, parks, and newsletter or newspaper. Descriptions of these communities are offered here, with references for additional information provided at the end of the section.

MINNEAPOLIS COMMUNITIES

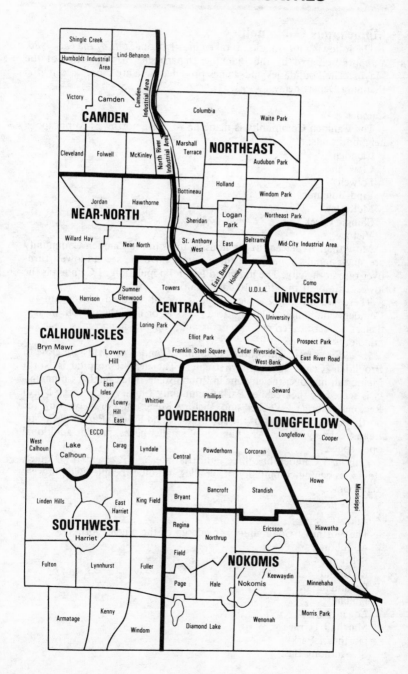

Shingle Creek
Lind-Behanon
Humboldt Industrial Area
Victory
Camden
CAMDEN
Camden Industrial Area
North River Industrial Area
Columbia
Waite Park
Cleveland
Folwell
McKinley
Marshall Terrace
NORTHEAST
Audubon Park
Holland
Windom Park
Jordan
Hawthorne
Bottineau
NEAR-NORTH
Sheridan
Logan Park
Northeast Park
Willard Hay
Near North
St. Anthony West
East
Beltrami
Mid-City Industrial Area
East Bank
Holmes
Como
Sumner Glenwood
Towers
U.D.I.A.
UNIVERSITY
Harrison
CENTRAL
University
Loring Park
Elliot Park
CALHOUN-ISLES
Bryn Mawr
Prospect Park
East River Road
Lowry Hill
Franklin Steel Square
Cedar Riverside
West Bank
East Isles
Seward
Lowry Hill East
Whittier
Phillips
POWDERHORN
West Calhoun
ECCO
Lake Calhoun
Carag
Lyndale
Central
Powderhorn
Corcoran
LONGFELLOW
Longfellow
Cooper
Howe
Linden Hills
East Harriet
King Field
Bryant
Bancroft
Standish
SOUTHWEST
Harriet
Regina
Ericsson
Hiawatha
Fulton
Lynnhurst
Fuller
Field
Northrup
NOKOMIS
Keewaydin
Page
Hale
Nokomis
Minnehaha
Armatage
Kenny
Windom
Diamond Lake
Wenonah
Morris Park
Mississippi

Minneapolis Communities

The following information is taken mostly from *State of the City 1980*, a report prepared by the Planning Department of the Office of the Mayor. The boundaries and names provided here are those used by the Planning Department.

Camden

The Camden Community is made up of these northwest Minneapolis neighborhoods:

Camden
Cleveland
Folwell
Lind-Bohanon
McKinley
Shingle Creek
Victory

More than 70 percent of the housing units in the Camden Community are single-family homes, and these homes have the second-lowest turn-over rate in the city. The unrelated (single) population of Camden is the lowest of any of the city's 10 communities.

There are no major concentrations of substandard housing in the Camden Community, and the area ranks at or near the bottom in incidences of serious crimes except assault, for which it ranks near the middle.

In addition to neighborhood shopping, Camden residents are close to Brookdale Center in Brooklyn Center. The nearest hospital is North Memorial, just over the city line in Robbinsdale. The Camden Community is served by the Webber Park Community Library and nearby North Regional Library. Webber and Victory Memorial Parkways ring the north and western edges of the community, and Folwell Park and Crystal Lake Cemetery, as well as a number of smaller parks, provide additional open space.

Although Camden has three industrial areas, it is essentially a quiet, stable residential community of families and older people living in well-kept homes.

Northeast

The Northeast Community is made up of these neighborhoods:
Audubon Park
Beltrami
Bottineau
Columbia
Holland
Logan Park
Marshall Terrace
Northeast Park
St. Anthony East

St. Anthony West
Sheridan
Waite Park
Windom Park

Northeast Minneapolis has an image: ethnic, blue-collar, a haven of respect for traditional institutions and values. Certainly that's part of the picture, but the Northeast Community is a large and varied area.

About half the community's housing units are single-family homes and an additional 30 percent are duplexes. Some neighborhoods closer to downtown have concentrations of substandard housing; neighborhoods nearer the city's north and east edges have a middle-class, almost suburban look. The Northeast Community has the lowest rate of residential burglaries of the city's 10 communities, and ranks near the bottom for incidences of other serious crimes, except for vandalism, where it is in the middle range.

The Central Av. corridor is Northeast's main business district. Nearby suburban shopping centers include Apache Plaza in St. Anthony and Rosedale Center in Roseville. The closest hospitals are in the downtown area.

The Northeast Community is served by the Northeast and Pierre Bottineau community libraries. Columbia Park, with an 18-hole public golf course, is the main recreational facility. St. Anthony Parkway and Stinson Boulevard are the community's scenic areas.

Northeast Minneapolis is known throughout the Twin Cities for its concentration of fine restaurants, most of them in the vicinity of University Av.

Near North

The Near North Community is made up of these neighborhoods:
Harrison
Hawthorne
Jordan
Near-North
Sumner-Glenwood
Willard-Hay

The Near North is a community in transition. Once a white, middle-class area, it now has a substantial black and Hispanic population. The movement now is toward a racially mixed, revitalized inner-city community.

Many of the area's substantial but decayed homes are being renovated under the city's Urban Homesteading program, which allows families meeting income guidelines to buy run-down houses for $1 and grants them low-interest loans for rehabilitation. In addition, some new suburban-style housing has been built. The West Broadway area, the Near North's major business district, is undergoing extensive redevelopment. The West Broadway redevelopment plan includes several hundred new townhouse units, as well as a refurbishing of the commercial area.

About 40 percent of the Near North's housing units are single-family homes.

The closest suburban center is Brookdale in Brooklyn Center. The nearest hospitals are those in the downtown area and North Memorial in Robbinsdale.

The Near North is served by the North Regional Library and the Sumner Community Library. Theodore Wirth Park, a major recreation area, is just across the city line in Golden Valley.

The Near North ranks at or near the top among Minneapolis communities in incidences of serious crime.

Central

The Central Community is made up of these neighborhoods:

Elliot Park-Franklin Steele Square

Loring Park

Stevens Square-Loring Heights

Towers

These neighborhoods include a polyglot of the city's most- and least-expensive housing, its newest and oldest. However, efforts to renew blighted areas of the community are planned or underway.

The Loring Park neighborhood, in particular, has seen construction of new town homes and high-rise condominiums. Although there has been some renovation of older apartment buildings as well, the neighborhood is undergoing a fundamental change of character.

Renovation, rather than replacement, of older buildings has been the focus of Stevens Court Inc., which has sought to improve housing in the Stevens Square neighborhood while keeping rents affordable for those with moderate incomes. General Mills Inc. has invested money in the effort.

The new domed stadium, located on the eastern edge of the Central Community in the Elliott Park neighborhood, is scheduled to open in the spring of this year. The dome will seat more than 62,000 people and will be home to the Minnesota Vikings, the Twins, and the Kicks. Parking for the dome is scattered throughout the downtown area.

The Towers neighborhood shares its name with its first high-rise condominium buildings. Additional housing has been constructed in the downtown part of the Towers neighborhood, and there are plans for a major development including housing along the Mississippi River north of Hennepin Av.

Central ranks at or near the top among the city's communities in incidences of serious crimes.

Hospitals in the Central Community are Eitel and Hennepin County and Metropolitan medical centers. The area is served by the Minneapolis Central Library, and Loring Park is the major recreational area.

The energy crunch and growth of downtown have caused increasing numbers of people to consider living in the Central Community. Displacement of present residents, many of them elderly and poor, as rents and property values skyrocket in some Central neighborhoods is likely to present considerable problems in the 1980s.

University

The University Community includes these neighborhoods:
Cedar-Riverside (West Bank)
Como
Holmes
Nicollet Island-East Bank
Prospect Park-East River Road
UDIA (University District Improvement Association)

The University of Minnesota's massive Minneapolis campus is part—and only part—of the University Community, which also includes the birthplace of the city, family oriented neighborhoods, and an industrial area.

The university's influence is strongest in the UDIA neighborhood, which includes Dinkytown, the major business area near campus. Apartment buildings and fraternity and sorority houses line University Av. and Fourth St. S.E. in the UDIA and Holmes neighborhoods, but they also have many single-family homes and duplexes.

Cedar-Riverside, named for the main avenues of its business district, has an identity as a sort of Greenwich Village of the Upper Midwest that predates the university's expansion to the West Bank. The future of Cedar-Riverside's housing, now mostly deteriorating rented houses, is uncertain following successful opposition to a plan that would have covered the neighborhood with high-rise apartment buildings.

Nicollet Island-East Bank consists largely of an old business district with the atmosphere of a typical Midwestern city of 20,000 or 30,000 people. Nicollet Island proper has been allowed to exist as a semi-ghost town for years, belonging neither to the lively city downtown to the south of it, nor to the resurrected areas on the East Bank. In the next year, plans for a riverfront park and both new and renovated housing may be finalized, making it possible for the Island to become a vital part of the city. The East Bank and adjacent parts of the Holmes neighborhood contain the old buildings that made up Minneapolis' first downtown. Several of these buildings have been restored, and now form the St. Anthony Main shopping and restaurant complex. New condominium towers have recently opened in this area, offering spectacular views of the river and downtown. A developing river park area provides recreation space for East Bank residents.

Prospect Park-East River Road is a neighborhood of stately older homes, many of them occupied by families of university faculty members. This area includes Tower Hill, with its witch's hat water tower, one of the highest points in the city. Stadium Village, another business area adjacent to the university, runs along Washington Av. and Oak St., S.E.

The Como neighborhood is an area of older, more modest but well-maintained single-family homes and duplexes.

University ranks in the low-middle range among Minneapolis communities in incidences of serious crimes, except for vandalism, for which it ranks at the top.

Fairview and St. Mary's hospitals on the West Bank and University Hospitals are within the University Community. The area is served by the Southeast Community Library. Park and recreation space is found along the Mississippi River.

Calhoun-Isles

The Calhoun-Isles Community includes these neighborhoods:

Bryn Mawr
Carag
Cedar-Isles-Dean
ECCO (East Calhoun Community Organization)
East Isles
Kenwood
Lowry Hill
West Calhoun

With three major lakes, quality housing, and a lively shopping and entertainment district, Calhoun-Isles has always been a desirable place to live. Now, thanks to the energy crunch, its proximity to downtown makes it more desirable than ever. Condominium conversions have begun to take place, and developers are eyeing the shores of Lake Calhoun as sites for high-rises. So far, community groups have blocked most proposed buildings, but some believe the new Uptown shopping mall at Hennepin Av. and Lake St. signals the inevitable urbanization of Calhoun-Isles.

At present the community consists of older, single-family homes, duplexes, and small apartment buildings, plus a few high-rises on the north shore of Lake Calhoun. Apartments, which make up three-quarters of the community's housing units, predominate in the Lowry Hill East, Carag, and ECCO neighborhoods. Kenwood and Lowry Hill are areas of large, well-maintained older homes; a Kenwood address is still the most prestigious in Minneapolis proper. East Isles has a variety of single-family and apartment housing. Bryn Mawr, a neighborhood of single-family homes, has an established suburban appearance.

Hospitals near Calhoun-Isles are Eitel in the Loring Park neighborhood, Methodist in nearby St. Louis Park, and those in the downtown area. Calhoun-Isles is served by the new Walker Community Library, an underground facility that is the first earth-sheltered building constructed by the city of Minneapolis. Major recreation areas are Kenwood Park and Cedar Lake, Lake Calhoun and Lake of the Isles parkways.

Calhoun-Isles ranks just above the median among Minneapolis communities in incidences of most serious crimes.

Powderhorn

The Powderhorn Community includes these neighborhoods:

Bancroft

Bryant
Central
Corcoran
Lyndale
Phillips
Powderhorn Park
Standish
Whittier

Powderhorn is a community of contrasts. Most of its housing consists of duplexes and apartments, but it also contains some of the largest and most stately homes in Minneapolis. Largely residential, it is the home of Honeywell Inc., the largest corporation headquartered in the city. Its population is black, white, and Indian; young and old; poor and middle class. In short, it's a very urban community, offering all the challenges and opportunities of life in the city.

The Phillips neighborhood has actually grown to become a community of its own, although separate Planning Department data are not available for it yet. In the Phillips neighborhood, blighted East Franklin Av. contrasts with the mansions on Park and Portland avenues. Many of the mansions have been converted to institutional use, and hospitals and office buildings have been built where other grand homes once stood. With Abbott-Northwestern, Minneapolis Children's, Lutheran Deaconess and Mount Sinai hospitals, Phillips is a major medical center for the metropolitan area. Because Phillips is relatively near necessary services and has affordable, if dilapidated, housing, it has become home to many Southeast Asian refugees.

There are more old mansions in the Whittier neighborhood, home of

Residential serenity in southwest Minneapolis.

the Minneapolis Society of Fine Arts complex. The nearby Nicollet Av. business area features ethnic restaurants and neighborhood shopping. Housing in Whittier is mostly smaller apartment buildings.

Separating Phillips and Whittier from the largely residential neighborhoods to the south is Lake St., a major business corridor. South of Lake St. there are more single-family homes and duplexes.

Powderhorn is served by the Franklin, Hosmer, and Roosevelt community libraries. Powderhorn Park is the major recreation area.

Powderhorn ranks in the high-to-middle range among Minneapolis communities in incidences of major crimes.

Longfellow

The Longfellow Community includes these neighborhoods:
Cooper
Hiawatha
Howe
Longfellow
Seward
Longfellow must be considered in two parts:
The southern four neighborhoods are the proverbial good places to raise children—quiet, middle class, conventional. But Seward has a different look. Mostly, what's different about Seward is its housing.

Not all its housing—there are plenty of conventional homes. But there are also solar homes. And earth-sheltered homes. And renovated homes. And new homes built to *look* like renovated homes.

What was once an area of run-down and abandoned houses has blossomed into the kind of neighborhood you'd expect to see just off the main street of Disneyland. The centerpiece of this area is Milwaukee Av., now a grassy mall flanked by brick cottages built in the late 19th century to house railroad workers and their families.

The main business district of the Longfellow Community is the Lake St. corridor. Hospitals are in the adjacent Phillips and Cedar-Riverside neighborhoods. Longfellow is served by the East Lake Community Library. Minnehaha Park and the West River Parkway are the major recreation areas.

Incidences of major crimes in Longfellow are in the low to middle range among Minneapolis communities.

Nokomis

The Nokomis Community includes these neighborhoods:
Diamond Lake
Ericsson
Field
Hale
Keewaydin
Minnehaha
Morris Park

Northrup
Page
Regina
Wenonah

Eighty-five percent of the housing units in Nokomis are single-family homes—the highest proportion of any community in the city. And they're nice homes—not unusually big or fancy or new or old, most of them, but very comfortable. Once people settle in the community, they tend to remain there, giving Nokomis the highest continuous residency rate in the city. Over the next two years, several condominium and townhouse projects are planned in the Nokomis area, including the conversion of two elementary school sites into townhomes and senior citizen cooperatives.

Nokomis is a community of lakes and parks. In addition to Lake Nokomis and the parkland around it, there is Lake Hiawatha with its 18-hole public golf course, East Minnehaha Parkway, and Diamond Lake.

Nokomis has no major business district, but shopping and other services such as hospitals are a quick drive by freeway to downtown or the Southdale area in Edina. The area is served by the Nokomis Community Library.

Nokomis ranks near the bottom among Minneapolis communities in incidences of major crimes, except vandalism and robbery, for which it ranks near the middle.

Southwest

The Southwest Community includes these neighborhoods:
Armatage
East Harriet
Fuller
Fulton
Kenny
King Field
Linden Hills
Lynnhurst
Windom

Remember those television shows from the early 1960s like *Leave It To Beaver* and *Father Knows Best*, where all the men wore suits to work and everyone lived in a big house on a quiet, tree-lined street? Well, the Southwest Community is still like that. Plus it's got Lake Harriet, West Minnehaha Parkway, and easy access to downtown and Edina, sections of which resemble Southwest.

The Fuller neighborhood contains an area known as "Tangletown," named for its winding, hilly streets that are unusual in Minneapolis. Tangletown is arranged around the Washburn Water Tower, an old structure that is decorated with eagles at the top and stern, medieval knights at its base.

In terms of land use, Southwest is the most heavily residential community in Minneapolis. There are neighborhood shopping areas around

ST. PAUL COMMUNITIES

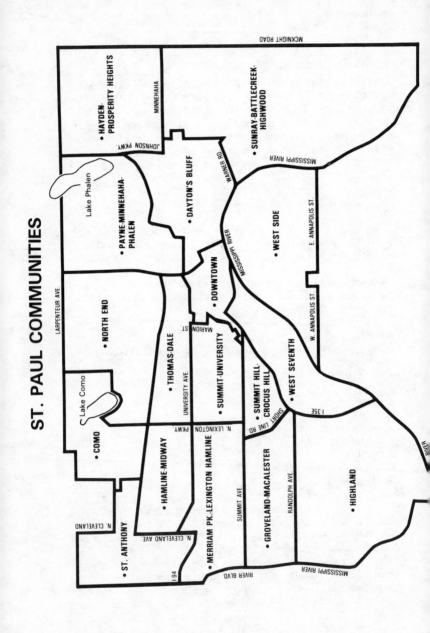

54

44th St. and Upton Av., and at various spots along 50th St. and Lyndale Av. Southwest is served by the Linden Hills and Washburn community libraries.

Southwest ranks at or near the bottom among Minneapolis communities in incidences of serious crimes.

St. Paul Communities

The district divisions that follow are those used by the city of St. Paul for planning purposes. The city uses different divisions for compiling crime statistics, so only a very general idea of the crime rate in each neighborhood is provided here. Information on incidences of crime in the immediate area of a particular address can be obtained by consulting a copy of *The Offense Summary Report* at any branch of the St. Paul Public Library. The report is published by the crime analysis unit of the St. Paul Police Department and details crime statistics over the past five years for 196 six-square-block areas of the city. If you need help interpreting the report, call 292-3515.

Hayden-Prosperity Heights

Hayden-Prosperity Heights is a predominantly middle-class residential district of well-kept single-family homes and duplexes. There are some apartment buildings in the southern part of the district. 3M Company, headquartered in neighboring Maplewood, is a major employer for the community. The main commercial areas are the Phalen Shopping Center at Prosperity and Maryland Avs. and Hillcrest Shopping Center on White Bear Av.

The nearest hospitals are Mounds Park and St. John's in the neighboring Dayton's Bluff district. Hayden-Prosperity Heights is served by the Hayden Branch Library. There are several small parks in the district, and Phalen Park, with a large lake and public golf course, is just to the southwest.

Hayden-Prosperity Heights has the highest percentage of households consisting of two-parent families among all 17 St. Paul planning districts. The area of the city that includes Hayden-Prosperity Heights has a relatively low rate of serious crime.

For more information on Hayden-Prosperity Heights, call 738-0489.

West Side

The West Side is actually *south* of downtown, but it is across the Mississippi River, which runs east-west in the area. Part of the West Side lies low along the river; inland there are steep bluffs. The Riverview Industrial Park and Holman Field, St. Paul's downtown airport, occupy some of the flats. The rest of the West Side is largely residential, although there are commercial areas at Concord and State Sts. and along Robert St. and Smith Av.

The West Side is an older district of smaller single-family homes, duplexes, and a few apartment buildings. It has been home to successive waves of immigrants—French-Canadian, German, Irish, Jewish, and Mexican-American. There remains a sizable Mexican-American population today, along with Scandinavians, Italians, blacks, Puerto Ricans, Poles, Hmongs and American Indians.

Riverview Memorial Hospital closed recently, making downtown hospitals the closest medical facilities. Riverview Branch Library serves the West Side. Cherokee Park and Harriet Island are the major recreation and open-space areas. West Side residents hold a "West Side Pride Day" celebration each June.

The rate of major crimes is relatively high in the part of St. Paul that includes the West Side.

Dayton's Bluff

Dayton's Bluff is a predominantly blue-collar community that's home to several major industries, including 3M and Whirlpool Corp. plants and the Hamm's brewery. About half of Dayton's Bluff's housing units are single-family homes; most of the rest are duplexes. There are areas of deteriorated housing in the older, western part of the district.

The major commercial area in Dayton's Bluff is along East Seventh St. The district has two hospitals, Mounds Park and St. John's, which is scheduled to move to Maplewood next year. The Arlington Hills Branch Library serves Dayton's Bluff. Indian Mounds Park, overlooking the Mississippi River, is the major recreation area and site of the Dayton's Bluff Community Festival each summer. The park contains several small hills that contained Indian graves. Not far from the park is a marker for Carver's Cave. This large cave was discovered in 1766, and was said to contain a lake about 20 feet from its entrance. The cave was decorated with Indian wall drawings. Construction and debris forced the cave's closing in 1958.

The rate of major crimes is somewhat higher in Dayton's Bluff than in the city as a whole.

For more information on Dayton's Bluff, call 772-2075.

Payne-Minnehaha-Phalen

Some of St. Paul's oldest homes are in the southwest corner of the Payne-Minnehaha-Phalen district, in a neighborhood called Railroad Island. And some of the city's newest homes are in the district as well, concentrated in its northern section and along Interstate Highway 35E. Housing of all ages is predominantly single-family and in excellent condition, except for some deterioration in the district's south section. New townhouse and apartment units are planned for western areas of the community.

This community's most interesting neighborhood no longer exists. Swede Hollow was a teeming immigrant settlement that accumulated in a deep ravine that runs along Payne Av. The first shack was built there in

1841, and the area was populated by new arrivals of various ethnic backgrounds until 1956, when the city razed the area as a health hazard. Ambitious explorers will still find signs of the settlement in the ravine, and there are plans to make a park out of the area.

In addition to its strong residential base, Payne-Minnehaha-Phalen has thriving commercial areas along Payne Av. and Arcade St., as well as industries that provide jobs for many who live in the district. Phalen Park, with its large lake and 18-hole public golf course, is the major recreational area.

The nearest hospitals to Payne-Minnehaha-Phalen are those in the downtown area and Mounds Park in the neighboring Dayton's Bluff district. The nearest public library is the Arlington Hills branch, also in Dayton's Bluff.

The rate of major crimes is in the low-middle range for the part of the city that includes most of Payne-Minnehaha-Phalen.

For more information on Payne-Minnehaha-Phalen, call 774-5234.

North End

St. Paul's North End has a variety of housing, including newer apartment buildings in its northern and central sections. Partly because of the concentration of apartment units, the North End has a high proportion of residents aged 18 to 24.

The main commercial area runs along Rice St., an older strip of stores and service establishments. Some housing in the Rice St. area is deteriorating, adding to the problems of traffic and inadequate parking in the area. A major goal of the North End's district plan is to improve simultaneously the commercial area and nearby housing. The community hosts a Rice St. Festival each August.

The nearest hospitals are those in the downtown area. The Rice St. Branch Library serves the North End. Como Park, just to the west in the Lake Como district, is the main recreation area.

Wheelock Parkway is the major scenic area for the North End. Parts of the parkway run along steep bluffs and provide a good view of the downtown area. The North End includes Oakland Cemetery, where prestigious early citizens like Alexander Ramsey are buried. Oakland is the oldest cemetery in St. Paul.

The rates of serious crimes in the areas of the city that include parts of the North End are about average for the city. However, the North End has a high rate of crimes against property committed by juveniles.

For more information on the North End district, call 488-0507.

Thomas-Dale

Thomas-Dale, also known as Frogtown, is a largely blue-collar community of older, single-family homes. Most housing in the district is in sound condition, although there are pockets of deterioration. Because the cost of homes in Thomas-Dale is relatively modest, it is expected to become increasingly attractive as a place to live. An outstanding landmark in Thomas-Dale is the Church of St. Agnes, built between the years

1900 and 1912. The church has an onion-shaped tower that is more than 200 feet tall.

Commercial areas in Thomas-Dale are on University Av., Rice St., and Dale St., and at Minnehaha Av. and Chatsworth St. Industries are located near the railroad tracks on the north edge of the district.

Bethesda Lutheran Medical Center is in the eastern end of Thomas-Dale, just north of the state capitol complex. Thomas-Dale's community facilities include the Lexington Branch Library just across University Av. and small parks and playgrounds. The nearest major recreation area is Como Park.

The rate of serious crimes in the area of the city that includes Thomas-Dale is relatively low.

For more information on Thomas-Dale, call 298-5068.

Summit-University

Spectacularly in some areas, almost imperceptibly in others, decay is giving way to renewal in Summit-University. Renovation of homes in the Historic Hill District has changed the once-deteriorated southeast section of Summit-University into a model of historic preservation and urban revitalization. But a few blocks away, along Selby Av., renewal has touched only a few of the deteriorating homes and commercial buildings.

The current population of Summit-University is as diverse as its physical environment and includes the largest Hmong population in the city. The gentrification of the Historic Hill District raises the question of what will happen to the poor, the minorities, the elderly, and the children who make up a significant part of Summit-University's population. Will redevelopment provide homes and jobs for them, or will they be forced to look elsewhere?

The nearest hospitals to Summit-University are those in the downtown area. The Lexington Branch Library serves the district. There are several small parks and playgrounds. A Summit-University Arts Festival is hosted each spring by the Martin Luther King Jr.-Hallie Q. Brown Community Center.

The rate of serious crimes in Summit-University is high.

For more information on Summit-University, call 646-6609 or 646-4162.

West Seventh St.

The West Seventh St. district is an older, working-class community built on the flats along the Mississippi River. The historic Irvine Park community, now undergoing extensive renovation, is part of the district. Major commercial areas are along West Seventh St., also known as Fort Road because it runs from downtown to Fort Snelling.

Hospitals in the district are United and Children's. The nearest public library is downtown. Recreation areas include small parks and playgrounds, open space along the river, and the unfinished Interstate 35E roadbed.

The West Seventh St. district is home to people of various ethnic backgrounds, including Czech, German, and Italian. Several churches and social clubs in the district sponsor "booyas," parties centering on the consumption of a large pot of stew.

Most of the West Seventh St. district is in an area of the city with a low rate of serious crimes.

For more information on the West Seventh St. district, call 224-9645.

Como

Como is a middle-class community of well-kept, mostly single-family homes. There is no major commercial area; a few retail stores are scattered throughout the district. There is some industry along the railroad tracks in the southwest part of the district. More than 40 percent of the land in Como is parks and open space.

The vast majority of that, of course, is Como Park, which includes a lake, zoo, 18-hole public golf course, conservatory and formal gardens. Como Park is a major recreation center for the entire metropolitan area.

The nearest hospitals are Samaritan in the Hamline-Midway district and Midway in the Merriam Park district. The nearest public library is the Lexington branch.

The rate of serious crimes in the Como district is relatively low. However, traffic and noise associated with Como Park and the state fair in neighboring Falcon Heights are occasional summer irritants.

For more information on the Como district, call 644-3889.

Hamline-Midway

Hamline-Midway is in the process of being transformed from a traditional commercial-residential area into the site of one of the most innovative mixed-use projects in the Midwest—St. Paul's Energy Park. The Energy Park project includes plans for more than 600 residential units, as well as office space and support services for energy-related businesses and a hotel-conference center. The development is designed for energy efficiency, and its purpose is to encourage innovative, energy-related ventures. Construction of Energy Park is expected to extend into 1985.

The Energy Park complex is being built on a 218-acre site that includes the old Midway Stadium area and portions of the old railway property that were never developed. Little of the existing residential or commercial areas of the community are being disturbed.

Homes in Hamline-Midway are generally in good condition, although there are pockets of deterioration. In recent years many young families have bought homes in the district, helping to balance a relatively large elderly population. Hamline University adds to the district's diversity.

The community's commercial areas run along Snelling and University Avs., two of the broadest and busiest thoroughfares in the Twin Cities. The Samaritan Hospital and Hamline Branch Library are within Hamline-Midway. There are several small parks and playgrounds.

The rate of serious crimes in the area of the city that includes Hamline-Midway is in the low-middle range.

For more information on Hamline-Midway, call 646-1986.

St. Anthony Park

The residential part of St. Anthony Park consists of two distinct communities. North St. Anthony Park, adjacent to the University of Minnesota's St. Paul campus in Falcon Heights, is a stable community of large older homes on curving streets. South St. Anthony Park, in the center of the district, is a smaller neighborhood in the final stages of a successful redevelopment and rehabilitation program. A quarter-mile band of railroad tracks separates the two areas.

The St. Anthony Park district also includes the West Midway commercial and industrial area south and east of the residential areas. This area will be affected by the Energy Park development. A separate neighborhood business district in North St. Anthony Park features attractive specialty shops. A festival is held the first Saturday of June at its crossroads, Carter and Como Avs.

The nearest hospitals to St. Anthony Park are Samaritan in the Hamline-Midway district and Midway on University Av. in the Merriam Park district. The elegant St. Anthony Park Branch Library, one of three Carnegie libraries in the city, serves the district. There are several small parks and playgrounds.

The rate of serious crimes in the area of the city that includes St. Anthony Park is in the low-middle range.

For more information on St. Anthony Park, call 646-8884.

Merriam Park

Merriam Park is a diverse district of single-family homes, duplexes, and apartments. Most of the housing dates back to the turn of the century. Homes along Summit Av. and near the Mississippi River are substantial; those to the north and east are more modest. Most of the district's housing is in sound condition.

Midway Center at Snelling and University Avs. is a major shopping area. There are neighborhood business districts at Selby and Snelling Avs., Lexington Parkway and University Av., and Cleveland and Marshall Avs. Interstate 94 through the northern part of the district provides easy access to downtown St. Paul and Minneapolis.

The College of St. Thomas and Concordia College are within Merriam Park, and many students at Macalester College just to the south live in the district.

Midway Hospital and the Merriam Park Branch Library are within the district. There are several small parks and playgrounds, and Summit Av. and the Mississippi River provide additional recreation space.

For more information on Merriam Park, call 645-0349.

Macalester-Groveland

Macalester-Groveland is a quiet residential district of large, well-kept homes dating back to the 1920s and '30s. There are some apartment buildings and small businesses along the district's main thoroughfares—Cleveland, Grand, St. Clair, and Snelling Avs. The major institutions, however, are educational—Macalester College and the St. Paul Seminary. The Colleges of St. Catherine and St. Thomas, which border the district, also contribute to its academic atmosphere.

The nearest hospital is Midway, and the nearest public library is the Merriam Park branch. Both are in the Merriam Park district. There are playgrounds but no parks in Macalester-Groveland; however, Summit Av. and the Mississippi River provide scenery and some recreation space. Highland Park is not far to the south.

The rate of serious crimes in Macalester-Groveland is relatively low.

Highland

Highland is a relatively new and prosperous community with several large parks, a suburban-style shopping area at Cleveland Av. and Ford Parkway, and two industrial plants. Its housing is predominantly single-family, although there are apartment buildings as well. The College of St. Catherine is a major cultural resource for the district.

The nearest hospital to Highland is Midway. The Highland Park Branch Library serves the district. Highland Park, which has an 18-hole public golf course, is the main recreation facility.

Highland is in the area of the city with the lowest rate of serious crimes.

Summit Hill-Crocus Hill

Since the late 19th century, Summit Hill and Crocus Hill have been favorite neighborhoods of St. Paul's prosperous merchants and professional people. Unlike areas to the north of Summit Av., these neighborhoods never deteriorated. The large Victorian homes remain today much as they were at the turn of the century, although a trend toward condo-

A sampling of residential restoration in St. Paul.

minium conversion is appearing. Renewed interest in city living and historic preservation bodes well for the area's future.

Businesses in the Summit Hill-Crocus Hill district, including many specialty shops and restaurants, are strung out along Grand Av., many of them occupying renovated houses and commercial buildings. There are also smaller homes and apartment buildings along Grand and St. Clair Av., another major thoroughfare. A "Grand Old Days" festival is held each June.

The nearest hospitals to Summit Hill-Crocus Hill are those in the downtown area. The nearest public libraries are the Lexington branch and the Central library downtown. Linwood Park is the district's major recreation area.

Comparative crime statistics for Summit Hill-Crocus Hill were not available at this writing.

For more information on Summit Hill-Crocus Hill, call 222-1222.

Downtown

Downtown St. Paul is coming alive. Apartment and condominium buildings are going up around the Science Museum of Minnesota and in Lowertown, where new construction and renovation of old warehouses around Mears Park is aimed at creating an "urban village" offering new housing, entertainment, and work environments. Lowertown hosts an Art and Music Festival every June and an Octoberfest in the fall.

The St. Paul-Ramsey Medical Center and St. Joseph's Hospital are located downtown, as is the Central Library. Mears and Rice Parks provide scenery and open space.

The rate of serious crimes in the downtown district is relatively high.

For more information on the Downtown district, call 221-0488.

Sun Ray-Battle Creek-Highwood

Sun Ray-Battle Creek-Highwood is the last developing area of St. Paul. Much of the housing south of the I-94 freeway was built in the last 10 years, and many of the neighborhoods have an almost suburban character. This area has been slow to develop because it is mostly hilly and wooded, and its western edge is mostly wetland. An absence of city utilities such as water and sewers also hindered development.

In addition to suburban-style single-family homes, much of the new development in the southern area consists of townhouses and condominiums. The portion of the community north of the freeway has mostly single-family homes in more mature neighborhoods. There is a concentration of apartments along I-94. Major commercial development in the area, including Sun Ray Shopping Center, is also along I-94.

Battle Creek Park and Pigs Eye Regional Park are the major scenic and recreational spaces for the area. The Mississippi River runs along the western edge of the community, and includes one of the few surviving heron rookeries in the state.

The nearest hospitals are Mounds Park and St. John's in the neighboring Dayton's Bluff district. The area is served by the Sun Ray Branch Library.

The district is within an area of the city that has a relatively low rate of serious crimes.

For more information on Sun Ray-Battle Creek-Highwood, call 739-5881.

TWIN CITIES RESIDENTIAL REAL ESTATE PRICES

The following information, compiled from data supplied by the Multiple Listing Service of the Greater Minneapolis Area Board of Realtors and the St. Paul Area Board of Realtors, provides a quick overview of single-family home prices in the Twin Cities. The community designations, listed here in alphabetical order, are those used by the Multiple Listing Service and may occasionally overlap.

Community	Average Sales Price 1980	Units Sold 1980	Average Sales Price 1979
Afton, Denmark, Lakeland	$ 79,671	52	$ 70,679
Anoka County West	59,856	263	63,610
Apple Valley, Rosemount, Lakeville	79,291	206	67,015
Arden Hills, New Brighton, Shoreview	80,434	504	74,393
Blaine, Lino Lakes, Circle Pines	60,993	154	59,030
Bloomington-East	65,342	322	59,372
Bloomington-West	92,670	796	79,743
Brooklyn Center, Brooklyn Park, Osseo	64,284	890	60,650
Burnsville	78,639	727	71,919
Calhoun-Harriet (Minneapolis)	75,795	451	66,644
Cedar-Isles, Loring (Minneapolis)	101,904	196	89,055
Cherokee, Riverview (St. Paul)	49,680	146	45,139
Como (St. Paul)	59,309	182	55,054
Coon Rapids, Anoka	62,757	731	56,776
Cottage Grove, St. Paul Park	64,263	390	58,617
Crocus Hill (St. Paul)	85,418	185	81,748
East Side, Hazel Park (St. Paul)	51,958	531	48,924
Eden Prairie	98,126	391	89,153
Edina	117,089	652	104,923
Eagan	76,368	197	72,005
Forest Lake	63,115	174	59,499

Community	Average Sales Price 1980	Units Sold 1980	Average Sales Price 1979
Fridley, Columbia Heights, Spring Lake Park	63,881	513	58,838
Golden Valley	84,439	298	77,022
Highland Park (St. Paul)	78,744	224	73,289
Hopkins, Minnetonka	91,445	703	78,139
Inver Grove Heights	65,456	123	59,182
Lake Minnetonka	105,942	802	89,050
Macalester, Groveland (St. Paul)	71,770	296	65,457
Maplewood-East	69,054	68	63,909
Maplewood-North	65,679	154	62,151
Merriam Park (St. Paul)	63,676	134	59,171
Midway, St. Anthony (St. Paul)	55,012	199	51,942
Miscellaneous Northeast Minneapolis Suburbs	59,856	273	56,462
Miscellaneous Northwest Minneapolis Suburbs	65,948	855	61,721
Miscellaneous South Minneapolis Suburbs	68,944	486	67,805
Miscellaneous Southwest Minneapolis Suburbs	67,727	248	63,298
New Brighton, Mounds View, St. Anthony	75,189	347	69,009
North Central (St. Paul)	43,464	324	39,491
North Central Suburban St. Paul	110,418	106	97,932
North Minneapolis	48,786	902	44,921
North St. Paul	61,862	90	55,903
North Washington County	85,390	11	89,700
Northeast Minneapolis	54,416	262	49,605
Parkway Central (Minneapolis)	64,570	376	59,856
Parkway South (Minneapolis)	56,600	413	51,837
Parkway West (Minneapolis)	73,785	331	66,765
Payne, Phalen (St. Paul)	52,439	271	46,881
Plymouth	94,694	675	86,860
Richfield	65,341	419	60,051
Robbinsdale, Crystal, New Hope	63,888	722	59,633
Roseville, Falcon Heights, Lauderdale	77,004	330	71,497
St. Louis Park	66,958	631	59,690
South Central Minneapolis	48,633	245	45,971
South Minneapolis	54,476	446	49,085
South St. Paul	55,927	185	53,426
Southeast Minneapolis	62,950	52	58,765
West St. Paul, Mendota Heights	80,610	209	80,013
White Bear	73,603	451	65,439

ADDITIONAL READING

Discover St. Paul, Ramsey County Historical Society, 1979. A short history of seven St. Paul neighborhoods, including Dayton's Bluff, Ramsey Hill, Frogtown, W. Seventh St., West Side, North End, and Payne Av. 50 pages, photos.

Historic St. Paul Buildings, H. F. Koeper, St. Paul City Planning Board, 1964. An older book that describes 85 St. Paul buildings and four historic sites. 116 pages, many photos.

The Lake District of Minneapolis: A History of the Calhoun-Isles Community, David A. Lanegran and Ernest R. Sandeen, Living Historical Museum, St. Paul. Indexed history of the community, including walking tours. 112 pages, photos.

Minneapolis, Barbara Flanagan, St. Martin's Press, New York, 1973. Chatty description of the Minneapolis downtown area. Many black and white photos.

Minneapolis Communities: A Bibliography, Minneapolis Public Library and Information Center, 1981. Lists relevant books, articles, and city reports by community. 16 pages, illustrated with maps.

St. Paul's Historic Summit Avenue, Ernest R. Sandeen, Living Historical Museum, St. Paul, 1978. Includes history and walking tours as well as indexed list of houses on Summit Av. by address, year built, original owner, style, and architect. 110 pages, photos.

St. Paul Is My Beat, Gareth Hiebert, North Central Publications, St. Paul, 1958. Collection of "Oliver Towne" columns from the *St. Paul Dispatch.* 154 pages.

St. Paul/Minneapolis: The Twin Cities, Ronald Abler, Ballinger Publishing Co., Cambridge, Mass., 1976. Overview of social conditions in the Twin Cities, with some planning statistics. 69 pages.

St. Paul Omnibus: Images of a Changing City, Patricia Kane, Old Town Restorations, Inc., 1979. Essays and three walking tours of St. Paul.

St. Paul: Saga of an American City, Virginia Brainard Kunz, Windsor Publications, Inc., 1977. Detailed history of St. Paul including historical profiles of St. Paul businesses. Author is executive director of the Ramsey County Historical Society. Indexed, 254 pages, black and white and color photos.

State of the City, 1980, City of Minneapolis Planning Department, 1981. Statistical portrait of Minneapolis, including housing and crime information. 244 pages

The Street Where You Live, Donald Empson, Witsend Press, 1975. This guide to street names in St. Paul gives some history as well. 181 pages, some photos.

The Twin Cities, Carol Brink, Macmillan Co., New York, 1961. Describes people and places in the Twin Cities. Published as part of Macmillan's "Cities of America" series.

The Twin Cities Perceived, Jean Adams Ervin, University of Minnesota Press, 1976. Indexed, narrative exploration of Twin Cities neighborhoods, landmarks, and other features. 143 pages, illustrated with drawings.

Chapter Four

THE SUBURBS

The suburban communities that ring Minneapolis and St. Paul have as much to offer as the cities themselves. Among the 85 cities and townships with populations over 2,500 in the metropolitan area, there is an environment to suit almost any lifestyle.

Tied together by an extensive freeway system, few of these communities are more than 45 minutes from either downtown Minneapolis or downtown St. Paul. While the level of services provided varies from suburb to suburb, most have their own park systems, excellent schools, and other amenities. More than two-thirds of the two-million-plus metropolitan population resides in the suburbs, and growth, particularly on the outer edges of the seven-county area, is expected to continue for some time.

The fastest-growing communities in the area are located in northwestern Dakota County and northeastern Hennepin County. Suburbs in these areas attract young families in search of the traditional Suburban Dream—affordable new homes and plenty of open space to raise children, within commuting distance to jobs in the city.

More sedate and exclusive communities are clustered around the two major suburban lakes—Lake Minnetonka, west of Minneapolis, and White Bear Lake, north of St. Paul. Some of the most expensive homes in the metropolitan area can be found nestled in scenic areas of these resort communities-turned suburbs. Both of the lakes are large enough to offer good sailing, and each has an active yacht club.

Many suburbs developed as independent communities, and still retain a

(See Locator Key Map, pages 8-9)

▶1 Mpls. Downtown
▶2 Mpls. Excluding Downtown
▶3 Mpls. North Suburbs
▶4 Mpls. Northwest Suburbs
▶5 Mpls. Southwest Suburbs
▶6 Mpls. South Suburbs

▶7 St. Paul Downtown
▶8 St. Paul Excluding Downtown
▶9 St. Paul North Suburbs
▶10 St. Paul Northeast Suburbs
▶11 St. Paul Southeast Suburbs
▶12 St. Paul South Suburbs

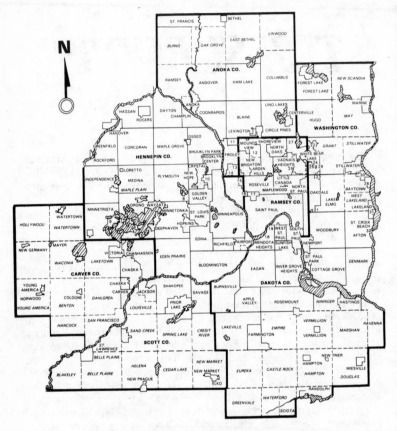

TWIN CITIES METROPOLITAN AREA
Political Boundaries

1 SPRING PARK	9 MOUND	17 FALCON HEIGHTS	25 GEM LAKE
2 ORONO	10 ROBBINSDALE	18 MENDOTA	26 BIRCHWOOD
3 MINNETONKA BEACH	11 SPRING LAKE PARK	19 LILYDALE	27 WHITE BEAR
4 TONKA BAY	12 U.S. GOVT	20 GREY CLOUD	28 BAYPORT
5 EXCELSIOR	13 HILLTOP	21 LANDFALL	29 WILLERNIE
6 GREENWOOD	14 COLUMBIA HEIGHTS	22 DELLWOOD	30 OAK PARK HEIGHTS
7 WOODLAND	15 ST. ANTHONY	23 PINE SPRINGS	31 LAKELAND SHORES
8 MEDICINE LAKE	16 LAUDERDALE	24 MAHTOMEDI	32 ST. MARY'S POINT

ANOKA — County Boundary

ORONO - Municipal Boundary

CAMDEN - Township Boundary

small-town flavor, in spite of the urban encroachment. The suburban inventory also includes typical Midwestern rivertowns lined up along the Mississippi, St. Croix, and Minnesota rivers. Some of these cities still serve as shipping centers for grain and lumber, and a few have particular historic significance.

There are predominately rural communities in the outer reaches of the area. Some of them are encouraging development, but most are zoned for agricultural preservation.

A more metropolitan lifestyle is available in the older, mature suburbs adjacent to Minneapolis and St. Paul. These communities have developed commercial and industrial centers of their own and may draw as many commuters in for jobs as leave for the big cities. Stabilizing in population after years of rapid urbanization, these communities are beginning to experience such central-city problems as declining school enrollments and commercial area decay. Most, however, remain viable and popular places to live.

Information on individual communities within the seven-county metropolitan area is provided on the following pages. The communities are listed in alphabetical order.

Population figures for 1980 are taken from preliminary 1980 census data supplied by the Metropolitan Council. Population projections for 1990 were made by the Metropolitan Council before the 1980 census was taken, and may not reflect the true growth potential of an area. Driving-time estimates are figured from the suburb to either downtown Minneapolis or downtown St. Paul.

Taxes on a $68,000 home are 1981 estimates made by the Citizens League for property that is fully homesteaded (owner-occupied). These figures do not represent actual taxes, and they will vary from year to year. The figures are presented as a means of comparison among communities. Tax rankings were also provided by the Citizens League, and do not include communities in Washington County, where data were not available. The local newspaper listed under each community is the one used for legal notices in that city. In fact, more than one newspaper may serve a particular community.

Some cities are in more than one school district. If this is the case, the school district listed is the one with jurisdiction over the majority of children in that community. This information, and most of the general information in each community profile, was supplied by city officials or the local chamber of commerce.

ANOKA (Anoka County) ►3

Pronounced A-*no*-ka. The county seat of Anoka County, Anoka straddles the Rum River at its confluence with the Mississippi. The city developed as a lumber-milling center in the 1860s and retains some of its historic flavor. The city has an extensive park system that includes a municipal golf course. Anoka has a strong central business district and a variety of housing—old and new, apartment and single-family. The Anoka Vocational-Technical Institute is in Anoka. The self-styled "Halloween Capital of the World," Anoka hosts a major celebration of that holiday each year. It is also headquarters of the Anoka County Fair held each August.

Population—	
1970:	13,591
1980:	15,541 (+14.4%)
1990:	15,000
Area (in acres)—	
Land:	4,170
Water:	289
Total:	4,459
Bus service:	MTC routes 26, 26B, 27B, C, D to Minneapolis
Half-hour drive or less to—	
Minneapolis:	No
St. Paul:	No
Shopping centers:	Northtown (Blaine), downtown Anoka
Hospital:	Mercy Medical Center (Coon Rapids)
Library:	Anoka City Library
Churches:	16 Protestant, one Catholic
School district:	11 (Anoka-Hennepin)
Schools:	One public high school, junior high, middle school, and four elementary; one private elementary
Taxes on $68,000 home:	$438
Tax rank 1 (high) to 90 (low):	37
Local newspaper:	*Anoka County Union*
City Hall phone:	421-6630
Chamber phone:	421-7130

APPLE VALLEY (Dakota County) ▶12

Apple Valley is a fast-growing residential community of mostly single-family homes. A relatively young suburb, it is more than 50 percent developed. The new Minnesota Zoo is in the northern part of the city. Apple Valley residents commute to jobs in nearby Bloomington as well as Minneapolis and St. Paul. The city sponsors a Fourth of July celebration and a "Midwinter Fest" each February.

Population—
1970:   8,502
1980:   21,806 (+156.5%)
1990:   36,500

Area (in acres)—
Land: 10,942
Water: 130
Total: 11,072

Bus service: MTC routes 32, 35M, 39, 64 to
                                           Minneapolis; 46 to St. Paul; 57
                                           Zoo-Minneapolis (summer only)

Half-hour drive or less to—
Minneapolis: No
St. Paul: Yes

Shopping centers: Burnsville (Burnsville), local centers
Hospitals: Apple Valley Clinic, Fairview
                                           Southdale (Edina), Divine
                                           Redeemer Memorial (South St.
                                           Paul)

Library: Dakota County (Burnsville)
Churches: 11 Protestant, one Catholic

School district: 196 (Rosemount)
Schools: One public high school, two
                                           middle schools, five elementary

Taxes on $68,000 home: $416
Tax rank 1 (high) to 90 (low):   49
Local newspaper: *Dakota County Tribune*

City Hall phone: 432-0750
Chamber phone: 432-8422

ARDEN HILLS (Ramsey County) ▶9

Arden Hills, a mostly residential suburb set on rolling hills north of St. Paul, is the home of the Twin Cities Arsenal, which takes up most of the northern third of the city. The city is still growing rapidly, and features several lakes, two colleges, and the new headquarters of Land O' Lakes, Inc., as well as several other major employers.

Population—
1970:   5,149
1980:   8,011 (+55.6%)
1990:   8,100

Area (in acres)—
Land: 5,785
Water: 498

Total:	6,283
Bus service:	MTC routes 38 to Minneapolis, and 35F to St. Paul; North Suburban Lines
Half-hour drive or less to—	
Minneapolis:	Yes
St. Paul:	Yes
Shopping centers:	Rosedale (Roseville), Arden Plaza
Hospitals:	Unity (Fridley), St. Paul-Ramsey Medical Center
Library:	Ramsey County branch
Church:	One Protestant
School district:	621 (Mounds View)
Schools:	One public high school, one elementary
Taxes on $68,000 home:	$407
Tax rank 1 (high) to 90 (low):	53
Local newspaper:	*New Brighton Bulletin*
City Hall phone:	633-5676
Chamber phone:	483-1313

BLAINE (Anoka County) ▶9

Blaine is growing quickly into a major suburb. It is about one-third developed, with single-family homes making up just over three-quarters of its housing units. More than 15 percent is multi-family. Blaine is the home of the Anoka County Airport, and hosts an Independence Day celebration each year called "Blaine's Blazing Fourth."

Population—	
1970:	20,568
1980:	28,488 (+38.5%)
1990:	39,300
Area (in acres)—	
Land:	21,775
Water:	40
Total:	21,815
Bus service:	MTC routes 10, 25, 27, 28, 29, 38 to Minneapolis, and 35F to St. Paul; North Suburban Lines
Half-hour drive or less to—	
Minneapolis:	Yes
St. Paul:	Yes
Shopping centers:	Northtown, neighborhood centers

Hospitals:	Unity (Fridley), Mercy Medical Center (Coon Rapids)
Library:	Anoka County Library
Churches:	Eight Protestant, one Catholic
School district:	11 (Anoka-Hennepin)
Schools:	Two public high schools, three junior highs, six elementary
Taxes on $68,000 home:	$465
Tax rank 1 (high) to 90 (low):	22
Local newspaper:	*Blaine & Spring Lake Park Life*
City Hall phone:	784-6700
Chamber phone:	755-3443

BLOOMINGTON (Hennepin County) ▶6

Bloomington is fast emerging as the third major urban center in the Twin Cities area. It is the home of several corporations, including Control Data, and its proximity to the Twin Cities International Airport and to downtown Minneapolis and St. Paul by freeway, has attracted both commercial and residential developers. Bloomington has no real downtown, but major office buildings, shopping centers, hotels, and restaurants are strung out along the Interstate 494 "strip" and, to a lesser extent, Interstate 35W. Professional hockey is played in Bloomington's Metropolitan Sports Center. There is a wide variety of housing, ranging from smaller and older homes in the eastern part of Bloomington to large new homes and expensive condominiums in the still-developing west. Bloomington is the home of Normandale Community College and the massive Hyland Park Preserve, as well as 90 other parks. This city is one of the few in the metro area that is served by cable television.

Population—	
1970:	81,970
1980:	81,640 (− 0.4%)
1990:	81,800
Area (in acres)—	
Land:	23,423
Water:	869
Total:	24,292
Bus service:	MTC routes 4, 5, 18, 35F, 35G, 35L, 35U, 35P, 39, 44A, B, C, D; 50 to St. Paul; 15, 48, 54, 64 to suburban destinations; Greyhound and Jefferson Lines
Half-hour drive or less to—	
Minneapolis:	Yes

St. Paul:	Yes
Shopping center:	Southtown
Hospital:	Fairview Southdale (Edina)
Library:	Two branches of the Hennepin County Library
Churches:	33 Protestant, three Catholic
School district:	271 (Bloomington)
Schools:	Three public high schools, two junior highs, 15 elementary; one private high school, four elementary
Taxes on $68,000 home:	$434
Tax rank 1 (high) to 90 (low):	38
Local newspaper:	*Bloomington Sun*
City Hall phone:	881-5811
Chamber phone:	888-8818

BROOKLYN CENTER (Hennepin County) ►4

Brooklyn Center is an almost completely developed suburb that borders directly on northwest Minneapolis. There is a new 6.6-acre arboretum in the city, as well as 20 parks. A new municipal building housing a library and offices for the city's courts and social services was opened in the fall of 1981. About one-third of Brooklyn Center's housing units are apartments. The city hosts "Early Bird Days" each June.

Population—	
1970:	35,173
1980:	31,167 (−11.4%)
1990:	33,500
Area (in acres)—	
Land:	5,201
Water:	233
Total:	5,434
Bus service:	MTC routes 5, 5D, E, K, L, M; 8B, C, D, E, F, G, H, J, L, M; 14, 14J; 26, 26A, X to Minneapolis
Half-hour drive or less to—	
Minneapolis:	Yes
St. Paul:	Yes
Shopping center:	Brookdale
Hospital:	North Memorial (Robbinsdale)
Library:	Hennepin County branch
Churches:	15 Protestant, one Catholic

School district:	286 (Brooklyn Center), 279 (Osseo)
Schools:	One public junior-senior high school, six elementary; one private high school, two elementary
Taxes on $68,000 home:	$422
Tax rank 1 (high) to 90 (low):	45
Local newspaper:	*Brooklyn Center Post*
City Hall phone:	561-5440
Chamber phone:	566-8650

BROOKLYN PARK (Hennepin County) ►4

Brooklyn Park is a fast-growing suburb with a variety of housing. Almost half of its housing units are rental apartments or townhouses. The northern half of Brooklyn Park is still very rural; the southern half is fully urbanized. A "downtown" area is developing around 77th and Zane Avs. N. The city boasts an award-winning park system, which includes an historical farm that is open for tours and demonstrations on designated days in the summer. Interstate 94 crosses the southern part of the city and will provide easy access to downtown Minneapolis when it's completed. The North Hennepin Community College and Suburban Hennepin County Technical College (north campus) are in Brooklyn Park.

Population—	
1970:	26,230
1980:	43,264 (+64.9%)
1990:	50,000
Area (in acres)—	
Land:	16,985
Water:	0
Total:	16,985
Bus service:	MTC routes 5E, K; 8D, M; 14H; 26; 45A, C, D, E to Minneapolis
Half-hour drive or less to—	
Minneapolis:	Yes
St. Paul:	Yes
Shopping centers:	Brookdale (Brooklyn Center), Brooklyn Park
Hospital:	North Memorial (Robbinsdale)
Library:	Hennepin County branch
Churches:	13 Protestant, one Catholic
School district:	279 (Osseo)
Schools:	One public high school, two junior highs, 10 elementary

Taxes on $68,000 home:	$444
Tax rank 1 (high) to 90 (low):	33
Local newspaper:	*Brooklyn Park Post*
City Hall phone:	425-4502
Chamber phone:	561-6280

BURNSVILLE (Dakota County) ►6

Burnsville is one of the metropolitan area's fastest-growing suburbs. Interstate 35W provides quick access to Bloomington and Minneapolis. Most of the new housing is single-family, but there is a variety of apartment and townhouse units as well. Burnsville has a major enclosed shopping mall, Burnsville Center, and its park system includes the first municipal ski hill designed for children. "Firemuster Days" are held in the city each September.

Population—	
1970:	19,940
1980:	35,681 (+78.9%)
1990:	51,000
Area (in acres)—	
Land:	16,390
Water:	502
Total:	16,892
Bus service:	MTC routes 32; 35K, M, N; 39, 64, 72
Half-hour drive or less to—	
Minneapolis:	Yes
St. Paul:	No
Shopping center:	Burnsville Center
Hospital:	Fairview Southdale (Edina)
Library:	Dakota County regional library
Churches:	16 Protestant, one Catholic
School district:	191 (Burnsville)
Schools:	One public high school, one junior high, six elementary schools
Taxes on $68,000 home:	$392
Tax rank 1 (high) to 90 (low):	63
Local newspapers:	*Dakota County Tribune; Burnsville Current*
City Hall phone:	890-4100
Chamber phone:	890-4455

CHANHASSEN (Carver and Hennepin counties) ►5

Chanhassen is home to the Chanhassen Dinner Theater, one of the largest and most successful dinner theater operations in the country. The city has several large lakes and the Lake Minnewashta Regional Park within its borders. There is a variety of housing, including five major apartment complexes. A new city hall was opened last year. This community has always had a rural character, but with new development the area is rapidly becoming urbanized. "Chanhassen" is a Sioux word meaning maple sugar.

Population—	
1970:	4,839
1980:	6,379 (+31.8%)
1990:	11,000
Area (in acres)—	
Land:	13,268
Water:	1,534
Total:	14,802
Bus service:	MTC routes 67E, F to Minneapolis; 53J to Eden Prairie
Half-hour drive or less to—	
Minneapolis:	Yes
St. Paul:	No
Shopping center:	Eden Prairie (Eden Prairie)
Hospitals:	St. Francis (Shakopee); Ridgeview (Waconia)
Library:	Carver County branch
Churches:	One Catholic, one Protestant
School district:	112 (Chaska)
Schools:	One public junior high, one elementary; one private elementary
Taxes on $68,000 home:	$413
Tax rank 1 (high) to 90 (low):	50
Local newspaper:	*Carver County Herald*
City Hall phone:	937-1900
Chamber phone:	934-3903

CHASKA (Carver County) ►5

Chaska, the county seat of Carver County, includes the "new town" of Jonathan as well as a traditional village and lots of rolling countryside. Chaska also is the home of the Minnesota Landscape Arboretum, a 560-acre education and research facility affiliated with the University of Minnesota. Chaska's annual festival is known as "River City Days."

Population—	
1970:	4,352
1980:	8,338 (+91.6%)
1990:	15,600

Area (in acres)—	
Land:	9,280
Water:	149
Total:	9,429

Bus service:	MTC route 53J to Eden Prairie; Zephyr Lines

Half-hour drive or less to—	
Minneapolis:	No
St. Paul:	No
Shopping centers:	Eden Prairie (Eden Prairie), Chaska
Hospitals:	St. Francis (Shakopee), Ridgeview (Waconia)
Library:	Carver County branch
Churches:	Six Protestant, one Catholic
School district:	112 (Chaska)
Schools:	One public high school, one junior high, one elementary; two private elementary

Taxes on $68,000 home:	$464
Tax rank 1 (high) to 90 (low):	23
Local newspaper:	*Carver County Herald*
City Hall phone:	448-2851
Chamber phone:	448-5000

COLUMBIA HEIGHTS (Anoka County) ►3

Columbia Heights is a mature suburb perched on the northeastern corner of Minneapolis. It surrounds the tiny city of Hilltop. The city's housing stock includes approximately 5,000 single-family homes and 2,500 rental or townhouse units. Downtown Columbia Heights is undergoing extensive redevelopment. A "Columbia Heights Jamboree" is held each June.

Population—	
1970:	23,997
1980:	19,931 (−16.9%)
1990:	20,000

Area (in acres)—	
Land:	2,061

Water:	189
Total:	2,250
Bus service:	MTC routes 1, 4, 10, 18, 28, 29 to Minneapolis; 52H, J, S to U of M
Half-hour drive or less to—	
Minneapolis:	Yes
St. Paul:	Yes
Shopping centers:	Apache Plaza (St. Anthony), downtown Columbia Heights
Hospital:	Unity (Fridley)
Library:	Columbia Heights City Library
Churches:	Seven Protestant, one Catholic
School district:	13 (Columbia Heights)
Schools:	One public high school, one junior high, two elementary; two private elementary
Taxes on $68,000 home:	$425
Tax rank 1 (high) to 90 (low):	43
Local newspaper:	*Columbia Heights-St. Anthony Sun*
City Hall phone:	788-9221

A shopping mall in downtown White Bear Lake.

COON RAPIDS (Anoka County) ▶3

Coon Rapids is a developing suburb; only a little more than half its land has been developed. The city provides extensive services and has a park system that includes two indoor swimming pools, an indoor ice arena, and a municipal golf course that has been ranked among the top municipal courses in the country. Two regional parks and two branches of the Anoka County Library are also located in Coon Rapids, as well as the Anoka-Ramsey Community College. The city hosts an annual "Snowflake Days" festival in February and a Fine Arts Week each September.

Population—	
1970:	30,505
1980:	35,838 (+ 17.5%)
1990:	46,200
Area (in acres)—	
Land:	14,538
Water:	117
Total:	14,655
Bus service:	MTC routes 10G; 27, 27A, 29 to Minneapolis
Half-hour drive or less to—	
Minneapolis:	Yes
St. Paul:	Yes
Shopping centers:	Northtown (Blaine), local centers
Hospital:	Mercy Medical Center
Library:	Two branches of the Anoka County Library
Churches:	14 Protestant, one Catholic
School district:	11 (Anoka-Hennepin)
Schools:	One public high school, two junior highs, 10 elementary; two private high schools, three elementary
Taxes on a $68,000 home:	$429
Tax rank 1 (high) to 90 (low):	42
Local newspaper:	*Coon Rapids Herald*
City Hall phone:	755-2880
Chamber phone:	755-1130

COTTAGE GROVE (Washington County) ▶11

Cottage Grove is an older residential, commercial, and industrial community that's still growing rapidly. Major employers are 3M's Chemolite plant and the Whirlpool Corp. Commercial development is concentrated along U.S. Highway 61, which bisects the city diagonally. The city is scenically situated near the confluence of the Mississippi and St. Croix rivers.

Population—	
1970:	13,419
1980:	18,925 (+41%)
1990:	28,500
Area (in acres)—	
Land:	22,962
Water:	88
Total:	23,050
Bus service:	MTC routes 17A, B; 18A, B, C to St. Paul
Half-hour drive or less to—	
Minneapolis:	No
St. Paul:	Yes
Shopping centers:	St. Paul, local centers
Hospitals:	Divine Redeemer (South St. Paul), Regina Memorial (Hastings)
Library:	Washington County branch
Churches:	10 Protestant, one Catholic
School district:	833 (South Washington)
Schools:	One public high school, four elementary; one private high school, two elementary
Taxes on a $68,000 home:	$486
Tax rank 1 (high) to 90 (low):	N.A.
Local newspaper:	*Washington County Bulletin*
City Hall phone:	458-2800
Chamber phone:	459-9779

CRYSTAL (Hennepin County) ►4

Crystal is a mature, mostly residential suburb with shopping and other services available in the Crystal Shopping Center, the community's "downtown." Both single-family homes and apartment units are available. "Crystal Frolics" are held each July.

Population—	
1970:	30,925
1980:	25,489 (−17.6%)
1990:	26,500
Area (in acres)—	
Land:	3,652
Water:	60

Total:	3,712
Bus service:	MTC routes 5L; 14D, J; 45 to Minneapolis
Half-hour drive or less to—	
Minneapolis:	Yes
St. Paul:	No
Shopping centers:	Brookdale (Brooklyn Center), Crystal
Hospital:	North Memorial (Robbinsdale)
Library:	Hennepin County branch
Churches:	Six Protestant, one Catholic
School district:	281 (Robbinsdale)
Schools:	Three public elementary; one private elementary
Taxes on a $68,000 home:	$445
Tax rank 1 (high) to 90 (low):	32
Local newspaper:	*North Hennepin Post*
City Hall phone:	537-8421
Chamber phone:	544-8439

DEEPHAVEN (Hennepin County) ▶5

Deephaven is a former resort town on Lake Minnetonka. It is now a settled, spacious community of older mansions and newer single-family homes. Deephaven has a city marina as well as the only paddleball court owned by a Minnesota municipality.

Population—	
1970:	3,853
1980:	3,689 (-4.3%)
1990:	4,200
Area (in acres)—	
Land:	1,526*
Bus service:	MTC routes 67D, E, H to Minneapolis
Half-hour drive or less to—	
Minneapolis:	Yes
St. Paul:	No

---

*Because a number of communities surrounding Lake Minnetonka extend their boundaries various distances into the lake, it is impossible to determine each community's portion of it. For this reason, only land area figures are given for these communities.

Shopping centers:	Ridgedale (Minnetonka), Excelsior
Hospital:	Methodist (St. Louis Park)
Library:	Hennepin County (Minnetonka)
Churches:	One Catholic, one Protestant
School district:	276 (Minnetonka)
Schools:	One public middle school, one elementary; two private elementary
Taxes on a $68,000 home:	$397
Tax rank 1 (high) to 90 (low):	62
Local newspaper:	*Southshore Sun*
City Hall phone:	474-4755

EAGAN (Dakota County) ▶12

Eagan is a fast-growing residential suburb with some industry along the Minnesota River. There is a variety of single-family, condominium, and rental housing. Lebanon Hills Park is in Eagan, and a new branch of the Dakota County Library is planned for the city. Interstate 35E will eventually be extended through Eagan, and will allow easy access to St. Paul.

Population—	
1970:	10,398
1980:	20,720 (+ 99.3%)
1990:	36,000
Area (in acres)—	
Land:	20,744
Water:	808
Total:	21,552
Bus service:	MTC routes 19A, 77E
Half-hour drive or less to—	
Minneapolis:	Yes
St. Paul:	Yes
Shopping center:	Burnsville (Burnsville), local centers
Hospital:	Divine Redeemer (South St. Paul)
Library:	Dakota County (Burnsville)
Churches:	Seven Protestant, one Catholic
School district:	191 (Burnsville); 196 (Rosemount)
Schools:	One public junior high, five elementary; one private elementary
Taxes on a $68,000 home:	$300
Tax rank 1 (high) to 90 (low):	78
Local newspaper:	*Dakota County Tribune; Eagan Chronicle*

City Hall phone:	454-8100
Chamber phone:	457-4921

EDEN PRAIRIE (Hennepin County) ►5

Eden Prairie is a scenic community that is undergoing both residential and industrial development. A variety of single-family and townhouse units are available. In addition to a major enclosed shopping mall (Eden Prairie Center), business activity includes headquarters for Gelco, Super Valu, and several other major companies. The new home of the Minnesota Vikings football team, which includes offices and training facilities, is located in Eden Prairie. Eden Prairie is trying to preserve its semi-rural character, and much of the new development respects the community's hills and lakes. Wetlands, virgin prairie, and portions of virgin Minnesota forest can still be found in the city. The Suburban Hennepin County Vocational-Technical Institute (south campus) is in Eden Prairie as is Flying Cloud Airport. Interstate 494 provides easy access to Minneapolis, St. Paul, and the Twin Cities International Airport. "Schooner Days" are hosted by the city each summer.

Population—	
1970:	6,938
1980:	16,259 (+134.4%)
1990:	25,000
Area (in acres)—	
Land:	21,270
Water:	1,190
Total:	22,460
Bus service:	MTC routes 53J, S to Minneapolis
Half-hour drive or less to—	
Minneapolis:	Yes
St. Paul:	No
Shopping centers:	Eden Prairie Center, Prairie Village Mall
Hospital:	Fairview Southdale (Edina)
Library:	Hennepin County branch
Churches:	Seven Protestant
School district:	272 (Eden Prairie)
Schools:	One public high school, one middle school, two elementary schools; one private high school, two elementary
Taxes on a $68,000 home:	$423
Tax rank 1 (high) to 90 (low):	44
Local newspaper:	*Eden Prairie News*

City Hall phone:	937-2262
Chamber phone:	944-2830

EDINA (Hennepin County) ▶5

Pronounced E-*di*-na. If Bloomington was everyone's suburb in the 1950s and '60s, Edina was claimed by the most prosperous and trend-conscious of those who moved out of the city. Now 90 percent developed, Edina remains a prestige address. There's more variety in housing now, particularly with new luxury apartments and condominiums. The area around Southdale, the world's first all-enclosed shopping mall (it opened in 1956), has become a major office and urban service center, and several smaller shopping centers and a discount department store have kept the area one of the most complete for shopping in the Twin Cities. In addition to the California-style Southdale area, Edina has a pedestrian-oriented downtown of mostly smaller shops around 50th St. and France Av. S. Edina's location allows easy access to downtown Minneapolis, Bloomington, and the Twin Cities International Airport. Edina hosts an art show each summer.

Population—	
1970:	44,046
1980:	46,000 (+ 4.4%)
1990:	50,000
Area (in acres)—	
Land:	9,947
Water:	121
Total:	10,068
Bus service:	MTC routes 4, 4C, F, G, J, L; 6A, B, C, D, E, H, J, K, L; 15A, D; 32; 35H, J, T; 42F; 48, 52B to Minneapolis; 50 to St. Paul
Half-hour drive or less to—	
Minneapolis:	Yes
St. Paul:	Yes
Shopping centers:	Southdale, 50th and France, smaller centers
Hospital:	Fairview Southdale
Libraries:	Hennepin County Area Library, Edina Public Library
Churches:	20 Protestant, two Catholic
School district:	273 (Edina)
Schools:	One public high school, two junior highs, four elementary; three private elementary

Taxes on a $68,000 home:	$399
Tax rank 1 (high) to 90 (low):	61
Local newspaper:	*Edina Sun*
City Hall phone:	927-8861
Chamber phone:	831-2713

EXCELSIOR (Hennepin County) ►5

Excelsior is an historic community on the south shore of Lake Minnetonka. The Excelsior-Lake Minnetonka Historical Society conducts walking tours of the city. An excursion boat runs between Excelsior and Wayzata on the north shore of the lake. Excelsior Commons is the only major lakefront park on Minnetonka. Downtown Excelsior businesses are mostly specialty shops. There is a high proportion of rental housing in Excelsior—highest in the metropolitan area, except for Minneapolis.

Population—	
1970:	2,563
1980:	2,507 (– 2.2%)
1990:	2,800
Area (in acres)—	
Land:	448
Bus service:	MTC routes 67C, D, G, H to Minneapolis
Half-hour drive or less to—	
Minneapolis:	Yes
St. Paul:	No
Shopping centers:	Ridgedale (Minnetonka), downtown Excelsior
Hospital:	Methodist (St. Louis Park)
Library:	Hennepin County branch
Churches:	Seven Protestant, one Catholic
School district:	276 (Minnetonka)
Schools:	One public elementary; two private elementary
Taxes on $68,000 home:	$464
Tax rank 1 (high) to 90 (low):	25
Local newspaper:	*Excelsior Maverick*
City Hall phone:	474-5233
Chamber phone:	474-6461

FALCON HEIGHTS (Ramsey County) ►9

Falcon Heights is a mature suburb on the northern border of St. Paul. It offers a mix of single-family and rental housing, and is the home of the

St. Paul Campus of the University of Minnesota, the Minnesota State Fairgrounds, and the Gibbs Farm Museum.

Population—	
1970:	5,530
1980:	5,291 (−4.3%)
1990:	5,200
Area (in acres)—	
Land:	1,422
Water:	0
Total:	1,422
Bus service:	MTC routes 4, 6, 12 to St. Paul
Half-hour drive or less to—	
Minneapolis:	Yes
St. Paul:	Yes
Shopping centers:	Rosedale (Roseville), local centers
Hospitals:	St. Paul-Ramsey Medical Center, Midway (St. Paul)
Library:	Ramsey County (Roseville)
Church:	One Protestant
School district:	623 (Roseville)
School:	One public elementary school
Taxes on a $68,000 home:	$500
Tax rank 1 (high) to 90 (low):	13
Local newspaper:	*St. Paul Dispatch, Pioneer Press*
City Hall phone:	644-5050
Chamber phone:	483-1313

FARMINGTON (Dakota County) ►6

Farmington, a trading center for the surrounding rural area, has become a Twin Cities suburb as well in the last decade. It retains a downtown business area, and there is some variety of single-family and apartment housing. The city has an extensive park system, an indoor ice arena, and a municipal golf course. The Dakota County Fair is held in Farmington each summer.

Population—	
1970:	3,464
1980:	4,362 (+25.9%)
1990:	5,550
Area (in acres)—	
Land:	7,364
Water:	0
Total:	7,364

Bus service:	Jefferson Lines
Half-hour drive or less to—	
Minneapolis:	No
St. Paul:	No
Shopping centers:	Burnsville Center (Burnsville), Farmington
Hospital:	Sanford Memorial
Library:	Dakota County branch
Churches:	Six Protestant, one Catholic
School district:	192 (Farmington)
Schools:	One public high school, one middle school, one elementary
Taxes on a $68,000 home:	$378
Tax rank 1 (high) to 90 (low):	69
Local newspaper:	*Dakota County Tribune*
City Hall phone:	463-7111

FOREST LAKE (Washington County) ▶10

Originally a resort community near the Twin Cities, Forest Lake has grown into a commercial center for the surrounding semi-rural area. Interstate 35, with branches to Minneapolis and St. Paul, allows Forest Lake residents to commute to jobs in the Twin Cities and their suburbs. The city retains a central business district for shopping which is supplemented by Northland Mall. There is a variety of single-family and rental housing. District Memorial Hospital is in Forest Lake. Masquers Theater Company, a community theater, holds several productions during the summer, and the Forest Lake Jaycees host a "Snowblast Weekend" each winter.

Population—	
1970:	3,213
1980:	4,588 (+42.8%)
1990:	6,100
Area (in acres)—	
Land:	1,848
Water:	0
Total:	1,848
Bus service:	Zephyr Lines
Half-hour drive or less to—	
Minneapolis:	No
St. Paul:	No
Shopping centers:	Maplewood Mall (Maplewood), Forest Lake

Hospital:	District Memorial
Library:	Forest Lake City Library
Churches:	Eight Protestant, one Catholic
School district:	831 (Forest Lake)
Schools:	Two public high schools, two elementary; one private high school, two private elementary
Taxes on a $68,000 home:	$484
Tax rank 1 (high) to 90 (low):	N.A.
Local newspaper:	*Forest Lake Times*
City Hall phone:	464-3550
Chamber phone:	464-3200

FRIDLEY (Anoka County) ▶3

Fridley is a mature suburb adjacent to northeast Minneapolis. The city is bordered on the west by the Mississippi, and the river's proximity provides many recreational opportunities. The Islands of Peace project sponsored by the city has made it possible for handicapped persons to enjoy the Mississippi park area. A variety of housing is available, with the housing stock made up of approximately 6,600 single-family homes and 2,500 rental units. Several light industrial plants operate in the city, and Interstate 694 provides easy access to both Minneapolis and St. Paul. Fridley is the home of the Columbia Ice Arena and is one of the few cities in the metropolitan area with cable television service. Fridley's annual summer festival is called "49er Days."

Population—	
1970:	29,233
1980:	30,089 (+2.9%)
1990:	34,500
Area (in acres)—	
Land:	6,548
Water:	232
Total:	6,780
Bus service:	MTC routes 10, 10E; 27; 28, 28E to Minneapolis
Half-hour drive or less to—	
Minneapolis:	Yes
St. Paul:	Yes
Shopping centers:	Northtown (Blaine), local centers
Hospital:	Unity Hospital
Library:	Anoka County branch
Churches:	11 Protestant, one Catholic
School district:	14 (Fridley)

Schools:	One public high school, one junior high, five elementary; one private high school

Taxes on a $68,000 home:	$404
Tax rank 1 (high) to 90 (low):	57
Local newspaper:	*Fridley Sun*
City Hall phone:	571-3450
Chamber phone:	571-9781

GOLDEN VALLEY (Hennepin County) ►4

Golden Valley is an established suburb directly west of Minneapolis. Single-family homes predominate, but there are more than 1,000 apartment units and 225 townhouse units among the city's 6,500 housing units. New senior citizen housing is available. The city is working on establishing a downtown area. At present there are businesses along U.S. Highway 12 and Minnesota Highway 55, the main routes into Minneapolis. General Mills' corporate headquarters is at the intersection of U.S. 12 and County 18.

In the fall of 1980, students in what had been Golden Valley School District 275 began attending schools in Robbinsdale District 281. Breck School, a private co-educational high school, will move from Minneapolis into the former Golden Valley High School at the start of the 1981-82 school year. Golden Valley Lutheran College is also located in the city.

Population—	
1970:	24,246
1980:	22,658 (−6.6%)
1990:	23,500
Area (in acres)—	
Land:	6,636
Water:	96
Total:	6,732
Bus service:	MTC routes 9C, D, E, K, L; 19A, C to Minneapolis; 34, 34A; 58, local routes; Medicine Lake Lines
Half-hour drive or less to—	
Minneapolis:	Yes
St. Paul:	No
Shopping centers:	Ridgedale (Minnetonka), Minneapolis, local centers
Hospitals:	Golden Valley Medical Center, North Memorial (Robbinsdale)
Library:	Hennepin County branch
Churches:	14 Protestant, one Catholic

School district:	281 (Robbinsdale)
Schools:	One public junior high, three elementary; one private high school
Taxes on a $68,000 home:	$441
Tax rank 1 (high) to 90 (low):	34
Local newspaper:	*North Hennepin Post*
City Hall phone:	545-3781
Chamber phone:	544-8439

HASTINGS (Dakota and Washington counties) ►12

Hastings, the county seat of Dakota County, is an old river town situated on the Mississippi at its confluence with the St. Croix. Although Hastings has an established downtown and retains its historic flavor, it is a fast-growing community with a variety of housing. Vermillion Falls and Lock and Dam #2 are two attractions along the river in Hastings.

Population—	
1970:	12,179
1980:	12,814 (+5.2%)
1990:	16,300
Area (in acres)—	
Land:	5,703
Water:	335
Total:	6,038
Bus service:	Greyhound
Half-hour drive or less to—	
Minneapolis:	No
St. Paul:	Yes
Shopping center:	Signal Hills (West St. Paul)
Hospital:	Regina Memorial
Library:	Dakota County branch
Churches:	Nine Protestant, two Catholic
School district:	200 (Hastings)
Schools:	One public high school, one junior high, four elementary; two private elementary
Taxes on a $68,000 home:	$368
Tax rank 1 (high) to 90 (low):	71
Local newspaper:	*Hastings Star and Gazette*
City Hall phone:	437-4127
Chamber phone:	437-6775

HOPKINS (Hennepin County) ▶5

Despite its suburban location, Hopkins in many ways is a typical Midwestern town. It has its own downtown business district as well as offices, factories, and warehouses that draw more people into Hopkins to work than commute from Hopkins to jobs elsewhere. Hopkins is headquarters of two supermarket chains—Red Owl and National, which owns Applebaums as well as National stores. Hopkins is a developed suburb with a wide range of single-family home sizes and prices and a major concentration of apartment housing. The Hennepin County Fair and "Raspberry Festival" are annual summer events.

Population—	
1970:	13,428
1980:	15,302 (+ 14.0%)
1990:	16,000
Area (in acres)—	
Land:	2,569
Water:	0
Total:	2,569
Bus service:	MTC routes 12A, B, C, D, E, F to Minneapolis
Half-hour drive or less to—	
Minneapolis:	Yes
St. Paul:	No
Shopping centers:	Knollwood (St. Louis Park), Hopkins
Hospital:	Methodist (St. Louis Park)
Library:	Hennepin County branch
Churches:	Five Protestant, two Catholic
School district:	274 (Hopkins)
Schools:	One public high school, two elementary; one private high school, two elementary
Taxes on a $68,000 home:	$459
Tax rank 1 (high) to 90 (low):	28
Local newspaper:	*Hopkins-Minnetonka Sun*
City Hall phone:	935-8474
Chamber phone:	938-6337

INVER GROVE HEIGHTS (Dakota County) ▶12

Inver Grove Heights is a fast-growing, mostly residential suburb south of St. Paul. The northeast corner of the city is where most of the population is concentrated—the remaining two-thirds of the community is basically undeveloped. About a quarter of the housing units are rental.

Inver Grove Heights is the home of Inver Hills Community College and the Macalester College Botanical Gardens. "Inver Grove Heights Days" are held each summer.

Population—	
1970:	12,148
1980:	17,154 (+41.2%)
1990:	24,000
Area (in acres)—	
Land:	18,546
Water:	912
Total:	19,458
Bus service:	MTC routes 5G, H; 8A, C, D, E; 11A, C; 29, 29A to St. Paul
Half-hour drive or less to—	
Minneapolis:	No
St. Paul:	Yes
Shopping centers:	Signal Hills (West St. Paul), local centers
Hospital:	Divine Redeemer Memorial (South St. Paul)
Library:	Dakota County branch (West St. Paul)
Churches:	Seven Protestant, one Catholic
School district:	199 (Inver Grove Heights)
Schools:	One public high school, one junior high, four elementary; one private elementary
Taxes on a $68,000 home:	$327
Tax rank 1 (high) to 90 (low):	76
Local newspaper:	*South St. Paul/Inver Grove Heights Sun*
City Hall phone:	457-2111

LAKEVILLE (Dakota County) ▶6

Lakeville is growing as both an industrial and residential community. A variety of housing is available, and the city's park system offers a range of recreational activities, including two public swimming beaches. Buck Hill ski area is on Lakeville's northern border. The "Panorama of Progress" festival that is held each summer in Lakeville features the state cow-chip throwing championships. The city has a new elementary school and a new fire station.

Population—	
1970:	7,196

1980:	14,760 (+ 105.1%)
1990:	18,300

Area (in acres)—
Land:	23,373
Water:	782
Total:	24,155

Bus service:	Greyhound, Zephyr, Jefferson

Half-hour drive or less to—
Minneapolis:	No
St. Paul:	No
Shopping centers:	Burnsville Center (Burnsville), Lakeville
Hospital:	Sanford Memorial (Farmington)
Library:	Dakota County (Farmington)
Churches:	Ten Protestant, one Catholic
School district:	194 (Lakeville)
Schools:	One public high school, one middle school, four elementary
Taxes on a $68,000 home:	$378
Tax rank 1 (high) to 90 (low):	70
Local newspaper:	*Dakota County Tribune*
City Hall phone:	469-4931
Chamber phone:	469-2020

LITTLE CANADA (Ramsey County) ►9

Little Canada has more than doubled its population in the last 10 years. Part of this growth may be attributed to its easy access to both Minneapolis and St. Paul. Situated just north of St. Paul, Little Canada is bisected by Interstate highways 35E and 694, which meet in the city. "Canadian Days" are held in Little Canada in July.

Population—
1970:	3,481
1980:	7,082 (+ 103.5%)
1990:	11,000

Area (in acres)—
Land:	2,575
Water:	248
Total:	2,843
Bus service:	MTC routes 2A, 35F; North Suburban Lines to St. Paul

Half-hour drive or less to—
Minneapolis:	Yes

St. Paul:	Yes
Shopping centers:	Rosedale (Roseville), Maplewood Mall (Maplewood)
Hospital:	St. Paul-Ramsey Medical Center
Library:	Ramsey County (Roseville)
Churches:	Two Protestant, one Catholic
School district:	623 (Roseville)
Schools:	One public high school, one junior high, one elementary
Taxes on a $68,000 home:	$267
Tax rank 1 (high) to 90 (low):	79
Local newspaper:	*Northern Suburban News*
City Hall phone:	484-2177
Chamber phone:	483-1313

MAHTOMEDI (Washington County) ►10

Pronounced Mah-to-*me*-di, this former resort community on White Bear Lake is undergoing new residential development. A variety of apartment and single-family housing is available. The city surrounds the tiny city of Willernie. The 961 Area Vocational-Technical school is in Mahtomedi.

Population—	
1970:	3,828
1980:	3,857 (+0.8%)
1990:	4,600
Area (in acres)—	
Land:	2,086
Water:	0
Total:	2,086
Bus service:	MTC routes 15D, E; 35D to St. Paul
Half-hour drive or less to—	
Minneapolis:	No
St. Paul:	Yes
Shopping centers:	Maplewood Mall (Maplewood), White Bear Lake
Hospitals:	Lakeview Memorial (Stillwater); St. Paul-Ramsey Medical Center
Library:	Washington County branch (Willernie)
Churches:	Four Protestant, one Catholic
School district:	832 (Mahtomedi)

Schools:	One public high school, one middle school, two elementary; one private elementary
Taxes on a $68,000 home:	$394
Tax rank 1 (high) to 90 (low):	N.A.
Local newspaper:	*White Bear Free Press*
City Hall phone:	426-3344

MAPLE GROVE (Hennepin County) ►4

Maple Grove is a fast-growing community of mostly single-family homes. The northwest corner is still very rural, but the remainder of the city is undergoing steady residential and commercial development. A new bond issue for park development was passed in Maple Grove recently and should lead to more city park resources. A portion of the Elm Creek Park Reserve is in the city. Interstates 94 and 494 meet in Maple Grove, providing easy access to Minneapolis, St. Paul, and the western suburbs.

Population—	
1970:	6,275
1980:	20,517 (+227.0%)
1990:	31,500
Area (in acres)—	
Land:	21,308
Water:	988
Total:	22,298
Bus service:	MTC routes 45B, C to Minneapolis; Medicine Lake Lines
Half-hour drive or less to—	
Minneapolis:	Yes
St. Paul:	No
Shopping centers:	Brookdale (Brooklyn Center), local centers
Hospital:	North Memorial (Robbinsdale)
Library:	Hennepin County (Osseo)
Churches:	Nine Protestant, one Catholic
School district:	279 (Osseo)
Schools:	Three public elementary
Taxes on a $68,000 home:	$418
Tax rank 1 (high) to 90 (low):	48
Local newspaper:	*Osseo-Maple Grove Press*
City Hall phone:	425-4521
Chamber phone:	425-1323

MAPLEWOOD (Ramsey County) ►9

Maplewood, draped around the northern and eastern borders of St. Paul, is home of the 3M Co., Minnesota's largest publicly held corporation. More than 10,000 people are employed at the 3M Center in Maplewood. The city has an extensive lake and park system, which includes the northern portion of Lake Phalen. Some 40 percent of Maplewood's land is undeveloped; the rest is covered mostly with single-family homes. Maplewood is the home of the Ramsey County Fair.

Population—	
1970:	25,186
1980:	26,954 (+7.0%)
1990:	34,000
Area (in acres)—	
Land:	11,062
Water:	378
Total:	11,440
Bus service:	MTC routes 3A, E, F; 9, 9B, C, D, G; 11B; 12A, B, C, D, E, H, J, K; 20; 35B; 36 to St. Paul
Half-hour drive or less to—	
Minneapolis:	Yes
St. Paul:	Yes
Shopping center:	Maplewood Mall
Hospital:	St. Paul-Ramsey Medical Center
Library:	Ramsey County branch
Churches:	11 Protestant, four Catholic
School district:	622 (North St. Paul-Maplewood)
Schools:	Two public junior high schools, four elementary; two private high schools, one junior high, six elementary
Taxes on a $68,000 home:	$494
Tax rank 1 (high) to 90 (low):	15
Local newspaper:	*Maplewood Review*
City Hall phone:	770-4520
Chamber phone:	483-1313

MENDOTA HEIGHTS (Dakota County) ►12

Extensions of both Interstates 35E and 494 are planned through Mendota Heights, making easier access from the city of Minneapolis and the southern suburbs. The city is a residential suburb of mostly single-family homes with some condominiums. It surrounds the tiny city of Mendota (pop. 266), which has a small downtown and the oldest church in Minnesota. Mendota Heights is near Minneapolis, St. Paul, and the Bloomington "strip."

Population—	
1970:	6,565
1980:	7,288 (+11%)
1990:	9,000
Area (in acres)—	
Land:	5,838
Water:	546
Total:	6,384
Bus service:	MTC routes 5D; 19A; 29C, D; 45; 46 to St. Paul
Half-hour drive or less to—	
Minneapolis:	Yes
St. Paul:	Yes
Shopping center:	Signal Hills (West St. Paul)
Hospital:	Divine Redeemer Memorial (South St. Paul)
Library:	Dakota County (West St. Paul)
Churches:	Two Protestant

Metropolitan life: at home in the Twin Cities.

School district:	197 (West St. Paul)
Schools:	One public high school, two elementary; one private high school
Taxes on a $68,000 home:	$325
Tax rank 1 (high) to 90 (low):	77
Local newspaper:	*West St. Paul-Mendota Heights Sun*
City Hall phone:	452-1850
Chamber phone:	457-4921

MINNETONKA (Hennepin County) ►5

Minnetonka is a newer suburb on the eastern edge of Lake Minnetonka. It has mostly single-family homes, although about 10 percent of its housing units are apartments. The city has emerged as a commercial and corporate center, with headquarters for the largest privately held corporation in Minnesota, Cargill. Toro is relocating to new headquarters in Minnetonka, and Fingerhut and Data 100 are already headquartered in the city. Ridgedale, a major enclosed shopping mall, and many smaller centers offer a variety of shopping experiences. U.S. Highway 12 and Minnesota Highway 7 are the major thoroughfares to Minneapolis; Interstate 494 provides access to suburbs north and south.

Population—	
1970:	35,776
1980:	38,699 (+8.2%)
1990:	42,700
Area (in acres)—	
Land:	17,425
Water:	558
Total:	17,983
Bus service:	MTC routes 12D, E; 67C, D, E, F, G to Minneapolis; 36B; 51, 51C (suburban routes)
Half-hour drive or less to—	
Minneapolis:	Yes
St. Paul:	No
Shopping center:	Ridgedale
Hospital:	Methodist (St. Louis Park)
Library:	Hennepin County branch
Churches:	Nine Protestant, two others
School district:	276 (Minnetonka)
Schools:	Two public high schools, three junior highs, seven elementary;

	one private high school, two elementary
Taxes on a $68,000 home:	$456
Tax rank 1 (high) to 90 (low):	29
Local newspaper:	*Hopkins-Minnetonka Sun*
City Hall phone:	933-2511
Chamber phone:	938-6337

MOUND (Hennepin County) ►5

Named for the Indian burial mounds found at the western end of Lake Minnetonka, Mound is a former resort town that's now an almost fully developed suburb. Tonka Toys are made in Mound. The city has mostly single-family homes, and it retains its old downtown.

Population—	
1970:	7,572
1980:	9,248 (+22.1%)
1990:	9,700
Area (in acres)—	
Land:	1,930
Bus service:	MTC routes 51S, 51N to Minneapolis
Half-hour drive or less to—	
Minneapolis:	No
St. Paul:	No
Shopping centers:	Ridgedale (Minnetonka), Mound
Hospitals:	Ridgeview (Waconia); North Memorial (Robbinsdale)
Library:	Hennepin County branch
Churches:	Four Protestant, one Catholic
School district:	277 (Westonka)
Schools:	One public junior high, two elementary; one private elementary
Taxes on a $68,000 home:	$455
Tax rank 1 (high) to 90 (low):	30
Local newspaper:	*The Laker*
City Hall phone:	472-1155
Chamber phone:	472-6780

MOUNDS VIEW (Ramsey County) ►9

Mounds View is a largely developed suburb with some variety of housing. New residential development planned for the city will include townhouses, duplexes, and condominiums as well as single-family homes. Mounds View has convenient freeway connections to both Minneapolis and St. Paul. The city holds a "Festival in the Parks" each July.

Population—
1970:   10,599
1980:   12,607 (+19%)
1990:   14,000

Area (in acres)—
Land: 2,910
Water: 20
Total: 2,930

Bus service: MTC routes 25B, 28 to Min-
                                neapolis; 35F to St. Paul; North
                                Suburban Lines

Half-hour drive or less to—
Minneapolis: Yes
St. Paul: Yes

Shopping centers: Northtown (Blaine), Mounds View
                                Square
Hospital: Unity (Fridley)
Library: Anoka County (Blaine)
Churches: Four Protestant

School district: 621 (Mounds View)
Schools: One public junior high, two
                                elementary

Taxes on a $68,000 home: $549
Tax rank 1 (high) to 90 (low): 5
Local newspaper: *New Brighton Bulletin*
City Hall phone: 784-3055

NEW BRIGHTON (Ramsey County) ▶9

New Brighton is a low-density suburb with single-family homes making up approximately 70 percent of its housing stock. Recent residential development has included condominiums and some apartments. The city's park system includes a municipal golf course. Interstates 35W and 694 intersect at the eastern edge of the city, providing easy access to both Minneapolis and St. Paul.

Population—
1970:   19,507
1980:   23,240 (+19.1%)
1990:   23,500

Area (in acres)—
Land:	4,380
Water:	370
Total:	4,750

Bus service: MTC routes 4D, G, F; 52S to Minneapolis

Half-hour drive or less to—
Minneapolis:	Yes
St. Paul:	Yes

Shopping centers: Rosedale (Roseville), Brighton Village

Hospital:	Unity (Fridley)
Library:	Ramsey County (Arden Hills)
Churches:	Six Protestant, one Catholic

School district: 621 (Mounds View)
Schools: One public high school, one junior high, four elementary; one private elementary

Taxes on a $68,000 home:	$460
Tax rank 1 (high) to 90 (low):	27
Local newspaper:	*New Brighton Bulletin*

City Hall phone:	633-1533
Chamber phone:	483-1313

NEW HOPE (Hennepin County) ►4

New Hope calls itself "the family-style city." It is a developed suburb of mostly single-family homes. It has an award-winning park system that includes an indoor ice arena. The community's annual July festival is called "Duk Duk Daze."

Population—
1970:	23,180
1980:	23,105 (− 0.3%)
1990:	21,500

Area (in acres)—
Land:	3,289
Water:	11
Total:	3,300

Bus service: MTC routes 5L; 14G, H to Minneapolis; Medicine Lake Lines

Half-hour drive or less to—
Minneapolis:	Yes
St. Paul:	No

Shopping centers:	Ridgedale (Minnetonka), Brookdale (Brooklyn Center), local centers
Hospital:	North Memorial (Robbinsdale)
Library:	Hennepin County (Crystal)
Churches:	Nine Protestant, one Catholic
School district:	281 (Robbinsdale)
Schools:	One public high school, one junior high, four elementary
Taxes on a $68,000 home:	$433
Tax rank 1 (high) to 90 (low):	39
Local newspaper:	*New Hope-Plymouth Post*
City Hall phone:	533-1521
Chamber phone:	544-8439

NORTH OAKS (Ramsey County) ▶9

North Oaks is a prestigious and secluded community of large single-family homes among several lakes. There is very little public land in the city, and services are minimal.

Population—	
1970:	2,002
1980:	2,849 (+42.3%)
1990:	3,900
Area (in acres)—	
Land:	4,718
Water:	767
Total:	5,485
Bus service:	North Suburban Lines
Half-hour drive or less to—	
Minneapolis:	Yes
St. Paul:	Yes
Shopping centers:	Maplewood Mall (Maplewood), White Bear Lake
Hospital:	St. Paul-Ramsey Medical Center
Library:	Ramsey County (White Bear Lake)
Church:	One Protestant
School district:	621 (Mounds View)
School:	One public junior high school
Taxes on a $68,000 home:	$484
Tax rank 1 (high) to 90 (low):	17
Local newspaper:	*White Bear Press*
City Hall phone:	484-5777

NORTH ST. PAUL (Ramsey County) ►9

North St. Paul developed as an independent community, and retains an active downtown business district. The atmosphere could be described as "small town." Most of the housing is single-family, but there are a substantial number of apartments—about 18 percent of total units. "Snow Frolics" are held each February, and "Round-up Days" are held each September.

Population—	
1970:	11,950
1980:	11,935 (– 0.1%)
1990:	12,500
Area (in acres)—	
Land:	1,889
Water:	134
Total:	2,023
Bus service:	MTC routes 9C, D; 31 to St. Paul
Half-hour drive or less to—	
Minneapolis:	Yes
St. Paul:	Yes
Shopping centers:	Maplewood Mall (Maplewood), North St. Paul
Hospitals:	St. John's (St. Paul), St. Paul-Ramsey Medical Center
Library:	Ramsey County branch
Churches:	Seven Protestant, one Catholic
School district:	622 (North St. Paul-Maplewood)
Schools:	One public high school, three elementary; two private elementary
Taxes on a $68,000 home:	$440
Tax rank 1 (high) to 90 (low):	36
Local newspaper:	*Ramsey County Review*
City Hall phone:	777-1346
Chamber phone:	483-1313

ORONO (Hennepin County) ►5

Orono's southern boundary is composed of the northern bays of Lake Minnetonka. There is a mix of old and new housing, with parts of the community semi-rural with large estates and some areas still being farmed.

Population—	
1970:	6,787
1980:	6,835 (+ 0.7%)

1990:	9,000
Area (in acres)—	
Land:	11,215
Bus service:	MTC route 51N (suburban)
Half-hour drive or less to—	
Minneapolis:	Yes
St. Paul:	No
Shopping centers:	Ridgedale (Minnetonka), Navarre
Hospitals:	North Memorial (Robbinsdale), Ridgeview (Waconia)
Library:	Hennepin County branch (Mound)
Churches:	Seven Protestant
School districts:	278 (Orono), 277 (Mound-Westonka)
Schools:	One public high school, one middle school, one elementary school
Taxes on a $68,000 home:	$400
Tax rank 1 (high) to 90 (low):	60
Local newspaper:	*Lake Minnetonka Area Sun*
City Hall phone:	473-7358

OSSEO (Hennepin County) ►4

Osseo is a small northern suburb sandwiched between Maple Grove and Brooklyn Park. It has an older downtown, a variety of housing, and an industrial park. The local Lions Club sponsors a festival called "Lions' Roar" each September.

Population—	
1970:	2,908
1980:	2,976 (+2.3%)
1990:	2,900
Area (in acres)—	
Land:	475
Water:	0
Total:	475
Bus service:	MTC routes 45B, C to Minneapolis; Greyhound
Half-hour drive or less to—	
Minneapolis:	Yes
St. Paul:	No
Shopping centers:	Brookdale (Brooklyn Center); Osseo

Hospital:	North Memorial (Robbinsdale)
Library:	Hennepin County branch
Churches:	Three Protestant, one Catholic
School district:	279 (Osseo)
Schools:	One public high school, one junior high, one elementary; two private elementary
Taxes on a $68,000 home:	$450
Tax rank 1 (high) to 90 (low):	31
Local newspaper:	*Osseo-Maple Grove Press*
City Hall phone:	425-2624 or 425-1111
Chamber phone:	425-1323

PLYMOUTH (Hennepin County) ►4

Plymouth is a fast-growing suburb that is about half developed. Housing is mostly single-family with some apartments. There are two large industrial parks and a smaller one. A downtown shopping center and regional park on Medicine Lake are planned.

Population—	
1970:	18,077
1980:	31,566 (+ 74.6%)
1990:	43,500
Area (in acres)—	
Land:	21,306
Water:	1,535
Total:	22,841
Bus service:	Medicine Lake Lines
Half-hour drive or less to—	
Minneapolis:	Yes
St. Paul:	No
Shopping center:	Ridgedale (Minnetonka)
Hospital:	North Memorial (Robbinsdale)
Library:	Hennepin County branch (Wayzata)
Churches:	One Protestant, one Catholic
School district:	284 (Wayzata)
Schools:	Two public high schools, two junior highs, seven elementary
Taxes on a $68,000 home:	$441
Tax rank 1 (high) to 90 (low):	35
Local newspaper:	*New Hope-Plymouth Post*
City Hall phone:	559-2800
Chamber phone:	544-8439

PRIOR LAKE (Scott County) ►6

Prior Lake is a resort area south of the Twin Cities that is fast becoming a year-round community. A variety of apartment and single-family housing has been built, and a scenic chain of lakes divides the city almost in half. Shopping centers are springing up along Highway 13, the main route through Prior Lake to the Twin Cities.

Population—	
1970:	4,127
1980:	7,109 (+72.3%)
1990:	9,100
Area (in acres)—	
Land:	8,276
Water:	1,241
Total:	9,517
Bus service:	MTC route 35N to Minneapolis
Half-hour drive or less to—	
Minneapolis:	No
St. Paul:	No
Shopping centers:	Burnsville Center (Burnsville), Prior Lake
Hospital:	St. Francis (Shakopee)
Library:	Scott County branch
Churches:	Seven Protestant, one Catholic
School district:	719 (Prior Lake)
Schools:	One public high school, one junior high, two elementary; two private elementary
Taxes on a $68,000 home:	$513
Tax rank 1 (high) to 90 (low):	8
Local newspaper:	*Prior Lake American*
City Hall phone:	447-4230

RAMSEY (Anoka County) ►3

Located just north of Anoka, Ramsey is growing rapidly, but is still semi-rural, with much open land. About one-third of the city is developed; 90 percent of the building took place during the last decade. All housing is single-family, and new residential development is limited to lots larger than two acres.

Population—	
1970:	2,360
1980:	10,084 (+327.3%)
1990:	13,900

Area (in acres)—

Land:	18,488
Water:	200
Total:	18,688

Bus service: None

Half-hour drive or less to—
Minneapolis: No
St. Paul: No

Shopping center: Northtown (Blaine)
Hospital: Mercy Medical Center (Coon Rapids)

Library: Anoka City Library
Churches: Four Protestant

School district: 11 (Anoka-Hennepin)
School: One public elementary

Taxes on a $68,000 home: $400
Tax rank 1 (high) to 90 (low): 59
Local newspaper: *Anoka Union*

City Hall phone: 427-1410

RICHFIELD (Hennepin County) ►6

Richfield is a mature suburb on the south edge of Minneapolis. About 10,000 of the city's 15,000 housing units are single-family homes; almost all the rest are rental apartments. The city has a fully developed park system, including a new 18-hole municipal golf course and a par-3 nine, plus a driving range. The city's commercial district along 66th Street between Nicollet and Lyndale is undergoing a major refurbishment. Richfield offers easy access by Interstates 35W and 494 to Minneapolis and Bloomington and by County Highway 62 (Crosstown) to Southdale and the Twin Cities International Airport. Richfield is home of the Wood Lake Nature Center. The city hosts an annual Fourth of July celebration.

Population—

1970:	47,231
1980:	37,789 (−20.0%)
1990:	39,000

Area (in acres)—

Land:	4,627
Water:	0
Total:	4,627

Bus service: MTC routes 4C, D; 5D, E, H; 15A, F; 18C; 19C; 35E, F, J, P, S; 39; 44; 47A, B, C, E, G, H; 57 to Minneapolis; 50 to St. Paul

Half-hour drive or less to—
Minneapolis: Yes
St. Paul: Yes

Shopping centers: Southdale (Edina), Hub
Hospital: Fairview-Southdale (Edina)
Library: Hennepin County branch
Churches: 15 Protestant, three Catholic

School district: 280 (Richfield)
Schools: One public high school, two middle
                                      schools, four elementary; two
                                      private high schools, five private
                                      elementary

Taxes on a $68,000 home: $482
Tax rank 1 (high) to 90 (low):   18
Local newspaper: *Richfield Sun*

City Hall phone: 869-7521
Chamber phone: 866-5100

General Mills' home office in Golden Valley.

ROBBINSDALE (Hennepin County) ►4

Robbinsdale is a smaller northwest Minneapolis suburb that is fairly mature. Some new commercial development is in progress, but there is very little residential building. The community hosts "Whiz Bang Days" in July.

Population—	
1970:	16,845
1980:	14,393 (−14.6%)
1990:	14,500
Area (in acres)—	
Land:	1,828
Water:	80
Total:	1,908
Bus service:	MTC routes 5A, B, H, J; 7B; 8, 8A, E, G, H, J, L, M; 11, 11A; 14A, B, C, D, G, H, J to Minneapolis
Half-hour drive or less to—	
Minneapolis:	Yes
St. Paul:	Yes
Shopping center:	Brookdale (Brooklyn Center)
Hospital:	North Memorial
Library:	Hennepin County branch (Crystal)
Churches:	Ten Protestant, one Catholic
School district:	281 (Robbinsdale)
Schools:	One public high school, two elementary; one private elementary
Taxes on a $68,000 home:	$558
Tax rank 1 (high) to 90 (low):	3
Local newspaper:	*North Hennepin Post*
City Hall phone:	537-4534
Chamber phone:	535-3522

ROSEVILLE (Ramsey County) ►9

Extensive shopping and other urban services make Roseville the center of activity in the suburbs north of St. Paul. Both Rosedale, a major regional shopping center, and Har Mar Mall are in the city, as well as several medium-sized corporations. There is a balance between residential and commercial-industrial activity in Roseville. The city's park system includes a municipal golf course. An Independence Day celebration is held in the city each year.

Population—
1970:   34,438
1980:   35,530 (+3.2%)
1990:   36,000

Area (in acres)—
Land: 8,463
Water: 321
Total: 8,784

Bus service: MTC and North Suburban Lines

Half-hour drive or less to—
Minneapolis: Yes
St. Paul: Yes

Shopping center: Rosedale
Hospital: St. Paul-Ramsey Medical Center
Library: Ramsey County branch
Churches: 10 Protestant, two Catholic

School district: 623 (Roseville)
Schools: One public high school, two junior
                                           highs; one private high school,
                                           two elementary

Taxes on a $68,000 home: $382
Tax rank 1 (high) to 90 (low):   66
Local newspaper: *Roseville Sun*

City Hall phone: 484-3371
Chamber phone: 483-1313

ST. ANTHONY (Hennepin and Ramsey counties) ▶9

St. Anthony is a developed suburb with mostly single-family housing. It adjoins Roseville and northeast Minneapolis. Interstate 35W passes along the city's southern border, providing easy access to both Minneapolis and St. Paul.

Population—
1970:   9,239
1980:   7,977 (−17%)
1990:   8,900

Area (in acres)—
Land: 1,363
Water: 117
Total: 1,480

Bus service: MTC routes 11, 28 to Minneapolis

Half-hour drive or less to—
Minneapolis: Yes

St. Paul:	Yes
Shopping center:	Apache Plaza
Hospital:	Unity (Fridley)
Library:	Hennepin County branch
Churches:	Three Protestant, one Catholic
School district:	282 (St. Anthony)
Schools:	One public high school, one middle school, one elementary; one private elementary
Taxes on a $68,000 home:	$478
Tax rank 1 (high) to 90 (low):	19
Local newspaper:	*New Brighton Bulletin*
City Hall phone:	789-8881

ST. LOUIS PARK (Hennepin County) ►5

St. Louis Park is a developed suburb adjacent to Minneapolis. Its growth has stabilized, although some commercial and light industrial development continues. About a third of the city's housing units are apartments, and there is a trend toward condominium conversions. Methodist Hospital is in St. Louis Park, and a newer feature in the city is the most extravagant store of the Byerly's luxury supermarket chain. U.S. 169-Minnesota 100 provides freeway access north and south, and U.S. 12 and Minnesota 7 are the main highways into Minneapolis. St. Louis Park has excellent services, including an active community education program and an extensive park system. The Westwood Hills Environmental Education Center is a unique feature of the park system.

Population—	
1970:	48,883
1980:	42,875 (-12.3%)
1990:	42,800
Area (in acres)—	
Land:	6,773
Water:	22
Total:	6,795
Bus service:	MTC routes 9C, D, H, L; 12F; 17C, E, F, H, J; 52P; 67A, B, C, D, E, F, G to Minneapolis; 46 (suburban)
Half-hour drive or less to—	
Minneapolis:	Yes
St. Paul:	Yes
Shopping centers:	Ridgedale (Minnetonka), Knollwood Plaza

Hospital:	Methodist
Library:	Hennepin County branch
Churches:	13 Protestant, four Jewish, two Catholic
School district:	283 (St. Louis Park)
Schools:	One public high school, one junior high, seven elementary; three private high schools, five private elementary
Taxes on a $68,000 home:	$521
Tax rank 1 (high) to 90 (low):	7
Local newspaper:	*St. Louis Park Sun*
City Hall phone:	920-3000
Chamber phone:	938-6337

ST. PAUL PARK (Washington County) ►11

St. Paul Park is a small southeastern suburb that is bounded on the west by the Mississippi River and on the east by Highway 61, a portion of the scenic Great River Road. An older, more established community, St. Paul Park has mostly single-family homes. The Ashland Oil refinery is the major industry in the city. St. Paul Park hosts an annual Fourth of July celebration each year.

Population—	
1970:	5,587
1980:	4,876 (−12.7%)
1990:	5,100
Area (in acres)—	
Land:	1,500
Water:	88
Total:	1,588
Bus service:	MTC routes 17, 18A, B, C to St. Paul
Half-hour drive or less to—	
Minneapolis:	No
St. Paul:	Yes
Shopping centers:	St. Paul, local centers
Hospital:	Divine Redeemer (South St. Paul)
Library:	Washington County branch (Cottage Grove)
Churches:	Five Protestant, one Catholic
School district:	833 (South Washington)
Schools:	Two public junior high schools,

one elementary; one private
elementary

Taxes on a $68,000 home:	$430
Tax rank 1 (high) to 90 (low):	N.A.
Local newspaper:	*Washington County Bulletin*
City Hall phone:	459-9785

SAVAGE (Scott County) ►6

Savage is a major grain-shipping terminal on the Minnesota River. Grain is brought to elevators in Savage and then loaded onto barges for transport to the Mississippi River. Savage was an independent community before it became a suburb, and it retains a downtown business district. There is new condominium development in the city, and GTA is building a new grain terminal on Highway 13. "Heritage Days" are held in Savage each summer.

Population—	
1970:	3,115
1980:	3,962 (+27.2%)
1990:	12,000
Area (in acres)—	
Land:	10,192
Water:	226
Total:	10,418
Bus service:	MTC routes 35N, 54
Half-hour drive or less to—	
Minneapolis:	Yes
St. Paul:	No
Shopping center:	Burnsville Center (Burnsville)
Hospital:	St. Francis (Shakopee)
Library:	Scott County branch
Churches:	One Protestant, one Catholic
School district:	191 (Burnsville); 719 (Prior Lake)
Schools:	One public elementary, one private elementary
Taxes on a $68,000 home:	$568
Tax rank 1 (high) to 90 (low):	2
Local newspaper:	*Prior Lake American*
City Hall phone:	890-1045

SHAKOPEE (Scott County) ►6

Pronounced *Shock*-o-pee, this city retains its small-town atmosphere in spite of rapid suburbanization. The south and southeast areas of the city remain mostly rural, with population concentrated in the northwest. Shakopee's industrial park is on the east side of the city. Shakopee is the county seat of Scott County. There is shopping downtown as well as in local centers. About 500 of Shakopee's 3,000 housing units are apartments. Tourist attractions and events in the Shakopee area include Valleyfair Family Amusement Park, Murphy's Landing, and the Renaissance Festival during late August and September weekends.

Population—
1970: 7,716
1980: 9,928 (+28.7%)
1990: 16,000

Area (in acres)—
Land: 16,874
Water: 727
Total: 17,601

Bus service: MTC route 53S to Eden Prairie Center

Half-hour drive or less to—
Minneapolis: No
St. Paul: No

Shopping centers: Eden Prairie Center (Eden Prairie)
Hospital: St. Francis
Library: Scott County branch
Churches: Eight Protestant, two Catholic

School district: 720 (Shakopee)
Schools: One public high school, one junior high, three elementary; one private elementary

Taxes on a $68,000 home: $468
Tax rank 1 (high) to 90 (low): 21
Local newspaper: *Shakopee Valley News*

City Hall phone: 445-3650
Chamber phone: 445-1660

SHOREVIEW (Ramsey County) ▶9

Shoreview is a developing suburb with mostly single-family housing and several major employers, including a Control Data Corp. plant and Deluxe Check Printers. There are several large lakes in or near the city. Interstate 694 provides easy access to other northern suburbs. Several Twin Cities radio and television stations have transmitting towers in Shoreview.

Population—
1970: 10,978

1980:	17,262 (+ 57.2%)
1990:	21,600

Area (in acres)—
Land:	7,045
Water:	1,006
Total:	8,060

Bus service:	MTC route 33B; North Suburban Lines

Half-hour drive or less to—
Minneapolis:	Yes
St. Paul:	Yes
Shopping center:	Rosedale (Roseville)
Hospitals:	Unity (Fridley), St. Paul-Ramsey Medical Center
Library:	Ramsey County branch (Arden Hills)
Churches:	Four Protestant, one Catholic
School district:	621 (Mounds View)
Schools:	One public junior high school, four elementary; one private elementary

Taxes on a $68,000 home:	$409
Tax rank 1 (high) to 90 (low):	51
Local newspaper:	*New Brighton Bulletin*
City Hall phone:	484-3353
Chamber phone:	483-1313

SOUTH ST. PAUL (Dakota County) ►12

South St. Paul is an established community with a small-town atmosphere. It is the home of the world's largest stockyards and the site of an annual rodeo. South St. Paul has its own hospital, library, and airport, as well as the Dakota County Historical Museum. The Mississippi River forms South St. Paul's eastern border, and Interstate 494 bisects the city. "Kaposia Days" are held in South St. Paul every summer.

Population—
1970:	25,016
1980:	21,216 (− 15.2%)
1990:	22,000

Area (in acres)—
Land:	3,466
Water:	214
Total:	3,680

Bus service:	MTC routes 8, 8A, C, D, E, G; 11A; 29, 29A to St. Paul
Half-hour drive or less to—	
Minneapolis:	No
St. Paul:	Yes
Shopping centers:	Signal Hills (West St. Paul), South St. Paul
Hospital:	Divine Redeemer Memorial
Library:	South St. Paul City Library
Churches:	23 Protestant, three Catholic
School district:	6 (South St. Paul)
Schools:	One public high school, one junior high, four elementary; three private elementary
Taxes on a $68,000 home:	$420
Tax rank 1 (high) to 90 (low):	47
Local newspaper:	*South St. Paul-Inver Grove Heights Sun*
City Hall phone:	451-2787
Chamber phone:	451-2266

STILLWATER (Washington County) ▶10

Stillwater, county seat of Washington County, is the oldest settlement in Minnesota, dating to 1841. Located on the St. Croix River, it was originally a lumbering center. Stillwater has a variety of housing, including old historic homes overlooking the river. The city's downtown, featuring restored buildings that house specialty shops, a few fine restaurants, and the Lowell Inn, has become a weekend drawing card for visitors from all over the metropolitan area. The city has its own library and Lakeview Memorial Hospital, and is the only Twin Cities suburb to have its own daily newspaper. "Lumberjack Days" are held in Stillwater each summer.

Population—	
1970:	10,208
1980:	12,255 (+20.1%)
1990:	13,500
Area (in acres)—	
Land:	3,065
Water:	584
Total:	3,649
Bus service:	MTC routes 12D, K; 94S to St. Paul; Valley Transit; Zephyr Lines

Half-hour drive or less to—	
Minneapolis:	No
St. Paul:	Yes
Shopping centers:	Maplewood Mall (Maplewood), Stillwater
Hospital:	Lakeview Memorial
Library:	Stillwater City Library
Churches:	15 Protestant, two Catholic
School district:	834 (Stillwater)
Schools:	One public senior high, one junior high, three elementary; two private elementary
Taxes on a $68,000 home:	$388
Tax rank 1 (high) to 90 (low):	N.A.
Local newspaper:	*Stillwater Gazette*
City Hall phone:	439-6121
Chamber phone:	439-7700

VADNAIS HEIGHTS (Ramsey County) ▶9

Pronounced *Vad*-ness, Vadnais Heights is a developing suburb that still has lots of open space. The Vadnais chain of lakes in the southwestern corner of the city supplies the city of St. Paul with drinking water. The lakes are surrounded by a park and forest preserve. There is some rental housing, and new development is moving toward more multi-family units. H.B. Fuller Co. is constructing its national headquarters and research facility in Vadnais Heights. Interstates 694 and 35E provide easy access to the northern suburbs and to downtown St. Paul.

Population—	
1970:	3,411
1980:	5,087 (+49.1%)
1990:	8,700
Area (in acres)—	
Land:	4,656
Water:	536
Total:	5,192
Bus service:	MTC routes 2A; 35F, D; North Suburban Lines
Half-hour drive or less to—	
Minneapolis:	Yes
St. Paul:	Yes
Shopping center:	Maplewood Mall (Maplewood)
Hospital:	St. Paul-Ramsey Medical Center
Library:	Ramsey County branch (White

	Bear Lake)
Churches:	Two Protestant
School district:	624 (White Bear Lake)
Schools:	One public elementary
Taxes on a $68,000 home:	$503
Tax rank 1 (high) to 90 (low):	10
Local newspaper:	*Vadnais Heights-Little Canada Free Press*
City Hall phone:	429-5343
Chamber phone:	483-1313

WAYZATA (Hennepin County) ▶5

Pronounced Wy-*zet*-a, and located on the northeast shore of Lake Minnetonka, Wayzata is one of the most prestigious addresses in the Twin Cities. Families such as the Daytons and the Pillsburys have mansions there. The thriving downtown business district features an unusual number of stock brokerage offices for a town of less than 4,000, along with specialty shops, professional services, and one of the most exclusive restaurants in the metropolitan area, Chouette. About one-third of the housing units are apartments, but condominium conversion is expected to cut into the supply of rental housing. U.S. Highway 12 (Wayzata Boulevard) provides access to Interstate 494 and downtown Minneapolis.

Population—	
1970:	3,700
1980:	3,642 (−1.6%)
1990:	4,200
Area (in acres)—	
Land:	2,010
Bus service:	MTC routes 51N, S, W (suburban)
Half-hour drive or less to—	
Minneapolis:	Yes
St. Paul:	No
Shopping centers:	Ridgedale (Minnetonka), Wayzata
Hospital:	North Memorial (Robbinsdale)
Library:	Hennepin County branch
Churches:	Three Protestant, one Catholic
School district:	284 (Wayzata)
Schools:	One public high school, one junior high, one elementary school; three private elementary schools
Taxes on a $68,000 home:	$381
Tax rank 1 (high) to 90 (low):	67

Local newspaper:	*Wayzata News, Minnetonka Sun*
City Hall phone:	473-0234
Chamber phone:	473-9595

WEST ST. PAUL (Dakota County) ►12

West St. Paul, like the adjacent West Side of St. Paul, is due south of downtown St. Paul. Nevertheless, because of the course of the Mississippi River in that area, West St. Paul is "west" of St. Paul. A compact, developed suburb, West St. Paul offers a variety of single-family and rental housing. It features the Dodge Nature Center, a good park system, and Signal Hills Shopping Center. Robert Street (U.S. 52) is a major shopping strip for the suburbs south of St. Paul. A "Summerfest" is held in the city each June.

Population—	
1970:	18,802
1980:	18,524 (−1.5%)
1990:	19,200
Area (in acres)—	
Land:	3,178
Water:	32
Total:	3,210
Bus service:	MTC routes 5, 5B, C; 7, 7D; 8, 8A, C, D, E; 29C, D to St. Paul
Half-hour drive or less to—	
Minneapolis:	Yes
St. Paul:	Yes
Shopping center:	Signal Hills
Hospital:	Divine Redeemer (South St. Paul)
Library:	Dakota County branch
Churches:	Six Protestant, two Catholic
School district:	197 (West St. Paul)
Schools:	One public junior high school, four elementary; three private high schools, four elementary
Taxes on a $68,000 home:	$345
Tax rank 1 (high) to 90 (low):	75
Local newspaper:	*West St. Paul Sun*
City Hall phone:	455-9671
Chamber phone:	457-4921

WHITE BEAR LAKE (Ramsey and Washington counties) ►10

White Bear Lake is an erstwhile resort town that has become a year-round residential community and commercial center. Downtown White Bear Lake retains a quaint, resort-like atmosphere, and the lake itself is popular with metropolitan-area sailors. Both Lakewood Community College and the White Bear Vocational-Technical Institute serve the community. "Manitou Days" are held each summer.

Population—	
1970:	23,290
1980:	22,551 (−3.2%)
1990:	24,500
Area (in acres)—	3,979
Water:	2,973
Total:	6,952
Bus service:	MTC routes 15A, B, C; 35B to St. Paul; Zephyr Lines
Half-hour drive or less to—	
Minneapolis:	No
St. Paul:	Yes
Shopping centers:	Maplewood Mall (Maplewood), White Bear Lake
Hospital:	St. Paul-Ramsey Medical Center
Library:	Ramsey County branch
Churches:	16 Protestant, two Catholic
School district:	624 (White Bear Lake)
Schools:	Two public high schools, two junior highs, eight elementary; two private elementary
Taxes on a $68,000 home:	$501
Tax rank 1 (high) to 90 (low):	12
Local newspaper:	*White Bear Lake Free Press*
City Hall phone:	429-8532
Chamber phone:	429-7666

FOR MORE INFORMATION

General

For more information on a particular community, call the city office or chamber of commerce, if one is listed, or see a realtor who does business in that area.

Bus Information

Twin Cities Transit Guide. Metropolitan Transit Commission, 801 American Center Bldg., 150 E. Kellogg Blvd., St. Paul 55101. 221-0939

Colorful map shows routes and numbers for all 130 MTC routes in the metropolitan area. Also indicates park and ride locations, gives routes for private bus companies, and lists MTC fares, services, and information numbers. Fifty cents plus 18 cents postage.

Church Information

Greater Minneapolis Council of Churches Denominational Directory, 1981. Greater Minneapolis Council of Churches, 122 W. Franklin Av., Rm. 218, Minneapolis 55404. 870-3660

Indexed, denominational listing of churches in Minneapolis and greater Minneapolis suburbs. Includes address and telephone number of church and pastor's name. Also has list of area chaplains and church ministries. 45 pages. $3.

St. Paul Area Council of Churches, 1980-81 Directory of Churches. St. Paul Area Council of Churches, 1671 Summit Av., St. Paul 55105. 646-8805

Indexed, denominational listing of churches in greater St. Paul. Includes directory of chaplains. 81 pages. $7.50

County Maps

Detailed county highway maps are available from the following offices:

Anoka County Highway Department, Anoka County Courthouse, 325 E. Main St., Anoka 55303. 421-4760. No charge.

Carver County Highway Department, Carver County Courthouse, Chaska 55318. 488-3435. No charge.

Dakota County Highway Department, Dakota County Government Center, 1560 W. Trunk Hwy. 55, Hastings 55033. 437-3191. No charge.

Hennepin County Public Service, 320 Washington Av. S., Hopkins 55343. 935-3381. No charge.

Ramsey County Public Works, 167 Ramsey County Courthouse, St. Paul 55102. 298-4127. No charge.

Scott County Highway Engineer, 428 Holmes St., Shakopee 55379. 445-7750. No charge for first map; 50 cents each for additional copies.

Washington County Highway Department, 11660 Myeron Rd. N., Stillwater 55082. 439-6058. No charge.

Chapter Five

GOVERNMENT

> **KEY NUMBERS**
> State Government Information: 296-6013
> Metropolitan Council Information: 291-6359
> Minneapolis City Hall: 348-3000
> St. Paul City Hall: 298-4012

The Twin Cities has a reputation for clean politics and grassroots political participation. The two major parties are the Democratic-Farmer-Labor Party (DFL), affiliated with the national Democratic Party; and the Independent-Republican Party (IR), which is affiliated with the national Republican Party. The DFL was formed in the mid-1940s, when the Democrats and the populist Farmer-Labor Party were joined through the efforts of a group of young politicians led by Hubert H. Humphrey.

Citizen involvement in state and local politics is traditional. In the late summer and fall before an election, campaign signs pop up like a crop of sunflowers on lawns in most Twin Cities neighborhoods. Citizen involvement is also the key to the success of the Metropolitan Council, a unique form of metropolitan government that provides services and policy guidance to city and county governments in the Twin Cities area. The Council is made up of citizen appointees who serve four-year terms.

The following list includes the names, party affiliations, addresses, and telephone numbers of elected officials whose constituencies include all or part of the Twin Cities. It is interesting to note that seven of Minnesota's eight Congressional districts touch some portion of the metro area.

FEDERAL GOVERNMENT

U.S. Senators

SEN. DAVE DURENBERGER, (IR), 353 Russell Senate Office Bldg., Washington, D.C. 20510. (202) 224-3244

Local office at 550 E. Butler Square, 100 N. Sixth St., Minneapolis 55403, 725-6111. Next election: November 1982.

SEN. RUDY BOSCHWITZ, (IR), 2109 Dirksen Senate Office Bldg., Washington, D.C. 20510.
(202) 224-5641
Local office at 210 Bremer Bldg., 419 Robert St., St. Paul 55101, 221-0904. Next election: November 1984.

U. S. Representatives

Term: Two years.
Next election: November 1982.

Descriptions of Twin Cities-area Congressional districts given here were written before the 1981 reapportionment process (required after the 1980 census) had been completed.

REP. ARLEN ERDAHL, (IR), First District, 1518 Longworth Office Bldg., Washington, D.C. 20515.
(202) 225-2271
Local office at 33 Wentworth Av. E., West St. Paul 55118, 725-7716. The First District includes Washington County and eastern Dakota County.

REP. TOM HAGEDORN, (IR), Second District, 2344 Rayburn Office Bldg., Washington, D.C. 20515.
(202) 225-2472
Local offices at 211 S. Newton Av., Albert Lea 56007, (507) 377-1676 and P.O. Box 3148, Mankato 56991, (507) 387-8226. To call toll-free from the Twin Cities: (800) 722-2245. The Sec-

ond District includes Carver, Scott, and southwest Hennepin counties.

REP. BILL FRENZEL, (IR), Third District, 1026 Longworth Office Bldg., Washington, D.C. 20515.
(202) 225-2472
Local offices at 110 S. Fourth St., Room 180, Minneapolis 55401, 349-5100, and 3601 Park Center Blvd., Minneapolis 55416, 925-4540. The Third District includes first- and second-ring Minneapolis suburbs in Hennepin County.

REP. BRUCE VENTO, (DFL), Fourth District, 230 Cannon Office Bldg., Washington, D.C. 20515.
(202) 225-6631
Local office at 405 Sibley St., St. Paul 55101, 725-7724. The Fourth District includes St. Paul and Ramsey County suburbs.

REP. MARTIN OLAV SABO, (DFL), Fifth District, 426 Cannon Office Bldg., Washington, D.C. 20515.
(202) 225-4755
Local office at 110 S. Fourth St., Room 462, Minneapolis 55401. The Fifth District includes almost all of Minneapolis and the suburbs of Columbia Heights, Fridley, Hilltop, and St. Anthony.

REP. VIN WEBER, (IR), Sixth District, 541 Cannon Office Bldg., Washington, D.C. 20515.
(202) 225-2331
Local office at 720 S. St. Germain St., St. Cloud 56301, 1-252-7580. The Sixth District includes northwestern Hennepin County.

REP. JAMES OBERSTAR, (DFL), Eighth District, 323 Cannon Office Bldg., Washington, D.C. 20515.
(202) 225-6211

Local office at 231 Federal Bldg., Duluth 55812, (218) 727-7474. The Eighth District includes all of Anoka County north of Fridley.

For other federal government offices, check telephone directories or call the Federal Information Center at 725-2073.

STATE GOVERNMENT

Legislature

The bicameral Minnesota Legislature meets at the state Capitol in St. Paul. 1981-82 marks the Legislature's 73rd session.

State Senate information: 296-0504.
Senate agenda and meetings hotline: 296-8088.
Senate bill information: 296-0269.
State House of Representatives information: 296-2146.
House of Representatives agenda and meetings hotline: 296-9283.
House of Representatives bill information: 296-6646.

State Government Officers

Term: Four years.
Next election: November 1982.

GOV. AL QUIE, (IR), 130 State Capitol, St. Paul 55155.
296-3391

LT. GOV. LOU WANGBERG, (IR), 122 State Capitol, St. Paul 55155.
296-2374

ATTY. GEN. WARREN SPANNAUS, (DFL), 102 State Capitol, St. Paul 55155.
296-6196

SEC. OF STATE JOAN GROWE, (DFL), 180 State Office Bldg., St. Paul 55155.
296-3266

AUDITOR ARNE CARLSON, (IR), 555 Park St., Suite 400, St. Paul 55103.
296-2551

TREASURER JAMES LORD, (DFL), 303 Administration Bldg., St. Paul 55155.
296-9623

COUNTY GOVERNMENT

The role of the region's seven county governments has changed as urbanization has decreased the need for such traditional county services as law enforcement in rural areas. Today counties, like cities, are involved in the delivery of urban services such as roads, libraries, and parks. The counties' most important role may now be as the main providers of social services.

Telephone numbers listed are for general information. Telephone directories list direct numbers for many county offices.

ANOKA COUNTY, Court

House, 325 E. Main St., Anoka 55303.
421-4760

CARVER COUNTY, Court House, Chaska 55318.
448-3435

DAKOTA COUNTY, Government Center, 1560 Hwy. 55, Hastings 55033.
437-3191

HENNEPIN COUNTY, Government Center, 300 S. Sixth St., Minneapolis 55487.
348-3000

RAMSEY COUNTY, Court House, 15 W. Kellogg Blvd., St. Paul 55102.
298-4012

SCOTT COUNTY, Court House, 428 S. Holmes St., Shakopee 55379.
445-7750

WASHINGTON COUNTY, 14900 N. 61st St., Stillwater 55082.
439-3220

METROPOLITAN GOVERNMENT

METROPOLITAN COUNCIL, 300 Metro Square Bldg., St. Paul 55101.
291-6359

The Metropolitan Council provides services to the entire metropolitan area and makes policy in matters that are significant to the metro region as a whole. The following commissions and boards deal directly with major metropolitan issues and are under the direction of the Metropolitan Council.

METROPOLITAN AIRPORTS COMMISSION, 6040 28th Av. S., Minneapolis 55450.
726-5770

METROPOLITAN HEALTH BOARD, 300 Metro Square Bldg., St. Paul 55101.
291-6352

METROPOLITAN PARKS AND OPEN SPACE COMMISSION, 300 Metro Square Bldg., St. Paul 55101.
291-6403

METROPOLITAN SPORTS FACILITIES COMMISSION, 330 Marquette Bldg., Minneapolis 55401.
332-0386

METROPOLITAN TRANSIT COMMISSION, 801 American Center Bldg., 160 E. Kellogg Blvd., St. Paul 55101.
221-0939

For transit information, call 827-7733.

TRANSPORTATION ADVISORY BOARD, 300 Metro Square Bldg.,
St. Paul 55101.
291-6347

METROPOLITAN WASTE CONTROL COMMISSION, 350 Metro Square Bldg., St. Paul 55101.
222-8423

CITY GOVERNMENT

Minneapolis, St. Paul, and most Twin Cities suburbs have mayor-council governments. St. Paul's seven council members have been elected at large; however, a recent referendum favored a ward system, and St. Paul's first ward elections will be in 1982. Minneapolis' 13 aldermen are elected from wards. Although recent charter reform has strengthened the Minneapolis mayor's office (a four-year mayoral term will begin in 1982), the city council retains much control over what in other U.S. cities are executive functions. Some suburban communities, like metropolitan counties, are run by appointed administrators.

Minneapolis

GENERAL OFFICES, City Hall, Minneapolis 55415.
348-3000

MAYOR DONALD FRASER, (DFL), 127 City Hall, Minneapolis 55415.
348-2100
Two-year term. Next election: November 1981.

Minneapolis Aldermen

CITY COUNCIL, 307 City Hall, Minneapolis 55415.
348-2200
Term: Two years.
Next election: November 1981.

WALTER DZIEDZIK, (DFL), First Ward.
348-2201

JUDY CORRAO, (DFL), Second Ward.
348-2202

PATRICK DAUGHERTY, (DFL), Third Ward.
348-2203

ALICE RAINVILLE, (DFL), Fourth Ward.
348-2204

VAN WHITE, (DFL), Fifth Ward.
348-2205

JACKIE SLATER, (DFL), Sixth Ward.
348-2206

PARKER TROSTEL, (IR), Seventh Ward.
348-2207

MARK KAPLAN, (DFL), Eighth Ward.
348-2208

TONY SCALLON, (DFL), Ninth Ward.
348-2209

SALLY HOWARD, (IR), 10th Ward.
348-2210

WALTER ROCKENSTEIN II, (IR), 11th Ward.
348-2211

DENNIS SCHULSTAD, (IR), 12th Ward.
348-2212

CHARLEE HOYT, (IR), 13th Ward.
348-2213

St. Paul

GENERAL OFFICES, City Hall, 15 W. Kellogg Blvd., St. Paul 55102.
298-4012

MAYOR GEORGE LATIMER, (DFL), 347 City Hall, St. Paul 55102.
298-4323
Two-year term. Next election: April 1982.

St. Paul City Council

COUNCIL OFFICES, Seventh Floor, City Hall, 15 W. Kellogg Blvd., St. Paul 55102.
Two-year term. Next election: April 1982.

BILL WILSON, (DFL).
298-4646

RUBY HUNT, (DFL).
298-5378

LEONARD LEVINE, (DFL).
298-4473

GEORGE McMAHON, (DFL).
298-5679

RONALD MADDOX, (DFL), President.
298-4475

JOANNE SHOWALTER, (DFL).
298-5289

VICTOR J. TEDESCO, (DFL).
298-5506

FOR MORE INFORMATION

State Government

The Minnesota Legislative Manual, Secretary of State's Office, 180 State Office Bldg., St. Paul 55155. Published each August and available on request by calling 296-2805, or by writing to the above address. Extensive description of the legislative, executive, and judicial branches of state government; also historical data and information on Minnesotans holding federal offices. Usually 600-plus pages.

Minnesota Guidebook to State Agency Services, 1980-1981. Office of the State Register, Suite 415, Hamm Bldg., 408 St. Peter St., St. Paul 55102. $6.50 per copy. Detailed but easy-to-read descriptions of the responsibilities of more than 150 state agencies. Indexed. 584 pages.

Metropolitan Government

Public Affairs Directory of the Twin Cities Metropolitan Area, Citizens' League, 84 S. Sixth St., Minneapolis 55402. Published annually. Contains names and addresses of state, county, and local office holders, as well as a variety of other information. 38 pages. Call 338-0791 to request a copy.

Chapter Six

THE MEDIA

NEWSPAPERS

ABC NEWSPAPERS, 4401 Coon Rapids Blvd., Coon Rapids.
421-4444

Publishers of the *Anoka County Union, Blaine & Spring Lake Park Life,* and *Coon Rapids Herald.* All weekly. Twenty-five cents each on newsstands. Subscription $10 one year, $18 two years.

AMERICAN JEWISH WORLD, 4820 Minnetonka Blvd., Minneapolis.
920-7000

News of and for the Jewish community. Weekly. Not on newsstands. Subscription $11 one year, $20 two years.

CATHOLIC BULLETIN, 244 Dayton Av., St. Paul.
291-4444

News of and for Catholics in the Archdiocese of St. Paul-Minneapolis. Weekly. Subscription $17.95 one year, $33.95 two years, $47.64 three years.

FINANCE & COMMERCE, 615 S. Seventh St., Minneapolis.
333-4244

Daily. Business news; Hennepin County and Minneapolis legal notices. Subscription $54 one year.

LARSON PUBLICATIONS, 200 Central Av., Osseo.
425-3323

Publishers of the *Osseo-Maple Grove Press, Champlin-Dayton Press,* and *Crow River News.* All

COMMUNITY NEWS

The major media in the Twin Cities are supplemented by a number of local and neighborhood publications that cover everything from politics to high school sports. Legal newspapers (usually weeklies) for each of the metro area's suburban communities are listed with the suburban profiles at the beginning of this book.

weekly. Subscription $9 one year, $17 two years.

LILLIE SUBURBAN NEWS-PAPERS, 2515 E. Seventh Av., North St. Paul.
777-8800

Publishers of the *Maplewood Review, New Brighton Bulletin, Ramsey County Review, Roseville Review, St. Anthony Bulletin, Shoreview Bulletin, Southwest Review,* and *Washington County Review.* All weekly. Thirty cents on newsstands. Subscription $14 one year.

MINNEAPOLIS DAILY AMER-ICAN, 1513 E. Lake St., Minneapolis.
721-6536

Daily newsletter. Not on newsstands. Subscription $2.50 one month, $30 one year. Mailing address: P.O. Box 729, Minneapolis, MN 55440.

MINNEAPOLIS LABOR RE-VIEW, 312 Central Av., Room 318, Minneapolis.
379-4725

Twice a month. News of and for members of AFL-CIO affiliated unions. Subscription $10 one year.

MINNEAPOLIS SPOKES-MAN/ST: PAUL RECORDER, 3744 Fourth Av. S., Minneapolis.
827-4021
Endicott Bldg., 350 Robert St., St. Paul.
222-0922

News of Twin Cities minority groups. Weekly. Twenty cents on newsstands. Subscription $8 one year.

MINNEAPOLIS STAR AND TRIBUNE, 425 Portland Av., Minneapolis.
372-4141

General-interest daily newspapers. *Star* M-F evenings. Twenty-five cents on newsstands. Subscription 80 cents one week. *Tribune* M-F mornings. Twenty-five cents on newsstands. Subscription 85 cents one week. *Tribune* Sat morning. Twenty-five cents on newsstands. Subscription 15 cents one week. *Tribune* Sun morning. Seventy-five cents on newsstands. Subscription 80 cents one week.

MINNESOTA DAILY, 10 Murphy Hall, University of Minnesota, Minneapolis.
373-3381

Student newspaper of the University of Minnesota—Twin Cities campus. Daily during school year; M, W, F summer. Distributed free on campus. Subscription $10 one quarter, $36 one year.

POST PUBLICATIONS, 8801 Bass Lake Rd., New Hope.
537-8484

Publishers of the North Hennepin (Crystal and Robbinsdale), Brooklyn Center, Brooklyn Park, Golden Valley, New Hope-Plymouth *Posts*. All weeklies. Thirty-five cents on newsstands. Subscription $14.50 one year.

ST. PAUL DISPATCH AND PI-ONEER PRESS, 55 E. Fourth St., St. Paul.
222-5011

General-interest daily newspapers. *Dispatch* M-F evenings, Sat morning combined paper with

Pioneer Press. Twenty-five cents on newsstands. Subscription 85 cents one week. *Pioneer Press* M-F mornings, Sat combined paper with *Dispatch.* Twenty-five cents on newsstands. Subscription 85 cents one week. *Pioneer Press* Sun morning, 75 cents on newsstands. Subscription 70 cents one week.

ST. PAUL DOWNTOWNER, 320 Cedar St., St. Paul.
222-5887

News for downtown workers. Once every two weeks. Free on newsstands downtown. Subscription $12 one year.

SKYWAY NEWS/FREEWAY NEWS, 80 S. Seventh St., Minneapolis.
332-8888

Three separate newspapers for 18-to-35-year-olds working in downtown Minneapolis and St. Paul and along I-494 in Bloomington. Free on newsstands. Subscription $15 one year.

STILLWATER GAZETTE, Stillwater 55082.
439-3130

Oldest daily paper in Twin Cities area. Fifteen cents on newsstands. Subscription $23 one year. Separate weekly published for St. Croix Valley.

SUN NEWSPAPERS (MINNESOTA SUBURBAN NEWSPAPERS INC.), 7401 Bush Lake Rd., Edina.
831-1200

Publishers of the Bloomington, Burnsville, Columbia Heights, Eden Prairie, Fridley, Hopkins-Minnetonka, Lake Minnetonka (north), Lake Minnetonka (south), Richfield, Roseville, St. Louis Park, South Minneapolis, South St. Paul, and West St. Paul *Sun Newspapers* and the *Sun Weekender.* All weeklies. Thirty-five cents on newsstands. Subscription $13 one year, except $9 one year in Fridley, Columbia Heights, and Roseville. *Sun Weekender* free on newsstands.

TWIN CITIES COURIER, 501 Syndicate Bldg., 84 S. Sixth St., Minneapolis.
336-9618

News of and for the black community, primarily aimed at 18-to-45-year-olds. Weekly. Twenty cents on newsstands. Subscription $7.50 one year.

TWIN CITIES READER, 100 N. Seventh St., Suite 300, Minneapolis.
338-2900

News, features, and entertainment listings. Aimed at 18-to-39-year-olds. Weekly. Thirty-five cents on newsstands (free on college campuses). Subscription $18 for one year.

UNION ADVOCATE, 440 W. Minnehaha Av., St. Paul.
488-6747

St. Paul area labor and union news. Weekly. Not on newsstands. Subscription $8.50 one year.

MAGAZINES

ARCHITECTURE MINNESOTA, 314 Clifton Av., Minneapolis 55403.
874-8771

Architecture and design in the Upper Midwest. Every two months. $2.50 on newsstands, $12 one year by subscription.

ARTS, Society of Fine Arts Membership Dept., 2400 Third Av. S., Minneapolis 55404.
870-3030

Arts attractions, focusing on the Minneapolis Institute of Arts and the Children's Theatre. Monthly. Free with society membership. Also available at the Institute.

COMMERCIAL WEST, 5100 Edina Industrial Blvd., Edina 55435.
835-5853

Banking and finance. Weekly. Not available on newsstands, $29 one year by subscription.

CORPORATE REPORT—MINNESOTA, 7101 York Av. S., Edina 55435.
835-6855

Business magazine for the Upper Midwest (Ninth Federal Reserve District). $2 on newsstands; $18 one year, $29 two years, $39 three years by subscription.

DESIGN QUARTERLY, Walker Art Center, Vineland Pl., Minneapolis 55403.
375-7600

Architecture and graphic design. $3 single copy, $6 double copy at the Walker bookstore; $9 four issues, $16 eight issues, $21 12 issues by subscription.

FINS AND FEATHERS MINNESOTA, 318 W. Franklin Av., Minneapolis 55404.
874-8404

Fishing and hunting. Monthly. $1.50 on newsstands, $11.95 one year by subscription.

GREATER MINNEAPOLIS, Greater Minneapolis Chamber of Commerce, c/o PRIME Publications, 1111 W. 22nd St., Suite 200, Minneapolis 55405.
377-9200

Each issue focuses on a single local topic. Every two months. Free to chamber members; available at libraries.

JAZZ, 430 First Av. N., Suite 406, Minneapolis 55401.
333-4371

Arts and entertainment monthly. $1 single copy in music and stereo stores; $12 one year by subscription.

MPLS./ST. PAUL, 512 Nicollet Mall Bldg., Suite 400, Minneapolis 55402.
339-7571

City magazine emphasizing local attractions and events. Monthly. $1.50 on newsstands, $8.95 one year by subscription.

MINNESOTA BUSINESS JOURNAL, 10800 Lyndale Av. S., Bloomington 55420.
884-6655

Minnesota business news. Free to managers in Minnesota, otherwise $19 for one year by subscription.

MINNESOTA MONTHLY, KSJN-Minnesota Public Radio, 45 E. Eighth St., St. Paul 55101.
221-1500

Public radio program guide, plus articles on the arts and public affairs, and sometimes fiction. Monthly. Free with MPR membership.

MINNESOTA SPORTSMAN, P. O. Box 3003, Oshkosh, WI 54903.
(414) 231-8160

Features and tips on hunting and fishing in Minnesota. Bimonthly. Subscription $7.50 for one year; $1.50 on newsstands.

SCENE—KTCA, KTCI, 1640 Como Av., St. Paul 55108.
646-4611

Program listings and information on Twin Cities public television. Issued monthly. Free with donation of $15 or more to Twin Cities Public Television.

SWEET POTATO, P. O. Box 8467, 711 W. Lake St., Minneapolis 55408.
827-8273

Music magazine also carrying some book and film reviews. Geared to 18-to-35-year-olds. Weekly. Free at music businesses and on college campuses. Subscription $16 for one year, $30 for two years.

TWIN CITIES, 7101 York Av. S., Edina 55435.
835-6855

Feature articles and photography about the Twin Cities area and its people. Monthly. $2.50 on newsstands; $24 one year, $48 two years by subscription.

WHERE MAGAZINE, 625 Second Av. S., Minneapolis 55402.
333-7793

Information on dining, shopping, entertainment, and special events. Weekly.

RADIO STATIONS

KBEM 88.5 FM, 1101 Third Av. S., Minneapolis.
348-4888

Affiliated with Minneapolis Public Schools. City council and school board meetings broadcast live. News, educational programming, including instruction in Laotian and Cambodian, and a variety of music.

KDAN 1370 AM, 6541 Military Rd., Woodbury.
459-1370

Jazz. Some Spanish programming on weekends.

KDWA 1460 AM, 18th and Vermillion Sts., Hastings.
437-1460

Adult contemporary music and Minnesota Gopher football games. Saturday Action Auctions, Paul Harvey. ABC affiliate.

KDWB 630 AM, 101.3 FM, Hwy. 12 and Radio Dr., Woodbury.
739-4000

AM—top 40. FM—album-oriented rock. *Robert Klein Radio Hour. 101 Underground*, featuring Twin Cities talent.

KEEY 1400 AM, 102.1 FM, 611 Frontenac Pl., St. Paul.
645-7757

"Easy listening."

KFAI 90.3 FM, 3104 16th Av. S., Minneapolis.
721-5011

"Fresh Air Radio." Noncommercial, listener-supported station with an emphasis on community affairs. Diverse programming, including shows for and about women, children, and gays. Minority and bilingual shows. Jazz and a variety of other music.

KMOJ 89.7 FM, 810 Fifth Av. N., Minneapolis.
374-5605
Community radio station. Programming includes cultural affairs, religion. Soul, jazz, blues, and a variety of other music.

KNOF 95.3 FM, 1347 Selby Av., St. Paul.
645-8271
Gospel music 24 hours a day.

KQRS 1440 AM, 92.5 FM, 917 N. Lilac Dr., Golden Valley.
545-5601
Adult-oriented rock; '60s music on weekends.

KRSI 104 FM, 950 AM, 11320 Valley View Rd., Eden Prairie.
941-5774
"The music of your life." Oldies from the 1940s-'70s, 24 hours a day. ABC affiliate.

KSJN 1330 AM, 91.1 FM, 45 E. Eighth St., St. Paul.
221-1500
Minnesota and National Public Radio affiliate. AM—news and information, including *All Things Considered* and *Morning Edition*. FM—classical music, news, Garrison Keillor, *Radio Theater*, and Studs Terkel, as well as a variety of other programming, 24 hours a day.

KSMM 1530 AM, 421 E. First St., Shakopee.
445-1866
Middle-of-the-road, memory music. Local sports, farm programming, some German/English programs. Local coverage of Scott and Carver counties.

KSTP 1500 AM, 94.5 FM, 3415 University Av., St. Paul.
646-5555
FM—adult contemporary music. AM—North Star hockey, *Marilyn Mason Show, Sports Talk*, and a variety of other news and talk shows as well as music.

KTCR 690 AM, 97.1 FM, 3701 Winnetka Av. N., New Hope.
544-1558
Country music. FM 24 hours a day.

KTIS 900 AM, 98.5 FM, 3003 N. Snelling Av., Roseville.
636-4900
Affiliated with Northwestern College. AM—religious programming and devotional music. FM—sacred and classical music 24 hours a day.

KTWN 1470 AM, 108 FM, 5215 Industry Av. N.W., Anoka.
421-4178 AM, 421-2600 FM
AM—country western. FM-pop, jazz. UPI news.

KUOM 770 AM, 550 Rarig Center, 330 21st Av. S., Minneapolis.
373-3177
A service of the University of Minnesota. Educational programming, news, and classical and contemporary music. National Public Radio affiliate.

KUXL 1570 AM, 5730 Duluth St., Golden Valley.
544-3196
Mornings: Christian programming. Afternoons: Christian contemporary music.

WAVN 1220 AM, Stillwater.
439-1220
Adult contemporary music. Mutual Broadcasting affiliate.

WAYL 980 AM, 94 FM, 2110 Cliff Rd., Eagan.
633-9667
Kicks soccer. "Beautiful music" 24 hours a day.

WCCO 830 AM, 625 Second Av. S., Minneapolis.
370-0611
An Upper Midwest institution for more than 50 years. Twins baseball, news, information, a variety of music, and other programming 24 hours a day. CBS affiliate.

WCCO 103 FM, 215 S. 11th St., Minneapolis.
339-1029
Adult contemporary music. News, weather, sports, and traffic reports.

WCTS 100.3 FM, 2105 Fremont Av. N., Minneapolis.
522-3628
"The Bible station."

WDGY 1130 AM, 1100 W. 104th St., Bloomington.
881-2633
Country western music, 24 hours a day. NBC affiliate.

WLOL 99.5 FM, 1370 Davern St., St. Paul.
698-5566
Adult contemporary music, 24 hours a day.

WMIN 1010 AM, 1995 Century Av. S., Maplewood.
739-4433
Country western and polka music. UPI news.

WWTC 1280 AM, 123 E. Grant St., Minneapolis.
333-2363
Golden rock (1950s-'80s) 24 hours a day. Mutual Broadcasting affiliate.

TV STATIONS

KMSP-TV (Channel 9), 6975 York Av. S., Edina.
925-3300
Independent.

KSTP-TV (Channel 5), 3415 University Av., St. Paul.
646-5555
ABC affiliate.

KTCA-TV (Channel 2), KTCI-TV (Channel 17), 1640 Como Av., St. Paul.
646-4611
Public television.

WCCO-TV (Channel 4), 50 S. Ninth St., Minneapolis.
330-2400
CBS affiliate.

WTCN-TV (Channel 11), 441 Boone Av. N., Golden Valley.
546-1111
NBC affiliate.

CABLE TV

Seven Twin Cities suburbs—Apple Valley, Bloomington, Farmington, Fridley, Lakeville, Rosemount, and St. Louis Park—are currently served by cable television. In addition, five Minneapolis suburbs—Eden Prairie, Edina, Hopkins, Minnetonka, and Richfield—awarded cable franchises in 1981 and should have complete cable service by December 1982. At this writing, most of the remaining suburbs, as well as the cities of Minneapolis and St. Paul, were in the process of awarding cable franchises. The Minneapolis City Council had in fact awarded a franchise, but the procedure was being challenged in court, and the city was about to embark on a new review process that could result in partial community ownership of a cable system. St. Paul was exploring the option of complete community ownership, but was not expected to make a franchise decision until well into 1982.

For a monthly fee, usually less than $10 per month for one receiver, cable adds entertainment, news, information, and community-access programs on many channels to the regular broadcasts received by television. In addition to the monthly fee, there usually is a one-time installation fee for hooking up to the cable.

Companies serving the Twin Cities suburbs now getting cable are:

Apple Valley, Farmington, Lakeville, and Rosemount—Metro Cable, Inc., 16900 Cedar Av., Rosemount 55068; 432-2610.

Bloomington—Northern Cablevision, 8946 Lyndale Av. S., Bloomington 55420; 888-9511.

Fridley—Northern Cablevision, 350 63rd Av. N.E., Fridley 55432; 571-8100.

St. Louis Park—Northern Cablevision, 3516 Beltline Blvd., St. Louis Park 55416; 925-6011.

The company installing cable service in Eden Prairie, Edina, Hopkins, Minnetonka, and Richfield is Minnesota Cable Systems, Inc., Suite 1001, Soo Line Bldg., Minneapolis 55402; 340-0525 and 941-9820.

Chapter Seven

EDUCATION

KEY NUMBER

Minnesota Department of Education: 296-6104

PUBLIC ELEMENTARY AND SECONDARY SCHOOLS

Public elementary and secondary schools in the Twin Cities generally are considered to be of relatively high quality. Those considering schools when deciding on a place to live should keep in mind that except for Minneapolis and St. Paul, school district and municipal boundaries rarely coincide in the metropolitan area. Not all of the Edina school district is in Edina, for example, and not all of Edina is in the Edina school district. A map showing metropolitan area school district and municipal boundaries as well as the locations of public school buildings is available from the Metropolitan Council, 300 Metro Square Bldg., E. Seventh and Robert Sts., St. Paul 55101, 291-6464.

For general information on public education in Minnesota, contact the state Department of Education, Capitol Square Bldg., 550 Cedar St., St. Paul 55101, 296-6104. Check telephone directories for local school district offices and school buildings.

(See Locator Key Map, pages 8-9)

- ►1 Mpls. Downtown
- ►2 Mpls. Excluding Downtown
- ►3 Mpls. North Suburbs
- ►4 Mpls. Northwest Suburbs
- ►5 Mpls. Southwest Suburbs
- ►6 Mpls. South Suburbs
- ►7 St. Paul Downtown
- ►8 St. Paul Excluding Downtown
- ►9 St. Paul North Suburbs
- ►10 St. Paul Northeast Suburbs
- ►11 St. Paul Southeast Suburbs
- ►12 St. Paul South Suburbs

MINNEAPOLIS PUBLIC SCHOOLS, Educational Service Center, 807 N.E. Broadway St., Minneapolis 55413.
348-6000

ST. PAUL PUBLIC SCHOOLS, 360 Colborne St., St. Paul 55102.
293-7621

Public elementary and secondary school facilities also serve as bases for adult community education programs in much of the Twin Cities. In Minneapolis and St. Paul, the public schools offer adult evening programs during the school year and throughout the summer. The curricula for these programs range from basic high school certification to auto mechanics and crafts and fine arts. Complete information on course offerings, registration, and fees (usually between $2 and $20) can be obtained by calling your local school district office.

POST-SECONDARY EDUCATION

Minneapolis-St. Paul is one of the few metropolitan areas in America served by the main campus of a major state university. With parts in Minneapolis and Falcon Heights (suburban St. Paul), the University of Minnesota offers programs to traditional students and adults in virtually every academic discipline. The U of M Twin Cities Campus, with some 40,000 students, is one of the largest in the United States, and a significant contributor to the quality of life, economy, and cultural activity in the metropolitan area.

But the U of M is hardly the area's only institution of higher learning. Metropolitan State University, an unusual "university without walls," serves working adults with classes throughout the Twin Cities. Several fine private colleges also offer programs for adults who can't attend day classes, in addition to serving traditional students who can. Community colleges and vocational-technical schools are conveniently located throughout the region to serve full- and part-time students.

Public Universities

METROPOLITAN STATE UNIVERSITY, 121 Metro Square Bldg., E. Seventh and Robert Sts., St. Paul 55101. ►7
296-3875
Other centers located at Hennepin Center for the Arts, 528 Hennepin Av., Minneapolis, 341-7250, and 7150 E. River Rd., Fridley, 571-9180.

UNIVERSITY OF MINNESOTA, Minneapolis and St. Paul 55455. ►2, 8
373-2851
Check telephone directories for public service and other frequently called numbers. Call 373-2851 for numbers or addresses of specific departments, programs, staff and faculty members.

Private Four-Year Colleges

AUGSBURG COLLEGE, 731 21st Av. S., Minneapolis 55454. 330-1000 ►2

Coed, liberal arts college affiliated with the American Lutheran Church. About 1,500 students.

BETHEL COLLEGE, 3900 Bethel Dr., Arden Hills 55112. ►9
638-6400
Coed, Baptist liberal arts college and seminary. About 2,000 students.

CONCORDIA COLLEGE, 275 N. Syndicate St., St. Paul 55104. 641-8278 ►8
Coed college affiliated with the Lutheran Church—Missouri Synod. Curriculum includes liberal arts, business and church vocations. About 700 students.

HAMLINE UNIVERSITY, 1536 Hewitt Av., St. Paul 55104. ►8
641-2800
Coed, liberal arts college affiliated with the United Methodist Church. About 1,200 students. Also offers Master of Liberal Studies Program. Law school has about 500 students.

MACALESTER COLLEGE, 1600 Grand Av., St. Paul 55105. 696-6000 ►8
Coed, liberal arts college affiliated with the National Presbyterian Council of Churches. About 1,700 students. Offers Adult Scholar Program for students over 25 years old.

MINNEAPOLIS COLLEGE OF ART AND DESIGN, 133 E. 25th St., Minneapolis 55404. ►2
870-3346
Coed. Affiliated with the Minneapolis Society of Fine Arts. Offers Bachelor of Fine Arts programs in seven fine arts areas and three design areas. About 600 students.

NORTH CENTRAL BIBLE COLLEGE, 910 Elliot Av., Minneapolis 55404. ►2
332-3491
Coed college affiliated with the Assemblies of God. Primarily religious curriculum. About 800 students.

NORTHWESTERN COLLEGE, 3003 Snelling Av. N., Roseville 55113. ►9
636-4840
Coed college offering liberal arts and Bible study. Unaffiliated. About 850 students.

COLLEGE OF ST. CATHERINE, 2004 Randolph Av., St. Paul 55105. ►8
690-6000
Catholic liberal arts college for women. About 2,300 students. Offers Continuing Education Program.

COLLEGE OF ST. THOMAS, 2115 Summit Av., St. Paul 55105. 647-5000 ►8
Coed, Catholic liberal arts college. Offers Master of Business Administration and graduate education program. About 5,500 students, 3,600 undergraduates. New College Program offers evening and weekend classes for undergraduates.

SCHOOL OF THE ASSOCIATED ARTS, 344 Summit Av., St. Paul 55102. ►8
224-3416
Coed. Offers three- and four-

year programs in graphic, commercial, and fine arts. About 100 students.

Private Professional Schools

APOSTOLIC BIBLE INSTITUTE, 6944 Hudson Blvd. N., St. Paul 55119. ►8
739-7686

LUTHER THEOLOGICAL SEMINARY, 2375 Como Av. W., St. Paul 55108. ►8
641-3456

NORTHWESTERN LUTHERAN THEOLOGICAL SEMINARY, 1501 Fulham St., St. Paul 55108. ►8
641-3456

ST. PAUL SEMINARY, 2260 Summit Av., St. Paul 55105. ►8
698-0323

UNITED THEOLOGICAL SEMINARY OF THE TWIN CITIES, 3000 N.W. Fifth St., New Brighton 55112. ►9
633-4311

WILLIAM MITCHELL COLLEGE OF LAW, 875 Summit Av., St. Paul 55105. ►8
227-9171

Community Colleges

ANOKA-RAMSEY COMMUNITY COLLEGE, 11200 Mississippi Blvd. N.W., Coon Rapids 55433.
427-2600 ►3

INVER HILLS COMMUNITY COLLEGE, 8445 College Trail, Inver Grove Heights 55075. ►12
455-9621

LAKEWOOD COMMUNITY COLLEGE, 3401 Century Av. N., White Bear Lake 55110. ►10
770-1331

MINNEAPOLIS COMMUNITY COLLEGE, 1501 Hennepin Av., Minneapolis 55403. ►1
341-7061

NORMANDALE COMMUNITY COLLEGE, 9700 France Av. S., Bloomington 55431. ►6
830-9300

NORTH HENNEPIN COMMUNITY COLLEGE, 7411 85th Av. N., Brooklyn Park 55445. ►4
425-4541

Private Junior Colleges

GOLDEN VALLEY LUTHERAN COLLEGE, 6125 Olson Memorial Hwy. (Hwy. 55), Golden Valley 55422. ►4
542-1216

ST. MARY'S JUNIOR COLLEGE, 2500 S. Sixth St., Minneapolis 55454. ►2
332-5521

Public Vocational-Technical Institutes

ANOKA VOCATIONAL-TECHNICAL INSTITUTE, 1355 W. Main St., Anoka 55303. ►3
427-1880

DAKOTA COUNTY VO-TECH, E. 145th St. and Akron Rd., Rosemount 55068. ►12
423-2281

HENNEPIN TECHNICAL CENTERS DISTRICT NO. 287, District Office, 1820 N. Xenium Lane, Plymouth 55441. ►4
559-3535

North Campus: 9000 77th Av. N., Brooklyn Park 55445, 425-3800; South Campus: 9200 Flying Cloud Dr., Eden Prairie 55344, 944-2222.

MINNEAPOLIS AREA VOCA-TIONAL-TECHNICAL INSTI-TUTE, 1415 Hennepin Av. S., Minneapolis 55403. ►1
370-9400

916 AREA VOCATIONAL-TECHNICAL INSTITUTE, 3300 Century Av. N., White Bear Lake 55110. ►10
770-2351

ST. PAUL TECHNICAL-VO-CATIONAL INSTITUTE, 235 Marshall Av., St. Paul 55102. ►8
221-1300

Private, Non-profit, Tax-Exempt Industrial and Technical Institutes

DUNWOODY INDUSTRIAL INSTITUTE, 818 Wayzata Blvd., Minneapolis 55403. ►1

NORTHWESTERN ELEC-TRONICS INSTITUTE, 3800 Minnehaha Av., Minneapolis 55406. ►2
721-2469

Private High Schools

ACADEMY OF THE HOLY ANGELS, 6600 Nicollet Av., Richfield 55423. ►6
866-8762
Coed, Catholic.

BENILDE-ST. MARGARET'S, 2501 Hwy. 100 S., St. Louis Park 55416. ►5
927-4176
Coed, Catholic.

On the Minneapolis campus of the University of Minnesota.

BLAKE SCHOOLS, 511 Kenwood Pkwy., Minneapolis 55403. 377-5998 ►2
Coed, non-denominational.

BRADY HIGH SCHOOL, 1200 Oakdale Av., West St. Paul 55118. ►12
457-8791
Coed, Catholic.

BRECK SCHOOL, 123 Ottawa Av. N., Golden Valley 55422. ►4
377-5000
Coed, non-denominational.

CONCORDIA ACADEMY, 2400 N. Dale St., Roseville 55113. ►9
484-8429
Coed, Missouri Synod Lutheran.

CRETIN HIGH SCHOOL, 495 Hamline Av. S., St. Paul 55116. 690-2443 ►8
Boys, Catholic.

DE LA SALLE HIGH SCHOOL, 25 Island Av. W., Minneapolis 55401. ►1
379-4671
Coed, Catholic.

DERHAM HALL, 540 Warwick Av. S., St. Paul 55116. ►8
698-0871
Girls, Catholic.

HILL-MURRAY HIGH SCHOOL, 2625 Larpenteur Av. E., St. Paul 55109. ►8
777-1376
Coed, Catholic.

MINNEHAHA ACADEMY, 3107 47th Av. S., Minneapolis 55406. ►2
729-8321
Coed, Evangelical Covenant Church.

REGINA HIGH SCHOOL, 4225 Third Av. S., Minneapolis 55409. 827-2677 ►2
Girls, Catholic.

ST. AGNES HIGH SCHOOL, 525 Thomas Av., St. Paul 55103. 225-1614 ►8
Coed, Catholic.

ST. BERNARD HIGH SCHOOL, 170 Rose Av. W., St. Paul 55117. ►8
489-1338
Coed, Catholic.

ST. PAUL ACADEMY AND SUMMIT SCHOOL, 1712 Randolph Av., St. Paul 55105. ►8
698-2451
Coed, non-denominational.

ST. THOMAS ACADEMY, 949 Mendota Heights Rd., Mendota Heights 55120. ►12
454-4570
Boys, Catholic.

TOTINO-GRACE HIGH SCHOOL, 1350 Gardena Av. N.E., Fridley 55432. ►3
571-9116
Coed, Catholic.

VISITATION HIGH SCHOOL, 2475 Dodd Rd., Mendota Heights 55120. ►12
454-6474
Girls, Catholic.

Chapter Eight

BUSINESS & INDUSTRY

Perhaps the easiest way to get at the major forces in the Minneapolis-St. Paul area economy is to go down the *Fortune 500* list of the largest U.S. industrial companies. There were 15 area companies on the list in 1980. Some of the Twin Cities firms on that list include 3M, Honeywell, General Mills, Control Data, Pillsbury, Land O'Lakes, International Multifoods—all of them either food or technology companies.

The Twin Cities is surrounded by a rich agricultural area, and Minneapolis—the Mill City—grew up around St. Anthony Falls, which supplied power for milling lumber and, later, wheat. Minneapolis is no longer a major milling center, but the companies that formed here to turn the region's wheat into flour—or successors of those companies—have maintained corporate headquarters in the area.

Also, because the Twin Cities lies between vast stretches of land producing crops and raw materials to the west and major industrial centers to the south and east, transportation quickly developed as an important part of the region's economy. First it was river

traffic, then rail, then truck and air. Today the Twin Cities is the base of a major railroad—the Soo Line—and two major airlines—Northwest and Republic.

In recent years the Minneapolis-St. Paul area has become the Midwestern center of high-technology industries such as computer and heart-pacemaker manufacturing. A recent study reported that there are 1,257 technology-intensive firms in the metropolitan area. Leaders of those industries credit the University of Minnesota and other local educational institutions with providing a supply of good engineers and scientists, as well as useful research.

Twin Cities companies in other fields also can be found on the *Fortune 500.* Bemis, for example, is a leader in packaging, graphics, specialty chemicals, and fabrics. Deluxe Check Printers does just that for banks in all 50 states. Josten's manufactures diplomas, class rings, and other recognition products for schools and businesses. Toro manufactures and distributes lawn mowers, tractors, and snowblowers.

In non-manufacturing categories as well, Twin Cities companies figure prominently in *Fortune*'s lists of national leaders. Northwest Bancorporation and First Bank System are among the nation's 50 largest commercial banking companies. Minnesota Mutual, Northwestern National, and IDS Life are among the 50 largest life insurance companies. The St. Paul Companies and Investors Diversified Services (now owned by Allegheny Corp.) are among the 50 largest diversified financial corporations. Northern States Power is among the country's 50 largest utilities. And Dayton Hudson and Gamble-Skogmo (now part of the Wickes Companies) are among the 50 largest retailing companies.

Other major forces in the Minneapolis-St. Paul area economy don't show up on the *Fortune* charts. Cargill, Inc., a merchandiser and processor of agricultural commodities, is reportedly the largest privately held company in the nation, with annual sales of $11 billion. The nine privately held Carlson Companies, like Cargill, employ a total of more than 25,000 people. With the state capital and University of Minnesota in the Twin Cities, the impact of public employment on the region's economy is considerable, too. So is the effect of the metropolitan area's role as the Upper Midwest's center for conventions, arts and entertainment, and wholesale and retail trade.

From the roots of agribusiness and transportation has grown a modern, diversified economy. Because of the variety of major businesses within its borders, the Twin Cities area is largely protected from downturns in a single industry, even in a large one such as motor vehicle manufacturing. And, although manufacturing—of light trucks at Ford's St. Paul plant, among other products—is part of the metropolitan area's economic activity, Minneapolis and St. Paul are essentially white-collar, corporate headquarters cities. Factory whistles and billowing smokestacks are not as common as in, say, Chicago or Cleveland. Nonetheless, labor unions play a significant role in the economy and politics of Minnesota and, therefore, in the Twin Cities region itself.

LARGEST PUBLICLY HELD COMPANIES BASED IN THE TWIN CITIES AREA
(Ranked by Sales)

Rank	Company	Revenues ($ millions)	Net Earnings ($ millions)	Employees
1.	3M	5,440.4	655.2	87,738
2.	Honeywell	4,209.5	260.5	94,620
3.	General Mills	4,170.3	170.0	66,032
4.	Super Valu	3,475.2	45.3	15,752
5.	Dayton Hudson	3,384.8	192.1	39,000

6. Control Data	3,250.0	124.2	58,000
7. Pillsbury	3,032.0	104.7	59,500
8. St. Paul Cos.	1,783.1	152.9	10,834
9. Northwest Airlines	1,310.6	72.5	12,814
10. Northwest Bancorp.	1,145.2	106.6	13,060
11. First Bank System	1,054.3	101.7	9,519
12. Northern States Power	1,048.2	120.7	6,700
13. Intl. Multifoods	1,012.2	25.6	8,549
14. Nash Finch	881.7	10.1	5,900
15. Peavey	734.8	22.6	6,073
16. Pac. Gamble Robinson	694.9	6.5	5,500
17. Modern Merchandising	678.8	12.7	7,000
18. Gelco	652.4	37.3	7,500
19. Bemis	648.5	26.6	8,800
20. Republic Airlines	609.2	13.1	9,800
21. Economics Laboratory	547.7	31.1	7,764
22. NW Natl. Life	513.6	30.8	993
23. American Hoist	508.6	20.7	7,846
24. Toro	402.0	5.3	4,000
25. Minnesota Gas	390.5	19.8	2,195
26. Deluxe Check	366.1	38.6	9,361
27. Josten's	295.1	21.7	5,600
28. Soo Line	290.5	27.6	4,684
29. Medtronic	270.4	38.7	4,485
30. H. B. Fuller	258.7	7.4	3,400
31. MEI	240.8	16.0	2,900
32. Donaldson	225.1	14.2	3,642
33. McQuay-Perfex	220.1	7.0	4,547
34. Pentair	192.8	11.8	1,850
35. K-Tel Intl.	167.0	3.7	700
36. Napco Industries	142.0	4.8	1,800
37. Munsingwear	131.2	1.5	5,205
38. Donovan Cos.	129.7	1.3	900
39. Tonka	129.1	3.4	3,000
40. Valspar	120.9	3.8	1,450
41. Webb	111.4	4.5	1,150
42. Cornelius	110.5	5.3	1,800
43. Graco	110.3	10.4	1,950
44. Van Dusen Air	109.7	3.6	812
45. Conwed	109.2	6.1	1,781
46. Apache	108.8	13.9	1,400
47. Tennant	97.8	8.8	1,541
48. IFG	84.2	5.3	1,109
49. Apogee	83.7	3.5	1,406
50. Murphy Motor	77.5	.5	1,579

SOURCE: *Corporate Report-Minnesota,* November 1980

HISTORY OF STATE UNEMPLOYMENT RATES,
1976-1980
(Annual Averages)

Year	Minnesota	National
1976	5.9%	7.7%
1977	5.5	7.0
1978	3.8	6.0
1979	4.2	5.8
1980	5.7	7.1

SOURCE: Minnesota Department of Economic Security

FOR MORE INFORMATION

Corporate Report Fact Book, Dorn Communications, Inc., Edina. Annual directory of publicly held corporations in the Ninth Federal Reserve District. Includes description of each firm, as well as a balance sheet and earnings history. Also includes a who's who of Upper Midwest business, and listings of regional facilities and privately held companies.

Corporate Report-Minnesota. Monthly magazine of business news and features in the Ninth Federal Reserve District. Dorn Communications, Inc., Edina, publisher.

Don W. Larson, *Land of the Giants: A History of Minnesota Business,* Dorn Books, Edina, 1979. History of business in Minnesota, including profiles of several major Minnesota companies, industries, and industrialists. 176 pages, photographs.

James J. Hill Reference Library, Fourth and Market Sts., St. Paul. 227-9531.

Chapter Nine

LODGING

Finding a place to stay in the Twin Cities is complicated only by the variety of establishments to choose from. Minneapolis and St. Paul both have their share of reliable national chain hotels, as well as a few excellent family-owned establishments. Hotels and motels can be found in the heart of both downtowns, as well as near the Twin Cities International Airport (many on Bloomington's "strip") and in suburban locations near corporate offices or industrial parks. If it's luxury accommodations you're looking for, you can find them in the Twin Cities, particularly in the newer "deluxe" hotels downtown. By the same token, there are many comfortable yet less expensive places for people watching their budgets. More adventurous sojourners may want to explore some of the less traditional lodging alternatives listed here.

Abbreviations for credit cards are: AE-American Express; CB-Carte Blanche; DC-Diners Club; MC-MasterCard (Master Charge); V-Visa (BankAmericard); and S-Shoppers Charge (a local card). Checks accepted generally means local checks with picture I.D.

HOTELS AND MOTELS

Room rates are subject to change. Inquire about current rates when calling for reservations.

Minneapolis Area

AMBASSADOR RESORT MOTOR HOTEL, Hwys. 12 and

(See Locator Key Map, pages 8-9)

▶1 Mpls. Downtown
▶2 Mpls. Excluding Downtown
▶3 Mpls. North Suburbs
▶4 Mpls. Northwest Suburbs
▶5 Mpls. Southwest Suburbs
▶6 Mpls. South Suburbs
▶7 St. Paul Downtown
▶8 St. Paul Excluding Downtown
▶9 St. Paul North Suburbs
▶10 St. Paul Northeast Suburbs
▶11 St. Paul Southeast Suburbs
▶12 St. Paul South Suburbs

The new Hyatt Regency in downtown Minneapolis.

100, St. Louis Park 55416. ►5
545-0441

Large indoor pool, sauna, shuffleboard. 199 rooms, $44 to $80. Camino Grill and Kashmiri Room restaurants. AE, CB, DC, MC, V cards accepted. Weekend packages available.

BILTMORE MOTOR INN, 5212 Vernon Av. S., Edina 55436. ►5
929-2601

Outdoor pool. 80 rooms, $22 to $38.50. Restaurant. AE, CB, DC, MC, V accepted.

CRICKET INN, BURNSVILLE, I-35W at Burnsville Pkwy., Burnsville 55337. ►6
894-8280

Free parking and coffee. 115 rooms, $25 to $37. AE, DC, MC, V accepted.

THE NEW CURTIS HOTEL AND MOTOR LODGE, 400 S. 10th St., Minneapolis 55404. ►1
340-5300

A collection of buildings covering almost a full block, the Curtis has undergone extensive remodeling. The new Palm Bar and Sunday brunch are popular attractions. Near the Minneapolis Auditorium and Convention Center. Indoor and outdoor pools, sauna, whirlpool, free parking. 824 rooms, $30 to $50; suites $60 to $125. Coffee shop, restaurant, two bars. AE, MC, V accepted.

GOLDEN VALLEY HOUSE (BEST WESTERN), 4820 Olson Memorial Hwy. (Hwy. 55), Golden Valley 55422. ►4
588-0511

Indoor pool, sauna, and free parking. 96 units, $33 to $37.

Restaurant, cocktail lounge. AE, DC, CB, MC, S, V accepted. Weekend package available.

GRANADA ROYALE HOME-TEL, 2800 W. 80th St., Bloomington 55431. ►6
884-4811

Guests at this new Spanish-style hotel receive complimentary cocktails every evening and a full, hot, cooked-to-order breakfast each morning. Indoor pool, whirlpool, sauna. All rooms are two-room suites. 119 rooms, $79 to $89. Woolley's Restaurant and Lounge. Eight minutes from the airport; complimentary limousine service. Weekend package available. AE, CB, DC, MC, V accepted. Weekend package available.

GUEST HOUSE BEST WESTERN MOTEL, 704 Fourth Av. S., Minneapolis 55415. ►1
370-1444

Free parking and in-room movies. Located across Seventh St. from the Hennepin County Government Center and a few blocks from the heart of downtown. 98 rooms, $34.50 to $44.50. Restaurant, coffee shop, bar. AE, CB, DC, MC, V accepted.

HOLIDAY INN AIRPORT #1, 7800 34th Av. S., Bloomington 55420. ►6
854-4000

Just off I-494 near the airport. Outdoor pool. 75 rooms, $37 to $43. Dining room, coffee shop, bar. AE, CB, DC, MC, V accepted.

HOLIDAY INN AIRPORT #2,

I-494 and Hwy. 100, Bloomington
55437. ►6
831-8000

Indoor pool, sauna, whirlpool,
in-room movies. 258 rooms, $46
to $54. Dining room, coffee shop,
bar. AE, CB, DC, MC, V accepted. Weekend package available.

**HOLIDAY INN BLOOMING-
TON CENTRAL,** 1201 W. 94th
St., Bloomington 55431. ►6
884-8211

Indoor pool, whirlpool, sauna.
173 rooms, $38 to $57. Restaurant, lounge, entertainment. AE,
DC, MC, V accepted.

HOLIDAY INN DOWNTOWN,
1313 Nicollet Mall, Minneapolis
55403. ►1
332-0731

Indoor pool, sauna, cocktail
lounge in dome above the city.
Near the Minneapolis Auditorium
and Convention Center as well as
Loring Park. 325 rooms, $49 to
$60. Two restaurants. AE, DC,
MC, V accepted. Weekend package available.

**HOLIDAY INN INTERNA-
TIONAL AIRPORT HOTEL,**
34th Av. at I-494, Bloomington
55420. ►6
854-9000

This new hotel features a
domed pool and three restaurants.
300 rooms, $49 to $57. AE, CB,
DC, MC, V accepted. Weekend
package available.

HOLIDAY INN PLYMOUTH,
3000 Harbor Lane (I-494 and
Hwy. 55), Plymouth 55441. ►4
559-1222

Located near General Mills'

corporate headquarters, this new
hotel features an indoor pool,
sauna, sundeck, and outdoor jog-
ging track. Winslow's Restaurant
and Lounge, entertainment. 120
rooms, $44 to $50. AE, CB, DC,
MC, V accepted.

**HOPKINS HOUSE BEST
WESTERN RESORT,** 1501 Hwy.
7, Hopkins 55343. ►5
935-7711

Indoor pool, sauna, whirlpool,
miniature golf. 170 rooms, $42.50
to $125. Two restaurants, three
lounges, entertainment. AE, CB,
DC, MC, V, S accepted. Weekend
package available.

HOTEL SEVILLE, at I-494 and
Hwy. 100, Bloomington 55437.
830-1300 ►6

Indoor pool, whirlpool, sauna,
game room, HBO in-room movies. 256 rooms, $44 to $55. Each
room of this new 18-story hotel
has its own balcony; room rates
vary depending on how high the
room is in the hotel. Located close
to the airport on Bloomington's
"strip." Antonio's Restaurant
and Lounge. AE, DC, DB, M, V
accepted. Call about weekend
packages.

HOWARD JOHNSON'S, 7801
Normandale Rd., Bloomington
55435. ►6
835-7404

Indoor pool. 150 rooms, $45 to
$55. Restaurant, bar. AE, CB,
DC, MC, V accepted.

HYATT REGENCY, 1300 Nicollet Mall, Minneapolis 55403. ►1
370-1234

New deluxe hotel in the heart of

downtown Minneapolis. Includes facilities of a complete athletic club, available to guests for a small fee. 540 rooms, $57 to $108. Extra-special services available to guests who reserve rooms on 22nd-floor Regency Club, including complimentary bathrobe, cordials, and concierge. Willows and Terrace restaurants. AE, CB, DC, MC, V accepted. Call about weekend packages.

HOTEL LEAMINGTON AND MOTOR INN, 1014 Third Av. S., Minneapolis 55404. ►1
370-1100

A favorite for large meetings and conventions. Near the Minneapolis Auditorium and Convention Center. 600 rooms, $40 to $59. Waikiki and Norse Room restaurants. AE, CB, DC, MC, V accepted. Several packages available.

L'HOTEL SOFITEL, 5601 W. 78th St. (I-494 and Hwy. 100), Bloomington 55435. ►6
835-1900

Formerly the L'hotel de France. Indoor pool, two saunas. 300 rooms, $63 to $110. Three French restaurants provide 24-hour service. Two bars, bakery, flower, art and gift shops. AE, CB, DC, MC, V, other major cards accepted. Several weekend packages available.

MARQUETTE HOTEL, IDS Center, 710 Marquette Av., Minneapolis 55402. ►1
332-2351

A contemporary deluxe hotel at the center of the Minneapolis skyway system. 282 rooms, $65 to $95. Five restaurants. AE, CB,

DC, MC, V accepted. Two weekend packages available.

MARRIOTT HOTEL, 1919 E. 78th St. at I-494 and Cedar Av., Bloomington 55420. ►6
854-7441

Indoor pool, sauna, whirlpool. 497 rooms, $61 to $81. Newly remodeled restaurant, coffee shop, gift shop. Complimentary limousine service to airport. AE, CB, DC, MC, V accepted. Weekend packages available.

MINNEAPOLIS HILTON INN, I-35W N. at Industrial Blvd., Minneapolis 55413. ►2
331-1900

New hotel with indoor pool, sauna, whirlpool. 245 rooms, $44 to $63. Anchorage Restaurant. AE, CB, DC, MC, V, Hilton cards accepted. Weekend package available.

NORMANDY MOTOR INN, 405 S. Eighth St., Minneapolis 55404. 370-1400 ►1

Tudor-style building with indoor pool, whirlpool. A few blocks from downtown shopping and the Minneapolis Auditorium and Convention Center. 150 rooms, $38.50 to $46.50. Dining room, coffee shop, bar. AE, DC, MC, V accepted. Weekend packages available.

RADISSON INN-PLYMOUTH, 2705 Annapolis Lane (Hwy. 55 and I-494), Plymouth 55441. ►4
553-1600

Japanese country-style inn with indoor pool, whirlpool. 163 rooms, $44 to $60. Tozai and Chikurin restaurants, coffee shop. AE, CB, DC, MC, V accepted.

Weekend packages available.

RADISSON NORTHSTAR INN,
612 Second Av. S., Minneapolis
55402. ►1
338-2288

Near the heart of downtown, the Radisson Northstar Inn is home of the Rosewood Room and three other fine restaurants. 226 rooms, $52 to $65. AE, CB, DC, MC, V accepted. Popular "Wine and Roses" weekend package available.

RADISSON SOUTH, I-494 and Hwy. 100, Bloomington 55435. 835-7800 ►6

Indoor pool, whirlpool, sauna. Large garden court and 22nd-floor cocktail lounge. 408 rooms, $50 to $70. Tiffany and Shipside restaurants, coffee shop. AE, CB, DC, MC, V accepted. Weekend package available.

RAMADA INN, 4200 W. 78th St. (off I-494), Bloomington 55435. 831-4200 ►6

Indoor pool. 186 recently re-modeled rooms, $48 to $85. Summerfield's Restaurant and cocktail lounge. Complimentary limousine service to airport. "Super Saver" family weekend rate available. AE, CB, DC, MC, V accepted.

REGENCY PLAZA, 41 N. 10th St., Minneapolis 55403. ►1
339-9311

Indoor pool, sauna. Just northwest of Hennepin Av., not far from Guthrie Theater and Walker Art Center. 200 rooms, $36 to

L'hotel Sofitel in suburban Bloomington.

$48. Dining room, coffee shop. AE, CB, DC, MC, V accepted. Weekend packages available. Free shuttle to downtown areas.

REGISTRY HOTEL, 7901 24th Av. S. (off I-494), Bloomington 55420. ►6
854-2244

Indoor pool, sauna, whirlpool. Near the airport. 336 rooms, $60 to $85. Grand Portage Restaurant, coffee shop. AE, CB, DC, MC, V accepted. Weekend rates available.

RODEWAY INN, 1321 E. 78th St. (off I-494), Bloomington 55420. ►6
854-3400

Indoor pool, sauna. 277 rooms, $51 to $63. Rodehouse Restaurant. AE, CB, DC, MC, V accepted. Special weekend family rate available.

SHERATON AIRPORT INN, 2525 E. 78th St. (off I-494), Bloomington 55420. ►6
854-1771

Domed indoor pool. 150 rooms, $49 to $63. Timbers Restaurant, coffee shop. AE, CB, DC, MC, V accepted. Weekend package available.

SHERATON INN NORTHWEST, I-94 and Hwy. 52, Brooklyn Park 55428. ►4
566-8855

Indoor pool, sauna, whirlpool, putting green, ping-pong, pinball machines. 220 rooms, $42 to $64; suites $70 to $150. Dining room, coffee shop, lounge with live entertainment. AE, CB, DC, MC, V accepted. Weekend packages available.

SHERATON PARK PLACE HOTEL, 5555 Wayzata Blvd., St. Louis Park 55416. ►5
542-8600

This 300-room hotel is scheduled to open in March 1982. It features a five-story glass atrium with indoor pool, sauna and whirlpool. Restaurant and lounge. Rooms $65 to $105. AE, CB, DC, MC, V accepted. Weekend package available.

SHERATON-RITZ HOTEL, 315 Nicollet Mall, Minneapolis 55401. 332-4000 ►1

Recently remodeled, indoor pool and health club, shops. 303 rooms, $53 to $80. Window Terrace Cafe, Stradivarius Restaurant. AE, CB, DC, MC, V accepted. "Ritz Package" weekend available.

THUNDERBIRD MOTEL, I-494 and 24th Av. S., Bloomington 55420. ►6
854-3411

On the "strip" in Bloomington. Indoor and outdoor pools, sauna, whirlpool, game room, limousine service. 263 rooms, $55 to $61. Dining room with live entertainment nightly, coffee shop. AE, CB, DC, MC, V accepted. Weekend package available.

St. Paul Area

CAPP TOWERS MOTOR HOTEL, Ninth and Minnesota Sts., St. Paul 55101. ►7
227-7331

Near the state Capitol, St. Paul-Ramsey Arts and Science Center, and the Science Museum of Minnesota. 98 rooms, $34 to $48.

Restaurant. AE, CB, DC, MC, V accepted. "Sweetheart Weekend" package.

HOLIDAY INN-CAPITOL, 161 St. Anthony Av. (off I-94), St. Paul 55103. ►7
227-8711

Indoor pool. 200 rooms, $41 to $58. Restaurant, entertainment. AE, DC, MC, V accepted. Weekend package available.

HOLIDAY INN-ROSEVILLE, 2540 Cleveland Av. N., Roseville 55113. ►9
636-4567

Indoor pool, sauna, whirlpool, wading pool. 259 rooms, $45 to $54. Dining room, lounge. AE, CB, DC, MC, V accepted.

HOWARD JOHNSON'S MOTOR LODGE, 6003 Hudson Rd. (Hwy. 12), St. Paul 55125. 739-7300 ►8

Located across the street from 3M Co. headquarters. Indoor pool, sauna. 164 recently remodeled rooms, $41 to $55. 24-hour restaurant. AE, CB, DC, MC, V accepted.

McGUIRE'S INN, Lexington Av. N. and County Rd. E, Arden Hills 55112. ►9
636-4123

Indoor pool, sauna, whirlpool. 154 rooms, $40 to $46. Continental dining room, two lounges with entertainment. AE, CB, DC, MC, V accepted. Special weekend rates.

MIDWAY TWINS MOTOR INNS, 1964 and 1975 University Av., St. Paul 55140. ►8
645-8681

Two inns located across the street from each other on St. Paul's University Av. Indoor and outdoor pools, sauna, whirlpool. 219 rooms, $30 single, $36 double. Two restaurants. AE, CB, DC, MC, V accepted.

RADISSON PLAZA ST. PAUL, 411 Minnesota St., St. Paul 55101. ►7
291-8800

This new 17-story hotel in St. Paul's Town Square project features a large glass solar-energy collecting atrium. Indoor pool. 252 rooms, $52 to $68. La Rotisserie Restaurant, lounge. AE, CB, DC, MC, V accepted.

RADISSON ST. PAUL HOTEL, 11 E. Kellogg Blvd., St. Paul 55101. ►7
292-1900

Indoor pool, revolving lounge and restaurant above the city. 475 rooms, $46 to $64. AE, CB, DC, MC, V accepted. Weekend package available.

COUNTRY INNS

Within an hour's drive of the Twin Cities are three fine, family-owned establishments with a country-inn atmosphere. A fourth such inn, though not exactly in the "country," is also listed below.

THE LOWELL INN, 102 N. Second St., Stillwater 55082. ►10
439-1100

The "Mount Vernon of the Midwest" has long been a favorite for romantic evenings and convenient retreats from city life.

Located in historic Stillwater on the St. Croix River 15 miles east of St. Paul, the inn retains its Old-World ambiance. No television. 21 rooms, $59 to $109. George Washington Room, Garden Room, and Matterhorn Room restaurants. AE, MC, V accepted.

NICOLLET ISLAND INN, 51 Merriam St. (just off the Hennepin Av. Bridge on Nicollet Island), Minneapolis 55401. ►1

Scheduled to open in December 1981, this 1893 limestone factory-turned-inn features a breathtaking view of the Mississippi River and a turn-of-the-century atmosphere. Furnishings include antique reproductions and custom-made European-style quilts. 24 rooms, $60 to $100. Continental breakfast included in room rate. Restaurant with view of the river; lounge includes authentic 1860s bar. AE, MC, V accepted. Call directory assistance for reservation number.

SCHUMACHER'S NEW PRAGUE HOTEL, 212 W. Main St., New Prague 56071. ►6
445-7285 (Twin Cities number)

About 30 miles south of the Twin Cities on Hwy. 13, the New Prague Hotel offers a quiet, television-free retreat from city life and a chance to enjoy fine German and Czech cuisine in the hotel's restaurant. Upstairs are 12 refurbished rooms, $55 to $79.50, each decorated differently in Old-World style. Weekday packages available. No credit cards, but Twin Cities checks are accepted.

ST. JAMES HOTEL, 406 Main St., Red Wing 55066. ►12

225-1400 (Twin Cities number)

Located in a pretty Mississippi River town southeast of the Twin Cities, this 1875 vintage hotel has recently been restored. Each room is named after a 19th-century Mississippi riverboat and decorated with Victorian-era antiques and reproductions. 60 rooms, 41 of them part of the original hotel, 19 in an addition added in 1981. All the newer rooms have a river view. Rates range from $32.50 to $70. Three restaurants, including an outdoor cafe. AE, MC, V accepted.

BED AND BREAKFAST

Long popular in Europe, the bed-and-breakfast concept is just beginning to take hold in the Twin Cities. These establishments include homey comfort and a continental breakfast in their room rates. Rates, as ever, are subject to change.

BLEICK HOUSE BED AND BREAKFAST, 2700 Fort Rd., St. Paul 55102. ►7
227-2800

This B & B, located near the heart of downtown St. Paul within walking distance of the Science Museum, Minnesota Museum of Art, and other attractions, is larger than most. 23 rooms; singles $19 to $23, doubles $26, triples $29. Six shared baths, hot running water in every room. Breakfast served on an enclosed porch, at patio tables, or in a winter dining room. This is a French Second Empire-style home built in 1873 for the first sheriff of St. Paul. There are antiques in every room and a garden in the summer. Free parking. Small pets may be acceptable.

EVELO'S BED AND BREAKFAST, 2301 Bryant Av. S., Minneapolis 55408. ▶2
374-9656

Located in the lake area of Minneapolis near the Guthrie Theater and Walker Art Center. Two rooms, $15 single, $25 double. Guests stay on the airy third floor of home. Breakfast is served in the room. Private bath, small refrigerator, coffee-maker. A lovely 1897 Victorian house with original woodwork and period furnishings.

KELMSCOTT BED AND BREAKFAST, 2648 Emerson Av. S., Minneapolis 55408. ▶2
377-7032

An 1885 Queen Anne home with completely restored exterior and original stained-glass windows. Located near Lake of the Isles and Lake Calhoun, as well as theaters and galleries. Easy bus access to downtown. One room, single $15, double $25. The room is on the second floor; shared bath. The hosts are interested in historic houses and restoration.

OGREN AND TRIGG BED AND BREAKFAST, 2616 Colfax Av., Minneapolis 55408. ▶2
377-2290

A late Victorian home with turret and classic Queen Anne-style front porch, complete with stained-glass windows, parquet floors, and golden oak woodwork. Located near lakes and the Guthrie Theater. Two rooms on the second floor; single $18, dou-

ble $25. Shared bath; breakfast is served in rooms or in a second-floor parlor. Hosts have a clock-repair shop in the house.

CONDOMINIUM RENTALS

CONDOMINIUM INNS, 7300 France Av. S., Edina 55435.
831-0335 or (800) 328-6384

Advertised as a "home away from home," Condominium Inns offers daily rates on one-, two-, and three-bedroom units that include full kitchens, linen, laundry facilities, housekeeping, and answering service. Some locations include recreational facilities such as tennis courts and swimming pools. Locations in Minneapolis, St. Paul, and suburbs. Minimum stay of four days required. Daily rates range from $40 to $65 for four to 29 days; rates decrease for stays longer than 30 days. AE, MC, V accepted.

HOUSEBOATS

If you're looking for a place to go to get away from it all, try a summer stay on a houseboat on the Mississippi River. Rentals are available within a short drive of the Twin Cities.

GREAT RIVER HARBOR HOUSEBOAT RENTALS, 731 Hennepin Av., Minneapolis 55403.
333-2088

A fleet of 17 boats is available May 15 through October 15. Pilot your own cruise on Lake Pepin in the heart of the Upper Mississippi

River Wildlife and Fish Refuge. Boats range from 30 to 50 feet, and will accommodate two to 10 people. Full showers, hot water, all appliances, bar. All you need to bring is food and recreational equipment. Rental periods range from midweek (M to Thu) and weekend (F to Sun) to week-long (M or F departure). Previous river experience not required. $340 to $1,100 depending on boat size and duration of trip. Reservations and $150 deposit required. No cards, no personal checks. Write for a free trip-planning kit.

CAMPING

There are seven public parks in the regional park system that have facilities for overnight camping for families and individuals. For information about private and municipal campgrounds write for the *Minnesota Camping Guide*, Minnesota Department of Economic Development, Tourism Bureau, 480 Cedar St., St. Paul 55101.

Anoka County

BUNKER HILLS REGIONAL PARK, in Coon Rapids off Hwy. 242 at Foley Blvd. ►3
755-4165
Horseback riding, but no swimming beach. 13 tent sites, 13 motor sites, flush toilets, cold running water; no showers or electricity. Open May-September, $3 per night, no parking fee; three-night limit on campers. Reservations required.

Carver County

BAYLOR REGIONAL PARK, on County Rd. 33, 2½ miles north of Hwy. 212 in Camden Township. ►5
467-3145
Swimming beach, tennis courts, volleyball, hiking trails. Both tent and motor camping; some sites have electrical hookups. Flush toilets, hot water, showers. $4, $5 with electricity, no parking fee. Reservations required for popular holidays.

Dakota County

LAKE BYLLESBY REGIONAL PARK, in Randolph Township. Take Hwy. 52 south to County Rd. 86, east to Harry Av., then south 1½ miles. ►12
437-6608
Near vintage dam. Has swimming beach, deep fishing lake. 17 tent sites, 13 motor sites, cold water, flush toilets; no electricity. Open all year. No charge; permits for camping can be obtained from evening park patrol. Camping on a first-come, first-served basis.

Hennepin County

BAKER PARK RESERVE, between Delano and Rockford on County Rds. 19 and 24. ►5
473-4693
Large sand swimming beach, paved bicycle trails, golf courses, boat launch, fishing. 80 tent sites, 161 motor sites, 21 with electricity. Open May to September. Hot showers, flush toilets, drinking

water. Sites $5, $7 with electricity. No parking fee for campers. First come, first served; no reservations.

CARVER PARK RESERVE, near Victoria on County Rd. 11. 473-4693 ▶5

Tent camping only. 10 lakes, nature center, many hiking trails. Open May to September. No electricity or hot water. Primitive toilets. Sites $3. No reservations; obtain permit at gate.

Scott County

MINNESOTA VALLEY STATE TRAIL, 3 miles southwest of Jordan on Hwy. 169. ▶6
492-6400

Hiking along river, but no swimming. 38 primitive sites; cold water pumps. Pay $5 camping fee at park office; state park vehicle sticker required. Open year-round.

Washington County

WILLIAM O'BRIEN STATE PARK, off Hwy. 95 in northeastern Washington County. ▶10
433-2421

Swimming beach, hiking trails, canoe rentals. 125 sites in two locations for both tents and motor campers. 43 sites with electricity. Flush toilets, hot water, showers. Sites $5, $6 with electricity; parking fee extra. First come, first served; Fridays always busy. Check in before 10 p.m.

Chapter Ten

DINING OUT

The following restaurant listing, arranged by specialty, is intended to provide a broad sampling of what the Twin Cities offers in the way of cuisine, settings, and prices. The editors have tried to include those establishments that have been recognized by critics and the public as worthy of a visit, as well as those we have enjoyed personally.

Restaurants can close or change menu, decor, or policies at any time, so we very strongly urge you to call before visiting. If reservations are suggested, it is probably very difficult to get a table without calling. And some restaurants that don't take reservations are extremely popular, so it is worth calling to check on the wait.

Because restaurant prices are changing rapidly, the designations of moderate, moderately expensive, expensive, and very expensive are best used for comparison only. At this writing, for a full dinner *not* including beverage, dessert, tax, or tip, moderate would be under $9; moderately expensive, $9 to $11.50; expensive, $11.50 to $14; and very expensive, over $14. Lunch prices in each category are roughly half of dinner prices.

The standard tip in the Twin Cities is 15 percent for fair to good service. Many feel 10 to 15 percent is adequate for middling service, and 20 percent is usually a reward for outstanding service.

Most Twin Cities restaurants will accept a personal check for the amount of your purchase, but they emphasize that the check must be local and accompanied by

(See Locator Key Map, pages 8-9)

▶1 Mpls. Downtown
▶2 Mpls. Excluding Downtown
▶3 Mpls. North Suburbs
▶4 Mpls. Northwest Suburbs
▶5 Mpls. Southwest Suburbs
▶6 Mpls. South Suburbs

▶7 St. Paul Downtown
▶8 St. Paul Excluding Downtown
▶9 St. Paul North Suburbs
▶10 St. Paul Northeast Suburbs
▶11 St. Paul Southeast Suburbs
▶12 St. Paul South Suburbs

picture identification, such as a Minnesota driver's license. Some restaurants require a second form of identification, such as a major credit card. If you have any doubt about whether your check will be accepted, call first—or bring cash.

Abbreviations used for credit cards are: AE-American Express; CB-Carte Blanche; DC-Diners Club; MC-MasterCard; S-Shoppers Charge; V-Visa (Bank-Americard).

AMERICAN

AL'S BREAKFAST, 413 Fourteenth Av. S.E., Minneapolis. ▶2
331-9991

The sign says this is the "Dinkytown Branch," but there is only one Al's, a University of Minnesota-area institution. It's one of the narrowest restaurants in the Twin Cities and serves only breakfast. No cards. No reservations. Checks accepted. Open Tue-Sat 6 a.m. to 1 p.m.; Sun 9 to 1.

BOBBIE'S 711 Third St., White Bear Lake. ▶10
429-7997

An old post office has been converted into an attractive restaurant with a straightforward menu. Spinach salads and noteworthy popovers come with dinners. AE, DC, MC, V. Reservations suggested. Checks accepted. Open M-F 11 a.m. to 2 p.m., 5:30 to 10 p.m.; Sat. 11 to 2, 5:30 to 10:30; Sun (buffet brunch) 11 to 2.

THE BOARDING HOUSE AND JUST DESSERTS, 653 Grand Av., St. Paul. ▶8
225-5441

Formerly the Restoration, the Boarding House serves fresh seafood and specialties like cheese fondue and lemon veal. Just Desserts, on the lower level, offers a fine selection of cheesecakes and other sweets. Restored Victorian house has a fireplace and a summer patio. Moderate to expensive. Reservations suggested. AE, MC, V. Checks accepted. Open Tue-Sat 11 a.m. to 2 p.m., 5 to 10 p.m.; Sun brunch 10 to 2.

BLUE FOX INN, 3833 N. Lexington Av. (Lexington at I-694), Arden Hills. ▶9
483-6000

Standard American menu featuring steaks and seafood. Moderate to expensive. AE, CB, DC, MC, V. Reservations accepted, checks accepted. M-Thu 11 a.m. to 9:30 p.m.; F, Sat 11 to 10:30.

CASTLE ROYAL, 215 S. Wabasha St., St. Paul. ▶8
227-8771

This subterranean bar and restaurant has been both an art deco speakeasy and a mushroom cave. It is reported to be haunted by a friendly ghost. Prime rib and Lebanese steak are specialties. AE, MC, V. Reservations suggested. Checks accepted. Open Tue-F 11:30 a.m. to 2 p.m., 6 to 9 p.m.; Sat 6 to 10.

THE COPPER HEARTH, Northstar Inn, 618 Second Av. S., Minneapolis. ▶1
338-2288

An American menu is featured in this popular lunch spot and bar. Moderately expensive. AE, CB,

DC, MC, V. Reservations suggested. Checks accepted. Open M-F 11:30 a.m. to 2 p.m., 6 to 10:30 p.m. Closed weekends.

DAYTON'S OAK GRILL and SKY ROOM, Dayton's Department Store, 700 Nicollet Mall, Minneapolis. ►1
375-2938

The Sky Room features a popular salad bar and view of the city. The Oak Grill's club-like atmosphere provides a relaxing respite from shopping. Soups, salads, hamburgers, and sandwiches are the mainstays of menus at both. Prices are moderate. Dayton's charge. Reservations accepted for eight or more. Checks accepted. Oak Grill open M, Thu 11:30 a.m. to 7 p.m.; Tue, W, F, Sat 11:30 to 5. Sky Room open M-Sat 11 a.m. to 2:30 p.m.

DeZIEL'S SUPPER CLUB, 6937 W. Hwy. 10, Anoka. ►3
427-8740

Popular north suburban gathering place that serves standard American food. Steaks and planked pike are specialties. Reservations required. No cards. Checks accepted. Open M-Thu 11 a.m. to 10 p.m.; F, Sat 11 to midnight.

EDDIE WEBSTER'S, 1501 E. 78th St. (off I-494), Bloomington. 854-4056 ►6

Straightforward meat and potatoes are prepared and served with care in an intimate atmosphere. New peanut bar serves chicken and hamburger baskets. Expensive. AE, CB, DC, MC, V. Reservations accepted. Checks accepted. Open M-Sat 11 a.m. to midnight; Sun 5 p.m. to midnight.

ENGINE HOUSE NO. 5, 498 Selby Av., St. Paul. ►8
227-0101

This 1880s firehouse is now a contemporary restaurant serving French and American food. Veal scaloppini and ice cream drinks are specialties. Reservations suggested. AE, CB, DC, MC, V. Checks accepted. Open seven days a week 11 a.m. to midnight.

FIRST STREET STATION, 333 S. First St., Minneapolis. ►1
339-3339

An historic old railroad building has been converted into this popular restaurant featuring a limited steak and seafood menu, salad bar, variety of a la carte vegetables (including fresh artichokes in season), and unusual desserts. Restaurant has view of Mississippi River and Minneapolis skyline. Moderately expensive. AE, MC, V. Reservations for lunch and for 12 or more for dinner. Checks accepted. Open M-Thu 11:30 a.m. to 2:30 p.m., 5:30 to 11 p.m.; F 11:30 to 2:30, 5:30 to midnight; Sat 5:30 to midnight; Sun 5:30 to 11.

FOREPAUGH'S, 276 S. Exchange St. (on Irvine Park), St. Paul. ►8
224-5606

An 1870 mansion across the street from the Alexander Ramsey House has been renovated into a collection of individual, attractively decorated dining rooms. The menu includes standard steak and seafood items, plus a few more adventurous selections. Expensive to very expensive. Checks accepted. AE, CB, DC, MC, V. Reservations suggested. Open

M-Thu 11 a.m. to 2:30 p.m., 5 to 9:30 p.m.; F 11 to 2:30, 5 to 10:30; Sat noon to 2:30, 5 to 10:30; Sun 11:30 to 2:30, 5 to 9.

THE FREIGHT HOUSE, 305 Water St., Stillwater. ►**10** 349-5718

A large, converted 1880s warehouse that overlooks the St. Croix River and houses a restaurant with an American menu emphasizing seafood. Moderate to expensive. Checks and V accepted. Reservations required for groups of five or more. Open M-Thu 11 a.m. to 10 p.m.; F, Sat 11 a.m. to 11 p.m.; Sun 10:30 to 9 p.m.

THE GALLERY, 710 Marquette Av. (in the IDS Tower), Minneapolis. ►**1**

Suspended over the Crystal Court in the IDS Tower, the Gallery was immortalized in the opening scenes of the *Mary Tyler Moore Show.* (Look for the plaque that designates the table she sat at.) Serves light meals, including the wild rice soup you pay more for upstairs in the Orion Room. AE, CB, DC, MC, V. Moderate to expensive. Checks accepted; reservations accepted. Open 7 a.m. to 11 p.m. seven days a week.

GRANDMA'S SALOON AND DELI, 1810 Washington Av. S., Minneapolis. ►**2** 340-0516

Newest addition to the Seven Corners restaurant scene. American menu served in a renovated building decorated with antiques and old advertising items. Moderate to expensive. AE, MC, V. No checks. No reservations. Open M-Sat 11 a.m. to midnight; Sun 11 a.m. to 11 p.m.

AL FRESCO DINING

When the summer sun comes out in the Twin Cities, so do the patio tables. There are dozens of restaurants in the metro area that offer full meals, cocktail service, or special menus outdoors. Start with the following list of al fresco establishments, and then discover your own favorites. Most restaurants open their outdoor areas in May and keep them open as long as the sun and warm weather last.

ANTHONY'S WHARF
ARBORETUM TEA ROOM
BLACK FOREST INN
THE BOARDING HOUSE
CAFE KARDAMENA

CHOUETTE
FREIGHT HOUSE
GALLERY 8
GRANDMA'S SALOON AND DELI
HART'S CAFE
JAX
JOSE'S
KOZLAK'S ROYAL OAK
KRAMARCZUK EASTERN EUROPEAN DELI
LA GRAND CREPE
LA TERRASSE
LORD FLETCHER'S
THE LOWELL INN
MAI TAI
MUFFULETTA
PRACNA ON MAIN
W. A. FROST & CO.

THE HANSON HOUSE, 1310 Wayzata Blvd., Long Lake. ►5 473-2452

Overlooking Long Lake, this restaurant provides a tranquil setting for enjoying soups, salads, and sandwiches at lunch, straight-forward meat and fish dishes at dinner. Moderate at lunch to expensive at dinner. AE, DC, MC, S, V. Reservations accepted. Checks accepted. Open M-Thu 11:30 a.m. to 3 p.m., 5 to 10 p.m.; F, Sat 11:30 to 3, 5 to 11; Sun brunch 11 am. to 2 p.m.; dinner 2:30 to 9:30. Longer hours in the summer.

JAX CAFE, 1928 University Av. N.E., Minneapolis. ►2 789-7297

The trout here are fresh—at least during the summer, when they're fished at your order from a pond in the patio, where al fresco dining is available. Live lobster, steaks, and prime rib round out the menu at this northeast Minneapolis favorite. AE, CB, DC, MC, V. Reservations accepted. Open M, Tue 11 a.m. to 11 p.m.; W, Thu 11 to 11:30; F, Sat 11 to midnight. Jax is also located at 604 N. Lilac Dr., Golden Valley.

J.P. MULLIGAN'S, 3005 N. Harbor Lane, Plymouth. 559-1595 ►4

Lots of mirrors and glass, an enormous chandelier in the bar, and an imaginative menu ranging from hamburgers to escargots are featured here. Moderately expensive. AE, DC, MC, V. No reservations. Checks accepted. Open M-Thu 11 a.m. to 10:30 p.m.; F, Sat 11 a.m. to 11:30 p.m.

JR, 1028 La Salle Av., Minneapolis. ►1 338-2424

No-nonsense food from a standard menu can be enjoyed near Orchestra Hall in dark, relaxing atmosphere here. Sandwiches, seafood, and steaks are served off an abbreviated late-night menu in the piano bar. Outdoor patio open in summer. AE, CB, DC, MC, V. Reservations accepted. Checks accepted. Open M-F 11 a.m. to 11:45 p.m.; Sat 4:30 to 11:45.

KASHMIRI ROOM, Ambassador Motel, 5225 Wayzata Blvd. (Hwys. 12 and 100), St. Louis Park. ►5 545-0441

The Kashmiri Room is the motel's formal dining area, providing a comfortable setting for business lunches and a more romantic ambiance at night. The menu is standard fare. Moderately expensive. AE, CB, DC, MC, V. Reservations accepted. Checks accepted. Open M-F 11:30 a.m. to 2:30 p.m., 6 to 11 p.m.; Sat 6 to 11 p.m.; Sun 5 to 10.

KOZLAK'S ROYAL OAK, 4785 Hodgson Rd., Shoreview. ►9 484-8484

A modern, tastefully designed dining area opens onto a flower-filled garden and patio. From the same family that brought you Jax Cafe. Moderately expensive. AE, CB, DC, MC, V. Reservations suggested. Checks accepted. Open Tue-Thu 11 a.m. to 2:30 p.m., 4 to 10:30; F, Sat 11 to 2:30, 4 to 11:30; Sun 11:30 to 2:30, 5 to 8:30. Kozlak's Oakwood Inn opened recently at 710 E. River Rd., Anoka..

MICKEY'S DINER, 36 W. Ninth St. (Ninth and St. Peter), St. Paul. ►7
222-5633

Mickey's is an authentic 1930s dining car located in downtown St. Paul. Among the last of its kind in the country, Mickey's is under consideration for nomination to the National Register of Historic Places. The food is traditional diner fare. No cards, no checks, no reservations. Open 24 hours, seven days a week.

MINNEAPOLIS TECHNICAL INSTITUTE RESTAURANTS, 1415 Hennepin Av., Minneapolis. 370-9410 ►1

As part of its food-service training programs, the Minneapolis Technical Institute operates four different types of restaurants that are open to the public. The most impressive of these is a dining room that offers a full seven-course meal M through Thu evenings, with seatings between 6 and 7 p.m. The entire meal costs about $9 (no liquor is served). Cash only. The other restaurants are a fast-food restaurant, a cafeteria, and another, less fancy full-service dining room. The fast-food restaurant serves breakfast and lunch; the other two, lunch and dinner. Call for hours.

MISSISSIPPI BELLE, 101 E. Second St., Hastings. ►12
437-5694

Straightforward food and homemade pies are served in a steamboat atmosphere for moderate prices. AE, DC, MC, S, V.

Reservations suggested. Checks accepted. Open Tue-Thu 11 a.m. to 2:30 p.m., 4:30 to 9 p.m.; F, Sat 11 to 2:30, 4:30 to 10; Sun noon to 6:30.

NIGHT TRAIN, 289 Como Av., St. Paul. ►8
488-2277

This chic new restaurant is a pair of converted Pullman coaches, elegantly appointed with a mahogany bar and brass fixtures. Menu changes seasonally and is composed of an eccentric mix of bar and grill food and light continental meals. Fine French pastry. Open M-Sat 11 a.m. to midnight. AE, CB, DC, MC, V, checks accepted.

NORMANDY INN/VILLAGE, 405 S. Eighth St., Minneapolis. 370-1400 ►1

Popovers, caesar salads, and a special that changes every month have made this a reliable downtown standby. Moderately expensive. AE, DC, MC, V. Reservations accepted. Checks accepted. Open M-Thu 11:30 a.m. to 2 p.m., 5 to 10:30 p.m.; F, Sat 11:30 to 2, 5 to 11:30; Sun 4 to 10:30.

ORION ROOM, IDS Tower, 80 S. Eighth St., Minneapolis. ►1
372-3772

The high ceiling, modern decor, and 50th-floor view make this a spectacular place to enjoy the well-rounded menu of steaks, seafood, and game. Dinner starts with a complimentary tray of fresh vegetables and bleu cheese dressing. Pheasant is a specialty. Very expensive. AE, CB, DC, MC, V. Reservations suggested.

Checks accepted. Open M-F 11:30 a.m. to 2 p.m., 6 to 10 p.m.; Sat 6 to 10; Sun brunch 11 a.m. to 2:30 p.m.

STONEWINGS, 8301 Normandale Blvd. (off I-494), Bloomington. ►6
831-4811

A popular steak and seafood restaurant, formerly Henrici's. AE, CB, DC, MC, V. Reservations accepted. Checks accepted. Open M-Thu 11 a.m. to 11 p.m.; F 11 to 11:30; Sat 5:30 to 11:30; Sun 11:30 to 9.

SUMMERFIELD'S, Ramada Inn, 4200 W. 78th (off I-494), Bloomington. ►6
831-4200

The Ramada's new restaurant features West Coast decor and lighter items along with traditional steak and seafood on the menu. Lunch and dinner are served from the same menu, so a wide range of appetites can be satisfied at either meal. Reservations accepted. AE, CB, DC, MC, V accepted. Checks accepted. Open seven days a week 7 a.m. to 10 p.m.

TIMBERS, Sheraton Airport Inn, 2525 E. 78th St. (off I-494), Bloomington. ►6
854-1771

Choose the monthly special or one of a variety of mostly American dishes. Expensive. AE, CB, DC, MC, V accepted. Reservations suggested. Checks accepted. Open M-Thu 11:30 a.m. to 10:15 p.m.; F 11:30 to 11:30; Sat 5 to 11:30; Sun 5 to 10:30.

TOP OF THE LIST, Calhoun Towers, 3430 List Pl., Minne-apolis. ►2
927-8731

Located on the 22nd floor of Calhoun Towers, Top of the List has more windows than walls and offers diners an excellent view of Lake Calhoun. The menu (standard American) and decor have been carried over from the restaurant's previous existence as the University Club. Moderately expensive. Reservations suggested. AE, CB, DC, MC, V, checks accepted. Open M-Thu 11:30 a.m. to 2 p.m., 5:30 to 9 p.m.; F 11:30 to 2, 5:30 to 10; Sat 5:30 to 10; Sun 5:30 to 8:30.

WHEBBE'S, 193 S. Robert St., St. Paul. ►8
227-4494

Located in an old firehouse, this pub-restaurant features an American and Middle Eastern menu. Moderate prices. Reservations suggested. DC, MC, V, checks accepted. Open M-Thu 6 a.m. to 10 p.m.; F, Sat 6 a.m. to 10:30 p.m.; Sun 8 to 8.

BEEF

BLACK ANGUS, 1029 Marquette Av. (across from Orchestra Hall), Minneapolis. ►1
336-8939

Prime rib and charcoal-broiled steaks are the specialty at this straightforward restaurant. An after-concert menu is available. Moderately expensive. AE, MC, V. Reservations accepted. Checks accepted. Open M-F 11:30 a.m. to 1 a.m.; Sat 5 to 1; Sun 5 to midnight.

CHEROKEE SIRLOIN ROOM,

886 Smith Av. S., West St. Paul. 457-2729 ►12

Oldest restaurant in West St. Paul. Steaks and other standard American menu items and daily specials are served. Dinners come with soup, relish tray, salad, and potato; excellent onion rings are available. Moderate prices. No cards. Reservations suggested. Checks accepted. Open M-Thu 11 a.m. to 2:30 p.m., 5 to 11:30 p.m.; F 11 to 2:30, 5 to midnight; Sat 5 to midnight; Sun 3 to 10 p.m.

CORK 'N CLEAVER AT STATION 19, 2001 University Av. S.E. (at Oak and University), Minneapolis. ►2
379-2510

The oldest fire station in Minneapolis and birthplace of softball has been renovated into an attractive restaurant serving mostly steaks and standard seafood accompanied by selections from a salad bar. AE, DC, MC, V. Reservations accepted. Checks accepted. Open M-Sat 5:30 p.m. to 11:15 p.m.; Sun 5 to 10.

Another Cork 'n Cleaver is located at 905 Hampshire Av. S., Golden Valley, 546-2594. The Golden Valley Cork 'n Cleaver is open for lunch M-Sat, and does not accept reservations.

GALLIVAN'S, 354 Wabasha St., St. Paul. ►7
227-6688

One of downtown St. Paul's most popular bars also serves up steaks, prime rib, and other substantial fare. Moderately expensive. AE, CB, DC, MC, V. Reservations suggested. Checks ac-

cepted. Open M-Sat 11 a.m. to 11 p.m.

GANNON'S, 2728 W. Seventh Blvd. (Gannon Rd.), St. Paul. ►8
699-2420

Dinners include a good selection of steak and seafood, plus Gannon's famous gigantic liver. A more limited menu including sandwiches is offered at noon. Moderately expensive. Gannon's charge, AE, DC. Reservations suggested. Checks accepted. Open M-Sat 11:30 a.m. to 11:30 p.m.

HORATIO HORNBLOWER, 345 Wabasha St., St. Paul. ►7
227-8781

This comfortable downtown bar and restaurant in the Lowry Hotel serves basic steaks, prime rib, and seafood. Moderately expensive. AE, DC, MC, V. Reservations accepted. Checks accepted. Open M-Sat 11 a.m. to midnight; Sun 4 to 10.

THE LEXINGTON, 1096 Grand Av. (at Lexington Pkwy.), St. Paul. ►8
222-5878

An elegant St. Paul institution, the Lexington offers standard beef and seafood dishes served on linen tablecloths in paneled, mirrored, and flocked surroundings. Expensive. Lexington charge only. Reservations suggested. Checks accepted. Open M-Sat 11 to midnight.

LINDEY'S PRIME STEAK HOUSE, 3610 Snelling Av. N., Arden Hills. ►9
633-9813

Steaks—enormous and well-prepared—are the only entree available at this no-nonsense, no-frills restaurant. Expensive. No cards. No reservations. Checks accepted. Open M-Thu 5 to 10:30 p.m.; F, Sat 5 to 11:30.

MURRAY'S, 26 S. Sixth St., Minneapolis. ►1
339-0909

The "silver butterknife steak," hickory-smoked shrimp, and house breads have made Murray's consistently popular with couples on a big night out and business people on an expense account. The atmosphere, service, and menu are right out of the 1940s. Moderately to very expensive. AE, CB, DC, MC, S, V. Reservations suggested. Checks accepted. Open M-Thu 11 to 11; F, Sat 11 to 11:30.

PRACNA ON MAIN, 117 S.E. Main St. (at St. Anthony Main), Minneapolis. ►1
379-3200

One of the first restorations of an old commercial building into a bar-restaurant in the Twin Cities, Pracna remains popular. Al fresco drinking and dining is available in the summer. Inside, it's an informal bar with a sandwich and burger menu except for the Steakhouse upstairs. Moderate (downstairs) to moderately expensive (upstairs). AE, CB, DC, MC, V. Checks accepted. Reservations accepted for Steakhouse only. Open M-Thu 11 a.m. to 11 p.m.; F-Sat 11 to midnight; Sun 11 a.m. to 10 p.m. Steakhouse open Sun-Thu 5 to 10 p.m.; F, Sat 5 to 11.

STEAK AND ALE, 6475 Wayza-

ta Blvd., St. Louis Park.
545-3800 ►5

Steaks accompanied by selections from the salad bar are the mainstays of the menu at this Old English-style restaurant. Moderately expensive. AE, CB, DC, MC, V. Reservations accepted. No checks. Open M-Thu 11:30 a.m. to 2 p.m., 5 to 10:30 p.m.; F 11:30 to 2, 5 to 11; Sat 5 to 11; Sun 5 to 9:30.

Steak and Ale also is located at 2801 Southtown Dr., Bloomington, 883-0124, and at 1893 Hwy. 36, Roseville, 633-9083.

VICTORIA STATION, 2300 Cleveland Av. N. (at Hwy. 36), Roseville. ►9
631-9410

A series of atmospheric train cars have been strung together to form a restaurant specializing in steak, prime rib, and some seafood accompanied by selections from a salad bar. Expensive. AE, CB, DC, MC, V. Reservations accepted. Checks accepted. Open M-Thu 11:30 a.m. to 2:30 p.m., 5 to 10:30; F, Sat 11:30 to 2:30, 5 to 11:30; Sun 11 to 10.

Victoria Station also is located at 4701 W. 80th St., Bloomington.

BRITISH

LORD FLETCHER'S OF THE LAKE, 3746 Sunset Dr. (on Lake Minnetonka), Spring Park. ►5
471-8513

This large, English-style restaurant is a favorite with yachters, who can dock right out back. Beef Wellington and other British-accented dishes are specialties here. Moderately expensive. AE, CB,

DC, MC, V. Reservations accepted. Checks accepted. Open M-Thu 11:30 a.m. to 2:30 p.m., 5 to 9:30 p.m.; F, Sat 11:30 a.m. to 2:30 p.m., 5 to 10 p.m.; Sun brunch 11 to 2, dinner 4:30 to 9. Summer dinner hours slightly longer.

BURGERS

ANNIE'S PARLOUR OF ICE CREAM, 406 Cedar Av., Minneapolis. ▶2
339-6207

Annie's serves hamburgers, salads, skin-on french fries, and fresh-fruit-flavored malts in an informal atmosphere. Moderate prices. No cards. No reservations. Checks accepted. Open M-Thu 11 a.m. to midnight; F, Sat 11 a.m. to 1 a.m.; Sun noon to midnight.

Annie's is also open in Dinkytown, at 313 15th Av. S.E., M-Thu 11 a.m. to 11 p.m.; F, Sat 11 a.m. to midnight; Sun noon to 11 p.m. Call 379-0744.

CLASSIC MOTOR COMPANY, 4700 Excelsior Blvd., St. Louis Park. ▶5
927-5666

One of the Twin Cities' busiest night spots also serves ribs, hamburgers, salads, sandwiches, and steaks that are particularly popular at lunch. Decorated with auto memorabilia and real antique cars. Moderately expensive. AE, CB, DC, MC, V. Reservations accepted. Checks accepted. Open M-F 11 a.m. to 1 a.m.; Sat noon to 1 a.m.; Sun noon to midnight.

CONVENTION GRILL, 3912 Sunnyside Av., Edina. ▶5
920-6881

Malts, hamburgers, and homemade soups are served in a decor right out of the 1940s. Moderate prices. Expect a wait. No cards. No reservations. Checks accepted. Open M-Thu 11 a.m. to 10 p.m.; F, Sat 11 to 11; Sun noon to 10.

HABERDASHERY, 1501 Washington Av. S., Minneapolis. ▶2
333-6303

Ribs, burgers, and salads are the mainstays of the menu at this popular casual peanut bar. Moderate prices. AE, CB, DC, MC, V. No reservations. Checks accepted. Open M-Sat 11 a.m. to 12:30 a.m.; Sun noon to 11:30.

Second location at 395 Wabasha St., St. Paul, 222-7855.

ICHABOD'S, 528 Hennepin Av. (in the Hennepin Center for the Arts), Minneapolis. ▶1
341-4009

Ichabod's new location in the Hennepin Center for the Arts makes it an ideal spot for downtown people-watching. Casual atmosphere; burger, steak, and seafood menu. AE, MC, V, checks accepted. Reservations not required. Open M-Thu 11 a.m. to 10:30 p.m.; F, Sat 11 to 11.

LAST FRONTIER, 2191 Snelling Av. N., Roseville. ▶9
631-0616

Amidst the fast-food franchises in the Rosedale-Har Mar area is this restaurant serving real hamburgers, sandwiches, chicken, and ice cream treats. The decor features Western artifacts, tastefully displayed. Moderate prices. V. Reservations accepted. Checks accepted. Open M-Sat 11:30 a.m. to 11 p.m.

T. WRIGHT'S, 3310 S. Hwy. 101, Wayzata. ►5
475-2215

Steaks, hamburgers, and the salad bar are the main attractions at this restaurant with a small-town supper club atmosphere. AE, CB, DC, MC, V. Reservations suggested. Checks accepted. Open M-Thu 11:30 a.m to 3 p.m., 5:15 to 11 p.m.; F, Sat 11:30 to 3, 5:15 to 11:30; Sun noon to 10:30.

CHINESE

THE EDGEWATER EAST, INC., 2420 N.E. Marshall St., Minneapolis. ►2
781-3444

Under new management (formerly the Edgewater Inn), this restaurant features a Cantonese menu and a view of the upper Mississippi River. AE, MC, V. Reservations suggested. Checks accepted. Open M-Sat 11:30 a.m. to 3 p.m., 5:30 p.m. to 10 p.m.

Pracna on Main, St. Anthony Main, Minneapolis.

Closed for Sat lunch June through mid-September.

THE GREAT WALL, 4515 France Av. S. (in the Morningside Shops), Minneapolis. ►2
926-4439

New Chinese restaurant with a predominantly Szechuan and Mandarin menu. Reservations on weekends only. AE, V, MC, checks accepted. Open M-Thu 11 a.m. to 11 p.m; F, Sat 11 to 11; Sun 4 to 10.

HOUSE OF LAI, 3412 S. Hwy. 101, Deephaven. ►5
473-1824

Appetizers are one of the strengths of this unpretentious Chinese restaurant in the Lake Minnetonka area. Beer and wine served. Moderate prices. AE, MC, V. Reservations accepted. Checks accepted. Open M-Thu 11 a.m. to 9 p.m.; F, Sat 11 to 10; Sun 5 to 9.

HOWARD WONG'S, 2701 Southtown Dr. (off I-494), Bloomington. ►6
888-8900

Cantonese, Szechuan, and some American dishes are served in an atmosphere that makes this one of the classiest Chinese restaurants in the Twin Cities. Full bar. Moderately expensive. AE, CB, DC, MC, S, V. Reservations accepted. Checks accepted. Open M-Sat 11 a.m. to 1 a.m.

HUNAN, 8066 Morgan Circle (behind Southtown), Bloomington. ►6
881-2280

A strictly Chinese menu featuring Peking and Szechuan dishes is served in ordinary Chinese-restaurant atmosphere. Liquor served. Moderate prices. No cards. Reservations for groups of six or more. Checks accepted. Open M-Thu 11 a.m. to 10 p.m.; F-Sat 11 to 11; Sun 3 to 10.

LEEANN CHIN, 1571 Plymouth Rd. (in Bonaventure Center), Minnetonka. ►5
545-3600

Elegant new Chinese restaurant with a Cantonese emphasis. Meals are served buffet-style. Specialties include lemon chicken and shrimp toast. Moderate to expensive. Reservations are suggested for dinner. AE, MC, V, checks accepted. Open M-Thu 11 a.m. to 2:30 p.m., 5 to 10 p.m.; F, Sat 11 to 2:30, 5 to 11; Sun 5 to 9 p.m.

MANDARIN YEN, 8625 Wayzata Blvd., St. Louis Park. ►5
544-5151

Ask about the dishes that aren't on the menu, particularly the triple crown seafood combination. Entrees are mostly Szechuan, served in a large, typically decorated dining room. Moderately expensive. AE, DC, MC, V. Reservations accepted. Checks accepted. Open M-Thu 11:30 a.m. to 2 p.m., 5 to 9:30; F 11:30 to 2, 5 to 11:30; Sat 5 to 11:30, 5 to 9:30.

NANKIN CAFE, 2 S. Seventh St., Minneapolis. ►1
333-3303

An extensive Chinese-American menu is served at this downtown Minneapolis institution, which is relocating to the new City Center building. Moderately expensive. No cards. Reservations accepted. Checks accepted. Open M-Sat 11 a.m. to midnight.

NEW CHINA INN, 328 Third St. S. (Third St. and Fourth Av. S.), Minneapolis. ►1
338-1022

Peking duck and sweet and sour pike (both require 24-hour advance order) are among the specialties of this dimly lit downtown restaurant. Moderately expensive. MC, V. Reservations accepted. Checks accepted. Open M-F 11 a.m. to 10 p.m.; Sat 5 to 10.

O'MEI MANDARIN CHINESE RESTAURANT, 25 W. Seventh St., St. Paul. ►8
226-1903

Short on atmosphere but long on quality food, O'Mei has both Mandarin and Szechuan offerings on the menu. On Seventh St. just west of downtown St. Paul. Open M-Sat 11 a.m. to 9 p.m. No cards. Checks accepted.

THE PALACE, 5340 Wayzata Blvd., Golden Valley. ►4
544-7017

One of the area's newer Chinese restaurants, the Palace emphasizes Cantonese dishes. Moderately expensive. No cards. Reservations accepted. Checks accepted. Open Tue-Thu 11 a.m. to 9 p.m.; Fri-Sat 11 to 10; Sun dim sum brunch 11 a.m. to 2:30 p.m.

PRINCESS GARDEN, 1665 Rice St. (at Larpenteur Av.), St. Paul. 488-0531 ►8

Authentic Cantonese and Szechuan dishes are served in a simple, casual atmosphere. Moderate prices. No cards. Reservations suggested. No checks. Open M-F 11 a.m. to 9:30 p.m.; Sat 11 to 11; Sun 4 to 9:30.

SZECHUAN STAR, Hazelton Rd. (next to Byerly's), Edina. ►5
835-7610

This attractively decorated restaurant specializes in spicy Szechuan dishes and serves a buffet M-F 11 a.m. to 2 p.m. and Sun 11 to 3. MC, V. Reservations accepted for six or more M-Thu. Checks accepted. Open M-Thu 11 a.m. to 10 p.m.; F, Sat 11 to 11; Sun 11 to 9.

TAIGA, St. Anthony Main, 201 S.E. Main St., Minneapolis. ►1
331-1138

Authentic Cantonese and Szechuan dishes are served in a tranquil, subtly decorated restaurant. Lunches and M dinners are always served buffet-style. Expensive. AE. Reservations suggested. Checks accepted. Open M-Thu 11:30 a.m. to 2:30 p.m., 5 to 9 p.m.; F, Sat 11:30 to 2:30, 5-10; Sun 5 to 9.

CONTINENTAL

THE BLUE HORSE, 1355 University Av., St Paul. ►8
645-8101

Consistent preparation of continental entrees has won the Blue Horse both awards and a reputation for excellence. Specialties include Dungeness crab, Pacific Coast salmon, and caesar salad. Ask about items not on the menu. Moderately expensive to very expensive. AE, CB, MC, V. Reservations suggested. Checks accepted. Open M-Thu 11 a.m. to 11 p.m.; F 11 a.m. to 11:30 p.m.; Sat 4 p.m. to 11:30 p.m.

THE CAMELOT, 5300 W. 78th

St. (Hwy. 100 and I-494), Bloomington. ►6
835-2455

Look for the moated castle. Inside is a formal, award-winning restaurant with a recently revamped menu. Expensive. AE, CB, DC, MC, V. Reservations suggested. Checks accepted. Open M-Sat 11:30 a.m. to 2:30 p.m., 6 to 10:30 p.m.

CHARLIE'S CAFE EXCEPTIONALE, 701 Fourth Av. S., Minneapolis. ►1
333-4646

A wide variety of consistently good food and comfortable, club-like atmosphere have made Charlie's a popular Twin Cities institution. At this writing, Charlie's was not open at lunchtime, due to heavy construction in the vicinity of the restaurant. Moderate to very expensive. AE, CB, DC, MC, V. Reservations suggested. Open M-Thu 5 p.m. to 10 p.m.; F, Sat 5 to 11:45.

510 HAUTE CUISINE, 510 Groveland Av., Minneapolis. ►2
874-6440

Continental cuisine is served in a quiet, refined Old World dining room. Dinner is fixed price and multi-course, including appetizer, soup, salad, choice of entrees, bread, and coffee. Specialties include roast duck breast with green peppercorn sauce and fresh seafood. Extensive wine list. Wine and dessert are extra. Very expensive. AE, CB, DC, MC, V. Reservations suggested. Checks accepted. Open M-F 11:30 a.m. to 2 p.m., 6 p.m. to 10:30; Sat 6 to 10:30.

GRAND PORTAGE, Registry Hotel, 7901 24th Av. S. (off I-494), Bloomington. ►6
854-2244

Continental cuisine and flaming desserts prepared tableside are specialties of the Grand Portage, which also serves from a standard American dinner menu. Salad bar at lunch and dinner. Hotel also has separate oyster bar. Live entertainment. Reservations recommended. Expensive to very expensive. AE, CB, DC, MC, V accepted. Checks accepted. Open M-F 11:30 a.m. to 2 p.m., 6 to 11 p.m.; Sat 6 to 11; Sun buffet brunch 11 to 2, dinner 6 to 10:30.

LA TORTUE, 100 N. Sixth St. (in Butler Square), Minneapolis. ►1
332-3195

This recent addition to the Twin Cities' collection of European-style restaurants is located in the new Butler Square expansion. A patio is open in the summer, and Bon Appetit, a deli, is open year-round. AE, DC, MC, V, checks accepted. Reservations suggested. Deli hours M-F 9 a.m. to 6 p.m.; Sat noon to 4. Restaurant open M-Thu 11:30 a.m. to 2:30 p.m., 5:30 to 10:30; F, Sat 11:30 to 2:30, 5:30 to 11.

LE CARROUSEL, Radisson St. Paul Hotel, 11 E. Kellogg Blvd., St. Paul. ►7
292-1900

Continental and American cuisine is served to diners slowly revolving at the top of the hotel. The view of St. Paul and the river is excellent. Expensive. AE, CB, DC, MC, V. Reservations required. Checks accepted. Open

M-Thu 11:30 a.m. to 2:30 p.m., 5:30 to 10:30 p.m.; F 11:30 to 2:30, 5:30 to 11:30; Sat 5:30 to 11; Sun 10:30 a.m. to 2 p.m., 5:30 to 10:30 p.m.

THE LOWELL INN, 102 N. Second St., Stillwater. ►10
439-1100

The Matterhorn Room features exquisite woodcarving and shrimp and beef fondue accompanied by escargots, all the wine you can drink, and grapes Devonshire (a coating of sour cream and brown sugar). The George Washington and Garden rooms offer regional cuisine. Moderately to very expensive. AE, MC, V. Reservations required. Checks accepted with major credit card. Matterhorn Room open Sun-Thu 6 to 8 p.m.; F-Sat 6 to 9:30; George Washington and Garden rooms open M-Thu noon to 2 p.m., 6 to 8 p.m.; F noon to 2, 6 to 10; Sat noon to 2, 6 to 10:30; Sun noon to 8.

MARQUIS ROOM, Marquette Hotel (IDS Tower), Minneapolis. ►1
332-2351

The IDS Tower Crystal Court below gives this restaurant an opulent setting. The menu features continental cuisine at very expensive prices. AE, CB, DC, MC, V. Reservations suggested. Checks accepted. Open M-Thu 11:30 a.m. to 2 p.m., 6 to 10 p.m.; F 11:30 to 2, 6 to 10:30; Sat 6 to 10:30. Sun 11:30 a.m. to 2:30 p.m.

SCHIEK'S, 115 S. Fourth St., Minneapolis. ►1
341-2332

Schiek's brings an international menu and a touch of the old elegance back to the site of the original Schiek's Cafe, a Minneapolis culinary landmark. Moderately expensive to expensive. Reservations recommended. AE, DC, MC, V accepted. Checks accepted. Open M-F 6:30 a.m. to 10 p.m.; Sat 5 to 10 p.m.

THE WILLOWS, Hyatt Regency Hotel, 1300 Nicollet Mall, Minneapolis. ►1
370-1234

Fine, formal restaurant with a continental menu. Features include a sample-a-bit-of-everything dessert bar, and a smorgasbord that can be visited for either an en-

DINING WITH A VIEW

The following is a sampling of Twin Cities restaurants that offer an interesting—in some cases, spectacular—view of rivers, lakes, or downtown skylines.

DAYTON'S SKYROOM
EDGEWATER EAST
FIRST STREET STATION
FREIGHT HOUSE
FUJI-YA
LORD FLETCHER'S
LE CARROUSEL
MINNESOTA MUSEUM OF ART
ORION ROOM
TOP OF THE LIST

tree or an appetizer. Very expensive. AE, CB, DC, MC, V, checks accepted. Reservations required. Open M-F 11 a.m. to 2:30 p.m., 6 to 11 p.m.; Sat 6 to 11; Sun 6 to 10.

CURRY

SRI LANKA CURRY HOUSE, 1824 Central Av. N.E., Minneapolis. ►2
781-0355

Hot, spicy food is the specialty at this tiny cafe. Most of the food served here is not available anywhere else in the Twin Cities. Reservations are required for banquets held the first Sunday of each month with seatings at 5:30 and 8 p.m. No Cards. Checks accepted. Open Tue, W, Sat 5 to 10 p.m.; Thu, F noon to 10.
10.

CZECH

SCHUMACHER'S NEW PRAGUE HOTEL, 212 W. Main St., New Prague. ►6
758-2133, 445-7285 (Twin Cities number)

Czech and German cuisine, including a variety of schnitzels, is the specialty of the dining room of this charming restored hotel. Twelve rooms are available for overnight stays. Expensive. No cards. Reservations required. Checks accepted. Open Sun-Thu 6 a.m. to 9 p.m.; F, Sat 6 to 11.

DELI

CECIL'S DELICATESSEN & RESTAURANT, 651 Cleveland Av. S. (Highland Village), St. Paul. ►8
698-9792

Kosher foods and homemade desserts at moderate prices are featured here. Potato latkes and sweet-sour cabbage borscht are specialties. Beer available. No cards. No reservations. Checks accepted. Open M-Thu, Sat, Sun 9 a.m. to 8 p.m.; F 9 a.m. to 3 p.m. Deli open M-Thu 9 to 9, F 9 to 6:30.

THE LINCOLN DEL, 5201 Wayzata Blvd. (at Hwy. 100), St. Louis Park. ►5
544-3616

Fluffy baked omelettes and sweet desserts are unusual draws for a deli, but they attract crowds here. Blintzes, reubens, and other standard deli fare also are offered. Moderate. No cards. Reservations for 12 or more. Checks accepted. Open M-Thu 7 to 1 a.m.; F 7 a.m. to 2 a.m.; Sat, Sun 8 a.m. to 1 a.m.

Other Lincoln Dels are located at 4100 W. Lake St., St. Louis Park, 927-9738, and I-494 near France Ave., Bloomington, 831-0780.

DUTCH

POULSSEN'S, 360 Wabasha St., St. Paul. ►7
222-4556

Dutch specialties, including a mixed vegetable dish called stampots, fill out an otherwise basic sandwich menu at this informal basement restaurant. Inexpensive. MC, V. Reservations accepted, required for six or more. Checks accepted. Open M-F 7 a.m. to 4 p.m.

FRENCH

CHEZ COLETTE, L'Hotel Sofitel, 5601 W. 78th St. (Hwy. 100 and I-494), Bloomington. ►6
835-1900

Provincial French cuisine is served in a bistro-like cafe. Moderately expensive. AE, CB, DC, MC, V. Reservations suggested. Checks accepted. Open M-Thu 6:30 to 11 a.m., 11:30 a.m. to 3 p.m., 5:30 to 10 p.m.; F 6:30 to 11, 11:30 to 3, 5:30 to 11; Sat 7 to 11:30, noon to 3, 5:30 to 11; Sun 7 to 3, 5:30 to 10.

CHOUETTE, 739 E. Lake St., Wayzata. ►5
473-4611

A fine French restaurant with an intimate, luxurious dining area. Menu changes two or three times a year. Courtyard dining available in the summer. Very expensive. MC, V. Reservations suggested. Checks accepted. Open M-Thu 11:30 a.m. to 2 p.m., 6 to 9 p.m.; F, Sat 11:30 to 2, 6 to 10.

THE FRENCH LOAF, 3640 W. 70th St. (in the Galleria), Edina. 929-8693 ►5

Attractive French restaurant that's become a favorite luncheon stop. No cards. Checks accepted. Reservations only for parties of five or more. Moderately priced. Open M-Sat 9 a.m. to 9 p.m.; Sun 10 to 4.

LA CAFE BRASSERIE, 618 Second Av., Minneapolis. ►1

Small French cafe located in the Northstar Inn. No reservations. Moderate to expensive. AE, CB, DC, MC, V, checks accepted. Open M-F 7 a.m. to 9 p.m.; Sat 7 a.m. to 2 p.m.

LA CREPERIE, 756 Cleveland Av. S. (Highland Village), St. Paul. ►8
698-8903

This intimate new French creperie also serves scallop, shrimp and beef specialties. Authentic French cooking using fresh ingredients. Dessert selections include flaming crepes. Regular French dinners are held the first Wednesday of each month, offering a full-course meal and French conversation. Reservations required for the monthly dinners and suggested at other times. Moderate prices. No credit cards. Checks accepted. Open Tue-F 11 a.m. to 2 p.m.; 5 to 8:30; Sat noon to 2, 5 to 8:30.

LA GRANDE CREPE, 1661 Grand Av., St. Paul. ►8
690-1401

Hearty meat, vegetable, and fruit crepes are offered here, along with dessert crepes. Menu also includes soups, salads, and croissants. Patio open in the summer. No cards, no reservations. Checks accepted. Open Tue-Thu 8 a.m. to 2 p.m., 5 to 10 p.m.; F, Sat 8 a.m. to 10 p.m.

LA TERRASSE, L'Hotel Sofitel, 5601 W. 78th St. (off I-494), Bloomington. ►6
835-1900

This bright cafe, open all night, offers al fresco dining during the summer and authentic French dishes the year round. Moderate prices. Large selection of French wines. AE, CB, DC, MC, V. No reservations. Checks accepted. Open seven days a week 11 a.m. to 6:30 a.m. the next day.

LE BISTRO, Yorktown Fashion Mall, 3433 Hazelton Rd., Edina. ▶5
835-7543

Sandwiches, crepes, quiches, and French pastries are served in a casual atmosphere at moderate prices. AE, MC, V. Reservations accepted for six or more. Checks accepted. Open M-Thu 11 a.m. to 10 p.m.; F-Sat 11 to 11; Sun 11 to 7:30. Check telephone book for four other Twin Cities locations.

LE CAFE ROYALE, L'Hotel Sofitel, 5601 W. 78th St. (off I-494), Bloomington. ▶6
835-1900

This is the most elegant of the three French restaurants at L'Hotel Sofitel. Specials vary by the month, and a four-course, set-price meal is available. Very expensive. AE, CB, DC, MC, V. Reservations suggested. Checks accepted. Open M-Thu 11:30 a.m. to 2 p.m., 6 to 10 p.m.; F 11:30 to 2, 6 to 11; Sat 6 to 11; Sun brunch 11 to 2.

LES QUATRE AMIS, Fifth and Hennepin (in the Lumber Exchange Building), Minneapolis. 332-9008 ▶1

Formerly in Northfield, Les

Le Carrousel, atop the Radisson St. Paul Hotel.

Quatre Amis relocated to Minneapolis last year. Features a full French menu and extensive wine list, offered in the elegant setting of the restored Lumber Exchange Building. Very expensive. Reservations required. AE, MC, V, checks accepted. Open M-F 11 a.m. to 2 p.m.; 5:30 to 10 p.m.; Sat 5:30 to 10.

NATHAN'S, 2809 Hennepin Av., Minneapolis. ►2
874-1171

Located in a frame house in the Uptown area of Minneapolis, Nathan's features a continental menu and front-porch dining in the summertime. French, German and Italian specialties. Seating is limited, so reservations are suggested. Open M-Thu 8 a.m. to 10 p.m.; F, Sat 8 a.m. to 11 p.m. Checks accepted. No cards.

THE NEW FRENCH CAFE, 128 N. Fourth St., Minneapolis. ►1
338-3790

French cuisine, some of it quite adventurous, is served with French bread baked on the premises. Extensive wine list. The atmosphere is stark with white walls, butcherblock tables, and the kitchen in full view. The menu at lunch is more limited, and prices are moderate. Continental breakfast also is served. Dinners are expensive to very expensive. AE, DC. Reservations suggested. Checks accepted. Open Tue-Sat 8 a.m. to 2:30 p.m., 6 to 9 p.m.; Sun 10:30 a.m. to 1:30 p.m.

ROSEWOOD ROOM, Northstar Inn, 618 Second Av. S., Minneapolis. ►1
338-2288

French and Scandinavian cuisine is served in a formal, modern dining room. Elegant service, harp music. Very expensive. AE, CB, DC, MC, V. Reservations required. Checks accepted. Open M-F 11:30 a.m. to 2 p.m., 6 to 10; Sat 6 to 10:30 p.m.; Sun noon to 2, 6 to 10.

TIFFANY, Radisson South Hotel, 7800 Normandale Blvd. (off I-494), Bloomington. ►6
835-7800

Steaks, prime rib, and a limited seafood selection are the mainstays at Tiffany. Some French dishes. Chateaubriand for two is a specialty. Expensive. AE, CB, DC, MC, V accepted. Reservations suggested. Checks accepted. Open M-F 11:30 a.m. to 2:30 p.m., 6 to 10:30 p.m.; Sat 6 to 10:30; Sun 6 to 10:30. Next to Tiffany is Shipside, a seafood restaurant (a couple of cuts of prime rib are also on the menu). Hours are the same as for Tiffany, except that Shipside is closed Sun.

WINE CELLAR, Northstar Center, 618 Second Av. S., Minneapolis. ►1
338-2288

This small, out-of-the-way French restaurant serves a fixed-price dinner menu featuring five entrees. Extensive wine list. AE, CB, DC, MC, V. Reservations suggested. Checks accepted. Open M-Thu 11:30 a.m. to 2:30 p.m., 6 to 10 p.m.; F 11:30 to 2:30, 6 to 10:30; Sat 6 to 10:30.

GERMAN

BLACK FOREST INN, 1 E. 26th

St. (at Nicollet Av.), Minneapolis. ►2
872-0812

The peasant-style German food and informal atmosphere have gained this informal bar-restaurant consistent popularity. An outdoor patio is open during the summer. Large onion rings are served after 9 p.m. only. Moderately expensive. AE, CB, DC, MC, S, V. Reservations accepted for five or more. No reservations for patio. Checks accepted. Open M-Sat 11 to 1 a.m.; Sun noon to midnight.

SCHONE'S GASTHAUS BAVARIAN HUNTER, 8390 Lofton Av. N. (on dirt road off County Rd. 15), Stillwater. ►10
439-7123

This out-of-the-way Bavarian inn complete with deer park serves peasant-style German food accompanied by pitcher-sized steins of imported beer. Moderate prices. No cards. Reservations suggested. Checks accepted. Open M-Thu 5 to 9 p.m.; F, Sat 5 to 10 p.m.; Sun noon to 8. Closed M October through April.

GREEK

ACROPOL INN, 748 Grand Av., St. Paul. ►8
225-1989

Greek restaurant with a fine family atmosphere. Gyros, lamb dishes are specialties. Moderate. No cards. Checks accepted. Reservations suggested. Open M-Thu 11 a.m. to 9 p.m.; F, Sat 11 a.m. to 10 p.m.

GEORGE IS IN FRIDLEY, 3720

E. River Rd., Fridley. ►3
781-3377

Greek specialties served to the accompaniment of belly dancing in the bar. Moderate prices. AE, DC, MC, V. Reservations accepted. Checks accepted. Restaurant open M 11 a.m. to 2 p.m.; Tue-Sat 11 a.m. to 1 a.m.; Sun 5 p.m. to midnight.

KING'S INN, 3901 Wooddale Av. (Hwy. 100 at Excelsior Blvd.), St. Louis Park. ►5
927-9921

One of the Twin Cities' most extensive salad bars and a sampling of Greek dishes among the standard American menu fare are the major attractions here. Full bar. Moderately expensive. AE, CB, DC, MC, S, V. Reservations accepted. Checks accepted. Open M-Sat 11 to 1 a.m.

NICKLOW'S, 3516 N. Lilac Dr. (off Hwy. 100), Crystal. ►4
529-7751

A complimentary appetizer, different each night, comes with dinner, which is chosen from a varied selection of Greek dishes. Moderately expensive. AE, CB, DC, MC, V. Reservations accepted. Checks accepted. Open M-Thu 11 a.m. to 11 p.m.; F, Sat 11 a.m. to midnight; Sun 11 a.m. to 3 p.m.

SHOREWOOD INN, 6161 N.E. Hwy. 65, Fridley. ►3
571-3444

Greek dishes supplement a strong American menu. Lamb dishes, a Greek appetizer tray, and Greek salad are features. Greek combination platters are served F and Sat nights only. Moderately expensive to expensive. AE, DC, MC, V. Reservations suggested. Checks accepted. Open M-Thu 11 a.m. to 11 p.m.; F, Sat 11 to midnight.

HOMESTYLE

BECKY'S CAFETERIA, 1934 Hennepin Av. S., Minneapolis. ►2
871-8500

Becky's serves standard American fare in an antique-filled parlor setting, complete with live organ music. No liquor. Moderate prices. No cards. Reservations accepted for 12 or more. Checks accepted. Open M-Sat 11:15 a.m. to 2 p.m., 4:45 to 7:30 p.m.; Sun 11:15 to 7:30.

CRABTREE KITCHEN, 19173 Quinnell Av. N. (2 miles north of O'Brien State Park), Marine-On-St. Croix. ►10
433-2455

Homestyle cooking, including baked chicken dinners and homemade rolls, make this river-town restaurant worth visiting. Family-style breakfast served Sat and Sun mornings. Inexpensive. No cards, no reservations. Checks accepted. Open M-Thu 9 a.m. to 7 p.m.; F, Sat 9 to 8; Sun 9 to 6:30.

HART'S CAFE, 700 E. Lake St. (on Lake Minnetonka), Wayzata. 473-9081 ►5

Home cooking and a homey atmosphere have made this cafe a long-time favorite. Patio tables in the summer. No reservations. Moderately priced. MC, V, checks accepted. Open winters M-Sat 6 a.m. to 8 p.m.; Sun 10 to 3. Summer hours M-Thu 6 a.m. to 8 p.m.; F, Sat 6 to 9; Sun 10 to 8.

LATHAM'S TABLE RESTAURANT, 3008 Lyndale Av. S., Minneapolis. ►2
823-9950

Offering large portions, reasonable prices, and excellent homestyle cooking, Latham's is a top-notch neighborhood eatery. Roast duck is a specialty. Operated by Freedom House; decorated with old barn wood and farm implements. No reservations. No cards. Checks accepted. Open M-Thu 11 a.m. to 8 p.m.; F 11 to 11. Closed weekends.

PETER'S GRILL, 85 S. Ninth St., Minneapolis. ►1
333-1981

Home-style cooking is served in what could have been the setting for a Norman Rockwell painting. The homemade apple pie served here is locally famous. Moderate prices—an exceptional value. No cards. No reservations. Checks accepted. Open M-F 11 a.m. to 8 p.m.

IRISH

McCAFFERTY'S, 788 Grand Av., St. Paul. ►8
227-7328

As the name implies, this bar and restaurant serves Irish specialties including Irish soda bread and mixed grill. Moderate prices. MC, V. Reservations accepted. Checks accepted. Open M-F 11 a.m. to 2:30 p.m., 5:30 to 9 p.m.; Sat 5:30 to 10; Sun 11 to 2:30, 5:30 to 9.

ITALIAN

CAFE DI NAPOLI, 816 Hennepin Av., Minneapolis. ►1
335-7373

A variety of Italian dishes is served for moderate prices at this straightforward downtown restaurant. Free parking behind the restaurant. AE, CB, DC, MC, V. Reservations accepted for eight or more. Checks accepted. Open M-Sat 11 a.m. to midnight.

DONATELLE'S SUPPER CLUB, 2400 N.E. Hwy. 10, New Brighton. ►9
784-7460

This is a neighborhood favorite that offers homemade pasta and Italian food. Moderate prices. AE, MC, V. Reservations required. Checks accepted. Open M-Thu 11 a.m. to 10 p.m.; F, Sat 11:30 to 11; Sun 4 to 10.

MANGINI'S RESTAURANTE, 345 Wabasha (in the Lowry Hotel), St. Paul. ►7
224-1331

A breakfast-and-lunch-only establishment that serves a full Italian menu, including a flat pizza. No cards. Checks accepted. Reservations for groups of six or more. Inexpensive. Open M-F 8 a.m. to 3 p.m.

MARIO'S RISTORANTE, 3748 23rd Av. S., Minneapolis. ►2
721-3355

A full Italian menu is offered, but the pizza is the main attraction at Mario's. A salad bar also is available. Patio umbrellas in the lobby give the entrance a sidewalk cafe atmosphere. Moderate prices. V. No reservations. Checks accepted. Open M-F 11:30 a.m. to midnight; Sat noon to 12:30 a.m.; Sun brunch 10:30 to 2, regular menu noon to 11 p.m. Mario's also has a take-out deli at 5201 Chicago Av. S. in Minneapolis.

PRONTO RISTORANTE, Hyatt Regency Hotel, 1300 Nicollet Mall, Minneapolis. ►1
333-4414

This new restaurant features a northern Italian menu and a pasta-making operation right in the dining room. Reservations suggested. AE, DC, MC, V accepted. No checks. Open seven days a week 11:30 a.m. to 11 p.m.

ROCCO'S, 1179 E. Minnehaha Av., St. Paul. ►8
776-9157

This neighborhood restaurant serves basic Italian cuisine at moderate prices. MC, V. No reservations. Checks accepted. Open Tue-Sun 11 a.m. to 10:30 p.m.

SAMMY D'S ITALIAN CUISINE, 1305 S.E. Fourth St. (Dinkytown), Minneapolis. ►2
331-5290

Informal lunches and more elaborate Italian dinners prepared according to Mama D's recipes are served at this Dinkytown mainstay. Moderate to moderately expensive. No cards. Reservations accepted. Checks accepted. Open M-Thu 10:30 a.m. to 10 p.m.; F, Sat 10:30 to midnight; Sun 11 to 10.

SORINI'S, 1569 University Av. (at Snelling Av.), St. Paul. ►8
645-6122

Deep-dish pizza and other standard Italian food is served in a plain environment at moderate prices. No cards. No reservations. Checks over #500 accepted.

SORREL'S RESTAURANT, 1919 E. 78th St., Bloomington. 854-7441 ►6

The Bloomington Marriott's Exchange restaurant has been transformed into a dining spot that features a northern Italian menu and Mediterranean decor. Veal and seafood are specialties. Reservations suggested. Checks accepted. AE, CB, DC, MC, V accepted. Open M-Thu 11:30 a.m. to 2 p.m.; 5:30 to 10 p.m.; F, Sat 11:30 a.m. to 2 p.m.; 5:30 to 11 p.m.; Sun 10 a.m. to 2 p.m.; 5:30 to 10 p.m.

STRADIVARIUS, Sheraton-Ritz Hotel, 315 Nicollet Mall, Minneapolis. ►1 332-4200

A new restaurant in the remodeled Sheraton-Ritz Hotel. Northern Italian menu. Expensive. Reservations suggested. Checks accepted. AE, CB, DC, MC, V. Open M-Thu 11:30 a.m. to 2 p.m.; 6 to 10:30 p.m.; F 11:30 to 2, 6 to 11 p.m.; Sat 6 to 11 p.m.

VITTORIO'S, 402 S. Main St., Stillwater. ►10 439-3588

Italian specialties are served in both a Family Dining Room and a more formal Grotto Blue Dining Room. Moderate to expensive. AE, MC, V. Reservations suggested for Grotto Blue Dining Room. Checks accepted. Family Dining Room open Tue-Sat 11 a.m. to midnight; Sun 3 to 11. The Grotto Blue Dining Room is open Tue-Sun 5 to 10:30 p.m.

THE WHITE HOUSE, 4900 Olson Memorial Hwy. (Hwy. 55), Golden Valley. ►4 588-0711

The standard American menu is accented by Chinese and northern Italian specialties. Rib dishes have recently been added. The restaurant is divided into a series of semi-formal dining rooms with a San Francisco motif throughout. Moderately expensive. AE, MC, V. Reservations suggested. Checks accepted. Open M-Thu 11:30 a.m. to 2:30 p.m., 5 to 10:30 p.m.; F 11:30 to 2:30, 5 to 11:30; Sun 5 to 11:30.

JAPANESE

ASUKA, 24 N. Seventh St., Minneapolis. ►1 333-2020

Authentic Japanese dishes are served in an informal atmosphere for moderate prices. No cards. Reservations for dinner only. Checks accepted. Open M-Thu 11 a.m. to 2:30 p.m., 4:30 to 9 p.m.; F 11 to 2:30, 4:30 to 10; Sat 5 to 10.

CHIKURIN TEPPANYAKI ROOM, Radisson Inn-Plymouth, 2705 Annapolis Lane, Plymouth. 553-1600 ►4

The Japanese food is prepared with lots of theatrics on grill-top tables in front of groups of diners. Expensive. AE, CB, DC, MC, V. Reservations suggested. No checks. Open M-Thu, Sun 6 p.m. to 10 p.m.; F, Sat 6 to 11.

FUJI INTERNATIONAL, 408 Cedar Av., Minneapolis. ▶2 333-7377

This simple, attractive West Bank restaurant offers authentic Japanese cuisine at moderate prices. No cards. No reservations. Checks accepted. Open M-Sat 11:30 a.m. to 2:30 p.m., 5 to 9 p.m.

FUJI-YA, 420 S. First St., Minneapolis. ▶2 339-2226

Fuji-Ya offers a magnificent view of the Mississippi River as well as two attractive dining rooms. Upstairs, Japanese specialties such as tempura and sukiyaki are served; downstairs teppanyaki chefs entertain as they prepare and grill the food at each table. A sushi (raw fish) bar is a recent addition. Expensive. AE. Reservations suggested. Checks accepted. Open M-Thu 11:30 a.m. to 2:30 p.m., 5 to 9 p.m.; F 11:30 to 2:30, 5 to 9:30; Sat 11:30 to 2:30, 5 to 10.

GENGHIS KHAN OF SAPPORO, 6534 Flying Cloud Dr. (off Hwy. 169), Eden Prairie. ▶5 941-5112

Country-style Japanese cooking is served in a traditional Japanese atmosphere. The decor includes private booths. Downstairs bar features American food, rock music. Moderate prices. AE, CB, DC, MC, V. Reservations suggested. Open M-F 11 a.m. to 2 p.m., 5 to 10:30 p.m.; Sat, Sun 5 to 10:30.

ICHIBAN JAPANESE STEAK HOUSE, 1333 Nicollet Av., Minneapolis. ▶1 339-0540

Diners watch as teppanyaki chefs prepare their meal. Lovely Japanese-garden-style surroundings. Unless you have a large party, be prepared to be seated with strangers. Expensive. Reservations suggested. AE, DC, MC, V, checks accepted. Open M-Thu 11:30 a.m. to 2 p.m., 5 to 10 p.m.; F 11:30 to 2, 5 to 11; Sat 5 to 11; Sun 5:30 to 9:30.

SAJI-YA RESTAURANT, 695 Grand Av., St. Paul. ▶8 292-0444, 292-1820

An elegant restaurant that features traditional Japanese country-style cooking. Emphasis is on fresh ingredients and attractive presentation. Sushi and sashimi available. Moderate to expensive. Reservations suggested. AE, MC, V, checks accepted. Open M-F 11 a.m. to 2:30 p.m., 5 to 10 p.m.; Sat, Sun 5 to 10 p.m.

KOREAN

KORAI KWAN RESTAURANT, 466 Lexington Av. N., St. Paul. 645-1694 ▶8

This may be the only Twin Cities restaurant with a Korean menu. Bulkoki (barbecue beef) and kimchi (Korean salad) are popular items. Moderately priced. Take-out service available. No cards or checks. No reservations. Open M, Wed-F 3:30 p.m. to 10 p.m.; Sat noon to 10; Sun 1 to 8.

LUNCH ONLY

ARBORETUM TEA ROOM,

Leon C. Snyder Education and Research Bldg., 3675 Arboretum Dr., Chaska. ►5
443-2460

Homemade soups and desserts complement the sandwiches served in this light, open cafeteria among the trees and plants of the arboretum. Patio dining available in the summertime. No cards. No reservations. Checks accepted. Open Tue-F 10 a.m. to 3 p.m.; Sat-Sun 11 to 4.

GALLERY 8, Walker Art Center, Vineland Pl., Minneapolis. ►2
374-3701

Homestyle cooking in bright, cheerful surroundings at moderate prices is available at the top of the Walker Art Center. Terrace tables available in the summer. Beer and wine available. No cards. No reservations. Checks accepted. Open Tue-Sun 11:30 a.m. to 3 p.m.

GLADSTONE CAFE, 75 W. Fifth St. (in the Landmark Center), St. Paul. ►7
227-4704

A cafeteria-style restaurant offering light lunches of soups, fruits, cheeses, salads, and desserts in an elegant setting just off the Landmark Center's cortile. Moderate prices. Wine and beer available. Checks accepted; no cards. Open for lunches only Tue-F 10:30 a.m. to 2:30 p.m.

THE LINK, Minneapolis Institute of Arts, 2400 Third Av. S., Minneapolis. ►2
870-3180

Soups, salads, and varying specials are the mainstays at this airy, modern cafe. Moderate. AE, MC, V. Reservations required. Checks accepted. Open Tue-Sat 11:30 a.m. to 2:30 p.m.; Sun buffet brunch 10:30 to 3.

MAYSLACK'S, 1428 Fourth St. N.E., Minneapolis. ►2
789-9862

Hold the atmosphere, hold the service, but, most of all, hold the plate with two hands as big Stan Mayslack piles the roast beef on your sandwich. That's the only item on the menu here, along with a salad bar, and you can expect a line. But it's the biggest, and many say the best, roast beef sandwich in town. No cards. No reservations. No checks. Open Tue-F 11:30 a.m. to 2 p.m.; Sat 11:30 a.m. to 3 p.m.

MINNESOTA MUSEUM OF ART, 305 St. Peter St. (St. Peter at Kellogg), St. Paul. ►7
224-7431

A buffet-style lunch including entree, wine, dessert, and coffee is served on the fourth floor. International luncheons third Wed of each month. Moderately priced. AE, MC, V. Reservations suggested. Checks accepted. Open Tue-F 11:30 a.m. to 2 p.m.; Sun 11:45 to 2:30. Closed during August.

MEXICAN

BOCA CHICA, 11 Concord St., St. Paul. ►8
222-9696

Plentiful, authentic Mexican food at moderate prices, not fancy atmosphere, is this restaurant's attraction. Liquor available, including Mexican beer. No cards. Reservations accepted. No checks. Take-out service for tacos available across the street at 407 S. Wabasha. Restaurant open M-Thu 11 a.m. to 10:30 p.m.; F, Sat 11 a.m. to 12:30 a.m.; Sun 11 a.m. to 10 p.m.

CHI CHI'S, 7717 Nicollet Av. (off I-494), Richfield. ►6
866-3433

Enormous margaritas, large portions, and moderate prices have made this a very popular restaurant. AE, CB, DC, MC, V. No reservations. Checks accepted. Open M-Thu 11 a.m. to 11 p.m.; F, Sat 11 to midnight; Sun 11 to 10.

Chi Chi's also is located at 7355 Regent Av. N., Brooklyn Park, 561-0550.

ESTEBAN'S, 903 Marquette Av., Minneapolis. ►1
338-3383, 338-3384

Potent margaritas and well-prepared Mexican food have made this a popular downtown dining spot. MC, V. No reservations. Checks accepted. Open M-Thu 11 a.m. to 11 p.m.; F, Sat 11 to midnight, Sun 3 to 11.

Check phone book for four other Twin Cities locations.

GARCIA'S OF SCOTTSDALE, 5600 Wayzata Blvd., St. Louis Park. ►5
546-7277

This nationally known Mexican restaurant chain has quickly become very popular in the Twin Cities. Moderately priced. AE, MC, V. No checks. No reservations. Open M-Thu 11 a.m. to 11 p.m.; F, Sat 11 a.m. to midnight; Sun noon to 10.

GUADALAHARRY'S, St. Anthony Main, 201 S.E. Main St., Minneapolis. ►1
378-2233

This popular Mexican restaurant features an elaborate south-of-the border decor and large portions of unique dishes at moderate prices. AE, MC, V. No reservations (prepare to wait). Checks accepted. Open Sun-Thu 11 a.m. to 11 p.m.; F-Sat 11 to midnight.

JOSE'S, 9920 Wayzata Blvd., St. Louis Park. ►5
546-6871

The former Amalgamated Underground has resurfaced as a Mexican restaurant. AE, CB, DC, MC, V. Reservations for lunch only. Checks accepted. Open M-Thu 11 a.m. to 11 p.m.; F, Sat 11 a.m. to midnight; Sun 11 to 10.

JOSE'S REFRIED BEANERY, 3746 Sunset Dr. (on Lake Minnetonka), Spring Park. ►5
471-8596

This restaurant in the basement of Lord Fletcher's (formerly The Beanery) serves large portions of popular Mexican dishes at moderate prices. AE, CB, DC, MC, V. No reservations. Checks accepted. Open M-Thu 4:30 p.m. to 10 p.m.; F, Sat 4:30 to 10:30; Sun 3 to 10.

MIDDLE EASTERN

ABDUL'S AFANDY, 2423 Nicollet Av., Minneapolis. ►2
872-0523

Abdul's serves authentic Middle Eastern food in an informal atmosphere for moderate prices. Beer and wine available. A second location in Butler Square, downtown Minneapolis, is called Amir Afandy's. No cards. No reservations. Checks accepted. Open Sun-Thu 11 a.m. to 11 p.m.; F, Sat 11 a.m. to midnight.

AWADA'S, 199 E. Plato Blvd., St. Paul. ►8
225-6341

A limited Lebanese menu is served along with basic American food, all for moderate prices. Cocktails, beer, and wine. AE, MC, V, CB. Reservations suggested for lunch. Checks accepted. Open M-Thu 11 a.m. to 2 p.m., 5 to 10 p.m.; F, Sat 11 a.m. to 2 p.m., 5 to 11 p.m.

CARAVAN SERAI, 2046 Pinehurst Av. (Highland Village), St. Paul. ►8
698-9941

Sit on the floor of this tastefully decorated restaurant serving foods of Afghanistan and other Middle Eastern lands. International wine list. Visit the Caravan's sweet room for a variety of coffees, Middle Eastern pastries, and other desserts. Moderately expensive. AE, CB, MC, V. Reservations accepted. Checks accepted. Open Tue-F 11:30 a.m. to 2 p.m., 5 to 9 p.m.; Sat 5 to 10 p.m., Sun 4 to 8.

EMILY'S LEBANESE DELI, 641 University Av. N.E., Minneapolis. ►2
379-4069

Moderately priced Middle Eastern food is available to eat in or

The Waikiki Room in downtown Minneapolis.

take out. Menu includes items like grape leaves, raw kibby, and lamb shishkabob. No cards. Reservations accepted for six or more. Checks accepted. Open M, W, Thu 9 a.m. to 9:30 p.m.; F-Sun 9 to 10:30.

JAVA, 503 Hennepin Av., Minneapolis. ►1
338-6810

This hole-in-the-wall restaurant offers Lebanese specialties and sandwiches at fast-food prices. Most popular is the shawirma (sliced hot beef on pita bread) sandwich. No cards. No reservations. Checks accepted. Open M-Sat 11 a.m. to 11 p.m.; Sun 1 to 9 p.m.

The Java is also open at 2801 Nicollet Av., Minneapolis, 870-7871.

MEDITERRANEAN CAFE, Knollwood Village, 8930 Hwy. 7, St. Louis Park. ►5
933-5833

This informal cafe, located in a shopping plaza, serves a Lebanese and Israeli menu. Inexpensive. Reservations for groups of eight or more. AE, MC, V accepted. Checks accepted. Open M-Thu 11 a.m. to 10 p.m.; F 11 a.m. to midnight; Sat 4:30 to midnight.

PIZZA

BROADWAY BAR & PIZZA, 2025 W. River Rd. (at Broadway), Minneapolis. ►2
529-7666

Popular flat pizza is served in a restaurant divided into a bar and family dining room. Look for the railroad car at the foot of the Broadway Bridge. Check phone book for other locations. No cards. Reservations accepted for six or more. Checks accepted. Open M-Sat 9:30 a.m. to 1 a.m.; Sun noon to midnight.

E.T. GRAFFITI, 502 N. Blake Rd. (off Hwy. 7), Hopkins. ►5
935-3444

Despite the Mexican decor, this is primarily a pizza place that also features soups, sandwiches, salads, and homemade desserts. Self-service lunches; table service at dinner. Prices are moderate. No cards. No reservations. Checks accepted. Open M-Thu 11 a.m. to 10:30 p.m.; F, Sat 11 to 12:30 a.m.; Sun 4:30 to 10.

THE GREEN MILL INN, 57 Hamline Av. S., St. Paul. ►8
698-0353

Seafood and sandwiches have joined the Green Mill's award-winning flat and deep-dish pizzas to attract big crowds to this casual restaurant. Moderate prices. AE, MC, V. No reservations. No checks. Open M-Sat 11 a.m. to midnight; Sun noon to 11.

There's Green Mill Too complete with oyster bar at 2626 Hennepin Av. S., Minneapolis, 374-2131. The newest Green Mill restaurant location is in the Hennepin Center for the Arts, downtown Minneapolis. There are also several Green Mill Box Offices (for take-out pizza) in the Twin Cities. Check the phone book for locations.

MY PIE, 5408 Wayzata Blvd., Golden Valley. ►4
544-5551

First-class pizza has made My

Pie a Twin Cities favorite. Call-in orders are taken at lunchtime; no reservations at dinner. Open M-Thu 11 a.m. to midnight; F, Sat 11 a.m. to 2 a.m.; Sun noon to midnight. Second location at 3501 W. 70th St., Edina, 920-4444; open M-Thu 4 to 9 p.m.; F, Sat 4 to 10 p.m.; Sun 4 to 8. Checks accepted. No credit cards.

PONTILLO'S PIZZERIA, 41 Cleveland Av. S. (at Grand Av.), St. Paul. ►8
690-4848

Thin-crust western New York state-style pizza and unusual hoagies are served at this tiny restaurant near the College of St. Thomas. Moderate prices. No cards. Reservations (telephone orders) accepted. Checks accepted. Open M-Thu 11 a.m. to 11 p.m.; F, Sat 11 to 2 a.m.; Sun noon to midnight. Check telephone book for four other Twin Cities locations.

VINCENZO'S, 2527 N.E. Harding St., St. Anthony. ►2
789-7555

This informal restaurant serves deep-dish and flat pizza and a variety of Italian specialties for moderate prices. No cards. Reservations accepted. Checks accepted. Open M-Sat 10:30 a.m. to 10 p.m.

POLISH

KRAMARCZUK EASTERN EUROPEAN DELI, 215 E. Hennepin Av., Minneapolis. ►1
379-3018

Sample sausages made on the premises and other eastern European fare are offered in this simple cafeteria. Outdoor tables are available during the summer. Moderate prices. No cards. No reservations. Checks accepted. Open M-Thu, Sat 8 a.m. to 6 p.m., F 8 to 8.

NYE'S POLONAISE, 112 E. Hennepin Av., Minneapolis. ►2
379-2021

American dishes as well as such Polish specialties as golabki (cabbage rolls), pierogi (pasta stuffed with cheese or prunes), spare ribs and sauerkraut, pork hocks, and Polish sausage are served for moderate prices. AE, DC, MC, V. Reservations required for F, Sat nights. No checks. Open M-Sat 11 a.m. to midnight.

POLYNESIAN

MAI TAI, 687 Excelsior Blvd. (Lake Minnetonka), Excelsior. 474-1183 ►5

Exotic drinks and appetizers are served from an outdoor pavilion on the lake. Inside, it's Polynesian dishes and decor. Moderately expensive. AE, DC, MC, V. Checks accepted. Reservations suggested. Open M-Sat 11 a.m. to 2:30 p.m., 5:30 to 11 p.m.; Sun 11 to 2:30, 5:30 to 10.

THE PEARL DIVER, 13700 Wayzata Blvd., Minnetonka. ►5
544-7211

The expensive, dimly lit decor is divided into intimate dining areas lavish in Polynesian detail. Drinks, appetizers, and entrees follow the theme. Moderate at noon to expensive at night. AE, CB, DC, MC, V. Reservations suggested. Checks accepted. Open

M-Sat 11 a.m. to 3 p.m., 5 to 11 p.m.; Sun 11 to 3.

WAIKIKI ROOM, Leamington Hotel, 10th St. and Third Av. S., Minneapolis. ►1
370-1100

Exotic drinks, varied hors d'oeuvres, and Polynesian entrees are served to the accompaniment of live Hawaiian music. Expensive. AE, CB, DC, MC, V. Reservations suggested. Checks accepted. Open W, Thu 5 to 10:45 p.m.; F, Sat 5 to 11:45; Sun 5 to 10:45.

RIBS AND SOUL FOOD

ART SONG'S WINGS, 3753 Nicollet Av. S., Minneapolis. ►2
822-0619

This south Minneapolis ribs-and-chicken spot sells over a ton of chicken wings a week. Eat-in or take-out menu includes curried or sweet-and-sour wings, ribs, rice, coleslaw, and egg rolls. Inexpensive. Open M-Thu 11 a.m. to 2 a.m.; F, Sat 11 a.m. to 3 a.m.; Sun noon to 2 a.m. No cards. Checks accepted.

BAR-B-Q-KING, 474 University Av., St. Paul. ►8
222-0751

One of the few soul-food eateries in the Twin Cities. New Orleans-style ribs, catfish, and chitterlings are mainstays here. Take-out and delivery service available. Moderate prices. No cards, no checks. Open Sun-W 4 p.m. to 4 a.m.; Thu-Sat noon to 5 a.m.

MARKET BAR-B-QUE, 28 Glenwood Av., Minneapolis. ►2
333-1028, 332-9980

A traditional favorite of visiting sports and entertainment personalities, the Market is an old-fashioned place that smokes its ribs and chicken over hardwood chips. Moderate prices. AE, DC. Reservations for five or more. Checks accepted. Open M-F 11:30 a.m. to 2:30 p.m., 5 p.m. to 2:30 a.m.; Sat 5 to 2:30; Sun 5 to 11 p.m.

RUDOLPH'S BAR-B-QUE, 1933 Lyndale Av. S. (at Franklin), Minneapolis. ►2
871-8969

Ribs and noteworthy cole slaw are served well into the night amidst showbiz memorabilia. Moderate prices. No cards. Reservations accepted for six or more. Checks accepted. Open 11 to 3 a.m. M-Sat; Sun 11 to 2 a.m.

ROMANIAN

LITTLE ROMANIA, 906 N. Concord Av., South St. Paul. 450-1844 ►12

The only Romanian restaurant in the Twin Cities. Cabbage rolls, dumplings, pork sausage, and other Romanian specialties add up to hefty meals here. This is a family operation where diners may encounter folk dancers, violin music, or the singing Romanian chef, depending on the day they visit. Moderately priced. Reservations accepted. MC, V, checks accepted. Open Tue-Sat 5 to 10 p.m.

RUSSIAN
THE RUSSIAN PIROSHKI TEA

HOUSE, 1758 University Av. (University and Fairview), St. Paul. ►8
646-4114

Hidden in an unassuming frame house, this take-out-only restaurant serves up homemade piroshkis ("Russian hamburgers"), borscht, cabbage rolls, tea cakes, and other traditional Russian foods. Inexpensive. No cards. Checks accepted. Open Tue-F 11 a.m. to 7 p.m.

SEAFOOD

ANCHORAGE, 1350 Industrial Blvd. (at I-35W north), Minneapolis. ►2
379-4444

This new restaurant at the Minneapolis Hilton Inn serves a variety of fresh seafood specialties. Decor includes fireplace and skylight area. Expensive. AE, CB, DC, MC, V. Reservations suggested for lunch and dinner. Checks accepted. Open M-F 6:30 a.m. to 10:30 p.m.; Sat 7:30 to 11; Sun 7:30 to 10:30.

ANTHONY'S WHARF, St. Anthony Main, 201 S.E. Main St., Minneapolis. ►1
378-7058

This extremely popular restaurant features fresh seafood specialties and large aquariums full of eels, piranhas, and other denizens of the deep. Moderately expensive. AE, MC, V. Reservations suggested. Checks accepted. Open M-Sat 11:30 a.m. to 3 p.m., 5 to 11 p.m.; Sun 5 to 10.

BOSTON SEA PARTY, 7801 Xerxes Av. S. (off I-494), Bloomington. ►6
883-3355

For a fixed price, you get a choice of lobster, steak, or prime rib and visits to various "piers" for all the seafood appetizers, vegetables, desserts, and fruits you care to eat. Wine and drinks are extra. Expensive. AE, DC, MC, V. Reservations suggested. Checks accepted. Open M-Thu 5 to 10 p.m.; F-Sat 5 to 11; Sun 4:30 to 9.

CRITERION, 5001 W. 80th St. (off I-494), Bloomington. ►6
835-5686

Live lobster and all-you-can-eat crab-leg specials are the big draws to this popular restaurant. Moderately expensive to expensive. AE, DC, MC, V. Reservations suggested (lobster reservations required). Checks accepted. Open M-Thu 11:15 a.m. to 2 p.m., 5 to 9:30 p.m.; F 11:15 to 2, 5 to 10:30; Sat 5 to 10:30.

RUSTY SCUPPER, 4301 W. 80th St. (off I-494 at France Av.), Bloomington. ►6
831-5415

The nautical theme is downplayed in favor of a tasteful decor of hanging plants, rattan chairs, tile-covered tables, and cloth napkins. Popular happy-hour gathering place. The menu consists of seafood and beef for dinner, salads, sandwiches, quiches, and omelettes at lunch. Moderately expensive to expensive. AE, MC, V. Reservations suggested. No checks. Open M-Thu 11 a.m. to 2 p.m., 5 to 10:30 p.m.; F, Sat 11 a.m. to 2 p.m., 5 to 11:30; Sun 4 to 9.

SPINNAKER, 14601 Hwy. 7, Minnetonka. ►5
935-8831

Meat and seafood dishes are served in a nautical decor. Sauteed scallops are the house specialty. There's an ample salad bar, and key lime pie for dessert. Prices are moderate (lunch) to expensive (dinner). AE, CB, MC, S, V. Reservations required. Checks accepted. Open M-Thu 11:30 a.m. to 2 p.m., 5:30 to 10 p.m.; F 11:30 to 2, 5:30 to 11; Sat 5:30 to 11. Sun 11:30 to 2, 5:30 to 9.

SOUPS, SALADS, SANDWICHES, ETC.

THE BUTTERY, Sixth and Robert Sts., St. Paul. ►7
222-5861

This casual downtown lunch spot has recently remodeled and is now serving dinners. Menu features homemade soups and chili, salad bar, and sandwiches you make yourself. Liquor available. Moderately priced. AE, DC, MC, V. Checks accepted. Reservations accepted. Open M-Sat 11:30 a.m. to 11 p.m.

DUDLEY RIGGS CAFE ESPRESSO, 1430 Washington Av. S., Minneapolis. ►2
332-6620

This popular late-night spot on the West Bank features homemade soups, sandwiches, and a variety of coffee drinks. A comedy theater as well as a cafe. Shows nightly at 8 p.m. Moderate prices. AE, MC, V. No reservations. Checks accepted. Open Tue-Sun 5 p.m. to 1 a.m.

D.B. KAPLAN'S, Butler Square, 100 N. Sixth St., Minneapolis. ►1
332-0903

Kaplan's offers 152 different sandwiches as well as omelettes, salads, and more. Ice cream drinks are specialties. Soft, three-dimensional art decorates this basement-courtyard restaurant that has been recently expanded. No cards. Reservations for 10 or more. Checks accepted. Open M-Thu 7:30 a.m. to 11 p.m.; F 7:30 a.m. to midnight; Sat 9 a.m. to midnight; Sun noon to 9.

GOOD EARTH, Galleria, 3460 W. 70th St., Edina. ►5
925-1001

Good Earth serves healthful soups, sandwiches, salads, and simple entrees accompanied by spiced tea, natural fruit drinks, and yogurt shakes. Moderate prices. No cards. No reservations. Checks accepted. Open seven days a week 9 a.m. to 10 p.m. Check phone book for other Twin Cities locations. Hours vary at other locations.

GREAT EXPECTATIONS, 1669 Selby Av., St. Paul. ►8
644-1836

A casual soup and sandwich place that also serves breakfasts featuring skin-on french fries, open-faced sandwiches, and homemade waffles and cakes on weekends. Moderate prices. No cards. Reservations accepted for six or more. Checks accepted. Open M-Thu 11 a.m. to 9 p.m.; F 11 to 10; Sat 8 a.m.to 10 p.m.; Sun 8 a.m. to 9 p.m.

THE MALT SHOP, 809 W. 50th

St. (at Bryant Av.), Minneapolis. 824-1352 ►2

Fruit-flavored malts, salads, pocket-bread sandwiches, quiche, and the like are served in an informal, plant-filled environment to live piano music. Moderate prices. No cards. Reservations accepted. Checks accepted. Open Sun-Thu 11 a.m. to 10:30 p.m.; F, Sat 11 to 11.

MUFFULETTA, 2260 Como Av., St. Paul. ►8
644-9116

The menu ranges from sandwiches and burgers to shrimp creole and fettucine Alfredo. Nice touches include lemon slices in the pitchers of water and fresh flowers on each table. Large sidewalk cafe in summer. Moderate prices. No cards. Reservations accepted for dinner, Sunday brunch. Checks accepted. Open M-Thu 11 a.m. to 10 p.m.; F, Sat 11 to 11; Sun 10:30 to 2:30.

ON STAGE CUISINE, 758 Grand Av. (Crocus Common), St. Paul. ►8
227-4244

A new restaurant with a theatrical atmosphere that includes seasonal changes in menu and decor. Soups, salads, quiches, light entrees. Wine bar. Moderate prices. Reservations suggested. AE, DC, MC, V, checks accepted. Open Tue-Thu 11 a.m. to 11 p.m.; F, Sat 11 a.m. to 1 p.m.; Sun brunch 11 to 4.

THE PANTRY, 5101 Arcadia (Hwy. 100 and 50th St.), Edina. 925-5628 ►5

Made-from-scratch sandwiches, soup, quiche, and salads are served in a restaurant decorated with huge photos of fresh fruit and vegetables. Moderate prices. MC, V. Reservations accepted for six or more. Checks accepted. Open M-Thu 11 a.m. to 11 p.m.; F 11 to 1 a.m.; Sat 9 to 1; Sun 8 a.m. to 11 p.m. Other locations at 2147 Ford Pkwy., Highland Park, and 7545 Lyndale Av. S., Richfield.

RAINBOW CAFE, 2916 Hennepin Av. S.,Minneapolis. ►2
825-4455

Burgers, sandwiches, seafood, and popovers are found on the varied menu at this popular, remodeled Uptown bar and restaurant. Moderate prices. V. Reservations accepted Sun-Thu for five or more. Checks accepted. Open M-Thu 7:30 a.m. to 11 p.m.; F, Sat 7:30 to midnight; Sun 8 to 11.

SGT. PRESTON'S, 221 Cedar Av., Minneapolis. ►2
338-6146

Hearty soups and made-to-order sandwiches are served at this popular bar and meeting place. Moderate prices. AE, CB, DC, MC, V. No reservations. Checks accepted. Open M-Sat 11 a.m. to 1 a.m.; Sun 6 p.m. to midnight.

TGI FRIDAY'S, 5875 Wayzata Blvd., St. Louis Park. ►5
544-0675

Typical fern bar/restaurant that caters to the cocktail-hour set, as the name implies. AE, MC, V. No reservations. No checks. Open M-Sat 11:30 a.m. to 1 a.m.; Sun 11:30 to 11.

THE TERRACE, Hyatt Regency Hotel, 1300 Nicollet Mall, Minneapolis. ►1
370-1234

This is the Hyatt's less-formal lunch and dinner spot. Sandwiches, soups, salads, light entrees. Moderately expensive. No reservations. AE, CB, DC, MC, V. Checks accepted with proper identification. Open seven days a week 6:30 a.m. to 11 p.m.

W.A. FROST AND CO., 374 Selby Av. (at Western Av.), St. Paul. 224-5715 ►8

A moderately priced menu features full dinners, sandwiches, and salads, accompanied by wine or fresh-squeezed fruit juices. Chocolate silk pie is a popular item. The decor is restored Victorian. Full bar. MC, V. Reservations suggested. Checks accepted. Open M-Sat 11:15 a.m. to 2:30 p.m., 5:30 to 11:45 p.m.; Sun 11 to 3, 5:30 to 10:45. Light meals are served on the patio from 2:30 to 5 p.m. summers.

WINDOW TERRACE CAFE, Sheraton-Ritz Hotel, 315 Nicollet Mall, Minneapolis. ►1
332-4000

Airy, indoor, European-style cafe serving such specialties as chilled fruit soups and open-faced sandwiches. Reservations suggested. AE, CB, DC, MC, V, checks accepted. Open seven days a week 6:30 a.m. to 11 p.m.

WINFIELD POTTER'S, St. Anthony Main, 201 S.E. Second St., Minneapolis. ►1
378-2660

An informal, Victorian bar-restaurant with greenhouse section features an eclectic menu of soups, sandwiches, burgers, quiche, steaks, chicken, seafood, and a few ethnic dishes. There's a well-stocked salad bar that costs extra to visit with lunch or dinner. Moderately expensive. AE, MC, V. Reservations accepted. Checks accepted. Open M-F 11 a.m. to midnight; Sat 10 a.m. to midnight; Sun brunch 10 to 3, dinner 4:30 to 11 p.m.

SPANISH

GARUDA, Victoria Crossing, 867 Grand Av., St. Paul. ►8
222-8806

Wood parsons tables, batik napkins, and fresh flowers accent this restaurant among the specialty shops of Victoria Crossing. The menu features Spanish and Filipino specialties, salads, and Bicyea ice cream treats. Moderate prices. AE. Checks accepted. Wine and beer available. Reservations accepted for five or more. Open M-Thu 11 a.m. to 10 p.m.; F 11 to 11; Sat 10 a.m. to 11; Sun 11 to 3 (desserts served until 5).

VEGETARIAN

BLUE HERON CAFE, 1123 W. Lake St., Minneapolis. ►2
823-4743

Ethnic specials are featured daily at this casual vegetarian restaurant in the Uptown area. Beer only. Moderate prices. No cards. Reservations accepted. Checks accepted. Open Tue-Thu 11 a.m. to 9 p.m.; F 11 a.m. to 11 p.m.; Sat 9 a.m. to 11 p.m.; Sun 10 to 9.

CAFE KARDAMENA, 364 Selby Av. (Dakota Bldg.), St. Paul. ►8
224-2209

Mediterranean-style vegetarian dishes served here include soups, salads, omelets, sandwiches, and daily specials accompanied by fresh-fruit drinks and homemade desserts, all at very moderate prices. Beer and wine available. No cards. Reservations accepted. Checks accepted. Open Tue-Sat 11:30 a.m. to 3 p.m. and 4 to 9 p.m.

FINLAYSON'S FINE FOODS, 2221 W. 50th St. (at Penn Av.), Minneapolis. ►2
927-4416

Fish specials, pizza, and iced herbal teas are among the unusual selections at this vegetarian restaurant. Casual 1930s atmosphere. Moderate prices. No cards. No reservations. Checks accepted. Open M, W, Thu 4 to 10 p.m.; F 4 to 10:30; Sat noon to 10:30; Sun 4 to 9.

MUD PIE VEGETARIAN RESTAURANT, 2549 Lyndale Av. S., Minneapolis. ►2
872-9435

Comfortable vegetarian restaurant with a menu that includes a large selection of Mexican items and the Mud Pie ice cream and carob dessert. Moderately priced. No cards, no reservations, no checks. Open M-Sat 11 a.m. to 10 p.m.; Sun noon to 9.

VIETNAMESE

BAMBOO VILLAGE QUAN TREE, Park Square Court, 400 Sibley St., St. Paul. ►7
298-1132

This informal restaurant in St. Paul's Lowertown serves Vietnamese cuisine at moderate prices. Beer and wine available. No cards. No reservations. Checks accepted. Open M-Thu 11 a.m. to 2:30 p.m., 5 to 9 p.m.; F 11 a.m. to 2:30 p.m., 5 to 10 p.m.; Sat 11 a.m. to 2:30 p.m., 5 p.m. to 1 a.m.

KIM LONG, 439 University Av., St. Paul. ►8
222-4615

Authentic Vietnamese specialties are served for moderate prices. No cards. Reservations accepted. No checks. Open M-F 11 a.m. to 2 p.m., 5 to 9 p.m.; Sat 5 to 9.

MATIN, 416 First Av. N., Minneapolis. ►1
340-0150

A stark remodeling of some old warehouse space provides a tasteful setting for this Vietnamese restaurant. Moderately expensive. No cards. Reservations for eight or more. Checks accepted. Open M-F 11 a.m. to 2 p.m., 5 to 10 p.m.; Sat 5 to 10.

PHOENIX, 1648 Grand Av. (in Mac Market), St. Paul. ►8
698-5015

Vietnamese food is served at this informal restaurant known for its egg rolls. Moderate prices. No cards. Reservations accepted for four or more. Checks accepted. Open M-Sat 11 a.m. to 2:30 p.m., 5 to 9:30 p.m.

SAIGON RESTAURANT, 317 W. 38th St. (at Grand Av.), Minneapolis. ►2
822-7712

The atmosphere is strictly American Main St. cafe, but the Vietnamese food is interesting, plentiful, and very reasonably priced. No cards. Reservations for F, Sat only. Checks accepted. Open seven days a week 11 a.m. to 10 p.m.

SODA FOUNTAINS

Ice cream comes in many forms in the Twin Cities, from the five-quart bucket of Kemp's at the local grocery to a heavenly 95-cent scoop of Häagen Dazs from an authentic Häagen Dazs store. A fast, inexpensive ice cream cone is available year-round at Byerly's and Lund's supermarkets. However, for a *real* soda fountain experience—including malteds, sundaes, and cherry Cokes served in traditional soda-fountain style—try the following establishments.

BRIDGEMAN'S.
Twenty-one Twin Cities locations. A hometown institution since 1936. The stores are large and of a standard decor. Call individual locations for information on hours.

ANNIE'S PARLOUR OF ICE CREAM, 406 Cedar Av. and 313 15th Av. S.E., Minneapolis. ►2
339-6207 and 379-0744

Annie's uses hard ice cream, has fruit-flavored malts, and brings your hot fudge sundae with the fudge on the side. Many portions are big enough for two.

Cedar Av. location open Sun-Thu 11 a.m. to midnight; F, Sat 11 a.m. to 1 a.m. 15th Av. location open M-Sat 11 a.m. to 10 p.m.

BUSSMANN'S ICE CREAM STORE, 722 Snelling Av. N., St. Paul. ►8
646-6604

An old-fashioned ice cream store that makes the ice cream it serves right on the premises. Prepares extravagant sundaes and double-egg malteds. Open M-Sat 9 a.m. to 9 p.m.

CLANCY'S, 3948 W. 50th St., Edina. ►5
926-7687

Good-sized soda fountain with reasonable prices. Open M-Sat 9 a.m. to 8 p.m.

CONVENTION GRILL, 3912 Sunnyside Av. (just off France Av.), Edina. ►5
920-6881

Run by the same people who operate Annie's Parlour, the Convention Grill offers the same large portions and extravagant treats. Open M-Thu 11 a.m. to 10 p.m.; F, Sat 11 to 11; Sun noon to 10.

HOISSER'S PHARMACY, 240 Snelling Av. S., St. Paul. ►8
698-8859

This tiny neighborhood fountain is right out of the 1940s—and so are its prices. Coffee is still a nickel a cup. Open M-F 8 a.m. to 9 p.m.; Sat 8 to 6; Sun 10 to 2.

TUTHILL'S GENERAL STORE, 2455 Hennepin Av. S., Minneapolis. ►2
377-4011

Tuthill's store, which sells gifts

and odds-and-ends as well as ice cream and other dishes, looks as though it's been on this Hennepin Av. corner for 80 years. It's really only three years old, and its soda fountain, taken from the old Rainbow Cafe down the street, was installed even more recently. Tuthill's serves Schwann's ice cream with a variety of trimmings. Open M-Sat 10 a.m. to 10 p.m.

TAKE-OUTS

Somewhere between cooking your own dinner and going out to eat is the option of sending out for a restaurant meal (or part of one). Most Oriental restaurants offer take-out service, and, like every other place in the country, the Twin Cities has plenty of choices for pizza-to-go. The following is a sampling of some of the more exotic take-out selections in the Twin Cities. Details on the restaurants can be found in this section. If the entries on this list don't satisfy your appetite, try calling your favorite restaurant. Many restaurants will prepare a take-out order on special request.

ART SONG'S WINGS
822-0619
Wings, ribs, egg rolls.

BAR-B-Q-KING
222-0751
Ribs, steaks, chicken, chitterlings.

BOCA CHICA
222-9696
Tacos.

CECIL'S DELI

698-9792
Jewish specialties.

EMILY'S LEBANESE DELI
379-4069
Middle Eastern specialties.

JAVA
338-6810
Middle Eastern specialties.

LE BISTRO
835-7543
Sandwiches, soup, quiche.

LE PETIT CHEF
926-9331
Fine French food.

MARIO'S DELI
825-2491
Italian food.

RUDOLPH'S
871-8969
Ribs.

THE RUSSIAN PIROSHKI TEA HOUSE
646-4114
Piroshkis, Russian specialties.

BANQUETS

The following special dinners offer an opportunity to sample food and company not usually available to regular restaurant diners.

BETHLEHEM LUTHERAN CHURCH SMORGASBORD, 4100 Lyndale Av. S., Minneapolis. ▶2
823-8281
A traditional all-you-can-eat Scandinavian smorgasbord that has been an annual event for more

than 35 years. Always held second Sat in March. Seatings at 4:30, 5:30, and 6:30 p.m. Tickets are sold in advance, beginning in January. Call for information.

CEDARHURST MANSION GOURMET DINNER TOUR, 6940 Keats Av. S., Cottage Grove. 459-9741 ►11

A six-course dinner with a changing international emphasis is served in this impressive mansion. Usually held third Tue of each month. Seatings at 6:30 p.m. A tour of the mansion is included with the meal. Reservations are required. No cards. Checks accepted.

DOWNTOWN COUNCIL OF ST. PAUL PROGRESSIVE DINNERS, 701 N. Central Tower, 445 Minnesota St., St. Paul. ►7 222-5561

In a variation on traditional progressive dinners where neighbors go house-to-house for a succession of courses, the St. Paul Downtown Council offers diners a chance to visit a series of St. Paul restaurants for different courses of a single meal. Offered once a month on a Tue or W evening, dinners include appetizer, salad, entree, and dessert or after-dinner drink. Reservations required. 50-100 persons can be accommodated. First seating is usually at 5:30 p.m. Price is in the $17 range and includes tax and tip. Call for dates.

DOWNTOWN COUNCIL OF MINNEAPOLIS PROGRESSIVE DINNERS, 15 S. Fifth St., Minneapolis. ►1 338-3807

Minneapolis Downtown Council progressive dinners are held four times a year, usually in February, May, August, and November. Seatings are limited to 60 persons, so advance payment and registration is required. Seatings are at 5:30, 6:15, and 7 p.m. Four-course meal at four restaurants within easy walking distance of each other. Wine included. Price is in the $17 range. Call for dates.

GOURMAND SOCIETY DINNERS, *Twin Cities Reader,* 100 N. Seventh St., Minneapolis. ►1 338-2900

Monthly Gourmand Society dinners are open to the public by reservation. Five-course meals are held at top area restaurants and usually feature special culinary efforts by the chef. Wine-tasting included. Call for dates, reservations, and prices.

LA CREPERIE, 756 Cleveland Av. S., St. Paul. ►8 698-8903

Dinners held the first W of every month are for people who enjoy French conversation as well as French food. Full-course French meal. Seating at 8 p.m. Reservations required. No cards. Checks accepted.

SRI LANKA CURRY HOUSE, 1824 Central Av. N.E., Minneapolis. ►2 781-0355

Banquet held first M of every month features curries that are the specialties of this unusual restaurant. Seatings at 5:30 and 8 p.m. Reservations required. No cards. Checks accepted.

Chapter Eleven

NIGHTSPOTS & ENTERTAINMENT

The following is a selective listing of Twin Cities-area bars and night clubs. Some of them feature regular entertainment; others are popular because of their atmosphere or because they have become a local tradition. In addition to the establishments listed here, many of the restaurants, hotels, and motels listed elsewhere in this book have bars and lounges.

Closing time in Minnesota M-Sat is 1 a.m.; bars open Sun close at midnight.

Abbreviations for credit cards are: AE-American Express; CB-Carte Blanche; DC-Diners Club; MC-MasterCard (Master Charge); V-Visa (BankAmericard); and S-Shoppers Charge (a local card). Checks accepted generally means local checks with picture I.D.

Establishments listed in this section can change their hours, prices, and programming at any time. Call ahead if you have any questions.

POPULAR BARS

BLACK FOREST INN, 1 E. 26th St., Minneapolis. ►2
872-0812

Bohemian atmosphere, outdoor patio open summer. Open seven nights a week. No entertainment, no specials. AE, DC, MC, V, S accepted. Checks accepted.

CASTLE ROYAL, 215 S. Wabasha St., St. Paul. ►8
227-8771

Grotto-like bar in former mushroom caves features eclectic, Art Deco-inspired interior. Open Tue-Sat. Piano bar. No cover. Happy

---

(See Locator Key Map, pages 8-9)

►1 Mpls. Downtown	►7 St. Paul Downtown
►2 Mpls. Excluding Downtown	►8 St. Paul Excluding Downtown
►3 Mpls. North Suburbs	►9 St. Paul North Suburbs
►4 Mpls. Northwest Suburbs	►10 St. Paul Northeast Suburbs
►5 Mpls. Southwest Suburbs	►11 St. Paul Southeast Suburbs
►6 Mpls. South Suburbs	►12 St. Paul South Suburbs

hour Tue-F 3:30 to 7 p.m. AE, V accepted. Checks accepted.

CHARLIE'S CAFE EXCEPTIO-NALE, 701 Fourth Av. S., Minneapolis. ►1
333-4646

Elegant, relaxed setting for enjoying carefully prepared drinks. Experienced barmen can rise to exotic challenges. Open M-Sat. AE, DC, MC, V accepted. Checks accepted.

COMMODORE HOTEL, 79 Western Av. N., St. Paul. ►8
227-8893

Intimate, Art Deco lounge with mirrored walls. Open seven nights a week. No credit cards. Checks accepted.

THE DOME, Downtown Holiday Inn, 1313 Nicollet Mall, Minneapolis. ►1
332-0371

Panoramic view of the city. Open M-Sat. AE, DC, MC, V accepted. Checks accepted.

ESTEBAN'S, 901 Marquette Av., Minneapolis. ►1
338-3383

Excellent margaritas and daiquiris (banana, peach, strawberry). Open seven nights a week. No entertainment. Check telephone directories for four other Twin Cities locations. AE, MC, V accepted. Checks over #500 accepted.

FIRST STREET STATION, 333 S. First St., Minneapolis. ►1
339-3339

Two comfortable lounges full of railroad artifacts; relaxing at-mosphere and view of the city. Backgammon boards available. Open seven nights a week. No entertainment. Happy hour M-F 4:30 to 7 p.m. AE, MC, V accepted. Checks accepted.

FELTY'S, Butler Square, 100 N. Sixth St., Minneapolis. ►1
339-6300

California-style bar with exposed brick, hanging plants, lots of sunshine. Huge working fireplace. Novel restrooms. Open seven nights a week, music on Sat. Happy hour M-Thu 4:30 to 7. AE, MC, V accepted. No checks.

GALLIVAN'S, 354 Wabasha St., St. Paul. ►7
227-6688

Piano bar M-Sat. Happy hour M-F 3 to 6 p.m. AE, CB, DC, MC, V, S accepted. Checks accepted.

GANNON'S, 2728 W. Seventh Blvd. (Gannon Rd.), St. Paul. ►8
699-2420

Open M-Sat. Piano bar Tue-Sat. No cover. Gannon's charge only. Checks accepted.

GLUEK BREWING CO., 16 N. Sixth St., Minneapolis. ►1
338-6621

Nicely restored former brewery offers substantial food as well as drink. Open M-Sat. No entertainment. MC, V accepted. No checks.

GREEN MILL TOO, 2626 Hennepin Av. S., Minneapolis. ►2
374-2131

Popular singles gathering place. Oyster bar, wine bar, deep-dish pizza. No entertainment. Always a drink special. Open seven nights a week. No checks. AE, DC, MC, V accepted.

ICHABOD'S WET GOODS, 528 Hennepin Av., Minneapolis. ►1
341-4009

On the ground floor of the recently renovated Hennepin Center for the Arts. Open M-Sat. AE, MC, V accepted. Checks accepted.

IMPROPER FRACTION, 712 Washington S.E., Minneapolis. 378-3838 ►2

Stadium Village hangout for college types. New game room, light entertainment M-Sat. Open seven days. Happy hour M-F 4 to 6. Checks accepted. MC, V accepted.

JIMMY HEGG'S, 420 Second Av. S., Minneapolis. ►1
336-8311

Theater crowd. Open M-Sat. No entertainment. Happy hour "all the time." Jumbo drinks. No credit cards. Checks accepted.

D.B. KAPLAN'S, Butler Square, 100 N. Sixth St., Minneapolis. ►1
332-0903

Bright, colorful decor and flavorful ice cream drinks to match. Open seven nights a week. No credit cards. Checks accepted.

THE LITTLE WAGON, 430 S. Fourth St., Minneapolis. ►1
332-4418

Favorite of *Star* and *Tribune* journalists. Open M-Sat. Amateur entertainment Tue. No cover. No happy hour. No credit cards. No checks.

MAYSLACK'S POLKA LOUNGE, 1428 N.E. Fourth St., Minneapolis. ►2
789-9862

Very potent drinks served in unpretentious surroundings. Juke box loaded with polka tunes. Open Tue-Sat. Happy hour until 8 p.m. No credit cards. No checks.

McCOLL PUB, 368 Jackson St., St. Paul. ►7
224-5421

Friendly basement bar in historic bank building. Open M-Sat. M, W are ladies' nights. Happy hour M-F 4 to 6 p.m. AE, MC, V accepted. Checks accepted.

NIGHT TRAIN, 289 Como Av., St. Paul. ►8
488-2277

Two elegant converted Pullman coaches, complete with mahogany bar and brass fixtures. Serves lunches and dinners as well as drinks. Classical jazz piano Tue-Sat. No cover. No happy hour. AE, MC, V accepted. Checks accepted.

PALM ROOM, Curtis Hotel, 10th St. and Third Av. S., Minneapolis. ►1
340-5300

Tasteful, understated green-and-neon decor. Open seven nights a week. Downstairs bar has light entertainment M-Sat; cover charge on weekends. AE, CB, DC, MC, V accepted. Checks accepted.

PRACNA ON MAIN, 117 S.E. Main St., Minneapolis. ►1
379-3200

The Twin Cities' first old building to be converted into a trendy bar-restaurant. Rooms on several levels; outdoor patio open summer. Open seven nights a week. No entertainment. Happy hour Sun-Thu 10 p.m. to midnight. AE, CB, DC, MC, V accepted. Checks accepted.

SGT. PRESTON'S, 221 Cedar Av., Minneapolis. ►2
338-6146

High-energy West Bank meeting place. Open seven nights a week. No entertainment. No happy hour. Occasional drink specials. AE, CB, DC, MC, V accepted. Checks accepted.

W.A. FROST AND CO., 374 Selby Av. (at Western Av.), St. Paul. 224-5715 ►8

Relaxed, nicely restored bar features fresh-squeezed fruit juices and a variety of imported beers. Back terrace open summer. No entertainment. No happy hour. MC, V accepted. Checks accepted.

DRINKS AND MUSIC

ARTIST'S QUARTER, 14 E. 26th St., Minneapolis. ►2
872-0405

Entertainment seven nights a week—blues, jazz, rock, bluegrass. $1 cover Thu-Sat. Happy hour M-Sat 4 to 6 p.m.; drink specials M, Thu 9 to 11 p.m. AE, MC, V accepted. No checks.

Lights in the night on Minneapolis' Hennepin Av.

BLUE OX NIGHT CLUB, 918 Third Av. S., Minneapolis. ►1 333-3541

Open M-Sat; mellow music every night. No cover. Happy hour M-Sat 4 to 7. No checks. AE, DC, CB, MC, V accepted.

BOYD'S ON THE RIVER, 1315 N. West River Rd., Minneapolis. 529-7737 ►2

Live rock music every night; two bands on weekend evenings. Open M-Sat 7 p.m. to 1 a.m. No cover M, Tue; cover $1 W, Thu; weekend cover varies. Drink specials vary. No cards, no checks.

BURNSVILLE BOWL, 1200 E. Hwy. 13, Burnsville. ►6 890-1200

Six separate lounges offer a variety of entertainment. Playpen features rock every night. Fanny Hill's, open every night, features music comedy Tue-Sat. Disco in the Silver Slipper W-Sat. Cover charge at Playpen F-Sat. Happy hour at Fanny Hill's until 6 p.m. AE, MC, V accepted. Checks accepted.

THE CABOOZE, 917 Cedar Av., Minneapolis. ►2 338-6425

Live rock and blues, including some of the best-known acts in the world, seven nights a week. Cover on W-Sat; charge varies. Variety of drink specials. No credit cards. No checks.

CHICAGO BAR AND RESTAURANT, 23 N. Sixth St., Minneapolis. ►1 340-0941

Food served downstairs, live entertainment upstairs Thu-Sun. Usually jazz from the '30s and '40s. Cover on weekends. AE, DC, MC, V accepted. Checks accepted.

CITY LIMITS, 7800 Computer Av. (Hwy. 494 and Hwy. 100), Bloomington. ►6 831-4498

Top 40s dance music seven nights a week. Jazz in the back room M-Thu. Cover varies; no cover if you eat in the restaurant. Happy hour M-F 3 to 7. AE, CB, MC, V accepted. Checks accepted.

DUFFY'S, E. 26th St. and 26th Av. S., Minneapolis. ►2 721-3301

Big-name reggae and rock 'n' roll acts seven nights a week. Cover varies depending on the band. No happy hour, always double drinks. New outdoor beer garden. No credit cards. Checks accepted.

EMPORIUM OF JAZZ, 400 D St., Mendota. ►12 452-1868

Hall Brothers New Orleans-style Jazz Band plays F-Sat; guest bands perform on occasion. Lounge open seven nights a week; cover F-Sat only, usually $2. AE, DC, MC, V accepted. Checks accepted.

GEORGE IS IN FRIDLEY, 3720 E. River Rd., Fridley. ►3 781-3377

Greek restaurant with a belly dancer and Greek music in the bar. Open Tue-Sun, show at 8 p.m. No cover. Happy hour every day from 4 to 6. AE, MC, V accepted. Checks accepted.

GULDEN'S ROADSIDE SUPPER CLUB, 2991 N. Hwy. 61, Maplewood. ►9
484-3396

Live country and jazz entertainment, dance music, Tue-Sat. No cover. Happy hour M-Sat 4:30 to 6:30. MC, V accepted. Checks accepted.

HORATIO HORNBLOWER, 345 Wabasha St., St. Paul. ►7
227-8781

Elegant, understated nautical decor. Open seven nights a week. Entertainment M-Sat. No cover. Happy hour M-F 4 to 7 p.m. Sun hours 4 to midnight. AE, DC, MC, V accepted. Checks accepted.

McCAFFERTY'S, 788 Grand Av., St. Paul. ►8
227-7328

Irish food and music. Open seven nights a week. Entertainment Tue-Sat. No cover, but drink prices increase when the band is playing. Happy hour M-F 4:30 to 6:30 p.m. MC, V accepted. Checks accepted.

MR. NIBS, 2609 26th Av. S., Minneapolis. ►2
729-2387

Rock and country bands seven nights a week. Cover F-Sat only. Drink specials Sun-W 4 to 7 p.m. AE, DC, MC, V accepted. No checks.

O'CONNELL'S, 656 Grand Av., St. Paul. ►8
226-2522

Entertainment M-Sat. No cover. No happy hour. AE, DC, MC, V accepted. Checks accepted.

PAYNE RELIEVER, 899 Payne Av., St. Paul. ►8
771-4215

Live entertainment M-Sat, usually rock 'n' roll or rhythm-and-blues bands. Disco on Sun. Cover Tue-Sun. Specials vary. No cards. Checks accepted.

RIVERVIEW SUPPER CLUB, 2319 W. River Rd. N., Minneapolis. ►2
521-7676

Twin Cities Jazz Society sponsors free jazz sessions in the front bar M, Tue. Out-of-town modern jazz bands featured Tue-Sun. Cover is usually $3. Happy hour M-F 4 to 7. No cards. Checks accepted.

RYAN'S CORNER, Fourth and Sibley Sts., St. Paul. ►7
298-1917

Live rock music Thu-Sun. Cover varies. Happy hour M-F 4 to 6. No cards, no checks.

THE ST. CROIX BOOM CO., 317 S. Main St., Stillwater. ►10
439-0167

Open seven nights a week. Entertainment W-Sun—rock, country, folk. Cover varies. Happy hour M-F 4 to 6 p.m.; Sun 4 to 10; no cover Sun before 7. Other drink specials vary. No cards. Checks accepted—$5 limit.

SUN BAR AND DISCO, 413½ Hennepin Av., Minneapolis. ►1
333-9501

Twin Cities' only drag revue is presented here F, Sat 10 p.m. to 1 a.m. Disco music the rest of the week. No cover. No cards, no checks.

THE UNION BAR, 507 Hennepin Av. E., Minneapolis. ►2
379-2858

Live rock, blues, country seven nights a week. Cover varies. Specials vary. No credit cards. Checks accepted.

WAIKIKI ROOM, Hotel Leamington, 1014 Third Av. S., Minneapolis. ►1
370-1100

Exotic drinks. Trio plays Hawaiian music on weekends. Happy hour W-Sun 5 to 6. AE, MC, V accepted.

WILLIAM'S PUB AND CAFE, 2911 Hennepin Av. S., Minneapolis. ►2
823-6271

Entertainment seven nights a week in the Pub; classical music Sun and jazz Tue. Other entertainment varies. Cover usually $1. Pub happy hour seven days a week 4 to 6 p.m. Other drink specials vary. Happy hour in Cafe M-F 4 to 7 p.m., in Peanut Bar M-F 4 to 6. Two-for-one Tue, Thu 9 to 11. AE, MC, V accepted. Checks accepted in Cafe only, not in Pub.

ZOOGIE'S, 14 S. Fifth St., Minneapolis. ►1
333-8108

Live rock 'n' roll M-Sat. Cover Thu-Sat. Happy hour M-Sat 4 to 7. Pizza available to 1 a.m. No credit cards. Checks accepted.

DANCING

BEL-RAE BALLROOM, Hwy. 10, Mounds View. ►9
786-4630

Ballroom dancing Thu, F 8:30 to 11:30; Sat 9 to 1; Sun 4:30 to 8:30. Cover depends on band. Setups and beer served.

COLISEUM BALLROOM AND SALTARI FOLK DANCE COFFEEHOUSE, 2708 E. Lake St., Minneapolis. ►2
724-9932

Ballroom dancing in the Coliseum F, Sat to big band sounds. Cover varies. Traditional square dancing and folk dancing, including instruction, Sun, Tue-Thu, usually at 8 p.m. Call for schedule and details.

GRAND PORTAGE, Registry Hotel, 7901 24th Av. S., Bloomington. ►6
854-2244

Floor show and soft rock music M-Sat. Ballroom dancing to big band music Sun. No cover. AE, MC, V accepted. Checks accepted.

MEDINA LANES AND BALLROOM, 500 Hwy. 55, Hamel. ►4
478-6661

Ballroom dancing to big band music W, F, Sat 9 to 1; Sun in the winter 3 to 10. Back 40 lounge has live country and rock music Thu-Sat 9 to 1. Bowling alley. MC, V, checks accepted.

OZ, A NIGHT CLUB, 345 Wabasha St., St. Paul. ►7
222-6858

Disco seven nights a week. Live entertainment in the C-Sharp Room Thu-Sat. Cover $5 F, Sat; $3 all other nights. Ladies free on W. Happy hour 4 to 7:30. AE, MC, V accepted. Checks under $20 accepted.

PENTHOUSE LOUNGE, IDS Tower, 80 S. Eighth St., Minneapolis. ▶1
332-2351

Fifty floors above downtown Minneapolis. Expect a wait F-Sat. Live dance music Tue-Sat. Cover $2.50 F, Sat after 9 p.m. Happy hour M-F 5 to 7. AE, CB, DC, MC, V accepted. Checks accepted.

PROM CENTER, 1190 University Av., St. Paul. ▶8
645-0596

Open to the public Sun night only for dancing to big band sounds. Cover $3.50. No cards. No checks.

SMUGGLER'S INN, 111 Kellogg Square, E. Fourth and Robert Sts., St. Paul. ▶7
291-1450

Dancing M-F, usually disco and rock 'n' roll. M is ladies' night. No cover. Happy hour M-F 4 to 6:30 p.m. AE, MC, V accepted. Checks accepted with credit card only.

THE TASTE SHOW LOUNGE, 14 N. Fifth St., Minneapolis. ▶1
332-2547

Disco six nights a week. Cover $3 F-Sat, $2 Sun-Thu, ladies free W. Happy hour 4 to 7 p.m. No credit cards. No checks.

UNCLE SAM'S, 29 N. Seventh St., Minneapolis. ▶1
332-1775

"Danceteria" in the huge main room playing a variety of recorded music. Open seven nights a week. No alcohol Sun. Seventh St. Entry lounge features live pro-

gressive rock and New Wave music M-Sat; closed Sun. Cover charges for both rooms vary. Drink specials vary. No credit cards. Checks accepted.

DINNER THEATERS

See page 223 for dinner theater listings.

MOVIES

The Twin Cities has a large selection of movie theaters offering everything from first-run films to adult triple-X features. Theaters are found in most suburban shopping centers and in the downtown areas of Minneapolis, St. Paul, and the larger suburbs. Check daily newspapers for up-to-date listings of first-run films. The only theater in the Twin Cities that has retained its large Cinerama screen and is still showing first-run films is the Cooper, 5755 Wayzata Blvd., St. Louis Park, 544-1506.

Theaters specializing in adult films can be found along Lake St. between 12th and 16th Avs. S., and downtown on Hennepin Av. in Minneapolis. Downtown St. Paul also has some theaters that show adult films.

For information on foreign, artistic, or classic films being shown in the Twin Cities, contact any of the film societies listed on page 235 of this guide.

The following listings are for theaters that offer special programming, prices, or atmosphere.

Foreign Films

CEDAR THEATER, 416 Cedar

Av., Minneapolis. ►2
338-6403

Unusual foreign films that are rarely screened elsewhere in the Twin Cities. Two shows per evening. Programming changes every few weeks, depending on the popularity of the film. Tickets $4 for adults, $1.25 for seniors and children. No ticket packages. Checks accepted.

Double Features

CAMPUS THEATER, 309 S.E. Oak St., Minneapolis. ►2
378-3770

Regular double features of almost anything but first-run films, including oldies and some foreign films. Tickets $3 for adults. Tue special $1.50.

PARKWAY THEATER, 4814 Chicago Av., Minneapolis. ►2
822-3030

Regular double features of popular films. One showing of each film each evening. All seats $1.50.

SUBURBAN WORLD, 3022 Hennepin Av. S., Minneapolis. ►2
825-6688

Located in the Uptown area. Double features of foreign films and popular American movies. No first-run movies. Tickets $3 adults, $1.50 children. Tue special $1.50.

UPTOWN THEATER, 2906 Hennepin Av. S., Minneapolis. ►2
825-4644

Double features of a variety of classic and popular films. Features change every night. *Rocky Horror*

Picture Show every F, Sat at midnight. Schedules available at the theater. Tickets $3 for adults, $1.50 children. Five-film ticket packages available.

VARSITY THEATER, Dinkytown, 1308 S.E. Fourth St., Minneapolis. ►2
331-4292

Double features of popular and classic films. Programming changes three times a week, with features running Sun-Tue, W-Thu, and F-Sat. Tickets $3 for adults, $1.50 for children and seniors. Five-film ticket packages available. Tue special $1.50.

Movie Bargains

ORPHEUM THEATER, Seventh and Wabasha Sts., St. Paul. ►7
277-1768

Recently refurbished and reopened after a long lull in activity, the Orpheum is a converted vaudeville house that can seat almost 2,000 people. It runs first-run, first-rate movies seven days a week. Tickets $1.50, Tue special $1.

The following Twin Cities theaters offer recently released movies (usually two to three months after the first showing) at bargain prices ranging from 99 cents to $1.50. Call the theater for program and price details.

BOULEVARD 1 and 2, 5315 Lyndale Av. S., Minneapolis. ►2
823-7471

CAMDEN, 4215 Webber Pkwy., Minneapolis. ►2
529-9669

HIGHLAND 1 and 2, 760 Cleveland Av., St. Paul. ►8
698-3085

RIVERVIEW, 3800 42nd Av. S., Minneapolis. ►2
729-7369

STUDIO 97, 9705 Lyndale Av. S., Bloomington. ►6
881-7980

ANOKA CINEMA, 420 E. Main St., Anoka. ►3
421-1414

THE HEIGHTS, 3951 Central Av. N.E., Minneapolis. ►2
788-9079

HOLLYWOOD THEATER, 2815 Johnson St. N.E., Minneapolis. ►2
781-3626

NILE THEATER, 3736 23rd Av. S., Minneapolis. ►2
724-5495

VILLAGE 4 THEATER, Village 10 Shopping Center, Hwy. 10 and Hanson Blvd., Coon Rapids. ►3
755-6980

Science and Natural History Films

OMNITHEATER, Science Museum of Minnesota, Wabasha and Exchange Sts., St. Paul. ►7
221-9400 information
221-9456 reservations
Impressive domed Omnitheater screen seems to engulf the viewer in the picture. Usually scientific features of interest to the general public. Programming changes two or three times a year. Shows are very popular, so buying tickets in advance is advised. Reservations accepted for an extra 50-cent charge. Tickets $4.50 for adults, $3.50 for seniors and students, $3 for children under 11. Admission to the Science Museum is only $1 for people attending the Omnitheater.

LIGHT SHOWS

LASER FANTASY, Northstar Theater, 28 W. Seventh St., St. Paul. ►7
227-2700
Laser light shows accompanied by classical and contemporary music. Shows Tue-Sun; usually two or three different shows offered in an evening. Shows change about every three months. Tickets $2.

LIVE RADIO

PRAIRIE HOME COMPANION, World Theater, 494 Wabasha, St. Paul. ►7
332-6960 tickets
221-1500 information
The Twin Cities' only live radio variety show, *Prairie Home Companion* features the humor of Garrison Keillor and a mixed bag of folk, bluegrass, and other music. Performances are broadcast live from the World Theater to the audience of National Public Radio. Shows every Sat 4:30 to 7 p.m. Tickets $4 adults, $3 students and seniors, $2 children under 11. Tickets may be purchased in advance at Odegard Books, 867 Grand Av., St. Paul, or at Hello Minnesota, Butler Square, 100 N. Sixth St., Minneapolis. No live performances when the show is on tour in late September and in early May.

THE ARTS

Art in the Twin Cities is a matter of civic pride. The Minneapolis-St. Paul metro area supports two major orchestras, three major art museums, and the Guthrie and Children's theaters—all nationally renowned. And community support extends past these major institutions to a remarkable number of smaller arts groups and organizations, as the following listings demonstrate.

ARTS INFORMATION

THE ARTS RESOURCE AND INFORMATION CENTER, Minneapolis Institute of Arts, 2400 Third Av. S., Minneapolis. ►2 870-3131

The Arts Resource and Information Center keeps files on more than 1,100 Minnesota arts organizations and is a good source of information on Twin Cities arts activities. Among the services offered by the center are daily events information for the Twin Cities area, job listings and notices of auditions and competitions, information on speakers and demonstrators in the arts, information on metropolitan-area arts classes, and information on major

(See Locator Key Map, pages 8-9)

►1 Mpls. Downtown	►7 St. Paul Downtown
►2 Mpls. Excluding Downtown	►8 St. Paul Excluding Downtown
►3 Mpls. North Suburbs	►9 St. Paul North Suburbs
►4 Mpls. Northwest Suburbs	►10 St. Paul Northeast Suburbs
►5 Mpls. Southwest Suburbs	►11 St. Paul Southeast Suburbs
►6 Mpls. South Suburbs	►12 St. Paul South Suburbs

cultural institutions, organizations, and programs across the nation, including traveling exhibitions.

The center also maintains a poster wall, a brochure rack filled with literature on arts organizations, and a subject index covering arts-related books, articles, organizations, and individuals. Publications on such subjects as exhibition and performing spaces in the Twin Cities, metropolitan art classes, and Minnesota art fairs are also available, for a slight charge. Open Tue, W, F, Sat 10 a.m. to 5 p.m.; Thu 10 to 9; Sun noon to 5.

ARTS ORGANIZATIONS

Several organizations work full-time to support and promote the arts in the Twin Cities.

COMMUNITY PROGRAMS IN THE ARTS AND SCIENCES (COMPAS), 308 Landmark Center, 75 W. Fifth St., St. Paul. ►7 292-3249

A member agency of the St. Paul-Ramsey Arts and Science Council, COMPAS was created to meet community demand for art opportunities for all citizens. It specializes in bringing arts activities to St. Paul neighborhoods and schools. COMPAS programs include Minnesota Writers in the Schools, St. Paul History Theater, Neighborhood Arts Program, Seniors and the Arts, Arts for the Handicapped, and a program for creating public art. The public art program, which involves community groups and businesses or public agencies as co-sponsors, produces murals and sculpture in St. Paul neighborhoods and the downtown area. During the first

---

THE MAT VOUCHER PROGRAM

One of the best arts bargains in the Twin Cities, the MAT (Metropolitan Arts Ticket) Voucher Program offers substantial discounts on performances by more than 90 local arts organizations. MAT vouchers may be purchased in sets of five for $10 a set. When presented at the box office of participating arts organizations, each voucher is good for a $4 discount (often full admission). Vouchers are transferable and may be used with family and friends.

The MAT Voucher Program is operated by the Twin Cities Metropolitan Arts Alliance as part of its program to increase access to the arts and to increase audience support for local arts organizations. Vouchers may be purchased by senior citizens, union members, physically disabled persons, teachers, and staff, and clients of social service and community programs. Persons who buy vouchers also receive a free monthly calendar of performing arts events.

For more information, and to receive a MAT voucher application form, call the Metropolitan Arts Alliance at 332-0471.

six years of the program, 67 murals and four sculptures were completed.

MINNEAPOLIS ARTS COMMISSION, 301 City Hall, Minneapolis. ►1
348-5486

Established in 1975 as an advocate for the arts and the arts consumer, and funded by the city of Minneapolis, the commission works with artists, arts organizations, and citizens to develop arts programs and services. It also serves as an advisory body to the city council and the mayor in regard to public use of the arts. The Minneapolis A.R.T. Exchange, a program of the arts commission, extends funding to organizations involved in arts activities.

MINNEAPOLIS INDEPENDENT CHOREOGRAPHERS' ALLIANCE, 400 First Av. N., Minneapolis. ►1
340-1900

MICA sponsors regular dance concerts by area choreographers, provides information on dance in the Twin Cities, and generally offers support to its choreographer members. Publishes a bimonthly calendar of dance events in Minnesota. Call for membership information and a concert schedule.

MINNEAPOLIS SOCIETY OF FINE ARTS, 2400 Third Av. S., Minneapolis. ►2
870-3046

Founded in 1883 to "foster and promote educational and artistic interests, particularly the knowledge, love and practice of the arts," the society is the governing and supporting body of the Minneapolis Institute of Arts and the Minneapolis College of Art and Design, and is affiliated with the Children's Theatre Company and School. By joining the society, you receive membership benefits for all three organizations.

MINNESOTA ASSOCIATION OF COMMUNITY THEATERS (MACT), P.O. Box 2317, Minneapolis 55402.
333-3010

This is a non-profit organization designed to promote community theater arts interests in Minnesota and to encourage, channel, and facilitate the exchange of ideas among community theaters and foster their growth and improvement. It sponsors conferences, workshops, a bimonthly newsletter, and a state community theater festival every two years as part of the national program sponsored by the American Community Theater Association (ACTA). Membership is open to amateur, non-profit community theaters, interested organizations, and individuals.

MINNESOTA CITIZENS FOR THE ARTS, 709 Pioneer Bldg., St. Paul. ►7
227-5963

An advocacy group organized throughout the state to encourage an understanding of the financial needs of the arts. More specifically, the group's aim is to communicate the financial need to the public and through the public to the legislature. The group educates the public about the roles of the arts within the community, provides a voice for citizens and artists in the programming of the arts, and supports programs and opportunities for the advancement of the arts in Minnesota. Minnesota Citizens for the Arts also researches bills coming into the legislature and lobbies on behalf of the arts community. Individual and group memberships are available.

MINNESOTA COMPOSERS FORUM, 302 Landmark Center, 75 W. Fifth St., St. Paul. ►7
225-4507

The Minnesota Composers Forum was established in 1973 to create both a forum and an audience for new music by Minnesota composers. One of the first organizations of its kind in the country, it commissions several new works each year, provides a "reading" service for composers, and sponsors about 10 major concerts of new music each year. It also holds information workshops and sponsors a regular monthly broadcast on Minnesota Public Radio. Call or write the forum for a schedule of its free concerts.

MINNESOTA STATE ARTS BOARD, 2500 Park Av., Minneapolis. ►2
341-7170

The Minnesota State Arts Board distributes grants to individual artists and arts organizations in Minnesota from funds it receives from the state legislature and the National Endowment for the Arts. The board's staff is also available to give advice, information, and technical assistance to organizations engaged in artistic activities. Call or write for information about its funding guidelines, to get on its mailing list, or to receive a copy of its annual report.

THE PLAYWRIGHTS' CEN-

CENTERS FOR THE ARTS

HENNEPIN CENTER FOR THE ARTS, 528 Hennepin Av., Minneapolis. ►1
332-4478

Formerly the old Masonic Temple, this Romanesque downtown landmark waited years for renovation. When it was refurbished and re-opened in 1979, it was considered a major factor in the effort to keep downtown arts activity alive. The Hennepin Center contains the Little Theater, which is a performing space used by a variety of groups; several smaller performing areas; and the offices of many non-profit arts groups. The top two floors house the Cricket Theater's offices and performing space. Two restaurants on the main floor look out on the activity of Hennepin Av. Open M-F 9 a.m. to 5 p.m. and during scheduled events.

TER, 2301 E. Franklin Av., Minneapolis, ►2
332-7481

The Playwrights' Center is an umbrella organization for the promotion and development of new plays. An outgrowth of the Playwrights' Lab, the center is composed of the Playwrights' Lab, the Midwest Playwrights' Program, Musical Project, and Storytalers, a traveling children's theater group. In addition to encouraging local playwrights, the center presents regular staged readings of original work. Call the center for schedules and information.

ST. PAUL-RAMSEY ARTS AND SCIENCE COUNCIL, 30 E. 10th St., St. Paul. ►7
292-3222

Umbrella organization for the Minnesota Museum of Art and Art School, the Schubert Club, the St. Paul Chamber Orchestra, the Chimera Theater Company, and COMPAS, the St. Paul-Ramsey Arts and Science Council was also instrumental in the renovation of Landmark Center. It provides funding for its member organizations and also administers an arts development fund for emerging arts organizations.

TWIN CITIES METROPOLITAN ARTS ALLIANCE, 305 Hennepin Center for the Arts, 528 Hennepin Av., Minneapolis. ►1
332-0471

Founded in 1974, the Metropolitan Arts Alliance aids the Twin Cities arts community by actively expanding arts audiences. The alliance encourages attendance at

CENTERS FOR THE ARTS

LANDMARK CENTER, 75 W. Fifth St., St. Paul. ►7
292-3232

This elegant Romanesque Federal Courts Building was renovated and re-opened in the fall of 1978 as a performing, meeting, and gallery space as well as the home for affiliates of the St. Paul-Ramsey Arts and Science Council. Landmark Center opens onto a first-floor cortile, used for concerts, exhibitions, and occasional gala "happenings." (The Gladstone Cafe is open for lunches Tue-F in the cortile.) The lower level includes Weyerhaeuser Auditorium, a gallery used by the Minnesota Historical Society, and the Schubert Club's keyboard instrument museum. The second floor serves as exhibit galleries for the Minnesota Museum of Art and has recently been expanded. The third and fourth floors house the offices of arts organizations and several former courtrooms that now are used for lectures, meetings, and receptions. The courtrooms are also available for public rental. The remaining two floors are still undergoing renovation and will open in late 1982 as classroom and studio space for the Minnesota Museum of Art's public education program. Landmark Center is open M, Tue, W, F 8 a.m. to 5 p.m.; Thu 8 to 8; Sat 10 to 5; Sun 1 to 5.

arts events by sponsoring the MAT Voucher Program and by providing cooperative marketing services for non-profit arts organizations. Write or call the alliance for MAT Voucher Program applications and for its monthly arts calendar, which is sent free to voucher program participants and is available to others at $5 per year.

THEATER

The Twin Cities has a vital and varied theater community. The following companies have indicated they will have an active 1981-82 season. Call the individual companies for program information.

ACTORS THEATRE OF ST. PAUL, 2115 Summit Av., St. Paul. ►8
227-0050

An ongoing professional company, the Actors Theatre is producing an eclectic season of six plays at the College of St. Thomas and one production at the Mixed Blood Theater in Minneapolis. Tickets $6 to $9; available at Dayton's and Donaldsons. MC, V accepted at the box office. MAT vouchers accepted. Michael Andrew Miner, artistic director.

AT THE FOOT OF THE MOUNTAIN, People's Center, 2000 S. Fifth St., Minneapolis. ►2
375-9487

At the Foot of the Mountain is a women's theater collective committed to producing plays, community events, and rituals by and about women while creating a professional workspace for women theater artists. Plays are produced year-round at the People's Center and on tour. Tickets $4 to $10 (depending on purchaser's income) at the door (telephone reservations accepted). MAT vouchers accepted.

AT RANDOM, 1455 Ashland, St. Paul.
646-2134

In its third season, At Random will produce three or four original works plus a touring show and a children's show. Performances at the Southern Theater and the Little Theater at the Hennepin Center for the Arts. Tickets $5. MAT vouchers accepted. Jim Slowiak, artistic director.

BLOOMINGTON EXPERIMENTAL THEATER (BET), Penn Community Center, 2501 W. 84th St., Bloomington. ►6
888-5328

BET, recently reorganized from the Bloomington Civic Theater, will specialize in new plays by local playwrights: three shows per season in October, February, and June. Tickets $3. MAT vouchers accepted. Classes on all aspects of theater taught September through May.

CAPITOL CITY THEATRE, 617 S. Smith, St. Paul. ►8
222-0957 or 774-1872

Capitol City Theatre is a community company that usually stages two musicals and two plays each season. Performances at Humboldt Senior High School in

St. Paul. Tickets $4 for adults, $3 for students and seniors. Maureen Nieman, artistic and music director.

CENTRE STAGE, 4330 S. Cedar Lake Rd., St. Louis Park. ►5 377-8330

The theater program of the Jewish Community Center of Minneapolis, Centre Stage produces six plays September through June, usually on Thursdays, Saturdays, and Sundays. Tickets $2.50 to $5.50. MAT vouchers accepted. Susan Schwaidelson-Siegfried, director of theater.

CHILDREN'S THEATRE COMPANY AND SCHOOL, 2400 Third Av. S., Minneapolis. ►2 874-0400

Plays for adults as well as children are part of the Children's Theatre's six-production season, which runs September through June. This year's season includes productions of *Puss in Boots, The Little Match Girl, Phantom of the Opera,* and *Alice in Wonderland.* The Children's Theatre has won several awards for its costumes and set designs, and has an international reputation as one of the leading theaters for young people. Tickets range from $5.95 to $9.95 for adults, $3.95 to $7.95 for children, students, and seniors; available at Dayton's and Donaldsons. MC, V accepted at the box office. MAT vouchers accepted. John Clark Donahue, artistic director.

The Children's Theatre School offers classes in performing and technical theater, and is the largest, fully professional theater school for young people (ages 11 to 18) in the nation. Admission to the school is by audition, held in

From 'The Marvelous Land of Oz' at the Children's Theatre.

September and January.

CHIMERA THEATER COMPANY, 30 E. 10th St., St. Paul. ►7
292-4311 (information)
292-4300 (tickets)

One of the largest community theaters in the country, Chimera is affiliated with the St. Paul-Ramsey Arts and Science Council. Nine mainstage plays are presented throughout the year. The emphasis is on family entertainment, including musicals. Performances are at the Crawford Livingston Theater in the St. Paul-Ramsey Arts and Science Center. Tickets $5.50, $6.50 for musicals, available at Donaldsons. AE, MC, V, S, Donaldsons charge accepted at the box office. MAT vouchers accepted. Student and senior discounts available for most performances.

COMMEDIA THEATER COMPANY, 1645 Hennepin Av., Room 311B, Minneapolis.
338-7952

Traveling throughout five states performing classical comedies by the likes of Shakespeare, Aristophanes, and Moliere, and spiced with improvisation, the Commedia Theater Company is at home in the Twin Cities during February, March, June, and August, performing free during the summer in Minneapolis and St. Paul parks. February and March performances are at the Southern Theater, 1420 Washington Av. S., Minneapolis. Tickets usually $5 to $5.50; available at Dayton's. MAT vouchers accepted.

COMPAS/ST. PAUL HISTORY THEATRE, Landmark Center, 75 W. Fifth St., St. Paul. ►7
292-3249

The St. Paul History Theatre produces original works that dramatize St. Paul history and life in the city's neighborhoods. Community participation is encouraged in all aspects of research, writing, and production. Four major productions a year. Performances are usually held at the Landmark Center. Call COMPAS for ticket information.

CRICKET THEATRE, 528 Hennepin Av., Minneapolis. ►1
333-2401

Performing "the classics of tomorrow," mostly contemporary American drama, the Cricket has become one of the Twin Cities' most exciting theater groups since its move to the Hennepin Center for the Arts. The Cricket's season runs from October to June. Tickets $8 and $9.50; $5 for students and seniors; available at Dayton's and Donaldsons. MC, V accepted at the box office. MAT vouchers accepted. Lou Salerni, artistic director. Cynthia Mayeda, managing director.

DUDLEY RIGGS' BRAVE NEW WORKSHOP, 2605 Hennepin Av. S., Minneapolis. ►2
377-2120

Famous for "instant theater," this professional company offers new, satirical revues written by company members about every 12 weeks year-round. Tickets $7; available at Dayton's and Donaldsons. AE, MC, V accepted at the box office. Student and senior discounts available. John Remington, director.

DUDLEY RIGGS' ETC. (EXPERIMENTAL THEATER COMPANY), 1430 Washington Av. S., Minneapolis. ►2
377-2120

Original musical comedies by the ETC. and the showcasing of new variety, comedy, and vaudeville performers are the mainstays at this West Bank institution, which is part theater, part bar and cafe. Tickets $7; available at Dayton's, Donaldsons. AE, MC, V accepted at the box office. Student and senior discounts available.

FLYING CARPET THEATER, 3255 Hennepin Av., Minneapolis. ►2
827-5362

This young professional theater company presents three shows a year, performing works involving European clown and mask work. It also presents workshops to a variety of groups, and performs for free in the city parks and at street festivals. Tickets to regular performances are $4. Rainer Dornemann, artistic director.

GUTHRIE THEATER, Vineland Pl., Minneapolis. ►2
377-2224

The Guthrie's decision to locate in Minneapolis in 1963 put the Twin Cities on the national theater map. "Committed to the classics," the Guthrie produces eight plays in repertory each season, including one by Shakespeare. The 1981-82 season, which runs June through March, includes *The Tempest, Don Juan, Our Town, Foxfire, Eve of Retirement, Eli: A Mystery Play, Candide,* and *As You Like It.* The company also offers slide shows on costuming and set and property construction; apprentice intern fellowships in acting, writing, directing, and design; a technical interning program; a variety of demonstrations after selected Tuesday evening performances and discussion of backstage construction and set changeovers following selected Saturday matinees. Tickets $5 to $15.95; available at Dayton's. AE, DC, MC, V, S, Amoco Torch Club accepted at the box office. Public rush M and student rush Tue-Sat—any seat $5. MAT vouchers accepted. Liviu Ciulei, artistic director.

HAMLINE UNIVERSITY THEATRE, 1536 Hewitt St., St. Paul. ►8
641-2297

Hamline productions offer hands-on experience to the university's theater arts students. Two major shows, two student productions, and a children's touring show are usually offered each year. Performances are held in Hamline's Drew Theater. Performances are free to Hamline students and faculty, and are open to the public.

ILLUSION THEATER, 528 Hennepin Av., Room 309, Minneapolis. ►1
339-4944

Experimental theater, especially plays that explore male-female relationships and roles, is the specialty of this professional theater group. Illusion's 1981-82 season features four major plays

THE GUTHRIE THEATER

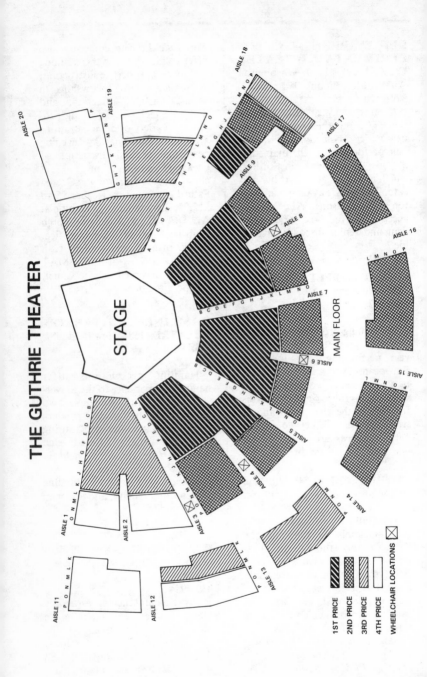

and will be interrupted by tours. Twin Cities performances will be at the Hennepin Center for the Arts. Tickets range from $4 to $6. MAT vouchers accepted. The Illusion Theater also tours with its production of *Touch,* part of the theater's program of sexual-abuse preventive education for parents, children, and school and community groups. Bonnie Morris and Michael Robins, artistic directors. Brooke Portmann, managing director.

LAKESHORE PLAYERS, 522 Stewart Av., White Bear Lake. ►10
426-3275 (information)
429-5674 (tickets)

This community theater performs two musicals and four other shows a year, including both comedy and mystery. Tickets $4.75, $3.50 for students and seniors. MAT vouchers accepted. Sherrie Tarble, administrative coordinator.

THE LOWER-LEVEL THEATER, 271 19th Av. S., West Bank Union, University of Minnesota, Minneapolis. ►2
373-5058

An ongoing program of the U of M West Bank Union, the Lower Level Theater presents three experimental theater productions per academic year. Tickets $3.50 for adults, $2.50 for students.

MASQUERS THEATER COMPANY, Forest Lake Senior High, Hwys. 61 and 97, Forest Lake. ►10
464-5828

The Masquers perform two musicals and a straight drama each summer. Performances Wednesday through Saturday at the Forest Lake Senior High School. Tickets $5 for adults, $4 for students, $3 for seniors and children. Patrick Voelker, technical director.

MINNETONKA THEATRE, 14300 Excelsior Blvd., Minnetonka. ►5
398-9467

A nationally recognized community theater that has become a serious teaching and performing company, the Minnetonka Theatre performs six plays for adults and four for young people September through April. Tickets $5.50, $6.50 for musicals; $3.50 for young people's productions. V, S accepted for season tickets. MAT vouchers accepted. David Allan, managing-artistic director.

MIXED BLOOD THEATRE COMPANY, 1501 S. Fourth St., Minneapolis. ►2
338-6131

This multi-racial company produces seven new plays September through May in the old West Bank Fire House. Tickets $5; available

---

Left: Guthrie Theater, Vineland Pl., Minneapolis. 377-2224. Used for Minnesota Opera performances and special arts events as well as for regular theater season. Price variations shown on diagram are for theater performances only. Paid parking in two lots north and south of the theater.

at Dayton's. MAT vouchers accepted. Jack Reuler, artistic director.

NEW HOPE MUSICAL THEATRE, 4401 Xylon Av. N., New Hope. ►4
332-7481

A program of the Playwrights' Center, the New Hope Musical Theatre produces one show for three or four weekends each summer in Civic Center Park, New Hope. All performances are free.

ORPHEUM THEATRE, 910 Hennepin Av., Minneapolis. ►1
339-1800

If you're looking for a touring Broadway show in the Twin Cities, chances are you'll find it at the Orpheum. It's the only local facility able to handle many major traveling productions. Call the Orpheum for current information on shows and ticket prices.

OUT-AND-ABOUT THEATRE COMPANY, 512 Nicollet Mall, Room 521, Minneapolis. ►1, 2
332-5747

This gay- and lesbian-oriented community theater group usually offers six productions a year at the Howard Conn Fine Arts Center of the Plymouth Congregational Church. Tickets $6; available at Dayton's. MAT vouchers accepted. Richard E. Rehse, artistic director.

PALACE THEATER, 1420 Washington Av. S., Minneapolis. 375-0343 ►2

A professional company, the Palace primarily performs original works by company members. Performances are at the Southern Theater. Three plays are scheduled for fall, winter, and spring of 1981-82. Tickets are $4 to $6. MAT vouchers accepted.

PARK SQUARE THEATRE, 400 Sibley St. (Park Square Court), St. Paul. ►7
291-7005

This community company with a professional staff specializes in classical theater and other plays of distinction. Seven plays are presented during the subscription season September through June, and there is an independent summer schedule. Ticket prices range from $3 to $5. Tickets available at Donaldsons. MAT vouchers accepted. Richard Cook, artistic director.

PENUMBRA, 270 N. Kent St., St. Paul ►8
224-4601

A semi-professional group affiliated with the Martin Luther King-Hallie Q. Brown Center, Penumbra presents a variety of mostly contemporary plays throughout the year at the center. Tickets $5. MAT vouchers accepted. Lou Bellamy, cultural arts director.

PERFORMER'S ENSEMBLE, 125 N. Washington Av., Minneapolis. ►1
338-2484

A professional company that performs ensemble works with a

multi-cultural emphasis. Four to five main productions per year, as well as monthly readings of works in progress. Acting, voice, and movement classes also offered. Tickets for main productions $5. MAT vouchers accepted. Susan Galbraith, artistic director.

PLAYS IN THE PARKS, 310 Fourth Av. S., Minneapolis. ►2 348-2226

Call or write for schedules of free summer performances by area theater groups in Minneapolis parks. Children's programs and movies in the parks also are offered.

PUNCHINELLO PLAYERS, 100 North Hall, University of Minnesota, St. Paul. ►9 373-1570

The University of Minnesota's community theater company, made up of students and community members, gives one production per quarter in North Hall on the St. Paul campus. Call for ticket or audition information.

REAL COMMUNITY THEATRE, 2700 12th Av. S., Minneapolis. ►2 871-8118

The Real Community Theatre performs three shows a year—spring, summer, and fall. The summer show, usually for children, tours Minneapolis parks. Admission to performances is by donation—$2 suggested, $1 for children. MAT vouchers accepted.

The theater has no office, but can be contacted through Stewart Park at the above address and telephone number.

SHOWBOAT, 120 Rarig Center, 330 21st Av. S., University of Minnesota, Minneapolis. ►2 373-2337

Docked south of the Washington Av. Bridge on the East Bank of the Mississippi River, the Showboat presents family entertainment performed by University of Minnesota students. One play is produced each summer. Tickets $5, $4 for students and seniors; available at Dayton's.

STORYTALERS, 2301 Franklin Av. E., Minneapolis. 332-6037

A program of the Playwrights' Center, Storytalers is a touring group of professional actors performing for children at shopping centers, parks, libraries, and schools. In addition to presenting classic children's stories and original plays, the group offers storytelling by a single performer using masks, mime, etc. Most performances are sponsored by outside organizations and are free. Denise Nienstadt, booking manager.

THEATRE IN THE ROUND PLAYERS, 245 Cedar Av., Minneapolis ►2 333-3010

This 29-year-old community group produces eight plays September through June, plus two summer shows. Works performed range from classical through contemporary dramas to comedies. Tickets $5; $4 for students and seniors F and Sun only; available Dayton's and Donaldsons. MC, V accepted at the box office. MAT vouchers accepted. Karen Knudsen, administrator.

THEATRE DE LA JEUNE LUNE, P.O. Box 1203, Minneapolis 55440.
333-6200

The French and American members of this bilingual company perform in the Twin Cities October to March and in Paris the rest of the year. Much of the group's work consists of pantomime and comedy. Minneapolis performances are held at the Hennepin Center for the Arts, the Southern Theater, and other Twin Cities locations. Call or write for ticket information and schedule. Diane Adair, general manager.

THEATRE FROM THE CENTER, P.O. Box 27073, Minneapolis 55427.
544-7588

A new avant-garde company that intends to produce two plays during the 1981-82 season. It will generally perform works written by company members. At this writing, performance locations had not been determined. Tickets $4, $3 for students. MAT vouchers accepted. Nitza Henig, artistic director.

THEATRE 1900, 1900 Nicollet Mall, Minneapolis. ►2
871-9020

This amateur company will perform four plays October through May in the Howard Conn Fine Arts Center of the Plymouth Congregational Church. Tickets $4 at the box office. MAT vouchers accepted.

THEATRE THREE, 3308 Colfax Av. S., Minneapolis. ►2
822-2803

This young professional theater group was founded by three women seeking to create greater opportunities for women in the theater. Four productions a year, presented at the Southern Theater and other locations in the Twin Cities. Tickets $6 for adults, $5 for students and seniors. MAT vouchers accepted.

UNIVERSITY OF MINNESOTA THEATRE, 120 Rarig Center, 330 21st Av. S., Minneapolis. ►2
373-2337

University of Minnesota students perform seven mainstage productions and a children's play each school year. Tickets $5, $4 for students and seniors; available at Dayton's. MAT vouchers accepted.

Right: Children's Theatre, 2400 Third Av. S., Minneapolis. 874-0500. Located in the Institute of Arts complex and featuring performances by the Children's Theatre Company. Free parking in ramp immediately south of theater on Third Av.

CHILDREN'S THEATRE

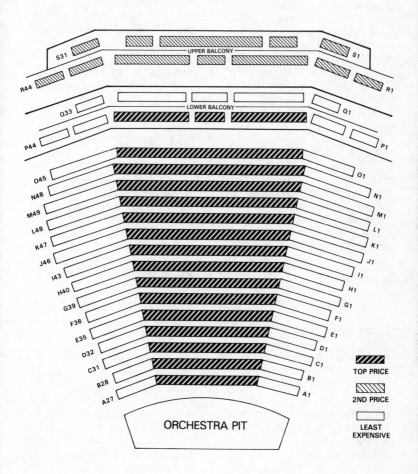

ORCHESTRA PIT

TOP PRICE

2ND PRICE

LEAST
EXPENSIVE

THE UP-AND-OVER THE-ATRE, 512 Nicollet Mall, Room 521, Minneapolis. ▶1
332-5747

A subsidiary of Out-and-About Theatre Company, Up-and-Over Theatre was established to produce all types of women's theater. Three productions each year, usually held in the Little Theater of the Hennepin Center for the Arts or at Plymouth Congregational Church. Tickets $6; available at Dayton's. MAT vouchers accepted. Sheila Reiser, artistic director.

WOMEN'S THEATER PROJECT, 731 Lincoln Av., St. Paul. 297-0298

A professional group committed to doing new plays written and produced by women. One major production a year, usually performed at the Hennepin Center for the Arts. Tickets $4 to $8. Carolyn Levy, artistic director.

Puppet Theater

The Twin Cities' "live" theater community is supplemented by a growing number of professional puppeteers who present shows for adults as well as children.

HEART OF THE BEAST PUPPET AND MASK THEATER, 1628 E. Lake St., Minneapolis. 724-9301 ▶2

Heart of the Beast, a professional company, performs throughout the year at the above address, at other Twin Cities locations, and on tour. The company produces the May Day Puppet Parade and Festival the first Sunday of May each year at Powderhorn Park in south Minneapolis. Heart of the Beast is the oldest puppet company in the Twin Cities. Tickets for most performances are $3 to $4 for adults, less for children. MAT vouchers accepted. Call to be put on mailing list for notification of future performances and workshops.

PANGOLIN PUPPET THEATER, 2436 First Av. S., Minneapolis. ▶2
871-1081

The Pangolin puppeteers use hand and rod puppets to produce original shows. Many of their puppet characters, such as Viola, the 400-year-old woman, reappear as stars of Pangolin productions. Human actors sometimes perform onstage with the puppets. The company gives annual staged performances at area theaters and tours schools, parks, and libraries. Call for program information.

ROSE AND THORN PUPPET THEATRE, 4751 Chicago Av., Minneapolis. ▶2
822-9525

The Rose and Thorn Puppet Theatre offers regular performances of family shows Saturdays October through May at their Chicago Av. location. During the summer the company appears at the Renaissance Fair and tours on independent bookings. A toystore is operated in conjunction with the theater, and classes in puppet construction and manipulation are offered as well. Call for ticket and schedule information.

UNITED PUPPET ARTISTS,

3516 Columbus Av. S., Minneapolis.
827-8976

An umbrella group rather than a performing organization, United Puppet Artists is a collective of Minnesota puppeteers who represent a variety of theatrical, literary, and visual disciplines. The group provides support for existing puppeteers and helps encourage new ventures. It is also working to establish a permanent puppet theater facility and to coordinate group puppet presentations in the Twin Cities area.

Dinner Theaters

CARLTON BACKSTAGE, 8350 24th Av. S., Bloomington. ►6
854-9292

Nationally known younger acts are presented Tue-Sun in this more intimate version of the Carlton Celebrity Room. Choice of three entrees. Dinner tickets and cocktail tickets available. Reservations advised. Two shows per evening. Checks, AE, DC, MC, V, S accepted.

CARLTON CELEBRITY ROOM, 8350 24th Av. S., Bloomington. ►6
854-9300

Las Vegas-style club offers top comedy, music, and dance acts with dinner or cocktails every night except M. Prices vary. AE, CB, DC, MC, V accepted. Reservations required.

CHANHASSEN DINNER THEATRES, Hwys. 5 and 101, Chanhassen. ►5
934-1535 (ticket information)

934-1525 (reservations)
800-362-3515 (toll-free number for greater Minnesota residents)

One of the largest and most successful Actors Equity operations in the country, Chanhassen has built a reputation for quality and adventurousness almost unheard of in dinner theaters. With four separate theaters (seating a total of 1,100) operating seven days a week year-round, Chanhassen can stage plays ranging from old-time musicals to contemporary drama. Tickets, from $14 to $25, include a complete dinner as well as the show; available at Dayton's. AE, DC, MC, V, S accepted at the box office. Howard Dallin, artistic director.

OLD LOG THEATER, 5175 Meadville St. (off Minnetonka Blvd.), Excelsior. ►5
474-5951

The Old Log, now in its 42nd year, is America's oldest professional theater with performances year-round. The primary attractions are Broadway comedies and English farces with an occasional drama or mystery. A children's play is also produced during the holiday season. Tickets are $6 Wed, Thu, F, and Sun; $6.50 Sat; available at Dayton's. Dinner and cocktails available prior to performances.

RADISSON PLAYHOUSE, I-494 and Hwy. 55, Plymouth.
553-1155 ►4

This professional dinner theater produces four or five musicals and comedies throughout the year at the Radisson Inn, Plymouth. Tickets available at Dayton's. AE,

MC, V, Dayton's charge accepted at the box office.

PERFORMING DANCE AND SCHOOLS

ANDAHAZY BALLET COMPANY AND ANDAHAZY CHOREOGRAPHIC SCHOOLS, 3208 Xenwood Av. S., St. Louis Park. 929-2801, 941-2567

Performances and instruction in classical, Russian-style ballet. At least one performance each year at Northrop Auditorium on the University of Minnesota's Minneapolis campus; religious ballet performed in area churches. Some performances free. Lorand Andahazy, artistic director.

COMMUNITY DANCE CENTER, 427½ Cedar Av., Minneapolis. 340-1306

Professionally taught classes in aerobic, ballet, jazz, ballroom and "jazz-xrcise" conducted in more than 25 metropolitan-area locations. Community Dance Center specializes in dance exercise classes. Call 24 hours a day for a free schedule.

CONTACTWORKS, 200 N. Third St., Minneapolis. 339-9398

Instruction and performances in contact improvisation. Performance schedule not set at this writing. Call for information. Tickets will cost about $4, $3.50 for students and seniors. MAT vouchers accepted.

ETHNIC DANCE THEATRE, 751 Goodrich Av., St. Paul. 226-6788, 227-1706

Performances and instruction in dance of various countries, with emphasis on dance of North America, the Balkan regions, other European nations. Six performances each year at various locations. Jonathan Frey, artistic director; Donald La Course, dance director.

INSTRUCTIONAL DANCE THEATER, 725 S.E. Fourth St., Minneapolis. 331-8563

This professional group performs modern dance for children and families. Performances and studio classes held at above address. Call for ticket information. Instructional Dance Theater also conducts a dance education program in the St. Paul schools and at other schools in Minnesota. Molly Lynn and Beverly Sonen, artistic directors.

MINNESOTA DANCE THEATRE, Hennepin Center for the Arts, 528 Hennepin Av., Minneapolis. 339-9150

A professional company that

Right: Northrop Auditorium, 84 Church St. S.E., Minneapolis. 376-8378. Site of performances of the Northrop Dance Season, the visiting Metropolitan Opera, and a variety of other productions. Diagram shows price variations for seating at Northrop Dance Season events only. Paid parking available in ramps, lots, and other U of M locations.

CYRUS NORTHROP MEMORIAL AUDITORIUM
UNIVERSITY OF MINNESOTA

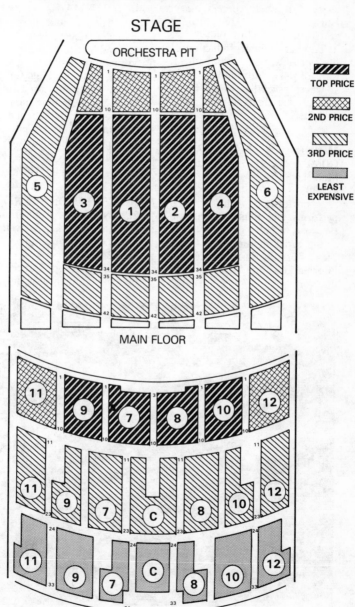

performs a variety of dance, classical through contemporary. Fall performances are scheduled at Northrop Auditorium, where its popular annual production of the *Nutcracker Suite* will be held. Call for ticket information. MAT vouchers accepted. Loyce Houlton, artistic director and choreographer.

MINNESOTA JAZZ DANCE COMPANY, 1815 E. 38th St., Minneapolis.
721-3031

A professional company that performs jazz dance throughout the year, usually giving fall and spring series in the Twin Cities. Tickets usually $4 to $6; call for information. Zoe Sealy, artistic director.

NANCY HAUSER DANCE COMPANY AND SCHOOL

Instruction and performances in modern dance, Spanish flamenco, and dance exercise. At this writing the dance company and school was searching for a new home. Check directory assistance for a new telephone number and address. Usually fall and spring performances. Ticket prices vary; some performances are free. MAT vouchers accepted. Nancy Hauser, artistic director.

NORTHROP DANCE SEASON, 229 Northrop Auditorium, 84 Church St. S.E., University of Minnesota, Minneapolis.
376-2345

The Northrop Dance Season brings a regular program of na-

From the 'Nutcracker' at Northrop Auditorium.

tionally and internationally known dance talent to the Twin Cities. The 1981-82 season extends from October to May and features seven major dance companies, including the American Ballet Theatre, Pilobolus Dance Theatre, and the National Ballet of Canada. Tickets range from $6 to $18.50, depending on the type of performance. Call for schedule information. MAT vouchers accepted.

OZONE DANCE SCHOOL AND REZONE DANCERS, 400 First Av. N. (sixth floor), Minneapolis.
338-1101

Instruction and performances by students in jazz and modern dance. Classes only in ballet and tap. Performances throughout the Twin Cities area. Tickets $3.50 to $4.50. MAT vouchers accepted. Linda Hendrick, director.

ST. PAUL CITY BALLET, 565 N. Kent St., St. Paul.
222-4676

Performances and instruction in classical ballet. School is known as the Classical Ballet Academy of Minnesota. Performances are generally during November, February, and April at locations throughout the Twin Cities. Tickets usually $4.50. MAT vouchers accepted. Jo Savino, director (company and school).

WHISPERS OF AMERICA, 2537 Aldrich Av. S., Minneapolis.
872-9523

This new company specializes in modern dance with an American theme. Its first performance schedule had not been set at this writing. Classes are offered. Call for ticket, performance, and class information.

MUSIC

In addition to two internationally recognized orchestras, the Twin Cities musical community can boast of a professional opera company, several fine choral organizations, and many symphony and chamber groups that range from a classical piano trio to full-fledged community orchestras. The music of our own performing groups is supplemented by visits from the Metropolitan Opera and other notable groups and individual artists.

Opera

METROPOLITAN OPERA IN THE UPPER MIDWEST, 105 Northrop Auditorium, 84 Church St. S.E., Minneapolis. ►2
373-2345

During its 38th annual festival in the Upper Midwest, the Metropolitan Opera will offer seven performances May 17 through 22. The 1982 season will include performances of Puccini's *Madame Butterfly,* Mozart's *The Magic Flute,* Verdi's *Rigoletto*, and Offenbach's *The Tales of Hoffman. Il Trovatore, Norma,* and *The Barber of Seville* will also be presented. The Met's annual spring tour is made up of six evening performances and one Saturday matinee. All performances are at Northrop Auditorium on the University of Minnesota's Minneapolis campus. Season tickets are available.

MINNESOTA OPERA COMPANY, 850 Grand Av., St. Paul.
221-0256

All of the Minnesota Opera Company's performances are in English. Six operas will be performed during the company's 1981-82 season, which runs November through May. *Hansel and Gretel* will be performed at the Orpheum Theater in downtown Minneapolis Nov. 22 through Dec. 12, 1981. A double bill of *Gianni Schicchi* and *The Village Singer* will be presented in February, followed by *The Barber of Seville* in March. A second double bill in May will feature *Feathertop* and *A Vampire Tale*. Except for *Hansel and Gretel*, performances will be at the Guthrie Theater in Minneapolis and O'Shaughnessy Auditorium at the College of St. Catherine in St. Paul. Tickets $6 to $17.50, available at Dayton's. MC, V accepted at the box office. MAT vouchers accepted. Artistic directors: Philip Brunelle, music; H. Wesley Balk, theater.

MINNESOTA SINGERS THEATRE, 2501 Pleasant Av., Minneapolis.
872-8362

Music between opera and Broadway—light opera and operetta, such as the works of Gilbert and Sullivan—is the repertoire of the Singers Theatre. Performances are Friday through Sunday, October through May (except around Christmas). At this writing, performance locations for the 1982 season had not been determined. Tickets $5, $3 for students and seniors, available at the door (telephone reservations accepted). MAT vouchers accepted. Edward Foreman, artistic director.

OPERA ST. PAUL, 485 Portland Av., St. Paul.
225-5541

This group was formed in 1980 to provide young professional singers in the Upper Midwest an opportunity to perform and work under professional direction. Traditional and light opera and musicals are performed in English. Three productions a year at various St. Paul locations. Tickets $8 to $10.

Orchestras and Ensembles

BLOOMINGTON SYMPHONY ORCHESTRA, 2215 W. Old Shakopee Rd., Bloomington. ►6
887-9601

Semi-professional orchestra performs six free concerts each year at Kennedy High School in Bloomington. Call for concert dates.

CIVIC ORCHESTRA OF MINNEAPOLIS, 305 Old Hwy. 8, #325, Roseville.
781-0878

Founded in 1953, this full symphony orchestra is made up of 93

Right: Orchestra Hall, 1111 Nicollet Mall, Minneapolis. 371-5656. Diagram shows price variations for regular Minnesota Orchestra series performances only. Seats at the side of the second- and third-tier balconies have partially obstructed views. Paid parking in Orchestra Hall ramp, with entrance at 11th and Marquette.

ORCHESTRA HALL

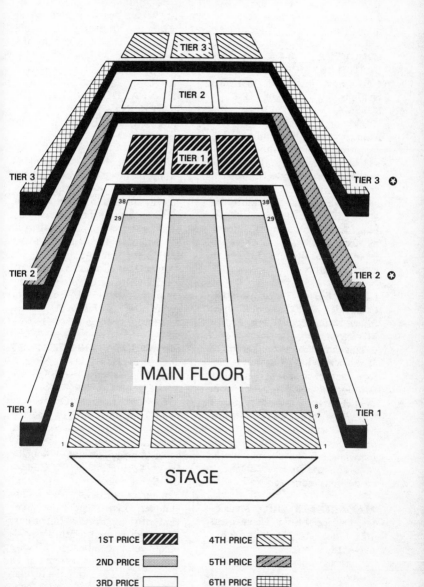

professional and semi-professional musicians. Twelve to 15 free
concerts are given each year at a
number of Twin Cities locations.

**GREATER TWIN CITIES
YOUTH SYMPHONIES,** 430
Oak Grove St., Suite 5-B, Minneapolis.
870-7611

Eight orchestras made up of elementary and high school students
perform concerts of mostly classical symphonic music throughout
the year. Formal concerts are held
at Orchestra Hall in Minneapolis
and O'Shaughnessy Auditorium
at the College of St. Catherine, St.
Paul. Admission to most concerts
by donation; MAT vouchers accepted. Dr. William L. Jones,
music director.

**KENWOOD CHAMBER OR-
CHESTRA,** 2020 Lake of the Isles
Pkwy., Minneapolis. ▶2
377-7699

This semi-professional group of
35 musicians has three major performances each year at the Walker
Art Center and three or four
smaller performances during their
September-through-May season.
Summer concerts are also presented. Its repertoire includes
both modern and classical music.
Most concerts are free. James Ric-
cardo, music director.

MACALESTER TRIO, Macalester College Music Department,
1600 Grand Av., St. Paul. ▶8
696-6518

Classical piano trio—piano,
violin, and cello—made up of
artists-in-residence at Macalester
College will perform three concerts in the fall and spring of

1981-82 in the Janet Wallace Concert Hall on the Macalester campus. Season tickets $8, individual
performance tickets $3; available
by calling or writing Jeanne
Holmquist at the Macalester Music Department.

**MINNEAPOLIS CHAMBER
SYMPHONY,** Rockler Bldg.,
Suite 700, 18 N. Fourth St., Minneapolis. ▶2
333-0985

Professional 23-piece symphony performs summer concert
series Sunday evenings. Performances are held in Willey Hall on
the west bank of the University of
Minnesota campus, 225 19th Av.
S., Minneapolis. Tickets $4.50
and $3 for students and seniors.
Available at Dayton's, Donaldsons, and the U of M's Coffman
Union bookstore. MAT vouchers
accepted. Jay Fishman, music
director.

MINNESOTA ORCHESTRA,
Orchestra Hall, 1111 Nicollet
Mall, Minneapolis. ▶1, 8
371-5656

The Minnesota Orchestra,
under the direction of Neville
Marriner, performs subscription
series at Orchestra Hall in downtown Minneapolis and O'Shaughnessy Auditorium at the College
of St. Catherine in St. Paul
September through May, plus
summer concerts under the direction of Leonard Slatkin. Klaus
Tennstedt is the orchestra's prin-
cipal guest conductor. Midday
Coffee Concerts are offered at 11
a.m. Thu and F during the regular
season. Tickets and series sub-
scriptions available at Dayton's
and Orchestra Hall. AE, MC, V,

S accepted at the box office. MAT vouchers accepted.

MINNETONKA SYMPHONY ORCHESTRA, 14300 Excelsior Blvd., Minnetonka. ►5
935-4615

This 60-member semi-professional orchestra performs an October-through-May season throughout the western Minneapolis suburbs. Three to four summer concerts also are given. All concerts are free. Roger S. Hoel, music director. The Minnetonka Orchestral Association also sponsors a chamber orchestra, adult chorale, children's choir, and civic orchestra.

ST. PAUL CHAMBER OR-CHESTRA (SPCO), 315 Landmark Center, 75 W. Fifth St., St. Paul.
291-1144

The Grammy Award-winning St. Paul Chamber Orchestra will perform six subscription series at seven Twin Cities area locations during its 1981-82 season from September through May. Among the series are the Capital, featuring guest artists, and the Perspectives, in which the 31 orchestra members will perform modern music. The season will also include a holiday concert. Tickets for individual performances are $5 to $15, available at the box office. MAT vouchers accepted. The SPCO is directed by Pinchas Zukerman.

Pinchas Zukerman directs the St. Paul Chamber Orchestra.

ST. PAUL CIVIC SYMPHONY, Macalester College Music Department, 1600 Grand Av., St. Paul. 696-6518

A full-size symphony made up of semi-professional and professional musicians. Performs mostly classical music at five or six concerts during its September-through-May season. Three of the performances are at the Janet Wallace Concert Hall at the college; the remaining concerts are held at other Twin Cities locations. All concerts are free, and are always held on Sunday evenings. Edouard Forner, director.

SFORZANDO, MacPhail Center for the Arts, 1128 LaSalle Av., Minneapolis. ►2
373-1925

Sforzando is a new professional music ensemble made up of 35 members of the faculty of the MacPhail Center. The group emphasizes the performance of music from the 20th century. Its 1981-82 season will feature a series of four concerts, November through May, called "New Composers of the Pacific Rim." Performances will be at the Walker Art Center. Tickets $4 at the Walker box office (375-7600). Richard Letts, managing director.

Renaissance Ensembles

CONCENTUS MUSICUS RENAISSANCE MUSIC AND

DANCE ENSEMBLES, 905 Fourth Av. S., Minneapolis. 338-4194

Three separate ensembles and Concentus Court Dancers seek to recapture and communicate to modern audiences the beauty and splendor of the music and dance of the Renaissance. The ensembles perform in period costumes and use replicas of historic instruments. Performances are held weekends October through June at various locations. Tickets $5 for adults, $3.50 for seniors and students; available at Dayton's. MC, V, and MAT vouchers accepted at the Concentus Musicus office. Dr. Arthur Maud, director.

Vocal Groups

APOLLO CLUB OF MINNEAPOLIS, INC., 3033 Excelsior Blvd., Minneapolis. 922-7671

Male choral group founded in 1895 performs two concerts each year, usually in November or December and April or May, usually in Orchestra Hall. Tickets $7 and $6 at the club's office. MC, V, S accepted. Roger S. Hoel, conductor.

BACH SOCIETY OF MINNESOTA CHORUS, P.O. Box 15021 Commerce Station, Minneapolis 55415. 373-1925

This semi-professional group

Right: O'Shaughnessy Auditorium, 2004 Randolph Av., St. Paul. 690-6703. Site of regular performances by the Minnesota Opera Company, Minnesota Orchestra, and the Schubert Club's music series. Price variations in diagram are for Minnesota Orchestra performances only. Obstructed views in row D, the first row of main-floor seating. On-street parking; paid lot southeast of the auditorium.

I. A. O'SHAUGHNESSY
AUDITORIUM
THE COLLEGE OF ST.
CATHERINE

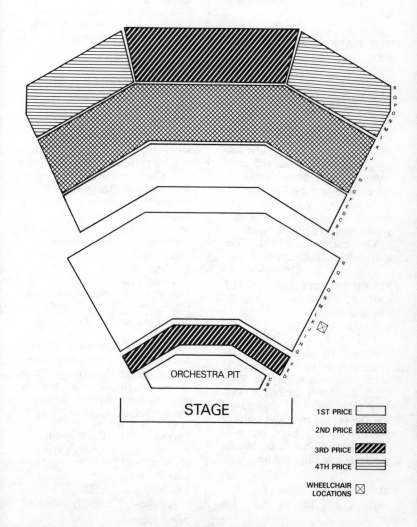

performs five or six concerts of choral music by Bach and other composers throughout the year at various locations. Call or write for information on performances. Tickets $6 to $15 available by telephone or mail. MAT vouchers accepted. A special Bach Easter Oratorio will be offered April 18, 1982. Henry Charles Smith, music director.

THE DALE WARLAND SINGERS, 1643 Wellesley Av., St. Paul.
292-9780

A 40-voice mixed professional choral ensemble organized in 1972. Singing an extensive repertoire of *a cappella* choral music, the group performs a regular season in the Twin Cities and internationally. Their 10th-anniversary season in 1982 will include five concerts, two of which will be given at Orchestra Hall in Minneapolis. Tickets $5, $3 for students. MAT vouchers accepted. Dale Warland, music director.

METROPOLITAN BOYS CHOIR, 7039 Morgan Av. S., Minneapolis.
866-2312

This 40-voice concert choir composed of nine- through 16-year-old boys performs about 35 concerts a season in the Twin Cities and tours nationally. Performances are held throughout the Twin Cities area, and many of them are free. A larger group of 125 boys aged six through 16 supplements the concert choir.

MINNESOTA CHORALE, Hennepin Center for the Arts, 528 Hennepin Av., Suite 216, Minneapolis.
227-3117

In its 10th season, the 150-voice Minnesota Chorale performs classics of choral literature. Five concerts are scheduled for the 1981-82 season, which runs from November to May. Performances are held at Orchestra Hall and other Twin Cities locations. Tickets $5 to $10; season tickets $32 and $40. MAT vouchers accepted.

Concert Series

BAKKEN LIBRARY MUSIC SERIES, 3537 Zenith Av. S., Minneapolis. ►2
927-6508

This October-through-April series will include regular Sunday evening performances by the Bakken Chamber Group and performances of Baroque music by Musica Primavera in January and April. Ticket prices had not been set at this writing. Call for ticket and program information. All performances are at the Bakken Library.

GLORIA DEI MUSIC SERIES, Gloria Dei Lutheran Church, 700 S. Snelling Av., St. Paul. ►8
699-1378

Series of free evening concerts featuring voice, organ, and instrumental groups. Performances held at the church. Call for program information. Robert Bobzine, music director.

PLYMOUTH MUSIC SERIES, Plymouth Congregational Church, 1900 Nicollet Av., Minneapolis. ►2
871-7400

A variety of music is presented

throughout the year. Performances are usually held at the church, but sometimes at other locations. Ticket prices and availability vary. Call for program information. Philip Brunelle, artistic director.

ST. MARK'S CATHEDRAL CONCERT SERIES, 519 Oak Grove St., Minneapolis. ▶2
870-7800

Full program of religious music performed by Gregorian singers and the cathedral choir, soloists, and orchestra offered September through May. Most performances on Sunday afternoons and evenings at the cathedral. Call for program information. Howard Don Small, music director.

SCHUBERT CLUB, 302 Landmark Center, 75 W. Fifth St., St. Paul. ▶7, 8
292-3268

Professional vocal and instrumental musicians perform classical works during the fall and winter at O'Shaughnessy Auditorium at the College of St. Catherine in St. Paul. The Schubert Club's 1981-82 International Artist Series will include performances by cellist Mstislav Rostropovich, mezzo-soprano Janet Baker, and pianist Jorg Demus. Ticket prices vary; tickets available at the Schubert Club office only. AE, MC, V, Dayton's charge accepted. MAT vouchers accepted.

THE THURSDAY MUSICAL, 4537 Drew Av. S., Minneapolis.
926-9644 ▶2

Founded in 1892, this group sponsors three-part classical concerts performed by its members, usually consisting of a piano solo, a vocalist and an instrumental ensemble. Bimonthly concerts held at the Walker Art Center Thursday mornings at 10:30 October to April. Admission by membership; $15, $12 for seniors, $6 for students.

FILM

The following organizations provide showings of classic, foreign, and other films not usually seen in local commercial moviehouses.

FILM IN THE CITIES, 2388 University Av., St. Paul. ▶8
646-6104

A major media center in the Twin Cities, Film in the Cities offers workshops, lectures, and an associate degree in filmmaking. Film series are offered almost every night of the week, including their Wednesday-night series called "Light and Form," which combines film screenings and a lecture. A second series, "Moving Image Makers," features works of regional film and video artists. Small fee for some series. Call for schedule.

THE MARX BROTHERHOOD, 951 S.E. 17th Av., Minneapolis. 331-7032 ▶2

Started by several Marx Brothers fans, this society shows six films a year, October through May. To supplement the 13 available Marx Brothers features, films starring W. C. Fields, Buster Keaton, and other vintage comedians are also offered. Cartoons and short-subject films are included in each showing. Donations of $1.75 are requested, and all proceeds are contributed to the American Heart Fund by the society. Showings are in 125 Willey Hall on the west bank of the Minneapolis campus of the University of Minnesota. Call or write for a schedule.

MINNEAPOLIS FILM FESTIVAL

Struggling to become an annual event, the Minneapolis Film Festival is a cooperative effort by the *Minneapolis Star* and *Tribune* and local arts and business organizations. Between 50 and 80 films of all types—American, foreign, independent, and retrospective—are scheduled to be shown in a number of local theaters over a 10-day period in January. Watch newspapers for schedules, admission prices, and other information.

MINNEAPOLIS INSTITUTE OF ARTS, 2400 Third Av. S., Minneapolis. ▶2
870-3046

The institute runs three film series throughout the year. Classic and other movies, some relating to museum exhibits, are shown Tue, W, F, Sat at 8 p.m. A family film festival is held weekends at 2 p.m. Children under 12 are admitted free; museum admission required for others. Admission to evening films is usually about $3, with a $1 discount for members. Call 870-3131 for program information.

MINNESOTA MUSEUM OF ART, 305 St. Peter St., St. Paul. 227-7613 ▶7

Regular Tuesday-night retrospective film series offering a variety of films. Most focus on a particular actor or subject. Screenings are in the Weyerhaeuser Auditorium of the Landmark Center, beginning at 7:30 p.m. Admission 50 cents for museum members, $1 for non-members.

RAMSEY COUNTY HISTORICAL SOCIETY FILM SERIES, 75 W. Fifth St., Landmark Center, St. Paul. ▶7
222-0701

The Ramsey County Historical Society runs three to four Wednesday-night film series each year, each one extending for about six weeks. All the films have an historical emphasis, and the 1982 series will concentrate on perspectives of urban life. Screenings are at Landmark Center. Admission usually $2 at the door.

SCHUBERT CLUB, 302 Landmark Center, St. Paul. ▶7
292-3268

Three or four ongoing film series during the year on a variety of themes. Screenings F, Sat at 8 p.m. at either the St. Paul-Ramsey Arts and Science Center Auditorium or the Landmark Center. Tickets $1.75 at the door.

SONG AND DANCE CINEMA SOCIETY, 1658 Rome Av., St. Paul.
698-6121

Showing seven classic Hollywood musicals each year and featuring the likes of Gene Kelly and Judy Garland, this society donates its proceeds to the Ronald McDonald Residence for families of cancer patients. Showings at 8 p.m. on selected Friday nights

September through May in 125 Willey Hall on the west bank of the University of Minnesota's Minneapolis campus. Donation $1.50. Call for program information.

UNIVERSITY OF MINNESOTA FILM SOCIETY, 3300 University Av. S.E., Minneapolis. ►2
373-5397

Foreign, experimental, popular current, and classic films are shown throughout the year in the Bell Museum of Natural History Auditorium, 10 Church St. S.E. (University and 17th Avs. S.E.), Minneapolis. International stars and critics occasionally appear as guest speakers. Admission usually $2.25 to $2.75; discount with membership, which costs $20 per year ($15 for students).

WALKER ART CENTER, Vineland Pl., Minneapolis. ►2
375-7600

Current, historical, and experimental films are shown throughout the year, generally in themed series. Scheduling is flexible, usually including weekend showings, often followed by a presentation or discussion. Admission is usually about $2.50 with a $1 discount for members and seniors. Calendars of film and other events at the Walker are available in the art center lobby.

ART

Art Museums
THE AMERICAN SWEDISH INSTITUTE, 2500 Park Av. S., Minneapolis. ►2
871-4907

The American Swedish Institute is an art and cultural museum housed in the castle-like mansion of the late Swan J. Turnblad, a successful Swedish-language newspaper publisher. The institute's collections are made up of art and artifacts that span more than 150 years of Swedish experience in America. They include more than 600 samples of Swedish glass, many works by important Swedish and Swedish-American artists, immigrant artifacts (trunks, weavings, looms, etc.), and rooms decorated in the traditions of particular Swedish provinces and time periods. Modern Swedish art is also displayed, and traveling exhibitions of Swedish glass, painting, and decorative arts are regularly featured.

The mansion in which the institute's collections are displayed was built in 1900. It contains 33 rooms and is decorated with intricately carved oak, walnut, and African mahogany panels and sculptures, plaster ceiling carvings, and unique tile stoves called *kakelugnar.*

Open Tue-Sat 1 to 4 p.m.; Sun 1 to 5. Admission is $1 for adults, 50 cents for students, 25 cents for children under six.

MINNEAPOLIS INSTITUTE OF ARTS, 2400 Third Av. S., Minneapolis ►2
870-3046

The Minneapolis Institute of Arts houses a collection of 65,000 objects representing nearly all schools and periods of art, including European and American paintings, sculpture, decorative arts, period rooms, prints and drawings, photography and Oriental, African, Oceanic, Ancient, and native North and South American arts.

Outstanding works in the collection include Rembrandt's *Lucretia*, Copley's *Mrs. Nathaniel Allen*, Goya's *Self Portrait*, Van Gogh's *Olive Trees*, Poussin's *Death of Germanicus*, the Pillsbury collection of ancient Chinese bronzes, the Gale collection of Japanese *ukiyo-e* prints, Paul Revere's Templeman Tea Service, and a collection of 40,000 prints and drawings representative of Rembrandt's works, 19th century French prints, and the Minnich collection of botanical, zoological, and fashion prints.

The museum maintains a continuous schedule of special exhibitions drawn from the permanent collection as well as from other museums and institutions. It also sponsors the Minnesota Artists Exhibition Program (see Galleries listings), a unique department administered by and for state artists.

The Minneapolis Institute of Arts was established in 1915 by the Minneapolis Society of Fine Arts. The museum's collection was housed in the Minneapolis Public Library from 1889 to 1915,

The Asian Galleries of the Minneapolis Institute of Arts.

when it was moved to the present location. The museum was expanded to 264,000 square feet, twice its original size, in 1974.

The museum also features a 25,000-volume non-circulating art reference library, a Museum Shop, and a Sales and Rental Gallery specializing in works by local artists. The Link Restaurant serves lunch, light refreshments, and Sunday brunch. Services offered by the museum include daily public tours, a monthly Expertise Clinic, and the Arts Resource and Information Center (870-3131). Wheelchairs and strollers are available at the museum entrance.

Open Tue-W, F-Sat 10 a.m. to 5 p.m.; Thu 10 to 9; Sun noon to 5. Admission is $2 for adults, $1 for students, and free for members, children under 12, seniors, scheduled school groups, and AFDC cardholders. Public admission is free Thu from 5 to 9 p.m. Free ramp parking is available for museum visitors at the corner of Third Av. S. and E. 25th St.

MINNESOTA MUSEUM OF ART, 305 St. Peter St. (Kellogg and St. Peter), St. Paul. ▶7
227-7613

The Minnesota Museum of Art, a member agency of the St. Paul-Ramsey Arts and Science Council, maintains a permanent collection at the above address and changing exhibitions on the second floor of the Landmark Center, 75 W. Fifth St., St. Paul. The permanent collection includes 20th century drawings, sculpture, and paintings; Asian art, including graphics, ceramics, and textiles; and African, Northwest Coast Indian,

and contemporary American crafts. In 1982 changing exhibitions will emphasize 20th century American art.

Activities of the permanent-collection gallery include changing exhibitions, Drawing USA (a biennial drawing competition), the Arts Awareness Program for the St. Paul schools, teacher training, and an internship program. The museum restaurant serves buffet lunches. The permanent collection gallery is open Tue-F 10 a.m. to 5 p.m.; Sun 10-5. The Landmark Center gallery is open Tue-Sat 10 a.m. to 5 p.m.; Sun 1 to 5 p.m. Admission to both is free.

WALKER ART CENTER, Vineland Pl., Minneapolis. ▶2
375-7600

The Walker Art Center, one of the most prestigious museums in the country, houses an extensive collection of 20th century arts with an emphasis on works by American artists. The Walker is particularly strong in contemporary sculpture, featuring works by George Segal, Claes Oldenburg, and Isamu Noguchi. Works of contemporary Minnesota artists such as Steve Beyers and Siah Armajani also are featured.

In 1982 the Walker will present two major exhibitions, along with its regular exhibition schedule. The first will feature more than 200 paintings, drawings, graphics, and architectural forms of the De Stijl period, an influential Dutch movement covering the years 1917-1931. Works in the exhibition will be from six major Dutch museums and from collections in France and America. The De Stijl works will be shown at only one other American museum in 1982. The second major exhibition will feature about 500 photographs from Sweden, Norway, Denmark, Finland, and Iceland comprising an ambitious display of images of experiences of Scandinavian cultures through successive generations. After its premiere at Walker, the Scandinavian photography exhibition will travel to the International Center of Photography, and several other museums in the United States and Scandinavia.

What is now the Walker Art Center began as the private art collection of Minneapolis lumberman T. B. Walker. The Walker Gallery opened to the public in roughly the present location in 1927. The widely acclaimed new Walker Art Center building opened in 1971.

The Walker sponsors public lectures and tours, plus film, dance, music, and poetry performances and events. It also publishes *Design Quarterly*, and maintains a gift shop and the Gallery 8 restaurant. Calendars of Walker Art Center activities are available in the lobby.

Open Tue-Sat 10 a.m. to 8 p.m. June through Feb.; 10 to 5 March through May; Sun 11 to 5 all year. Free admission.

Sales Galleries

Unless otherwise noted, works at the following galleries are for sale and admission is free.

ALLAN F. GALLERY, 2821 Hennepin Av. S., Minneapolis. ▶2
872-7712

Original works by 20th century European, Mexican, and North American artists. Some sculpture. Open Tue-Sat 10 a.m. to 7:30 p.m. (closed Sun and M).

AMERICAN WILDLIFE ART GALLERIES, 926 Plymouth Bldg., 12 S. Sixth St., Minneapolis. ▶1
338-7247

All wildlife and Western art; mostly oils, watercolors, and prints by Americans. Open M-F 9 a.m. to noon and 2 to 4:30 p.m.

BREAM GALLERY, 961 Grand Av. (between Lexington and Victoria Crossing), St. Paul. ▶8
221-0020

Contemporary works by national, regional, and local artists displayed in an old Victorian house. Monthly shows feature an individual artist. Open M-F 10 a.m. to 5 p.m.; Sat 10 a.m. to 4 p.m.

VERN CARVER GALLERY, 1018 LaSalle Av., Minneapolis. ▶1
339-3449

Mostly prints and posters, as well as works by local artists. Occasional shows by Minnesota artists. Open M-F 9:30 a.m. to 5:30 p.m.; Sat 9:30 a.m. to 2 p.m.

DEAN GALLERY, 2815 Hennepin Av. S., Minneapolis. ▶2
872-4976

Posters and graphics. Located in Uptown area near several other galleries. Open M and Thu 10 a.m. to 8 p.m.; T, W, F 10 to 6; Sat 10 to 5.

ELAYNE GALLERIES, INC., 6111 Excelsior Blvd., St. Louis Park. ▶5
926-1511

A "one-stop" gallery featuring all kinds of art, including works by Norman Rockwell, Leroy Neiman, and Richard Guindon (former Minnesota cartoonist). Open M-W, F-Sat 10:30 a.m. to 6 p.m.; Thu 10:30 to 8:30.

THE DOLLY FITERMAN ART GALLERY, Plymouth Bldg., Suite 935, 12 S. Sixth St., Minneapolis. ▶1
370-8722

Contemporary originals: prints, drawings, graphics, some paintings and sculpture. Shows every month. Open Tue-F 10 a.m. to 4:30 p.m.; Sat noon to 4; Sun and M by appointment.

FRIENDS GALLERY, MINNEAPOLIS INSTITUTE OF ARTS, 2400 Third Av. S., Minneapolis. ▶2
870-3160

Major works of prominent Midwestern painters and sculptors. All works subject to curatorial approval. Rentals to Society of Fine Arts members. Open Tue-W, F-Sat 10 a.m. to 5 p.m.; Thu 10 to 8; Sun noon to 4:30.

GROVELAND GALLERY, 25 Groveland Terrace, Minneapolis. ▶2
377-7800

Works of regional, professional artists for sale or rent. Works lean toward recognizable imagery rather than the abstract. Oils, acrylics, watercolors, some sculpture; clay and glass fill one room. Shows change every month. Located in

an old mansion behind the Walker Art Center. Open Tue-F noon to 5 p.m.; Sat noon to 4 p.m.

GLEN HANSON GALLERY, 130 N. Fourth St., Minneapolis. ▶1
339-5154

Contemporary work by regional, though some national, artists. Shows change about every five weeks. Open Tue-Sat 11 a.m. to 4 p.m.

IMAGES GALLERY, 5050 Excelsior Blvd., Suite 313 (Citizens Bank Building), St. Louis Park.
927-5565 ▶5

Original early American and contemporary oils, watercolors, sculptures, bronzes, and etchings. Emphasis on Western and American Indian themes. Open Tue-F 11 a.m. to 5 p.m.; Sat 11 to 4; and by appointment.

FLOYD JOHNSON GALLERY, 420 First Av. N., Minneapolis. ▶1
332-6012

Paintings, prints, drawings, and posters on Western, sports, and Viking themes. Monthly rentals available. Open Tue-Sat 11 a.m. to 5 p.m.

KLABAL GALLERY INC., 1716 Mt. Curve Av., Minneapolis. ▶2
377-6290

Open by appointment only, this gallery features limited editions of prints and sculptures by 20th-century European masters.

KRAMER GALLERY, 229 E. Sixth St., St. Paul. ▶7
225-0863

Late 19th- and early 20th-century European paintings, watercolors, and prints, as well as fine antiques. Specialties also include early Minnesota artists and American Indian artifacts. Open M-F 9 a.m. to 5 p.m.; Sat 10:30 to 2:30.

LESCH GALLERY, 122 Butler Square, Minneapolis. ▶1
332-4992

Paintings, silkscreens, and sculpture by regional and national artists. Shows change once a month. Open M-Thu 10 a.m. to 9 p.m.; F-Sat 10 to midnight; Sun noon to 5.

LORING GALLERY, 705 Douglas Av., Minneapolis. ▶1
374-4004

All original works. Mostly contemporary oils and watercolors by regional artists. Six shows a year. Open W-Sun noon to 6.

MILLS GALLERY, 12926 Minnetonka Blvd., Minnetonka. ▶5
933-8803

Variety of paintings, watercolors, and sculpture by regional and national artists. Also displays ceramics, fibers, and jewelry. Open M-Sat 10 a.m. to 5 p.m.

MINNESOTA ARTISTS' GALLERY, 29 University Av. S.E., Minneapolis. ▶2
378-9668

A cooperative displaying the works of its 35 to 40 members, Minnesota Artists' Gallery shows china and pottery as well as traditional and contemporary two-dimensional works. New shows every month. Open Tue-Sat noon to 5 p.m.

OSBORNE GALLERY, 1074 Grand Av. (Grand at Lexington), St. Paul. ▶8
224-3801

Mostly works by local artists including pottery, graphics, and sculpture. Open M-F 9 a.m. to 5:30 p.m.; Sat 9 to 4.

C.G. REIN GALLERIES, 3646 W. 70th St., Edina. ▶5
927-4331

More than 10,000 paintings, graphics, and sculptures by regional and world artists. Open M-F 10 a.m. to 9 p.m.; Sat 10 to 6; Sun noon to 5.

BARRY RICHARD GALLERY, 102 Lumber Exchange Building, 10 S. Fifth St., Minneapolis. ▶1
333-7620

Eclectic mix of paintings, prints, drawings, sculpture, and multimedia works by regional and national artists. New show every month. Open Tue, Thu, F noon to 9 p.m.; W, Sat noon to 5:30.

PETER M. DAVID GALLERY, 430 Oak Grove St., Minneapolis. ▶1
870-7344

Contemporary works, mostly on paper, by local and national artists. Prints, drawings, photography, artists' books. Some sculpture and paintings on canvas. Shows change every six weeks. Open Tue-F 11 a.m. to 5 p.m.; Sat noon to 4 (September to May only).

SUZANNE KOHN GALLERY, 1690 Grand Av., St. Paul. ▶8
699-0477

Contemporary paintings and prints by regional artists. Open M-Sat 1 to 5 p.m.; by appointment only July and August.

JOHN C. STOLLER & CO., 400 Marquette Av. (Marquette Building), Minneapolis. ►1
871-7060

Contemporary American paintings, drawings, sculpture, and graphics. Open by appointment, M-Sat 10 a.m. to 5:30 p.m.

UNICORN GALLERIES, 53 S. Ninth St. (at Nicollet Mall), Minneapolis. ►1
332-0931

Contemporary sculpture, paintings, and graphics by international artists. Usually four shows per year lasting six weeks each. Open Tue-Sat 10 a.m. to 6 p.m.

W.A.R.M. (Women's Art Registry of Minnesota), 414 First Av. N., Minneapolis. ►1
332-5672

Art by Minnesota women, mostly by members of W.A.R.M., although works by invited artists are also displayed. Shows change about every five weeks, and two or three shows usually run concurrently. The art registry, available for examination at the gallery, is a catalog of slides and samples of works of member artists. Open Tue-F 11 a.m. to 4 p.m.; Sat noon to 5.

WESTLAKE GALLERY, 1612 W. Lake St., Minneapolis. ►2
822-0600

Cooperative gallery of 14 artists working in oils, acrylics, watercolors, pottery, weaving, and other media. New shows every six weeks by member or guest artists. "Pots

and knots" room downstairs. Open Tue-Sat 11 a.m. to 5 p.m.

WYER-PEARCE GALLERY, 201 Mill St., Excelsior. ►5
474-6966

Realism by Minnesota artists, including landscapes, sculpture, and lithographs. Works for sale or rent. Shows change about every six weeks. Located in a restored Victorian mansion overlooking Lake Minnetonka. Open M-Sat 9 a.m. to 5 p.m.; other times by appointment.

Specialty Galleries

While the majority of Twin Cities galleries feature a variety of art, including art of a particular period or by a particular group of artists, a few center their offerings on a specific theme or medium. The following list is a sampling of these more specialized galleries. Unless otherwise noted, admission is free and all works are for sale.

Native American Art

THE RAVEN GALLERY, 3825 W. 50th St., Minneapolis. ►2
925-4474

Tribal art by Eskimos, Native American, and other Indian artists. Paintings, prints, sculpture, weavings, wall-hangings, masks, and other art forms. Shows change at irregular intervals. Call about mailing list. Open M-Sat 10 a.m. to 5:30 p.m.

JUDITH STERN GALLERY, 118 N. Fourth St., Minneapolis. ►1
338-5292

Works by living American Indian artists from the Upper Midwest and Southwest. Paintings, sculpture, lithographs, weavings, and posters. Also a unique collection of Indian-inspired clothing. Occasional shows. Open Tue-Sat 9 a.m. to 3 p.m.

Photography

J. HUNT GALLERY, 3015 E. 25th St., Minneapolis. ►2
721-3146

Minnesota's only privately owned photography gallery, featuring works of national, international, and some local photographers; some sculpture. Open Sat-Sun 1 to 5 p.m. and by appointment.

Textiles

TEXTILE ARTS ALLIANCE, 1721 Mt. Curve Av., Minneapolis. ►2
377-5688

Only gallery in Minnesota showing strictly textile art. Wall-hangings, baskets, weavings, and soft sculpture displayed in a Mt. Curve mansion. Features museum-quality work of Hmong refugees. Open by appointment only.

Theater Art

OPENING NIGHT, 920 Nicollet Mall, Suite 228, Minneapolis. ►1
339-1576

Sketches and watercolors of original set and costume designs. Lots of photography and a line of erotic sketches. Open M-F 9 a.m. to 5 p.m.; Sat 10 to 3 (sometimes closed on Sat).

College and University Galleries

Hamline University
LEARNING CENTER GALLERY, 1536 Hewitt Av., St. Paul. 641-2296 ►8

Teaching gallery for the Fine Arts Department of Hamline University. Features works relating to subjects being taught. All types of artists represented. Most work for sale. Shows change every month; no shows in the summer. Open M-F 8 a.m. to 8 p.m. during the school year.

Macalester College
MACALESTER GALLERIES, Janet Wallace Fine Arts Center, 1600 Grand Av., St. Paul. ►8
696-6416

Exhibitions of contemporary works by regional artists; historical and special topics. Student exhibitions each spring. Indoor garden gallery. Shows change monthly. Open M-F 9 a.m. to 9 p.m.; Sat hours vary.

Minneapolis College
of Art and Design
MINNEAPOLIS COLLEGE OF ART AND DESIGN GALLERY, 133 E. 25th St., Minneapolis. ►2
870-3285

Works by regional and national artists most of the year; faculty and student shows in April and May. Shows change monthly and open with free public receptions. Call or write for schedule. Exhibition only; nothing for sale. Open M-F 9 a.m. to 9 p.m.; Sat 9 to 5; Sun noon to 5.

University of Minnesota
COFFMAN UNION GALLERY,

University of Minnesota, 300 Washington Av. S.E., Minneapolis. ►2
376-1660, 373-7600

First and third floors of Coffman Memorial Union. Unusual work by regional artists and students. New shows every three weeks with the public invited to opening nights. Most works for sale. Open during the school year M-F 10 a.m. to 3 p.m.; Thu 10 to 7. Call about summer hours.

GOLDSTEIN GALLERY, 241 McNeal Hall, 1895 Buford Av., St. Paul. ►8
373-1032, 376-1488

Student, graduate, and faculty shows relating to subjects taught in the Department of Home Economics. Decorative arts, design, some studio art, and items from the historic costume collection are shown. Exhibition only. Open M-F 8 a.m. to 4:30 p.m.

JAQUES GALLERY, Bell Museum of Natural History, 10 Church St. S.E. (University Av. at 17th Av. S.E.), Minneapolis. ►2
373-2423

Four to six shows each year of natural history art including works by Minnesota museum artist Francis Lee Jaques. Subjects include plants, animals, and natural environments. Exhibition gallery only—nothing for sale. Open during shows Tue-Sat 9 a.m. to 5 p.m.; Sun 1 to 5 p.m.

KATHERINE E. NASH GALLERY, Lower level, Willey Hall, 225 19th Av. S., Minneapolis. ►2
376-1185

On the University of Minnesota's West Bank campus, just north of the Washington Av. Bridge and east of Cedar Av. Mostly contemporary art by local, national, and student artists. Many works for sale. Shows change about once a month. Open M, Tue, F 9 a.m. to 4:30 p.m.; Wed, Thu 9 to 7; Sat, Sun noon to 4.

ST. PAUL STUDENT CENTER GALLERIES, 2017 Buford Av., St. Paul. ►8
373-1051

Lower level and second floor of St. Paul Student Center. All kinds of works by staff, student, and outside artists. Most work for sale. Shows change monthly. Open M-F 10 a.m. to 7 p.m.; Sat, Sun noon to 5.

UNIVERSITY GALLERY, Northrop Auditorium, 84 Church St. S.E., Minneapolis. ►2
373-3424

Third and fourth floors of Northrop Auditorium. Permanent collection of early 20th-century American works and some 17th- and 18th-century prints. Shows of mostly two-dimensional works by national and international artists change every six weeks. Exhibition gallery only; nothing is for sale. Prints, watercolors, and some oil paintings from a special collection can be rented for a nominal fee per academic quarter. Rental office at M-16 Northrop Auditorium, 373-5685. Catalogs from major exhibitions can be purchased at gallery office. Open M, W, F 11 a.m. to 4 p.m.; Tue, Thu 11 to 8; Sun 2 to 5.

Normandale Community College
NORMANDALE COMMUNITY COLLEGE GALLERY, 9700 France Av. S., Bloomington. ►6
830-9340

Work of local, regional, and national artists. Paintings, drawings, heavy emphasis on photography. Usually two shows running concurrently. Some work for sale. Open during academic seasons M-Thu 8 a.m. to 10:30 p.m.; F-Sat 8 to 4.

College of St. Catherine
CATHERINE G. MURPHY GALLERIES, Visual Arts Building, 204 Randolph Av., St. Paul. 690-6520 ►8

Features works by student, faculty, and other artists. One show per month, closed parts of June and August. Some works for sale. Open M-F 8 a.m. to 8 p.m.; Sat, Sun 1 to 8. Call about summer hours.

Community Center Galleries

Most of the following centers offer art classes, cultural programs, or other community activities as well as providing display space for local and regional artists. Most are non-profit. Unless otherwise noted, admission to these galleries is free and some of the art work displayed is for sale.

AFRICAN AMERICAN CULTURAL CENTER GALLERY, 2429 S. Eighth St., Minneapolis. ►2
332-3506

Paintings, photographs, sculpture, and other media. Mostly works by black artists, often with an ethnic perspective. Occasional displays of African artifacts. Open M-Tue 9 a.m. to 5 p.m.; W-F 9 to 8; Sat 10 to 3.

ART CENTER OF MINNESOTA, 2240 Northshore Dr., Crystal Bay. ►5
473-7361

Main gallery has two or three shows of established area or regional artists per year. Two smaller galleries feature work by center students and instructors. Open M-Thu 9 a.m. to 4:30 p.m. and 7 to 10 p.m.; F 9 to 4:30; Sat 9 to noon. Gourmet lunch served M-F noon to 1 p.m. at the Center Cuisine.

BLOOMINGTON ART CENTER, 10206 Penn Av. S., Bloomington. ►6
887-9667

Features emerging local artists working in a variety of media. Open M-F 10 a.m. to 5 p.m., and most evenings (closing hours vary according to class schedules); Sat 9 to noon; Sun 1 to 4.

DAKOTA CENTER FOR THE ARTS (Sky Gallery), 222 N. Concord Exchange (above Globe Publishing), South St. Paul. ►12
457-1220

Oil paintings, watercolors, ceramics, jewelry, cards, etc., mostly by local artists. Shows change about once a month. All works are for sale. Rental service available. Open M-F 10 a.m. to 4:30 p.m.; first Sun of the month, 1 to 4 p.m.

EDINA ART CENTER, 4701 W. 64th St., Edina. ►5
929-4555

Original art in a variety of media by art center instructors, students, and other regional artists. Monthly exhibits, plus special events. Located in a large country house at the edge of Cornelia Park in Edina. Open M, Tue, Thu 9 a.m. to 10 p.m.; Wed 9 to 3:30 and 7 to 10 p.m.; F 9 to 3:30; Sat 10 to noon.

GALLERY C, Jewish Community Center of Greater Minneapolis, 4330 S. Cedar Lake Rd., St. Louis Park. ►5
377-8330

Works by national and regional artists working in a variety of media. Occasional exhibits of artifacts of ancient Judaic culture. Usually seven shows a year, with concurrent shows often mounted in two smaller exhibition spaces at the center. Most work for sale. Open Sun-Thu 9 a.m. to 10:30 p.m.; F 9 to 5. Call about summer hours.

MINNEAPOLIS REGIONAL NATIVE AMERICAN CENTER GALLERY, 1530 E. Franklin Av., Minneapolis. ►2
871-9421

Native American paintings, drawings, photos, and artifacts. Shows change about every six weeks. Although this is a display gallery only, there is a craft shop at the center. Open M-F 10 a.m. to 5 p.m.

MINNESOTA ARTISTS EXHIBITION PROGRAM, Minneapolis Institute of Arts, 2400 Third Av. S., Minneapolis. ►2

Although not located in a community art center, this gallery does have a distinct community emphasis. It is a gallery within the Minneapolis Institute of Arts showing all kinds of works by Minnesota artists. Although this is an exhibition gallery, visitors may contact artists to purchase works on display. Shows change at least every two months. Museum admission required for visit. Open Tue-W, F-Sat 10 a.m. to 5 p.m.; Thu 10 to 9; Sun noon to 5.

PILLSBURY-WAITE NEIGHBORHOOD CULTURAL ARTS DEPARTMENT, 3501 Chicago Av. S., Minneapolis. ►2
824-0708

This community center gallery displays works by community and professional artists as well as works by students at the center. Some works for sale. Open M-F 9 a.m. to 9 p.m.

SONS OF NORWAY CULTURAL CENTER GALLERY, 1455 W. Lake St., Minneapolis. ►2
827-3611

Although a second-floor gallery features artwork with a Scandinavian influence, other types of work are displayed. New shows monthly. Open M-F 8 a.m. to 10 p.m.; Sat 10 to 5. All works are for sale.

Special Collections

Many fine collections of art exist in the Twin Cities that are rarely seen. The following is a sampling of these collections to which some public access is allowed.

DAYTON HUDSON CORP. ART COLLECTION, IDS Tower, 800 S. Eighth St., Minneapolis. ►1
370-6657

This corporate art collection

consists of more than 100 works, most of them done by artists currently living and working in Minnesota. The works are displayed throughout the offices of the Dayton Hudson corporate headquarters in the IDS Tower in downtown Minneapolis. The public can view parts of the collection by visiting the corridors and reception areas of the Tower's 15th floor during regular business hours. Call for a copy of a brochure that describes several of the works in the collection.

NINTH FEDERAL RESERVE BANK ART COLLECTION, 250 Marquette Av., Minneapolis. ▶1 340-2279

Besides four major sculptures displayed on the plaza outside the Federal Reserve Bank in downtown Minneapolis, there is a collection of more than 150 art works displayed throughout the bank, mostly for employee enjoyment. The collection includes only works by artists who have lived or worked in the Ninth Federal Reserve District; the works have been acquired mostly since 1973 with an eye toward decorating the new building and supporting the regional art community. A short tour of the collection is available to groups of four or more by pre-arranged appointment only.

GENERAL MILLS CORPORATE ART COLLECTION, 9200 Wayzata Blvd., Golden Valley. ▶4 540-7269

This 1,100-work collection features 20th-century masters like Picasso and Toulouse-Lautrec. General Mills started collecting the art in 1958, mostly for the enjoyment of its employees. A majority of the works are by contemporary artists, and recently the company has been concentrating on collecting works of living artists whose art reflects the world in which General Mills operates. Because the works are displayed throughout the hallways and offices of the headquarters building, visitors should inquire about an appointment for a short tour. Several large sculptures are displayed on the lawn for unrestricted public viewing.

JAMES J. HILL REFERENCE LIBRARY, Fourth St. at Market St., St. Paul. ▶7 227-9531

Hidden in the cool, vaulted domain of this business reference library is a collection of more than 70 watercolors of North American Indian life done by artist Seth Eastman, at one time a resident of Fort Snelling. A collection of lithographs by Karl Bodmer, used to illustrate a volume entitled *Travels in the Interior of North America, 1832–1834,* are also housed at the Hill Library. Both collections are filed in a restricted area and are not on display, but private viewings may be arranged by appointment. The library also has copies of the books both Eastman's and Bodmer's works have been printed in, and these are more accessible. A very large collection of Edward S. Curtis photographs of American Indians, taken in the late 1800s, may also be seen at the library. Library hours are M-Thu 9 a.m. to 9 p.m.; F-Sat 9 to 5 in the winter; M-Tue 9 a.m. to 8 p.m., W-F 9 to 5:30 summers.

Chapter Thirteen

THINGS TO SEE, THINGS TO DO

KEY NUMBERS

Minnesota Department of Tourism: 296-5029
Greater Minneapolis Chamber of Commerce: 370-9132
Minneapolis Convention and Tourism Commission: 348-4313
St. Paul Chamber of Commerce: 222-5561
St. Paul Convention, Exhibition and Tourism Commission: 297-9303

TOUR SERVICES

GRAY LINE SIGHTSEEING BUS TOURS, 3118 Nicollet Av., Minneapolis.
827-4071

Buses pick up sightseers (individuals or groups) at the Minneapolis Bus Depot, Downtown Holiday Inn, and Radisson, Leamington and Curtis hotels in Minneapolis. Tickets available at all of the above. Tours given Memorial Day through Labor Day only. Fees are $13.50 for Twin Cities tour, which begins at 9 a.m. and lasts all day; $9.50 for Minneapolis tour only, which begins at 1 and runs to 3:30 p.m.; and $6.50 for the two-hour St. Paul-only tour, which begins at 8:45 a.m.

JEFFERSON TOURS, 1206 Currie Av., Minneapolis.
335-8745

Motor coach day tours to areas

(See Locator Key Map, pages 8-9)

▶1 Mpls. Downtown
▶2 Mpls. Excluding Downtown
▶3 Mpls. North Suburbs
▶4 Mpls. Northwest Suburbs
▶5 Mpls. Southwest Suburbs
▶6 Mpls. South Suburbs

▶7 St. Paul Downtown
▶8 St. Paul Excluding Downtown
▶9 St. Paul North Suburbs
▶10 St. Paul Northeast Suburbs
▶11 St. Paul Southeast Suburbs
▶12 St. Paul South Suburbs

surrounding the Twin Cities. Groups only. Fees begin at $28 per person, which includes lunch. Call for reservations as far in advance as possible.

LIEMANDT'S TOUR AND CONVENTION SERVICES, 1010 Second Av. S., Minneapolis. 339-2302

Custom-designed tours, groups only. Call for details.

MAGIC CARPET TOURS, 212 River Woods Lane, Burnsville. 890-0686

Custom tours for small groups (four-person minimum). Twelve Twin Cities tour plans; transportation by van. Average fee is $10 per person. Call for information.

TAILOR MAID TOURS, 427 Woodlawn Av., St. Paul. 699-7317

Tours of the metropolitan area for large groups only. Half-day sightseeing tours, full-day excursions, trips to evening events. Transportation by bus.

TWIN TOWN TOURS, 1111 Nicollet Mall, Minneapolis. 377-4921, 371-5654

Custom-designed bus tours for groups only. Twin Cities area, with some outstate tours available. A program of the Women's Association of the Minnesota Orchestra (WAMSO), Twin Town Tours' proceeds go to the Minnesota Orchestra.

VALLEY TOURS, INC., Stillwater. 439-6110

Bus and walking tours of historic river towns from Taylors Falls to Winona and excursions to other Minnesota and Wisconsin towns. Small group walking tours of Stillwater; larger groups required for bus trips.

CITY VIEWS AND OVERLOOKS

IDS TOWER OBSERVATION DECK, IDS Tower, 80 S. Eighth St., Minneapolis. ►1 333-6656

The tower's 51st-floor deck offers a spectacular bird's eye view of Minneapolis, the Mississippi, and St. Paul. On a clear day parts of 12 Minnesota counties are visible, with the view extending as far as 35 miles. Open daily 10 a.m. to 7 p.m. in winter, 10 to 10 during the summer months. Admission $2.75 for adults, $1.50 for children and seniors.

INDIAN MOUNDS PARK, Earl St. and Mounds Blvd., St. Paul. ►8

This park, which is the site of several Indian burial mounds, sits on a bluff above West St. Paul and the Mississippi River. River traffic and industrial areas along the river can be viewed from here.

LOCK AND DAM #1, E. 50th St. and the Mississippi River, Minneapolis. ►2 724-2971

Closed for construction until July 1982, Lock and Dam #1 provides a good perspective from which to view the river, dam, and a functioning lock. Located near Minnehaha Park, the revamped lock-and-dam area will have a visitors building and interpretive signs.

LOCK AND DAM #2, off Hwy. 61 in Hastings. ►12
437-3150

Lock and Dam #2 also offers a view of a working lock, located south of the Twin Cities on the Upper Mississippi. Open daylight hours March through November.

SCENIC DRIVES

The following are among several urban routes that provide a scenic drive in any season.

MINNEHAHA PKWY. ►2

Pick up the parkway at Hiawatha Av. (Hwy. 55) near Minnehaha Park in south Minneapolis. Follow the elm-shaded route along Minnehaha Creek through several attractive residential neighborhoods. Lake Nokomis can be seen from the parkway just south of the Cedar Av. intersection. After about five miles, the parkway joins the parkways that circle Lake Harriet, Lake Calhoun, Lake of the Isles, and Cedar Lake. Wirth Park, north of Cedar Lake, provides a logical end point for this drive.

SUMMIT AV. ►8

Pick up Summit at the St. Paul Cathedral, on the hill just west of downtown St. Paul. Summit jogs south and then proceeds due west past some of the most elegant and historic residences in the city. Summit extends more than four miles west to the Mississippi River, becoming a wide, tree-lined boulevard as it moves away from the cathedral. Finish the drive at the campus of the College of St. Thomas, or continue north or south along scenic Mississippi River Blvd. at the western terminus of the avenue.

THE RIVER PARKWAYS ►2, 8

Parkways following the banks of the Mississippi River can be picked up near the Franklin Av. Bridge just south of the University of Minnesota's Minneapolis campus. On the west bank, pick up West River Pkwy. and follow it south to Minnehaha Park. You will pass both residential and park areas. On the east bank, take River Rd. South until it joins Mississippi River Blvd. Follow Mississippi River Blvd. south for views of the river and many fine homes. End the drive at Hidden Falls Park, or continue on Shepard Rd. to downtown St. Paul.

HISTORIC SITES AND MUSEUMS

CEDARHURST MANSION, 6940 Keats Av. S., Cottage Grove. 459-9741 ►11

Historic 1860s mansion on a 10-acre estate. Now a private home, the mansion is open for public tours Tue at 10:30 a.m. and 1 p.m. 1½-hour tour includes a lecture on the history of the house and a pipe organ demonstration. Admission $2.25.

DAKOTA COUNTY HISTORICAL MUSEUM, 130 Third Av. N., South St. Paul. ►12
451-6260

This museum has three 19th-century period rooms, as well as

exhibits of fossils, farm tools, military items, and Minnesota birds. Open Tue-F 8 a.m. to 4:30 p.m., Sat 8 to 1. Admission is free.

THE FILLEBROWN HOUSE, 303 Lake Av., White Bear Lake. 426-0479 ►10

One of the last cottages remaining from the period when White Bear Lake served as a summer resort for the wealthy families of St. Paul's Summit Av. Open Sun 1 to 4 p.m. June through September. Admission $1, 50 cents for children.

W.H.C. FOLSOM HOUSE, Government Rd., Taylors Falls. ►10 465-3125

A well-preserved 1855 house with original furnishings in a St. Croix River town north of Stillwater. The five-bedroom house was built by lumber magnate W.H.C. Folsom and was occupied by members of his family until it was sold to the state of Minnesota in 1978. Open seven days a week 1 to 4:30 p.m. June through mid-October. Admission $1.50, 50 cents for children.

FORT SNELLING, Hwys. 5 and 55. ►8 726-1171

Self-guided tours of the "birthplace of Minnesota" start with orientation in the schoolhouse. Visitors then proceed to tour other parts of the restored military outpost on their own. Employees are strategically placed to guide visitors and answer questions. Each hour there are guard drills and musket- and cannon-firing.

Craft shops feature skilled laborers in authentic costumes. Orientation begins every 15 minutes. Open daily June through Labor Day 10 a.m. to 5 p.m. Open May, September, and October M-F 9 to 4:30; Sat, Sun 10-5. Fee $1.50 for adults, 25 cents for children five to 16; children under five admitted free.

ARD GODFREY HOUSE, Richard Chute Square, at 28 S.E. University and S.E. Central Avs., Minneapolis. ►2 870-8001

Oldest remaining frame house in Minneapolis, recently restored by the Minnesota Women's Club. Open M, F noon to 3; Sat, Sun 1 to 4 June 1 to October 15. Admission $1, 25 cents for students.

HENNEPIN COUNTY HISTORICAL SOCIETY MUSEUM, 2303 Third Av. S., Minneapolis. 870-1329 ►2

Thirty rooms of exhibits include miniature village of the early 1900s, antique doll collection, blacksmith's shop, early doctor's and dentist's offices, a Victorian parlor, 1920s kitchen, antique clocks and watches, china, silver, glassware, and pioneer and Indian artifacts. Museum also has archives and library. Open Tue-F 9 a.m. to 4:30 p.m.; Sat-Sun 1 to 5 p.m. Closed Sat June through August. Free admission.

JAMES J. HILL HOUSE, 240 Summit Av., St. Paul. ►8 296-7129

Opulent red sandstone mansion built by Minnesota railroad builder James J. Hill. The house, which is being restored, is expected to be open for tours sometime in 1982. Call for updated information.

OLIVER H. KELLY FARM, Hwy. 10, 2½ miles east of Elk River. ►3
726-1171

This was the experimental farm of the founder of the national Grange movement. Farmhouse, working farm with animals. Open seven days a week, May through October, 10 a.m. to 5 p.m.; November through April Sat 10 to 5, Sun noon to 5. Admission is free.

MINNEHAHA DEPOT, Minnehaha Av. near E. 49th St., Minneapolis. ►2
721-1171

Attractive old train depot once used by Minneapolis residents visiting Minnehaha Park and the now-defunct Longfellow Zoo. Open June through September Sun 1 to 5 p.m. Admission is free.

MINNESOTA HISTORICAL SOCIETY, 690 Cedar St. (across from state Capitol), St. Paul. ►8
296-6126

Regularly changing exhibits on Minnesota history, plus a library with an outstanding collection of historical photographs, provide a wealth of knowledge about Minnesota's past. Minnesota newspaper collection, genealogy reference library. Open M-Sat 8:30 a.m. to 5 p.m.; Sun 1 to 4 p.m. Free admission.

MINNESOTA TRANSPORTATION MUSEUM, P. O. Box 1300, Hopkins 55343
890-2830

Without a home at this writing, the Minnesota Transportation Museum collects and restores old trains, streetcars, motor buses— almost anything that ran on rails or has some local significance. Museum members operate the Lake Harriet Trolley (see page 258). Some of the museum's collection is displayed at different times at various Twin Cities locations. Call for information on current displays.

MURPHY'S LANDING (MINNESOTA VALLEY RESTORATION), Hwy. 101 east of Shakopee. ►6
445-6900

Eighty-seven-acre site with some 20 buildings shows a cross-section of 19th-century Minnesota life. Open summer only except for special Christmas program December 1-23. Hour-and-a-half tours given Tue-F 9 a.m. to 4 p.m.; Sat, Sun 1 to 5 p.m. Fees are $3.50 for adults and $2.50 for students and seniors; children under six admitted free. Group rates available.

ALEXANDER RAMSEY HOUSE, 265 S. Exchange St. (off Irvine Park), St. Paul. ►8
296-0100

The home of Minnesota's first territorial governor, built in 1872, still has many of its original furnishings. Special Christmas programs should not be missed. Fee is $1.50; children under 16 free with parents. Tours given M-F 10 a.m. to 4 p.m.; Sat, Sun 1 to 4:30 p.m. Reservations required for groups of 10 or more. Gift shop.

RAMSEY COUNTY HISTORI-

CAL SOCIETY—GIBBS FARM, Cleveland Av. N. and Larpenteur Av., Falcon Heights. ►9
646-8629

Displays include 1870 farm house and artifacts, red barn with tools and animals, blacksmith's and woodworkers' shop, 1870s schoolhouse. Crafts demonstrations are held Sundays. Open Tue-F 10 a.m. to 4 p.m.; Sun noon to 4. Tours available to groups of 10 or more by calling six weeks in advance. Closed January through mid-April except for tours. Admission is $1.50 for adults, $1.25 for seniors, $1 for teenagers, and 50 cents for children 12 and younger.

SIBLEY HOUSE MUSEUM, Water St. (block north of Hwy. 13), Mendota. ►12
452-1596

The house of Henry Hastings Sibley, first governor of the state of Minnesota, is the oldest private home in the state, dating to 1836. Restored in 1909, the house contains some furnishings dating to the 1850s. Hour-and-a-half tour also includes the adjacent Jean Faribault House. Faribault was an early 19th-century fur trader and guide to Col. Henry Leavenworth, the first commander of Fort Snelling. His house, built in 1837, is now a museum for Indian artifacts. Open May 1 to October 31. Tours given Tue-Sat 10 a.m. to 4 p.m.; Sun 1 to 6 p.m. Fees are $1.50 for adults and 50 cents for children six to 15; children under six admitted free. Reservations required for groups of 10 or more.

WASHINGTON COUNTY HISTORICAL SOCIETY MUSEUM AND WARDEN'S HOUSE, 602 N. Main St., Stillwater. ►10
439-5956

This 16-room house was the warden's residence for Minnesota's first state prison. Period furniture, costumes, a pioneer kitchen, and handmade lumberjack tools are displayed. Many of the items relate to Stillwater's history. Open May 1 to November 1; Tue, Thu, Sat, Sun 2 to 5 p.m. Admission $1 for adults, 50 cents for children. Group tours can be arranged.

SCIENCE MUSEUMS

BAKKEN LIBRARY, 3537 Zenith Av. S., Minneapolis. ►2
927-6508

A cross between a rare-book library and a museum of antique medical and electrical machines, the Bakken Library is an excellent place to study the development of the medical applications of electricity. Located in an old mansion near Lake Calhoun. By appointment only, M-F 9 a.m. to 5 p.m.

BELL MUSEUM OF NATURAL HISTORY, 10 Church St. S.E. (at 17th and University Avs. S.E.), University of Minnesota, Minneapolis. ►2
373-2423

Exhibits feature habitats and many birds and mammals of Minnesota. Touch and See Room allows handling of bones, pelts and other natural objects. Oil paintings, watercolors, and sketches by Minnesota wildlife artist Francis Lee Jaques are housed in the Museum's Jaques Gallery. Open Tue-Sat 9 a.m. to 5 p.m.; Sun 1 to 5 p.m. Free admission. Free guided tours for eight or more with two weeks advance notice.

SCIENCE MUSEUM'S CHILDREN'S CENTER AND PLANETARIUM, Minneapolis Public Library, 300 Nicollet Mall, Minneapolis. ►1
372-6543

Affiliated with the Science Museum of Minnesota, the Children's Center features exhibits on the natural history of Minnesota, has a small-animal lab, a "how things work" lab where visitors can participate in exhibits, and a popular trading post where children can bring in natural "treasures" to swap for similar items. Saturday storytelling programs. Open Tue-Sat 9 a.m. to 5 p.m.; Sun 1 to 5. Admission to Children's Center only is $1.50 for adults, $1 for students and seniors.

Planetarium schedule varies. There are usually shows during the school year for groups only Tue-F at 11 a.m., 1 and 3 p.m.; and for the general public Sat at 11 a.m., 1, 2, and 3 p.m.; Sun 2 and 3 p.m. Summer schedule varies. Call for show times. Admission to planetarium only is $2 for adults, $1.50 for children six to 12 and for seniors. Combined admission for both Children's Center and Planetarium is $2.50 for adults, $2 for seniors and students. Museum members free.

SCIENCE MUSEUM OF MINNESOTA, 30 E. 10th St. (at Wabasha St.), St. Paul. ►7
221-9488

The new Science Museum features the William L. McKnight-3M Omnitheater, perhaps the most advanced space theater in the United States. In the Omnitheater, huge images are projected on a dome surrounding the audience, putting those watching "in the picture." Museum exhibits include dinosaurs, displays of several Native American cultures,

The Science Museum of Minnesota, downtown St. Paul.

and examples of the impact of such modern technologies as lasers and computers on society. About half the exhibits are permanent and half are changing. Guided tours of the museum are available by reservation. Exhibits emphasize hands-on experience. Open M-Sat 9:30 a.m. to 9 p.m.; Sun 11 to 9. Closed M Labor Day to Memorial Day. Admission to museum only is $3 for adults, $2 for seniors and children 12 and younger. Admission to the Omnitheater only is $4.50 for adults, $3.50 for seniors and children. Combined admission is $5.50 for adults, $4 for seniors and children. For Omnitheater information and tickets, call 221-9400.

MUSICAL INSTRUMENT MUSEUMS

KEYBOARD INSTRUMENT MUSEUM, 75 W. Fifth St. (Landmark Center), St. Paul. ►7
392-3268

Small but fine exhibits of 19th-century keyboard instruments from the Schubert Club's collection displayed in the basement of Landmark Center. Exhibit changes annually. Open M-F 11 a.m. to 3 p.m. Admission is free.

MUSICAL INSTRUMENTS MUSEUM, 1124 Dionne St. (near Lexington and Larpenteur Avs.), Roseville. ►9
488-4303

Bill and Dr. Ida Kugler have gathered more than 1,300 musical instruments from around the world for the museum they run in their home. On display is everything musical from an ostrich-egg sitar to nickelodeons, calliopes, and hurdy-gurdies. Two-hour tour—by reservation only—includes a talk on music history and a chance to play some of the instruments. Museum was closed during much of 1981, but was expected to reopen by 1982. Call as far in advance as possible for tour reservations. Tours are given to groups of 30 to 60 only, but smaller groups and individuals will be combined. Admission is $1.50 for adults, 75 cents for high school students, and 50 cents for grade school children.

ZOOS AND ANIMALS

ANIMAL HUMANE SOCIETY, 845 N. Meadows Lane, Golden Valley. ►4
522-4325

Tours of the animal shelter and a film highlighting the Humane Society's work. Groups of 10 to 50 only; reservations required. The general public can visit the Humane Society daily, M-Sat 9:30 a.m. to 6 p.m., Sun noon to 6.

COMO PARK ZOO, Como Park off Lexington Pkwy., St. Paul. 488-4041 ►8

This Twin Cities favorite has been undergoing a facelift. New features in 1982 will include a marine mammals building and a bear exhibit. The cat exhibit, ape house, and seal shows (summers) have long been popular. The Como Park conservatory, gardens, and amusement park are nearby. Open seven days a week: summer 8 a.m. to 8 p.m. (buildings open 10 a.m. to 5 p.m.); winter 8 a.m. to 6 p.m. Parking and admission are free. Ten-cent charge to enter some of the exhibit buildings.

UNIVERSITY OF MINNESOTA ANIMAL BARNS, St. Paul campus, 1420 Eckles Av., St. Paul. 373-1099 ►8

Free tours, by reservation only, of the university's dairy, swine, and sheep barns. Tours given M-F 8:30 a.m. to 4 p.m.

MINNESOTA ZOO, 12101 Johnny Cake Ridge Rd., Apple Valley. 432-9010 ►12

One of the major family attractions in Minnesota, the Minnesota Zoo features more than 1,200 animals in close-to-natural environments. The award-winning zoo complex is only four years old. Animals from the ocean, tropics, and northern habitats can be seen along exhibit trails, with a special trail for Minnesota animals and a "discovery" trail that includes an introduction to the zoo. Set on 480 acres, the zoo can be explored on foot, on skis, or on the all-weather monorail that passes over the Northern Trail, which includes a family of Siberian tigers.

Zoo programs include regular whale- and dolphin-feeding shows, a children's petting zoo, theater programs, and live animal demonstrations. Cross-country ski rentals are available in the winter. There are picnic areas in and around the zoo grounds.

The Minnesota Zoo is open every day of the year except Christmas. Summer hours 9:30 a.m. to 6 p.m.; winter hours 9:30 to 5. Admission $3 for adults, $1.50 for children 12-16 and seniors, children six-11 $1, five and under free. Parking fee is $1. Monorail tour is $2 for adults, $1 for children; 50 cents extra on weekends.

OUTDOOR CONCERTS

Music in the parks has a long tradition in the Twin Cities. Free concerts are usually presented during the summer months at the Lake Harriet bandstand and in Nicollet Island Park in Minneapolis, and at the Como Lakeside Pavilion in St. Paul. Fair weather also allows free music in downtown plazas and other city parks. Call the Minneapolis (348-2121) and St. Paul (488-7291) parks departments for 1982 summer music schedules. Daily newspapers list times and locations of downtown concerts.

BOAT EXCURSIONS

One of the best ways to take advantage of the rivers and lakes in the Twin Cities area is to go for a ride on them. The following list is a sampling of excursion services. Call ahead to confirm times and fees. Check your telephone book for other listings.

JOSIAH SNELLING, JONATHAN PADELFORD, AND VIKING EXPLORER, Harriet Island, St. Paul. ►8
222-0000 (information)
227-1100 (reservations)

Regular sightseeing cruises on the Mississippi from downtown St. Paul to Fort Snelling, and dance, dinner, and lock trips available. The Viking Explorer cruises all the way to New Orleans on special charters. Boats run Memorial Day through Labor Day. Regular cruise lasts one hour 45 minutes, and leaves Harriet Island (right at sign off S. Wabasha St. across bridge from downtown) seven days a week at 10 a.m., noon, 2, and 4 p.m. Lock trip lasts four hours, and leaves Sun 1 p.m. Dance trip lasts four hours, and leaves F-Sat at 8 p.m. Dinner trip lasts three hours, and leaves Tue, Sun at 7:30 p.m. Tickets are $4.50 for adults, $2.25 for the regular cruise, more for others. Tickets can be picked up half hour before cruise except for dinner cruise, which requires reservations.

JUBILEE I, Stillwater. ▶10
439-7311

Private charter sternwheeler open to the public holidays only for cruises on the St. Croix River. Reservations must be made 10 days in advance. Charter parties can be arranged. Fees are $8 for adults, $5 for children under 12. Cruises are from 2 to 5 p.m., and include live music and a bar.

LADY OF THE LAKE, at Water and Lake Sts., Excelsior. ▶5
929-1209

Narrated cruises of Lake Minnetonka. One-and-a-half-hour public cruises from Excelsior W and Sun 1 p.m.; from Wayzata Tue and Sat 11 a.m. Bring your own lunch. Public dinner cruises June through August by reservation only. Regular cruises $3 for adults, $2 for children. Dinner cruise $24 per person. Boats oper-

ate May through mid-October.

QUEEN OF THE LAKES CRUISE, Lake Harriet, Minneapolis. ▶2
348-2243

This small sternwheeler leaves the Lake Harriet bandstand area every 45 minutes from 1 to 8:15 p.m. seven days a week, June 15 to Labor Day. Adults $1, children 50 cents.

TAYLORS FALLS SCENIC BOAT TOURS, off Hwy. 8, Taylors Falls. ▶10
291-7980

Follow the St. Croix River past several unusual stone formations. Departures from near the Taylors Falls Minnesota-Wisconsin bridge (Hwy. 8). Tours daily from May to October. Thirty-minute ride $3 for adults, $2 for children. Ninety-minute ride $5 for adults, $3 for children. Call ahead to confirm times and fees.

STREETCAR RIDES

LAKE HARRIET TROLLEY, W. Lake Harriet Blvd. and 42nd St., Minneapolis. ▶2
348-2243

Ride these authentically restored, old-fashioned streetcars on a two-mile, 20-minute round trip between Lake Harriet and Lake Calhoun. Informative brochure included in the price of the ride. Forty cents per person. Operates May 25 through Labor Day M-F 6:30 p.m. to dusk; Sat 3:30 to dusk; Sun and holidays noon to dusk. Weekends only April, September, and October.

TOURS

The following business and community organizations offer public tours of their facilities. Many of the tours are offered only to groups, and most require at least two weeks notice before a visit. In some cases, individuals can be included with a scheduled group on short notice.

Theater and Arts Tours

CHILDREN'S THEATRE, 2400 Third Av. S., Minneapolis. ►2
874-0500

Hour-long group tour—by reservation only—features a look backstage at lighting, props, costumes, and scene shop. Groups of fewer than 25 only; $5 fee per group. Tours given M-Tue 10 a.m. to 5 p.m. Reservations must be made at least two weeks in advance.

CHIMERA THEATER, 30 E. 10th St., St. Paul. ►7
292-4311

Hour-long tour—by reservation only—includes backstage areas, lighting booth, costume and prop preparation, green room and short history of the Chimera. Free. Tours given M-F 10 a.m. to 3 p.m. Reservations must be made two weeks in advance.

GUTHRIE THEATER, Vineland Pl., Minneapolis. ►2
377-2824

Half-hour to hour-long tour—by reservation only—includes visits backstage, below stage, and to dressing rooms. Fees for groups are $20. Free open-house tours for the public are held Wed mornings at 10:30 a.m. during the Guthrie season. Call for details and reservations.

LANDMARK CENTER, 75 W. Fifth St., St. Paul. ►7
292-3233

Open to the public during regular business hours, Thu evenings, Sat 10 a.m. to 5 p.m., and Sun 1 to 5. Visitors can arrange 45-minute guided tours by calling the Landmark Center office.

MINNEAPOLIS INSTITUTE OF ARTS, 2400 Third Av. S., Minneapolis. ►2
870-3140

Public tours featuring the permanent collection and the "object of the month" are given Tue-Sun at 1 and 2 p.m. and Thu at 7 p.m. Private tours by appointment, three-weeks notice required. Museum admission required.

ORCHESTRA HALL, 1111 Nicollet Av., Minneapolis. ►1
371-5600

Tours—by reservation only—given to groups of 10 or more. Tours include visits to backstage, rehearsal, and office areas, and information about the building and its acoustics. Arrange time of tour when calling for reservations.

Community Tours

CATHEDRAL OF ST. PAUL, 293 Selby Av., St. Paul. ►8
225-6563

Forty-five-minute narrated tour highlights the art and architecture of this Twin Cities landmark. Groups of 10 or more only. Tours given M-F, usually at 1 p.m. Reservations required. Free.

CHILDREN'S HEALTH CENTER AND HOSPITAL, 2525 Chicago Av., Minneapolis. ►2 874-6200

Hour-long tour—by reservation only—for groups of 10 to 30 given October through May. Tour includes visits to admitting, x-ray, laboratory, and some floor areas of the hospital. Free. Reservations must be made at least three weeks in advance.

CHILDREN'S HOSPITAL, 311 Pleasant Av., St. Paul. ►8 298-8666 ext. 8874

Forty-five-minute tour—by reservation only—includes visits to admitting, newborn nursery, playroom, and other areas of the hospital. Free.

COURAGE CENTER, 3915 Golden Valley Rd., Golden Valley. ►4 588-0811

See occupational and physical therapy areas, therapeutic preschool, ham radio system, and art by the handicapped during one-hour-15-minute experiential tour. By reservation only. Tours given Tue-F.

DUNWOODY INDUSTRIAL INSTITUTE, 818 Wayzata Blvd., Minneapolis. ►2 374-5800

Forty-five-minute tour—by reservation only—includes visits to various shops and labs where vocational skills are taught and practiced. Free. Tours given M-F 9 a.m. to 3 p.m. Best time to visit

is September through June, when the institute is most active. Reservations must be made at least two days in advance.

HENNEPIN COUNTY GOVERNMENT CENTER, 300 S. Sixth St., Minneapolis. ►1 348-5596

Hour-long tour includes explanation of architectural highlights, county government and court system, and visits to the county board room and a court room. Free. Public tours given M-F at 2 p.m. Tours for groups of 10 to 60, reservations required, given M-F 9 a.m. to 3 p.m.

METROPOLITAN AIRPORTS COMMISSION, Minneapolis-St. Paul International Airport. ►6 726-5574

Hour-long tour—by reservation only—includes a look at terminal operations and a chance to step inside a plane. Tours given M-F 9 a.m. to 2:30 p.m. Groups of 15 to 50 only; individuals can be included with scheduled groups.

MINNEAPOLIS CITY HALL, 350 S. Fifth St., Minneapolis. ►1 348-7528

Forty-five-minute tour includes a visit to the City Council chambers and the Mayor's office, and highlights the building's architecture. By appointment only. Groups or individuals.

MINNEAPOLIS FIRE DEPARTMENT Check telephone directory for nearest station.

Tours given of neighborhood fire stations only. Call one to arrange a tour.

MINNEAPOLIS PUBLIC LIBRARY AND INFORMATION CENTER, 300 Nicollet Mall, Minneapolis. ►1
372-6667, 372-6500

Forty-five-minute tour of open departments includes an introduction to the library and instruction on using card catalogs. Closed department tour adds visits to the rare book section, bindery, and administration areas, for a total of one-and-a-half hours. Tours given to individuals W, Thu noon, and to groups by reservation made at least two weeks in advance.

MINNESOTA STATE CAPITOL, Aurora and Park Avs., St. Paul. ►8
296-2881 (reservations)
297-3521 (information)

Guided tours of the Capitol's art and architecture include a visit to the state Supreme Court chambers. Thirty-five-minute tour; reservations required. Tours on the hour year-round (except on major holidays) M-F 9 a.m. to 4 p.m., Sat 10 to 3, Sun 1 to 3. Separate tours outlining the legislative process are also offered. Free.

ST. PAUL FIRE DEPARTMENT, 101 E. 10th St., St. Paul.
224-7811 ►7

Half-hour tour—by reservation only—includes close-up looks at engines, the watch office, and, if available, an ambulance. Free. Arrange time of tour when calling for reservation.

ST. PAUL POLICE DEPARTMENT, 101 E. 10th St., St. Paul 55101. ►7

Write the chief of police at the above address three weeks in advance to request a tour. Hour-long tour includes visits to the communications center, crime lab, detective division, artists' area, practice shooting range, and administrative offices. Free.

ST. PAUL POST OFFICE, 180 E. Kellogg Blvd., St. Paul. ►7
725-7216

Fifty-minute tour highlighting the stages of mail processing. Visitors can bring their own letters to follow through sorting. Groups preferred, though individuals can be accommodated. Two-week notice required. Tours given M-F 9 a.m. to 2:30 p.m. Free.

Media Tours

BROWN INSTITUTE, 3123 E. Lake St., Minneapolis. ►2
721-2481

Hour-long tour—by reservation only—can include visits to three different areas: a new computer facility, radio and television studios, and the electronics laboratory. Free. Tours given M-F 9 a.m. to 3 p.m. Reservations must be made at least one week in advance.

KTCA/KTCI-TV, 1604 Como Av., St. Paul. ►8
646-4611

Schedule for tours of the Twin Cities public television studios varies. Call for details and reservations.

KSTP-TV AND RADIO, 3415 University Av., St. Paul. ►8
642-4375

Half-hour tour—by reservation

only—includes visits to *Twin Cities Today* studios, control booth, AM radio facilities, and weather center. Free. Tours given M, Tue, Thu at 10:15 a.m.

MINNEAPOLIS STAR AND TRIBUNE, 425 Portland Av., Minneapolis. ▶1
372-4163

Hour-long tour—by reservation only—shows how a newspaper comes together from the newsrooms and advertising department through composing, the press room, and distribution. Also includes a film. Free. Tours given M-F at 10:30 a.m. and 1:15 p.m. Limit of 60 in the morning, 30 in the afternoon. Two-week notice required.

WCCO-TV, 50 S. Ninth St., Minneapolis. ▶1
330-2492

Tours for groups of 10 to 30 only, by reservation. Visitors see master control room, news department, weather center, and studios. Tours given M-F 10 a.m. to 4 p.m. Free.

Business Tours

BACHMAN'S FLORISTS, 6010 Lyndale Av. S., Minneapolis. ▶2
861-7692

Thirty-minute tour includes walk through greenhouses, gift shop, and design areas. Groups of five or more, by reservation only. Tours given M-F 9 a.m. to 2 p.m. Free.

BETTY CROCKER KITCHENS, General Mills, Inc., 9200 Wayzata Blvd. (Hwy. 12 at County Rd. 18),

Golden Valley. ▶4
540-2526

Hour-long walking tour—by reservation only—includes multi-image slide presentation, refreshments, and visits to seven test kitchens. Free. Tours given M-F 10 and 11 a.m.; 1, 2, 3 p.m. Call three days before visiting, if possible.

FEDERAL RESERVE BANK, 250 Marquette Av., Minneapolis. 340-2345 ▶1

Hour-long tour—by reservation only—includes an introduction to the Federal Reserve Bank, slide show, and visits to the money and check departments. Free. Tours given Tue-F at 8:45 and 10 a.m.; 1 and 2:15 p.m. Call a week in advance for reservations, if possible.

A. GEDNEY PICKLE FACTORY, County Rd. 10 off Hwy. 212, Chaska. ▶5
448-2612

Thirty-minute tours of pickle-processing factory for school groups only.

MAID OF SCANDINAVIA, Hwys. 7 and 100, St. Louis Park. ▶5
927-7996

Hour-and-a-half tour—by reservation only—includes a cake-decorating demonstration and a visit to the Maid of Scandinavia retail store. Tours given M-Thu 9 a.m. to 2 p.m. Groups of 20 to 40 only. Free.

MARVEL FOODS INC. INTERNATIONAL HOUSE, 75 W. Island Av., Minneapolis. ▶1
379-2335

Hour-and-a-half tour—by

reservation only—includes a lecture on Far Eastern foods, an opportunity to sample some foods, and a visit to the retail store. Tours were suspended after a fire in 1981. Tours may be resumed at a new location. Call for reservations and other details.

MEDTRONIC INC., 6972 Old Central Av., Fridley. ►3
574-3543

Hour-and-a-half tour—by reservation only—includes a history of the company and a look at its major product—heart pacemakers and other biomedical-engineering products—being made and tested. Background in anatomy and physiology helpful; tours limited to people 16 and older. Free. Tours given M-Thu at 9 a.m. and 1 p.m. Reservations must be made at least two weeks in advance.

MINNEAPOLIS GRAIN EXCHANGE, Fourth St. and Fourth Av. S., Minneapolis. ►1
338-6212

Hour-long tour includes film on grain-marketing, explanation of how price quote board and trading work, and an opportunity to watch trading and have questions answered. Free. Reservations required. Tours given M-F at 8:45 and 10 a.m. Visitors' balcony open M-F 9:30 a.m. to 1:20 p.m.

NORTHERN STATES POWER PLANT TOURS PROGRAM, 414 Nicollet Mall, Minneapolis. 330-6677 ►1

Tours open for groups only, by reservation. Visitors have a choice of three tours, each highlighting a particular means of power pro-duction. Actual walking tours through power plants. Call for a brochure with tour descriptions. Times and days of tours can be arranged when calling for reservations. Free.

NORTHWESTERN BELL TELEPHONE, 200 S. Fifth St., Minneapolis. ►1
344-7619

Tour directory assistance, network control, and the annoyance-call bureau areas of the phone company. Reservations required. Tours given M-F 8 a.m. to 4 p.m. and usually last an hour. Free.

NORTHWESTERN NATIONAL BANK, Seventh St. and Marquette Av., Minneapolis. ►1
372-8122

Forty-five-minute tour—by reservation only—includes visits to the safe-deposit and gold vaults, convenience bank, directors' room, and weather-ball room. Free. M-F; arrange time of tour when calling for reservations.

REPUBLIC AIRLINES INC., 7500 Airline Dr. (I-494 at 34th Av. S.), Bloomington. ►6
726-7921

Forty-five-minute tour—by reservation only—includes visits to the airline's computer and reservations centers, hangars, and maintenance shops. Free. Groups of 25 to 50 only. Reservations should be made six weeks in advance.

ST. PAUL UNION STOCKYARDS, 100 Exchange Bldg., South St. Paul. ►12
455-2991 ext. 183

See livestock auctions at the nation's largest stockyards. Mostly cattle, swine, and sheep. Tour not recommended for young children. Reservations required two weeks in advance. Tours usually given Tue-Thu at 9 and 10:30 a.m. and last about an hour. Free.

JACOB SCHMIDT BREWING CO., 582 W. Seventh St., St. Paul. ►8
226-3471

Twenty-minute tour of brewing and bottling operations at the Schmidt brewery. Tour includes a visit to the Rathskellar, where samples are offered. Tours M-F at 10 a.m. and 2 p.m. Free.

H.M. SMYTHE CO., INC., 1085 Snelling Av. N., St. Paul. ►8
646-4544

Forty-five-minute tour of the Smythe printing facility. For groups only; reservations required. Free.

TONKA TOYS TOUR, 5300 Shoreline Blvd., Mound. ►5
472-8000

This popular tour follows the manufacture of a Tonka toy from stamping to painting and packaging. Reservations required far in advance. Tours given February through November on Tue and F at 9:30 and 10:45 a.m.; 12:30 and 2 p.m. Tour book and small toy given to each visitor. Free.

WOODS CHOCOLATE FACTORY, 225 E. Sixth St., St. Paul.
227-7800 ►7

Reservations are not required to visit this factory and candy store. Visitors can view the candy-making process through a large observation window. Open M-F 9 a.m. to 2 p.m. Most interesting to visit during the busy holiday seasons; slow during summer. Candy for sale on the premises.

GARDENS AND NATURAL SPOTS

COMO PARK CONSERVATORY, off Lexington Pkwy. in Como Park, St. Paul. ►8
488-7291

Built in 1915, the conservatory is a St. Paul landmark. Blooming flower displays are open to the public all year. Nearby is a formal Japanese garden. Open seven days a week; summer 10 a.m. to 6 p.m.; winter 10 a.m. to 4 p.m. Admission is free.

ELOISE BUTLER WILDFLOWER GARDEN AND BIRD SANCTUARY, on Wirth Pkwy. north of Hwy. 12, Minneapolis. ►2
374-4305

Twenty acres of wildflower habitat with separate woodland, upland, and bog flower areas set on hilly terrain. A descriptive brochure and numbered stakes allow visitors to take self-guided tours. The area is also a bird sanctuary. Open April 1 to October 31 from 10 a.m. to 6 p.m. Admission is free.

THE FRESHWATER BIOLOGICAL INSTITUTE, 2500 Shadywood Rd., Navarre.
471-8407 ►5

Located about 20 miles west of Minneapolis on Lake Minnetonka, the Freshwater Biological Institute is mainly a research facility. Visitors, however, can see a small museum and its award-winning modern building, and view marsh wildlife from its outdoor decks. No fish tanks or other live displays. Open to the public, by reservation only, M-F 8 a.m. to 4 p.m. Admission is free.

LAKE HARRIET ROSE GARDENS AND THOMAS SADLER ROBERTS BIRD SANCTUARY, on Roseway Rd. off W. 40th St., Minneapolis. ►2

See more than 3,000 rosebushes plus annual and perennial flowers in the formal gardens on the northeast shore of Lake Harriet. The roses are all identified, and the gardens are decorated with trees and fountains. The bird sanctuary, just north of the rose gardens, was damaged by the June 1981 tornado. Restoration is in progress, however, and marshland birds can still be seen. Open during daylight hours; flower displays June through September. Admission is free.

UNIVERSITY OF MINNESOTA LANDSCAPE ARBORETUM, 3675 Arboretum Dr., Chaska. 443-2460, 443-2773 ►5

Five-hundred-sixty acres of hills, lakes, and marshland set with rare and unusual trees and plantings. Six miles of walking trails. There is also a conservatory with flowering plants and a restaurant that serves lunch. Cross-country skiing on marked trails in the winter. Open M-F 8 a.m. to 4:30 p.m., weekends and holidays 11 to 4:30. Individual memberships $15; admission for non-members $1.50 for each car and 50 cents per person, children under 16 free, seniors free second and fourth Fridays of each month.

NOERENBERG MEMORIAL PARK, off County Rd. 15 on County Rd. 51 between Crystal and Maxwell Bays on Lake Minnetonka. ►5
475-0050

These formal gardens were once part of a wealthy brewer's estate. The house has been destroyed, but the gardens, with more than 3,000 blooming plants, are freshly landscaped every year and are open to the public. Open Memorial Day to Labor Day, M-F 8 a.m. to 4:30 p.m.; Sat, Sun noon to 4. Admission is free.

NORTHRUP-KING GARDENS, 13410 Research Rd. off Hwy. 169, Eden Prairie. ►5
941-3870

The public can visit these experimental flower gardens on an informal basis during daylight hours. Picking is not allowed. Best displays are in mid-July, though flowers bloom until the first major frost.

TOWN SQUARE PARK, in Town Square, downtown St. Paul. ►7

Although not a conventional garden, this indoor park features four levels of greenery in an open, airy setting complete with waterfall. Part of St. Paul's new downtown shopping and office complex. Open year-round during shopping hours.

NATURE CENTERS

The following nature centers are open to drop-in visitors most of the year. Call for information on hours and programs.

COON RAPIDS DAM REGIONAL PARK, 9750 Egret Blvd., Coon Rapids. ►3
757-4700 or 425-4683

EASTMAN NATURE CENTER, ELM CREEK PARK RESERVE, 13351 Elm Creek Rd., Osseo. ►4
425-2324

FRIDLEY NATURE CENTERS: Innsbruck Nature Center, 5815 Arthur St. N.E., Fridley. ►3; Springbrook Nature Center, 100 85th Av. N.E., Fridley. ►3.
571-3450

LOWRY NATURE CENTER, CARVER PARK RESERVE, Carver Co. Rd. 11, near Victoria, Excelsior. ►5
472-4911

MAPLEWOOD NATURE CENTER, 2659 E. Seventh St., Maplewood. ►9
738-9383

MINNESOTA VALLEY NATIONAL WILDLIFE REFUGE, 4101 E. 78th St., Bloomington.
854-5900 ►6

RICHARDSON NATURE CENTER, HYLAND PARK RESERVE, 8737 E. Bush Lake Rd., Bloomington. ►6
941-7993

WESTWOOD HILLS ENVIRONMENTAL EDUCATION CENTER, 8300 W. Franklin, St. Louis Park. ►5
920-3000

WOODLAKE NATURE CENTER, 735 Lake Shore Dr., Richfield. ►6
861-4507

The beluga whale and friend at the Minnesota Zoo.

Chapter Fourteen

SPECIAL EVENTS

The following descriptions of some of the Twin Cities' major annual events should be considered tentative. Consult magazine or newspaper listings, or contact the sponsoring organizations listed, for confirmation or changes. Information on events throughout Minnesota is available from the Minnesota Department of Economic Development, Tourism Bureau, 480 Cedar St., St. Paul 55101, 296-5029.

NOVEMBER 1981

COMO PARK CONSERVATORY FALL SHOW, Eastbrook Dr. at Aida Pl., St. Paul. ▶8
489-1740

Two Sundays before Thanksgiving through the holiday weekend (Nov. 14-28), the Como Park Conservatory presents a special fall show. Just as the trees and shrubs outside are shedding their last leaves, the conservatory is filled with flowers and greenery. Open regular hours. Free admission.

DAYTON'S ANNUAL CHRISTMAS SHOW, 700 Nicollet Mall, Minneapolis. ▶1
375-3018

The Sunday before Thanksgiving through Christmas Eve, Dayton's presents a special Christmas show in its eighth-floor auditorium during regular store hours. This year's show will have a *Hansel and Gretel* theme. Free admission.

A CHRISTMAS CAROL, Guth-

(See Locator Key Map, pages 8-9)

▶1 Mpls. Downtown	▶7 St. Paul Downtown
▶2 Mpls. Excluding Downtown	▶8 St. Paul Excluding Downtown
▶3 Mpls. North Suburbs	▶9 St. Paul North Suburbs
▶4 Mpls. Northwest Suburbs	▶10 St. Paul Northeast Suburbs
▶5 Mpls. Southwest Suburbs	▶11 St. Paul Southeast Suburbs
▶6 Mpls. South Suburbs	▶12 St. Paul South Suburbs

rie Theater, Vineland Pl., Minneapolis. ►2
377-2224

This annual Guthrie classic will be presented in 47 performances beginning Nov. 23 and running to Jan. 2. Tickets are usually sold out quickly, so reserve yours as far in advance as possible. Tickets run $8.95 to $15.95.

TOYMAKERS FAIR, Walker Community Church, 3104 16th Av. S., Minneapolis. ►2
729-3922

Old-fashioned and modern handmade toys and soft sculpture will be on sale at Walker Community Church Nov. 28. Ethnic food will also be available. Twenty exhibitors are expected. No admission fee.

DECEMBER 1981

THE NUTCRACKER SUITE, Minnesota Dance Theater, Northrop Auditorium, 84 Church St. S.E., Minneapolis. ►2
339-9150

The Minnesota Dance Theater's production of the *Nutcracker* is a perennial holiday favorite. 1981 performances will be held Dec. 10-20. Call for ticket information.

CHRISTMAS PARTY AT GIBBS FARM MUSEUM, Cleveland Av. N. and Larpenteur Av., Falcon Heights. ►9
646-8629

Gibbs Farm will present a "Currier and Ives Christmas" Dec. 13th. The 1870s farmhouse will be decorated with traditional ornaments; baked goods and hot cider will be served. Carol singing,

other activities. Party is from noon to 4. Admission $1.50 for adults, $1.25 for seniors, 50 cents for children.

JANUARY 1982

BOAT SHOW, Minneapolis Auditorium, 1403 Stevens Av. S., Minneapolis. ►1
827-5833

The 1982 boat show will be held Jan. 27-31. All kinds of boats, from canoes to cruisers, will be exhibited, and there will be special features. Last year 60,000 people visited the show to see some $10 million worth of floating hardware. Admission $3.50 for adults, $1.50 for children.

ST. PAUL WINTER CARNIVAL, Winter Carnival Association of St. Paul, Bremer Bldg., 98 E. Seventh St., St. Paul 55101.
222-4416

Begun in 1886 to show that Minnesota during winter was not, as an Eastern newspaper had reported, "another Siberia, unfit for human habitation," the St. Paul Winter Carnival has grown into a 10-day festival of more than 100 events. The 1982 carnival will run Jan. 29 through Feb. 7. Major events will include the world's largest pancake breakfast at the Civic Center, ice-carving contest, and King Boreas Grande Day Parade downtown, all on Saturday, Jan. 30; the International 500 snowmobile race from Winnipeg ending in St. Paul Friday, Jan. 29; treasure hunt starting Sunday, Jan. 31; Torchlight Parade Saturday, Feb. 6 downtown; and the Carnival Park Family Recreation

Center at Highland Park offering sleigh rides and other activities at Highland Park throughout the carnival.

DeSTIJL EXHIBIT, Walker Art Center, Vineland Pl., Minneapolis. ▶2
375-7600

A major exhibition of Dutch art and architecture from the DeStijl movement (1917-1931) will open at the Walker Jan. 30, and will run until March 28. Call the Walker for information about special events connected with the exhibit.

FEBRUARY 1982

SHRINE CIRCUS, Minneapolis. 871-3555 ▶1

The local Shriners will be bringing a real three-ring circus to the Minneapolis Auditorium (1403 Stevens Av. S.) Feb. 27 through March 7. This may be the only circus in town this year. Animal acts, acrobats, clowns, and high-wire acts will be among the features on the program. Tickets should range from about $3 to $7. Twenty performances are planned.

MARCH 1982

MINNESOTA STATE HIGH SCHOOL HOCKEY TOURNAMENT, Minnesota State High School League, 2621 Fairoak Av., Anoka 55303.
427-5250

Eight high school hockey teams will play off Thursday, March 11, through Saturday, March 13, in the St. Paul Civic Center Arena

for the state championship. Tickets are sold out, and there's a long waiting list, but the tournament will be broadcast over KSTP-TV, Channel 5.

METROPOLITAN AUTO SHOW, Minneapolis Auditorium, 1403 Stevens Av. S., Minneapolis. ▶1
831-8019

Everything from current-model domestic cars to imported sports cars and antique beauties will be displayed at the Metropolitan Auto Show March 13-21. More than $3 million worth of cars and accessories will be exhibited. Admission.

ST. PATRICK'S DAY PARADES, Downtown St. Paul and Minneapolis. ▶7, 1

Parades through both downtowns generally start at noon March 17. Daily newspapers carry maps of parade routes in advance. The big event is in St. Paul, where the Catholic archdiocese had succeeded in banning the parade from 1911 to 1966. It was revived in 1967 by then-Mayor Tom Byrne, and has become the third-largest St. Patrick's Day parade in the United States (after those in New York and Chicago). Some 100,000 people participate in St. Paul's celebration each year.

MINNESOTA STATE GIRLS' HIGH SCHOOL BASKETBALL TOURNAMENT, Minnesota State High School League, 2621 Fairoak Av., Anoka 55303.
427-5250

Eight teams each in Class A and Class AA will compete Thursday,

March 18, at the Minneapolis Auditorium, and the winners will advance to competition Friday, March 19, and Saturday, March 20, at the Met Center for the state championship titles. Tickets are available from the Minnesota State High School League, and cost $4.50 for adults and $2.50 for students for each two-game session. Adult "season tickets" for the entire tournament are available for $18. WTCN-TV, Channel 11, will broadcast Saturday's games only.

DAYTON'S ANNUAL FLOWER SHOW, 700 Nicollet Mall, Minneapolis. ►1
375-3018

Just when it seems that spring will never arrive, Dayton's fills its eighth-floor auditorium with a full summer's worth of flowers. The theme for this year's show had not been set as of this writing, but it will be held March 20 through April 3. Free admission.

MINNESOTA STATE BOYS' HIGH SCHOOL BASKETBALL TOURNAMENT, Minnesota State High School League, 2621 Fairoak Av., Anoka 55303.
427-5250

Eight teams each in Class A and Class AA will compete Thursday, March 25, at Williams Arena at the University of Minnesota, and winners will advance to competition Friday, March 26, and Saturday, March 27, at the St. Paul Civic Center for the boys' state championship titles. Tickets are available at the same prices as for the girls' tournament. WTCN-TV, Channel 11, will broadcast the entire tournament. (Tradition-

ally, the Twin Cities' last major snowstorm of the winter hits during this tournament.)

NORTHWEST SPORTS SHOW, Minneapolis Auditorium, 1403 Stevens Av. S., Minneapolis. ►1
827-5833

The Sports Show is said to be the second most heavily attended event in Minnesota, after the State Fair. The 1982 show, to be held March 26-April 4, will be the event's 50th anniversary. Marine, recreational-vehicle, fishing, and sports-equipment exhibits are regular features of the show. There is also a stage show and special exhibits. Ticket prices had not been set at this writing.

APRIL 1982

COMO PARK CONSERVATORY SPRING SHOW, Eastbrook Dr. at Aida Pl., St. Paul. ►8
489-1740

A special flower show will be presented at the conservatory during regular hours Palm Sunday, April 4, through Sunday, April 18. The theme had not been chosen as of this writing. Free admission.

MINNESOTA TWINS HOME OPENER, Hubert H. Humphrey Metrodome, Minneapolis. ►1
854-4040

The Twins will inaugurate the 1982 season—and the new downtown Minneapolis domed stadium—on April 6. The dome will eliminate the uncertainty of the Minnesota weather, but not necessarily the uncertainty of the club.

Call the Twins for 1982 ticket information.

MINNEAPOLIS HOME AND GARDEN SHOW, Minneapolis Auditorium, 1403 Stevens Av. S., Minneapolis. ►1
475-2237

Springtime is home-improvement time, and Home Show promoters will bring the latest in home design, building supplies, and gardening gear to the auditorium April 8-14. More than 300 exhibitors are expected. Six landscaped gardens will decorate the lower floor, and special features will include a seed store, a collection of the work of Minnesota furniture craftsmen, and "the idea house." Admission $3; $1 for children.

NORTHROP DANCE SEASON, Northrop Auditorium, 84 Church St. S.E., Minneapolis. ►2
373-2345

The National Ballet of Canada will give three Twin Cities performances April 16-18 as part of the Northrop Dance Season. Tickets $7 to $13. Call for performance times and other details.

FESTIVAL OF NATIONS, International Institute of Minnesota, 1694 Como Av., St. Paul 55108.
647-0191

Foods of 40 ethnic groups, folk dancing, exhibits, and bazaars will fill the St. Paul Civic Center Friday, Saturday, and Sunday, April 30, May 1, and 2, during the Festival of Nations. Ticket prices had not been set at this writing, but tickets will be available at the International Institute, Dayton's, and the door.

MAY 1982

SCOTTISH COUNTRY FAIR, Macalester College, 1600 Grand Av., St. Paul. ►8
696-6261

For hundreds of years, clans from all over Scotland have united in a fair-like atmosphere for entertainment, competition, banquets, and barter. On Saturday, May 1, a similar gathering will be held at Macalester College. Caber (log)-tossing, stone-putting, and hammer-throwing competitions are among the events. Dancers perform the fling, sword dance, and the Seann Truibhas. Crafted items and Scottish food specialties are sold. Admission is $2 for adults, free for children.

NATIONAL HISTORIC PRESERVATION WEEK, Minnesota Historical Society—James J. Hill House, 240 Summit Av., St. Paul 55102.
296-0104

Contact the state historical society for a calendar of local events to be held during National Historic Preservation Week, May 9-15.

NORWEGIAN CONSTITUTION DAY (SYTTENDE MAI), Sons of Norway, 1455 W. Lake St., Minneapolis 55408. ►2
827-3611

A parade in downtown Minneapolis and craft, book, and organization displays on Nicollet Mall are planned for Sunday, May 15, in celebration of Norwegian Constitution Day. A dance will be held that evening.

METROPOLITAN OPERA IN THE UPPER MIDWEST, Northrop Auditorium, 84 Church St. S.E., Minneapolis. ►2
373-2345

New York's Metropolitan Opera makes its annual visit to the Twin Cities, giving seven performances May 17-22. These performances are eagerly awaited, so reserve your tickets early. Call for information.

JUNE 1982

EDINA ART FESTIVAL, 50th St. and France Av. S., Edina. ►5

Annual outdoor art show sponsored by the 50th and France Business Association in downtown Edina. Show will run June 4-6 from about 10 a.m. to 6 p.m. daily. About 200 artists are expected to show and sell their work.

DANISH DAY, Danish American Fellowship, 4200 Cedar Av., Minneapolis 55406. ►2
729-3800

Music, folk dancing, pony rides and clown shows for children, and an address by a guest speaker will highlight Danish Day activities, tentatively scheduled for Sunday, June 6, in the Waubun Picnic Area of Minnehaha Park in Minneapolis. Admission will be charged.

GRAND OLD DAY, Grand Avenue Business Association, 2142 St. Anthony Av., St. Paul 55104. ►8
644-2948

St. Paul's avenue of craft and specialty shops will host a 1 p.m. parade, children's parade, art show, food booths, and bands and orchestras Sunday, June 6. The 1981 Grand Old Day celebration attracted 150,000 people. Grand Avenue merchants also host an annual Grand Meander the first Sunday in December. Hot drinks and refreshments are served in some shops, and Santa Claus entertains the children. Most stores and restaurants along the avenue are open for both events.

GREATER LAKE ST. INTERNATIONAL BAZAAR, Greater Lake Street Council, 1518 E. Lake St., Minneapolis 55407. ►2
721-7458

All six miles of Lake Street from the Mississippi River to Lake Calhoun will be lined with ethnic food stands and dancing and antiques and crafts displays. In 1982, the celebration will probably be held the first weekend in June.

DEUTSCHER TAG (GERMAN DAY), Volkfest Association of Minnesota, 301 Summit Av., St. Paul 55102. ►8
222-7027

Authentic German food and music and dancing by the Minnesota Schuhplattlers, Edelweiss Dancers, and Bavarian Dancers will highlight this celebration in St. Paul's Highland Park Sunday, June 13. Free admission.

ICE CREAM SOCIAL AT THE RAMSEY HOUSE, Alexander Ramsey House, 265 S. Exchange St. (at Irvine Park), St. Paul. ►8
296-0100

Relax in a chair on the lawn of

the home of Minnesota's first territorial governor while you enjoy an ice cream sundae or glass of lemonade and listen to the live entertainment from 1 to 4:30 p.m. Sunday, June 13. Admission to the grounds is free; tours of the house are $1.50 for adults, free for children under 16 with parents. The Ramsey House also hosts special events during the Christmas season, when guest cooks prepare ethnic specialties in the kitchen and music performances are held.

LOWERTOWN ART FAIR AND MUSIC FESTIVAL, Lowertown Community Council, 320 Cedar St., St. Paul. ►7
222-5887

Continuous entertainment, authentic ethnic food, booths for local organizations, and art and craft displays by regional artists will fill and surround Mears Park Friday, Saturday, and Sunday, June 4, 5, and 6. A concert is planned for Saturday night. Free admission, except for the Saturday night concert.

ROSE FETE, Minneapolis Institute of Arts, 2400 Third Av. S., Minneapolis. ►2
870-3072

Patterned after the summer festival held at Villa Rosa, a house that once occupied what are now the institute grounds, the Rose Fete features arts and crafts displays, family entertainment, food and drink, and free admission to the museum. It will be held from noon to 6 p.m., Sunday, June 20. Free admission.

TANBARK CAVALCADE OF

ROSE HORSE SHOW, Minnesota State Fairgrounds, Falcon Heights. ►9
937-8916

A multi-breed horse show featuring more than 300 horses will be presented at the Fairgrounds June 24-27. Friday shows will be held at 1 and 7 p.m., Saturday shows at 9 a.m., 4 and 7 p.m.; Sunday shows at 9 a.m. and 1 p.m. Harness and saddle competitions. Admission $2.50.

OLD ST. ANTHONY HERITAGE FESTIVAL, Minneapolis Park and Riverfront Development Boards, 1940 Penn Av. S., Minneapolis 55405. ►1
222-5887

The riverbanks where Minneapolis began (the S.E. Main St. area) will host a festival featuring art exhibits, entertainment, ethnic foods, and an animal fair Saturday and Sunday, June 26 and 27. In 1980, about 80,000 people attended the festival. Free admission.

MINNESOTA CRAFTS COUNCIL FESTIVAL, College of St. Catherine, 2004 Randolph Av., St. Paul. ►8
333-7789

Juried crafts show featuring 150 top craftsmen and their work. The 1982 show, to be held Saturday and Sunday, June 26 and 27, will be the 10th anniversary of the event. Exhibits are on the campus of the College of St. Catherine. Food will be sold, and there will be musicians, street players, and other entertainment. No admission charge.

SVENSKARNAS DAG (MID-

SUMMER FESTIVAL), 1605 Louisiana Av. S., Minneapolis 55426. ►2
545-9294

This traditional Swedish celebration of the longest day of the year will include folk dancing, singing, a band contest, queen contest, and Swedish food specialties Sunday, June 27, at Minnehaha Park in Minneapolis. Free admission.

JOE DUFFY CELEBRITY TOURNAMENTS, 310 Fourth Av. S., Suite 610, Minneapolis 55415.
339-8675

Local and national celebrities compete in golf and tennis for the benefit of such local charities as the Minnesota Heart Association, Kidney Foundation of the Upper Midwest, and Children's Heart Fund. The 1982 events will be scheduled on a Saturday and Sunday at the end of June. Locations for the events had not been chosen at this writing. Admission will be $2.50 for both days.

CIVIL WAR WEEKEND, Minnesota Historical Society, Bldg. 25, Fort Snelling 55111. ►2, 8
726-1171

The First Minnesota Regiment will land by riverboat, set up camp, and recreate the fort's days as a Civil War recruiting and training center one weekend in late June or early July. Special activities will include a military ball, reading of Civil War letters, and operation of the fort's hospital and recruiting office. Regular admission will be charged.

JULY 1982

SOUTH ST. PAUL KAPOSIA DAYS, South St. Paul. ►12
451-2266

South St. Paul will sponsor fireworks, bingo, a street dance, music in the park, and a grand parade during its Kaposia Days celebration Friday, Saturday, and Sunday, July 2, 3, and 4. A South St. Paul men's organization will also prepare the traditional pot of booya (stew) to be served to the public.

TRADITIONAL 1820s MILITARY FOURTH OF JULY, Minnesota Historical Society, Bldg. 25, Fort Snelling 55111. ►2, 8
726-1171

Dress parades, an oration by the commander, dances, cannon- and musket-firing, and sampling of roast pig highlight this recreation of July Fourth on the frontier. Fort Snelling will be open 10 a.m. to 5 p.m.; regular admission will be charged. Later in the summer, look for announcements of the Fort Snelling open house. Admission to the fort will be free that weekend, probably in August, and special programs will be presented.

SOUTH ST. PAUL RODEO, Rodeo Arena, St. Paul Stockyards, South St. Paul. ►12
451-2266

Big-time rodeo featuring the top 10 money-winners in the country is held in South St. Paul every year. This year the rodeo will be held July 7-11 and will consist of five events, including saddle- and bareback-bronc riding, bulldogging, bull riding, and women's barrel riding. 1981 prices were $7.50 for reserve seating, $5 for adults, $2.50 for children.

NORWAY DAY, Norwegian National League of Minnesota, 2871 Humboldt Av. S., Minneapolis 55408. ►2
823-6692

Church services, a noon concert, children's flag parade, demonstrations of Norwegian arts and crafts, food specialties, and crowning of the Sons of Norway Queen will all be part of Norway Day festivities Sunday, July 11, in Minnehaha Park. Free admission.

MINNEAPOLIS AQUATENNIAL, 702 Wayzata Blvd., Minneapolis 55403.
377-4621

The Minneapolis Aquatennial was conceived on a rainy afternoon in 1939 when a group of Twin Cities men were in Winnipeg for a parade honoring Britain's King George VI. If Winnipeg could attract a million people to pay homage to a king, they thought, why couldn't Minneapolis crown its own royalty to preside over a summer festival? The next year the Aquatennial was born. Now it is the largest civic celebration in the United States, including some 250 family-oriented events. Highlights of the Aquatennial, which will run July 16-25, are the Grande Day Parade downtown Saturday, July 17; coronation Friday, July 23; and Torchlight Parade downtown Wednesday, July 21. Other activities include hydroplane and canoe races,

Big-time rodeo in South St. Paul.

craft displays, musical entertainment, and a milk-carton boat race.

MERRIAM PARK MUSIC AND ARTS FESTIVAL, 2000 St. Anthony Av., St. Paul. ►8
645-0349

The 10th-annual Merriam Park Music and Arts Festival will be held at the park Tuesday, July 20, from 6 to 9 p.m. The festival will feature an outdoor concert by the Minnesota Orchestra, as well as an art fair and other entertainment. Six-thousand people attended in 1981. Tickets will be $10.

RAMSEY COUNTY FAIR, Ramsey County Agricultural Society, 2702 Reardon Pl., North St. Paul 55109.
770-2626, 777-2330

Minnesota's smallest county in area finds room each year to display poultry, rabbits, vegetables, clothing, crafts, and furnishings produced within its borders. The fair will be held July 21-25 at the fairgrounds in Maplewood. Admission is free, but there is a charge for parking.

HENNEPIN COUNTY FAIR, Hennepin County Agricultural Society, 23185 County Rd. 10, Rogers 55374.
498-8502

A horse show, exhibits of 4H activities, fruits, and vegetables, and other traditional activities highlight the Hennepin County Fair, which will be held July 22-25 at the fairgrounds in Hopkins. No admission fee, no parking fee.

VICTORIAN CRAFTS FESTI-
VAL, Alexander Ramsey House, 265 S. Exchange St. (at Irvine Park), St. Paul. ►8
296-8719

Victorian crafts will be shown and sold on the lawn of the Alexander Ramsey House July 31 and Aug. 1. Thirty different craftsmen will demonstrate their work. Admission to the grounds will be 50 cents. Regular house admission will be charged.

AUGUST 1982

LUMBERJACK DAYS, St. Croix Valley Chamber of Commerce, 408 E. Chestnut St., Stillwater 55082. ►10
439-7700

This four-day celebration scheduled for the first week in August will include the National Log-rolling Championships, a parade, a 10,000-meter footrace, barbershop chorus and quartets' jamboree, kiddie carnival, sidewalk sales, dances, tours of historic Stillwater, float-plane rides, and cruises on the sternwheeler Jubilee. Many events will be free. Admission probably will be charged for events in Lowell Park; tickets for the plane and boat rides can be purchased in advance from the local chamber of commerce.

ANOKA COUNTY SUBURBAN FAIR, Anoka County Fair Board, 1144 Fifth Av. S., Anoka 55303.
427-4920, 427-4070 ►3

Tractor and truck pulls, demolition derbies, a diaper derby baby race, historical farm exhibit, beer garden, grandstand shows, livestock and horse shows, and other traditional activities will all be part of the Anoka County Suburban Fair Monday through Sunday, Aug. 2-8, at the fairgrounds north of Anoka at Ferry St. and Hwy. 47. Admission probably will be $1.50, and there will be a charge for parking.

DAKOTA COUNTY FAIR, Box 73, Farmington 55024.
463-8818

Rodeos, more than 300 commercial exhibits, food stands, continuous entertainment, produce and animal exhibits, tractor pulls, demolition derbies, and carnival rides will be among the attractions at the Dakota County Fair at the fairgrounds, Hwy. 3 and County Rd. 74 south of Farmington, Aug. 9-15. Free admission.

UPTOWN ART FAIR, E. A. Nieland, 7201 Shannon Dr., Minneapolis 55435.
941-3985

This 19th Uptown Art Fair will feature 600 artists from across the United States displaying paintings, pottery, sculpture, ceramics, macrame, and other arts and crafts objects. One of the Midwest's largest art fairs, the Uptown Art Fair drew some 150,000 people to the area of Hennepin Av. S. and Lake St. in Minneapolis in 1980. The 1982 fair will be held Friday through Sunday, Aug. 13-15.

MINNESOTA RENAISSANCE FESTIVAL, Route 3, Box 117, Shakopee 55379.
445-7361

A variety of artisans and performers come together Saturdays and Sundays from Aug. 21 through Sept. 26 (and Labor Day) to recreate the atmosphere of a medieval European marketplace. Artisans include candlemakers, jewelers, painters, and potters. Performers include clowns, jugglers, magicians, mimes, musicians, and puppeteers, all in period dress. Admission to horse races and jousts is included with general admission. Displays are set in shops and studios of rough wood, stone, and thatch. Unusual and imaginative food is available everywhere. Tickets in 1981 were $6.95 for adults and $3 for children at the gate, slightly less if bought in advance; available at Dayton's and Twin Cities Fotomat stores.

MINNESOTA STATE FAIR, Falcon Heights 55108.
642-2200, 645-1241

The 12 days ending on Labor Day compose State Fair time in Minnesota, and 1.3-million people visited the fairgrounds on Snelling Avenue in Falcon Heights in 1980 to eat the food, check out the latest in farm machinery, sample the midway rides and attractions, and visit the numerous commercial exhibits. A wide variety of entertainment including big-name musicians, demolition derbies, and a fine arts exhibition is always part of one of the largest fairs in the United States. If you can't attend in person, watch for radio and television broadcasts from the fairgrounds. Admission in 1981 was $3 for adults and $1 for children 5 to 15 years old. Children under 5 are admitted free.

Minnehaha Falls, a symbol of the Twin Cities' parks.

278

Chapter Fifteen

PARKS

Parks are often singled out as important contributors to the quality of life in the Twin Cities. Not surprisingly, lakes form the heart of the metropolitan park system (there are more than 800 lakes in the seven-county metropolitan area, at least 25 of them within the city limits of Minneapolis and St. Paul), and provide visual and recreational variety year round. Paved bike trails, ball fields, playgrounds, and hockey rinks are also standard attractions in Twin Cities neighborhoods. Community park buildings serve as neighborhood meeting spots, and park programming reaches community residents of all ages.

Besides the ever-popular lakes, Twin Cities recreational resources include four major scenic rivers. Portions of the Mississippi, the Minnesota, and the Rum rivers have been declared state Wild and Scenic Rivers. Highways along the Mississippi near the Twin Cities are part of a system known as the Great River Road, suitable for scenic traveling. The St. Croix River, on the eastern edge of the metropolitan area, has been declared a National Scenic River.

The parks listed below are part of a regional park network established by the Metropolitan Parks and Open Space Act of 1974. Their planning, acquisition, development, and operation are carried out by counties, a few municipalities, and, in some cases, the state. The Metropolitan Council is responsible for the planning of the overall system, and it supplied the following information. Many municipal and county parks and

---

(See Locator Key Map, pages 8-9)

▶1 Mpls. Downtown
▶2 Mpls. Excluding Downtown
▶3 Mpls. North Suburbs
▶4 Mpls. Northwest Suburbs
▶5 Mpls. Southwest Suburbs
▶6 Mpls. South Suburbs
▶7 St. Paul Downtown
▶8 St. Paul Excluding Downtown
▶9 St. Paul North Suburbs
▶10 St. Paul Northeast Suburbs
▶11 St. Paul Southeast Suburbs
▶12 St. Paul South Suburbs

some trails and wildlife refuges are not part of the regional park system and are not listed here. Contact your county and municipal offices for more information on parks in your area.

BAKER PARK RESERVE, County Rds. 19 and 24, north of Maple Plain. ►4

Largest natural sand beach in the area. Seven miles of paved bike and hiking trails. Two nine-hole golf courses. 214 campsites, boat launch, all water sports. Ski touring and snowmobiling. Parking fee. For more information, call the Hennepin County Park Reserve District, 473-4693.

BALD EAGLE-OTTER LAKE REGIONAL PARK, Hugo Rd. and Overlake Av., White Bear Twp. ►9

Three lakes. Picnic area next to beach on Bald Eagle. Boat launch. Snowmobiling. Bus service. For more information, call the Ramsey County Parks Dept., 777-1361.

BATTLE CREEK REGIONAL PARK, McKnight and Upper Afton Rds., Maplewood. ►9

Hike trails through the river bluff site of the last battle between the Chippewa and Sioux. Picnic at 3,000-year-old Indian burial grounds that overlook spectacular vistas of the Mississippi River and St. Paul. Ski, ski tour, snowshoe. Bus service. For more information, call the Ramsey County Parks Dept., 777-1361.

BAYLOR REGIONAL PARK, County Rd. 33, Camden Twp. ►5

Farm museum offers home-made maple syrup. Hike a boardwalk marsh trail. Camping, fishing, ski touring. 2½ miles north of Hwy. 212. For more information, call Carver County, 467-3145.

BRYANT LAKE REGIONAL PARK, Shady Oak Rd., Eden Prairie. ►5

Rent horses and explore valleys, hills, and the lake, or swim off the sandy beach. Boat launch, all water sports. For more information, call the city of Eden Prairie, 937-2262.

BUNKER HILLS REGIONAL PARK, Hwy. 242 at Foley Blvd., Coon Rapids. ►3

Walk a field archery range; shoot at targets as they appear. Horseback riding stables, picnic shelters, stone fireplace for groups. Camping, ski touring, snowmobiling. For more information, call the Anoka County Park and Recreation Dept., 757-3920.

CARVER PARK RESERVE, County Rd. 11, near Victoria. ►5

Ten lakes and 3,500 acres compose a superb sanctuary for deer, geese, ducks, and recently reintroduced trumpeter swans. Extensive trails include one with "touch and feel" markers for the visually disabled. Nature center. Biking, boat launch, all water sports, camping, ski touring, snowmobiling, snowshoeing. For more information, call the Hennepin County Park Reserve District, 472-4911.

CLEARY LAKE REGIONAL PARK, County Rd. 27, southwest of Prior Lake. ►6

Playground, nine-hole golf course, and small, pleasant beach. Non-power boating. Pavilion for groups. Biking, ski touring. For more information, call the Hennepin County Park Reserve District, 447-2171.

COMO REGIONAL PARK, Lexington Pkwy., St. Paul. ►8

The most visited site in the Twin Cities, this century-old park offers golf, tennis, canoeing, paddleboats, a zoo, conservatory, gardens, and an amusement park. Skiing, skating, snowshoeing. Bus service. For more information, call the city of St. Paul, 488-7291.

COON RAPIDS DAM REGIONAL PARK, between Coon Rapids and Brooklyn Park. ►4

Walk across the Mississippi River on a 1,000-foot-long hydroelectric dam built in 1913. Excellent fishing. Summer river ecology programs. Boat launch. Ski touring. Parking fee. Bus service. For more information, call the Hennepin County Park Reserve District, 473-4693.

CROW-HASSAN PARK RESERVE, off County Rd. 19, North of Hanover. ►4

Canoe the meandering Crow River bordering the park for seven miles. Look for great horned owls, red-tailed hawks, and newly reintroduced trumpeter swans. Ski touring, snowmobiling. From County Rd. 19 north, take County Park Access Rd. 203 2½ miles to park. Parking fee. For more information, call the Hennepin County Park Reserve District, 473-4693.

ELM CREEK PARK RESERVE, County Rd. 202, northwest of Osseo. ►5

Spring-fed artificial swimming pond with 1,500-foot sand beach. Longest hike and bike trail system in area parks. Nature center. Ski touring, snowmobiling, snowshoeing. Parking fee. For more information, call the Hennepin County Park Reserve District, 425-0993.

FORT SNELLING STATE PARK, Post Rd. off Hwy. 5, Fort Snelling. ►2, 8

The park is split by a spectacular bluff. Above is a reconstruction of the original Fort Snelling outpost, the first white settlement in Minnesota. Below is the confluence of the Mississippi and Minnesota rivers. Picnic or swim at spring-fed Snelling Lake or walk Pike Island trails to a nature center. Boat launch, all water sports, ski touring. Bus service. Motor vehicle entrance fee. For more information, call the Minnesota Dept. of Natural Resources, 727-1961.

GRASS-VADNAIS LAKE REGIONAL PARK RESERVE, Snail Lake Blvd. at Mackubin St., Shoreview. ►9

Four lakes offer good shore fishing. Boat launch, swimming beach on Snail Lake. Forest has 50-foot pine trees and hiking trails. Snowmobiling. Bus service. For more information, call the Ramsey County Parks Dept., 777-1361.

HIDDEN FALLS-CROSBY FARM REGIONAL PARK, along the Mississippi River, near

Hwy. 5 and Shepard Rd., St. Paul. ►8

The falls are in a secluded, sandstone cliff area. Downriver at Crosby Farm, hike at mid-level along a 150-foot bluff or navigate a swamp by boardwalk and marvel at monster cottonwood trees. Boat launch and ski touring. Bus service. Hidden Falls Park is north of Hwy. 5 off E. River Rd. Crosby Farm Park is south of Shepard Rd. at the end of Mississippi Blvd. For more information, call the City of St. Paul, 488-7291.

HYLAND-BUSH-ANDERSON LAKES, Bloomington and Eden Prairie. ►5, 6

The Hyland Lake Park Reserve offers a secluded lake surrounded by hills. Hiking, biking. Isolated picnic areas and nature center. Canada goose and duck habitat. Non-power boating only. Skiing and ski touring. E. Bush Lake Rd. off I-494, Bloomington. For more information, call the Hennepin County Park Reserve District, 835-4604. Bush Lake has a popular beach, good bass fishing, and waterfowl observation sites. Boat motors restricted to six horsepower. 9140 E. Bush Lake Rd., Bloomington. For more information, call the city of Bloomington, 881-5811, ext. 230. Three Anderson Lakes provide waterfowl habitat and opportunities to observe nature. South of I-494 and west of County Rd. 18, Eden Prairie. For more information, call the city of Eden Prairie, 937-2262.

LAKE BYLLESBY REGIONAL PARK, off County Rd. 86, Randolph Twp.. ►12

A dam on the Cannon River formed this wide, deep fishing lake with a swimming beach. Boat launch. All water sports. To reach Lake Byllesby, take Hwy. 52 south to County Rd. 86, then east to Harry Av., then south 1½ miles. For more information, call Dakota County, 437-6608.

LAKE GEORGE REGIONAL PARK, off County Rd. 9, Oak Grove Twp. ►3

Natural sand beach, boat launch, good fishing. For more information, call the Anoka County Park and Recreation Dept. 757-3920.

LAKE REBECCA PARK RESERVE, County Rd. 50, between Delano and Rockford. ►4

Swimming beach, bike trails, canoe and paddleboat rental, creative play area. Restored wildlife habitat attracts swans, geese, and ducks. Horseback riding, ski touring, snowmobiling. Parking fee. For more information, call the Hennepin County Park Reserve District, 473-4693.

LEBANON HILLS REGIONAL PARK RESERVE, Cliff and Pilot Knob Rds., Eagan and Apple Valley. ►12

A glacier-made park with three lakes, steep hills, deep valleys. Canoeing, fishing, biking. Hiking and horse trails. Ski touring, snowmobiling, snowshoeing. Adjacent to the new Minnesota Zoo. For more information, call Dakota County, 437-6608.

LILYDALE-HARRIET ISLAND REGIONAL PARK, along the Mississippi River, south of downtown St. Paul. ►7, 8

From Harriet Island watch tugs, barges, and pleasure craft on the Mississippi pass downtown St. Paul. Picnic on Cherokee Bluffs overlooking the river. Bus service. For more information, call the City of St. Paul, 488-7291. Explore clay pits for rocks and fossils in Lilydale Regional Park near the river. Boat launch. Ski touring. Call the interpretive center for required group reservations. Bus service. For more information, call the Ramsey County Parks Dept., 777-1361.

LUCE LINE STATE TRAIL, Vicksburg Lane, Plymouth. ►4

Hike, bike, or ride horseback along a route Dakota Indians traveled two centuries ago, today an abandoned railroad corridor. Ski touring, snowmobiling. The 30-mile trail starts at Gleason Lake in Plymouth, ends at Winsted. For more information, call the Minnesota Dept. of Natural Resources, 296-9115.

MARTIN-ISLAND-LINWOOD LAKE REGIONAL PARK, County Rds. 22 and 26, northeastern Anoka County. ►9

Hike nature trails or a long boardwalk through marshes to see waterfowl. Boat launch, all water sports. For more information, call the Anoka County Park and Recreation Dept., 757-3920.

MINNEAPOLIS CHAIN OF LAKES, Minneapolis. ►2

This urban park system includes Cedar Lake, Lake of the Isles, Lake Calhoun, and Lake Harriet. Seven beaches. Rose garden, bird sanctuary. Performances four nights a week during the summer at the Lake Harriet bandstand. Ride a trolley from Lake Harriet to Lake Calhoun. Rent canoes, rowboats. Good fishing. Bike, hike, rollerskate, or jog 12 miles of virtually continuous off-road trails. Ski touring, skating, snowshoeing. Bus service. Locations—Cedar Lake: Cedar Lake Pkwy.; Lake of the Isles: W. 26th

A summer afternoon in the Twin Cities.

St. and Lake of the Isles Pkwy.; Lake Harriet: 4135 W. Lake Harriet Pkwy.; Lake Calhoun: 2701 W. Lake St. For more information, call the Minneapolis Park and Recreation Board, 348-2142.

MINNEHAHA REGIONAL PARK, E. 48th St. and Minnehaha Av., Minneapolis. ►2

Explore Minnehaha Creek from above the falls to the Mississippi River or watch boats and barges go through the Ford Dam locks. Two large picnic areas with pavilion and electric cooking equipment. Skating and snowshoeing. Bus service. For more information, call the Minneapolis Park and Recreation Board, 348-2142.

MINNESOTA VALLEY STATE TRAIL, along Hwy. 169, near Jordan and Shakopee. ►6

As wide as five miles and as deep as 300 feet, the Minnesota Valley receives more than 40,000 migratory birds each fall. Look for herons, pheasant, and large woodpeckers. Includes Minnesota Valley National Wildlife Refuge. Carver Rapids (three miles southwest of Shakopee) and Lawrence (three miles southwest of Jordan) Trail Sites have a total of 15 miles of foot trails. Canoeing, fishing, camping, horseback riding, ski touring, snowmobiling. For more information, call the Minnesota Dept. of Natural Resources, 296-4776.

MINNESOTA ZOOLOGICAL GARDEN, 12101 Johnny Cake Ridge Rd., Apple Valley. ►12

Watch animals in their natural habitat outdoors or inside a spectacular tropical pavilion. Monorail ride. Ski touring. Bus service. For more information, call the Minnesota Zoo, 432-9000.

MISSISSIPPI RIVERFRONT REGIONAL PARK, Nicollet Island, Minneapolis. ►1

Explore ancient logging troughs, early flour mills, river locks, and Nicollet Island. View the historic Stone Arch Railroad Bridge. Outdoor concerts two nights a week in the summer. Bus service. For more information, call the Minneapolis Park and Recreation Board, 348-2142.

NOKOMIS-HIAWATHA REGIONAL PARK, Cedar Av. and Minnehaha Pkwy., Minneapolis. ►2

Nokomis, the larger of the two lakes, has two beaches, a fitness trail, bike and walking paths. Nearby Hiawatha (E. 44th St. and 26th Av. S.) is more secluded, with a family beach and 18-hole golf course. Canoeing, sailing, skating, ski touring. Bus service. For more information, call 348-2142.

WILLIAM O'BRIEN STATE PARK, off Hwy. 95, north of Marine on St. Croix. ►10

Picnic grounds in spacious wooded area, many hiking trails, swimming in lake or river. Bicycling, all water sports, ski touring. Motor vehicle entrance fee. For more information, call the Minnesota Dept. of Natural Resources, 433-2421.

PHALEN-KELLER-GERVAIS REGIONAL PARK, Keller and Wheelock Pkwys. at Arcade St.,

St. Paul and Maplewood. ▶8, 9

Completely redeveloped since 1976, these urban parks offer three lakes, two golf courses, archery, boat launches, bicycling, ski touring, and snowshoeing. Bus service. For more information, call the St. Paul Parks and Recreation Dept., 292-7400 (Phalen), or the Ramsey County Parks Dept., 777-1361 (Keller-Gervais).

RICE CREEK-CHAIN OF LAKES REGIONAL PARK RESERVE, County Rd. 14 off I-35E, Lino Lakes. ▶9

Four shallow lakes and wetlands attract many bird species. Park also features Hopewell Indian burial mounds and a nine-hole golf course. For more information, call the Anoka County Park and Recreation Dept., 757-3920.

RUM RIVER CENTRAL REGIONAL PARK, County Rds. 7 and 55, west-central Anoka County. ▶3

Canoe the Rum River, designated a state Wild and Scenic River. Park also has a Sioux Indian burial mound. For more information, call the Anoka County Park and Recreation Dept., 757-3920.

RUSH LAKE-LONG LAKE REGIONAL PARK, I-694 and Long Lake Rd., New Brighton. ▶9

Swimming beach at Long Lake. Access via Beach Rd. at I-694 and Long Lake Rd. For more information, call the New Brighton Park and Recreation Dept., 633-8906, or the Ramsey County Parks Dept., 777-1361.

SOUTH WASHINGTON COUNTY REGIONAL PARK RESERVE, Hwy. 61 and County Rd. 19, Cottage Grove. ▶11

See downtown St. Paul rise up as you hike out of a steep and spectacular creek gorge. Ski touring. For more information, call Washington County, 439-6058.

SPRING LAKE REGIONAL PARK RESERVE, off County Rd. 42, Nininger. ▶12

Spectacular view of the Mississippi River valley from a picnic area on high bluffs overlooking backwater formed by a dam at Hastings. To reach Spring Lake, take Hwy. 55 to County Rd. 42, turn left at Idell Av., then left at E. 127th St. For more information, call Dakota County, 437-6608.

SQUARE LAKE REGIONAL PARK, County Rd. 7, six miles north of Stillwater. ▶10

One of the region's clearest swimming lakes and a favorite of scuba divers. Boat launch, all water sports. For more information, call Washington County, 439-6058.

THEODORE WIRTH REGIONAL PARK, Glenwood Av. and Xerxes Av. N., Minneapolis. ▶2

Hike or bike paved trails or pleasure drive through wooded areas. Visit the secluded Eloise Butler Wildflower Garden and Bird Sanctuary. Swimming, canoeing, sailing, golf, skiing, ski touring, snowshoeing. Bus service. For more information, call the Minneapolis Park and Recreation Board, 348-2142.

REGIONAL PARKS AND ACTIVITIES

	BIKING	BOAT LAUNCH	POWER BOATING	CANOEING	SAILING	CAMPING	FISHING
Coon Rapids Dam*		•	•	•			•
Bunker Hills						•	
Rum River Central				•			•
Lake George		•	•	•	•		•
Martin-Island-Linwood Lake		•	•	•	•		•
Rice Creek-Chain of Lakes							
Rush Lake-Long Lake							•
Grass-Vadnais Lake*		•	•	•	•		•
Bald Eagle-Otter Lake*		•	•	•	•		•
William O'Brien State Park	•	•	•	•		•	•
Square Lake		•	•	•	•		•
Como*	•			•			
Phalen-Keller-Gervais*	•	•	•	•	•		•
Battle Creek*							
South Washington County							
Spring Lake							
Lake Byllesby		•	•		•	•	•
Lebanon Hills	•			•			•
Minnesota Zoological Garden*							
Lilydale-Harriet Island*		•	•	•			•
Hidden Falls-Crosby Farm*	•	•	•	•			•
Fort Snelling State Park*	•	•	•	•	•		•
Minnehaha*							
Nokomis-Hiawatha*	•	•		•	•		•
Cleary Lake	•			•	•		
Minnesota Valley State Trail				•		•	•
Hyland-Bush-Anderson Lakes	•	•		•	•		•
Bryant Lake	•	•	•	•	•		•
Baylor						•	•
Carver	•	•	•	•	•	•	•
Minneapolis Chain of Lakes*	•	•		•	•		•
Theodore Wirth*	•	•		•	•		•
Mississippi Riverfront*	•			•			•
Luce Line State Trail	•						
Baker	•	•	•	•	•	•	•
Lake Rebecca	•	•		•	•		•
Crow-Hassan							
Elm Creek	•						

*Parks reached by Metropolitan Transit Commission buses. For exact schedules call MTC Transit Information, 827-7733.

GOLF	HIKING	HORSEBACK RIDING TRAILS	SUMMER NATURE INTERPRETATION	PICNICKING	SWIMMING	ICE FISHING	WINTER NATURE INTERPRETATION	SKATING	SKIING, DOWNHILL	SKI TOURING	SNOWMOBILING	SNOWSHOEING
	•		•	•		•	•			•		
•	•	•	•	•						•	•	
	•											
				•	•	•						
	•			•	•	•						
•												
				•	•							
	•			•	•	•						•
	•			•	•	•						•
	•		•	•	•					•		•
•	•			•	•	•		•	•			•
•	•			•	•	•		•		•		•
	•			•					•	•		•
	•			•						•		
	•			•						•		
	•			•	•	•						
	•	•	•	•		•				•	•	•
	•		•	•			•			•		
	•			•						•		•
•	•		•	•	•		•			•		•
	•			•				•				•
•	•			•	•	•		•		•		
•	•			•	•					•		
	•	•		•						•	•	
	•		•	•	•	•	•		•	•		•
	•	•		•	•					•		
	•			•	•					•		•
	•	•	•	•		•	•			•	•	•
	•		•	•	•	•		•		•	•	•
•	•		•	•	•					•		•
	•			•								
	•	•								•	•	
•	•	•		•	•	•				•	•	
	•	•		•	•	•				•	•	
	•	•								•	•	
	•	•	•	•	•		•			•	•	•

Sailing in the Land of Lakes.

Chapter Sixteen

RECREATION

> **KEY NUMBERS**
> Ramsey County Parks Department: 777-1361
> Minneapolis Park Board: 348-2121

In the Twin Cities, the weather is seldom a barrier to outdoor fun. Every season has its activities, and facilities for most forms of outdoor recreation are close at hand.

The following is a list of resources for popular recreational activities. Call your local park office for more information about programs and facilities in your part of the metropolitan area.

ARCHERY

MINNESOTA STATE ARCHERY ASSOCIATION, Stephen Redmann, 3050 Lisbon Av. N., Lake Elmo 55042.
770-6328

Annual membership ($8) includes subscription to bimonthly *Minnesota Arrow,* a publication listing all archery events in Minnesota. There are several local archery associations in the Twin Cities area.

The Minneapolis Park Board (348-2248) maintains archery butts for public use near Wirth Park at the corner of Glenwood and Plymouth Avs.; on the northwest edge of Lake Nokomis; on

(See Locator Key Map, pages 8-9)

- ►1 Mpls. Downtown
- ►2 Mpls. Excluding Downtown
- ►3 Mpls. North Suburbs
- ►4 Mpls. Northwest Suburbs
- ►5 Mpls. Southwest Suburbs
- ►6 Mpls. South Suburbs
- ►7 St. Paul Downtown
- ►8 St. Paul Excluding Downtown
- ►9 St. Paul North Suburbs
- ►10 St. Paul Northeast Suburbs
- ►11 St. Paul Southeast Suburbs
- ►12 St. Paul South Suburbs

the southeast edge of Lake Calhoun; and on the southeast corner of Columbia golf course. Ramsey County maintains three or four archery ranges in and around St. Paul. Call 777-1361 for information.

AUTO RACING

ELKO SPEEDWAY, 20 miles south of Minneapolis on I-35W, Elko. ►6
461-3321

Five classes of late-model stock-car races on a three-eighths-mile asphalt track. Occasional demolition derbies. Sat 7:30 p.m. in the summer (Memorial Day-Labor Day). Admission $4.50 adults, $2 children under 15, children under 7 free.

RACEWAY PARK, Hwy. 101, between Savage and Shakopee.
445-2257 ►6

Hobby, late-model, and figure-eight stock cars race Sun and holidays at 7 p.m. summer. Admission $5 for adults, $2 for children 7 to 15, free for children 6 and under with parents.

BIKING

AMERICAN YOUTH HOSTELS (Minnesota Council), 475 Cedar St., St. Paul 55101.
292-4121

Sponsors bike trips, including one through China last year, and maintains hostels (inexpensive overnight accommodations for people traveling under their own power). Membership ($14 for adults, $7 for juniors and seniors,

$21 for families) includes handbook of hostels throughout the United States and the *Hosteler* newspaper.

GOPHER WHEELMEN, Gary L. Johnson, 4124 21st Av. S., Minneapolis 55407.
721-5849

Amateur racing club schedules tours and training rides. Membership $10 per year open to beginning through advanced racers, men and women, teen-age and older.

Bike Trails

There are hundreds of miles of well-maintained bike trails in the metropolitan area. In Minneapolis, the most popular trail follows Minnehaha Creek. A continuous path for bikes only, the trail runs from Minnehaha Park through south Minneapolis and around Lake Harriet, Lake Calhoun, and Lake of the Isles. See the Parks section of this book (page 278) for information on other public parks with bike trails.

The most complete and detailed sources of bike-route information for both the metropolitan area and the state are the Minnesota Department of Transportation *Minnesota Bikeways* maps. These maps are available for 52 regions of the state, eight of them for the metro area. They detail each roadway in the area they cover and provide a roadway evaluation (suitability for biking) by color code. Prices for the maps were not set at this writing. For an order form, write *Minnesota Bikeways,* Minnesota Department of Transportation, John Ireland Blvd., Room B-20, Transportation Bldg., St. Paul 55155, or call 296-2216.

BOWLING

The following organizations can provide information on Twin Cities bowling leagues and events.

MINNEAPOLIS DISTRICT BOWLING ASSOCIATION, 3701 Fremont Av. N., Minneapolis.
522-7100

MINNEAPOLIS WOMEN'S BOWLING ASSOCIATION, 6125 Cloverdale Av. N., Crystal.
537-0306

ST. PAUL DISTRICT BOWLING ASSOCIATION, 1022 Arkwright St., St. Paul.
774-0960

ST. PAUL WOMEN'S BOWLING ASSOCIATION, 48 W. Jessamine, St. Paul.
489-6521

CAMPING

For information on campgrounds in public parks in the metropolitan area see the Lodging section of this book (page 147). For information on public and private campsites throughout the state, write for the free *Minnesota Camping Guide,* Department of Economic Development, Tourism Bureau, 480 Cedar St., St. Paul 55101, or call 296-5029.

CANOE RENTALS AND ROUTES

A good source of information on rivers to canoe in Minnesota is Greg Breining's book, *A Gathering of Waters: A Guide to Minnesota Rivers* (Minnesota Department of Natural Resources, 1977). Book includes maps, color photos, and descriptions of 18 popular state rivers. 106 pages.

MINNESOTA DEPARTMENT OF NATURAL RESOURCES/PARKS AND RECREATION, Space Center Bldg., Second Floor, 444 Lafayette Rd., St. Paul 55101.
296-4776
Provides information on canoe routes and rentals in state parks.

LAKE CALHOUN BOAT HOUSE, 3000 E. Calhoun Blvd., Minneapolis. ►2
823-8386
Rents canoes and rowboats to the public Memorial Day through Labor Day. Rentals require $10 deposit. Rates for canoes are $3 for first hour, 75 cents each additional 15 minutes; for rowboats $5 first four hours, $10 all day. Open seven days a week 11 a.m. to 8 p.m.

PHALEN BEACH, south shore of Lake Phalen, Wheelock Pkwy., St. Paul. ►8
776-9833
Canoe rentals to the public Memorial Day through Labor Day. Rentals $3.50 an hour, no daily rates. Driver's license or other identification required as a deposit. Open seven days 11:30 a.m. to 8 p.m.

CROSS-COUNTRY SKIING

The information listed here for metro-area cross-country ski areas is adapted from data supplied by the Minnesota State Tourism Bureau, 480 Cedar St., St. Paul 55101. For a map with information on cross-country and downhill ski areas around the state, write the Tourism Bureau, or call 297-2525.

BAKER PARK RESERVE, Medina. ►4
473-4693
North of County Rd. 24 in Medina. 9.3 km marked and groomed, beginner to advanced trails. Ski rental, instruction by reservation, trail map, chalet, snack bar, barn with picnic area, toilets. Parking fee.

BATTLE CREEK, St. Paul. ►8
777-1361
Off Winthrop St., one block south of Upper Afton Rd. Two miles marked and groomed advanced trail. Instruction, trail map, downhill ski chalet with snack bar and restrooms.

BIG WILLOW PARK, Minnetonka. ►5
933-2511
East of I-494 and west of County Rd. 73 along Minnetonka Blvd. Two miles marked and groomed, beginner to intermediate trail. Trail map.

BUNKER HILLS SKI TRAILS, Anoka. ►3
757-3920
Nineteen-km marked and groomed beginner to advanced trail. Ski rentals and instruction; trail map, restaurant, restrooms, shelter.

CARVER PARK RESERVE, Victoria. ►5
472-4911
West of Victoria between Hwys. 5 and 7. 9.9 km marked and groomed, beginner to advanced trail. Ski rental and instruction by reservation, trail map, tent camping, Lowry Nature Center, picnic areas, restrooms, barn with stove, patrol on trails. Parking fee.

CENTRAL PARK NINE MILE CREEK TRAIL, Bloomington. ►6
887-9638, 887-9601
104th St. and Morgan Av.; 5 miles marked, intermediate to advanced trail. Instruction available through city; trail map, shelter.

CIVIC CENTER TOURING TRAIL, Burnsville. ►6
890-4100
Trail runs east of Nicollet Av. along 130th St. Trail maps, lodging, and food in area.

CLEARY LAKE REGIONAL PARK, near Prior Lake. ►6
447-2171
County Rd. 27 south of County Rd. 12. 6.8 km marked and groomed, beginner to intermediate trail. Ski rental, instruction by reservation, trail map, toilets, snack bar. Parking fee.

COLUMBIA SKI TOURING AREA, 33rd and Central Avs. N.E., Minneapolis. ►2
348-2121

2.2-km beginner to intermediate trails. Ski rental and instruction; food service, restrooms, chalet.

CROW-HASSAN PARK RE-SERVE, north of Hanover. ►4
473-4693

County Rd. 15, south from I-94, west on County Rd. 116, west on Hassan Pkwy. 9.3 km marked and groomed, intermediate to advanced. Trail maps, pit toilets, trail shelters. Parking fee.

ELM CREEK PARK RESERVE, northwest of Osseo. ►4
425-2423

Hwy. 152 and Territorial Rd. 9.3 km marked and groomed, beginner to advanced trails. Ski rental, instruction by reservation, trail map, Eastman Nature Center, toilets, picnic area. Parking fee.

EVERGREEN PARK, Minnetonka. ►5
933-2511

South of Minnetonka Blvd. and W. Williston Rd. on Victoria St. Two miles marked and groomed, beginner to intermediate trail. Trail map.

FORT SNELLING STATE PARK, St. Paul. ►8
727-1961

Hwy. 5 and Post Rd.; 15.8-mile marked and groomed beginner trail. Trail map, toilets. Connects to Minnesota Valley Trail Nature Center.

FRIENDLY HILLS PARK, Mendota Heights. ►12
452-1850

Two-mile marked beginner to advanced trail. Trail map, restrooms, warming house, and skating facilities.

GIRARD LAKE PARK TRAIL, Bloomington. ►6
887-9638, 887-9601

84th St. one block east of France Av.; one-mile marked beginner trail. Instruction through city; trail map.

HIAWATHA SKI TOURING AREA, 46th St. and Longfellow Av. S., Minneapolis. ►2
348-2121

Three lighted trails up to three km each, marked and groomed. Ski rental and instruction, trail map, chalet with fireplace, toilets, and food service.

HIGHLAND GOLF COURSE, Edgecumbe Rd. and Montreal, St. Paul. ►8
699-6082

3.5 miles marked and groomed, beginner to intermediate trail. Ski rental and instruction, trail map, food service, restrooms.

HYLAND LAKE PARK RE-SERVE, Bloomington. ►6
941-7993

E. Bush Lake Rd. near 96th St. 6.6 km marked and groomed, beginner to advanced trail. Ski rental, instruction by reservation, trail map, Richardson Nature Center, picnic area, toilets. Parking fee.

JONATHAN-CHASKA, Chaska. ►5
448-4700

Nine miles beginner to advanced trails. Association-sponsored lessons, trail map.

KELLER GOLF COURSE, Maplewood. ►9
484-3011

Two-mile beginning to advanced trail. Parking, equipment sales, rentals, instruction, toilets.

LAKE REBECCA PARK RESERVE, near Rockford. ►4
473-4693

County Rd. 55, one mile west of Hwy. 55. Eight km marked and groomed, beginner to advanced trail. Trail map, picnic areas, fireplaces, toilets, shelters. Parking fee.

LAWRENCE WAYSIDE, Jordan. ►6
492-6400

5.8 miles marked and groomed, beginner trail. Trail map, toilets, shelter, parking.

LEBANON HILLS PARK, near Hastings. ►12
437-6608

One mile west of Hwy. 3 on Cliff Rd. Eight miles marked and groomed. Maps at park office, toilets.

LONE LAKE PARK, Minnetonka. ►5
933-2511

Shady Oak Rd., south of Excelsior Blvd. Two miles marked and groomed, beginner to intermediate trail. Trail map.

LUCE LINE TRAIL, Plymouth to Orono. ►4, 5
296-2553

Six-mile marked and groomed beginner trail. Trail map at state Department of Natural Resources office. Second segment from Orono to Watertown; 12-mile marked

Cross-country skiing through a Twin Cities park.

and groomed beginner trail. Trail map at DNR office.

MEADOW PARK, Minnetonka. ►5
933-2511

On Oakland Rd., east of I-494 and west of County Rd. 61, north of Minnetonka Blvd. and south of Hwy. 12. Two miles marked and groomed, beginner to intermediate trail. Trail map.

MINNESOTA VALLEY TRAIL, Jordan. ►6
492-6400

Trails at Carver Rapids. Six-mile marked and groomed intermediate trail. Trail map, toilets, shelter, parking.

MINNESOTA ZOOLOGICAL GARDEN NORTHERN TRAIL, Apple Valley. ►12
432-9010

12.5 km of marked and groomed beginner to expert trails. Rental available. Toilets, parking, shelter in Tropics Bldg., food. Regular admission to zoo covers skiing. All exhibits open during winter. Trail map, information available.

MINNREG SKI TOURING CENTER, Honeywell Country Club, Minnreg. ►6
435-6166, 435-7685

Minnreg exit off I-35W. Fifteen miles marked and groomed, beginner to advanced trails; 10 km lighted trails. Ski rental and instruction, trail map, parking, clubhouse, ski shop. Trails connect with Ritter Park. Trail use fee.

MURPHY-HANREHAN PARK RESERVE, Burnsville. ►6
447-2171

Located approximately two miles southwest of the junction of I-35 and County Rd. 42 in Burnsville. Fifteen km of marked and groomed intermediate to advanced trails. Trail map, parking, toilets.

WILLIAM O'BRIEN STATE PARK, Marine-on-St. Croix.
433-2421 ►10

9.8 miles marked and groomed, beginner to advanced trails. Trail map, limited pack-in camping, pit toilets, parking lot, water.

PHALEN PARK, St. Paul. ►8
778-0424 or 645-4631

Ten miles marked and groomed, beginner to intermediate trail. Ski rental and instruction; food, toilets, shelter, parking.

PINE POINT, Stillwater. ►10
439-6058

Junction of County Rd. 19A and Hwy. 61. Five-mile marked and groomed beginner to advanced trail. Trail map, picnic tables, barbecue grills, toilets.

PURGATORY CREEK PARK, Minnetonka. ►5
933-2511

On Excelsior Blvd., a quarter-mile east of Hwy. 101. Two-mile marked and groomed beginner to intermediate trail. Trail map.

RITTER PARK, 195th St., west of I-35W, Lakeville. ►6
469-5354

Fifteen-km marked and groomed

beginner to advanced trail. Trail map, restrooms. Trails connect with Minnreg Ski Touring Center trails. Parking fee.

SOUTH WASHINGTON COUNTY PARK, Stillwater.
439-6058 ►10

Junction of County Rd. 19A and Hwy. 61. 5.3-mile beginner to advanced marked trail. Trail map, picnic tables, barbecue grills, toilets.

SPRING LAKE PARK, Hastings.
437-6608 ►12

Two miles west of Hastings on Co. Rd. 42, north on Idell one-half mile to 127th St. E. Five miles marked and groomed. Toilets, maps at park office.

SUNFISH LAKE PARK, Sunfish Lake. ►10

Hwy. 212 between I-694 and Lake Elmo. Four miles marked, beginner to advanced trails; three loops. Trail map, parking.

TERRACE OAKS SKI TRAIL, Burnsville. ►6
890-4100 ext. 150

Near Ville Du Parc Skating Area, one mile south of Cliff Rd. at the end of Kennelly Rd. Five miles of groomed trails. Toilets, parking, maps.

VALLEY PARK, Mendota Heights. ►12
452-1850

2.5-mile marked beginner to advanced trail. Trail map, open-air pavilion; parking.

VALLEYWOOD SKI TRAIL, Cottage Grove. ►11
458-2828

5.1 miles of connecting loops between Cottage Grove, Oakwood Park, Pine Tree Pond Park. Trail maps, shelters, and parking in area.

WIRTH PARK 3 SKI TOURING AREA, Minneapolis. ►2
348-2121

Theodore Wirth Pkwy. and Plymouth Av. 2.2-km beginner to intermediate lighted trail. Ski rental and instruction; food service, restrooms, chalet.

WOOD LAKE NATURE CENTER TRAIL, 735 Lake Shore Dr., Richfield. ►6
861-4507

Three-mile beginner to intermediate trail. Ski rental, toilets, shelter, parking.

DOWNHILL SKIING

AFTON ALPS SKI AREA, County Rds. 20 and 21 (off Hwy. 12 East), Denmark Twp. ►11
436-5245

Thirty-two runs, 18 chairs, two tow ropes. Longest run, 3,000 feet; vertical drop, 330 feet. Night skiing, snowmaking. Three rental shops, ski school. Four chalets with food, bar with food, and band weekends. Prices not set at this writing. MC, V accepted.

BATTLE CREEK SKI AREA AND JUMP, 2080 Upper Afton Rd., St. Paul. ►8
738-2577

Six runs, three rope tows. Night skiing. Rental equipment, lessons, snacks. Prices not set at this writing.

BUCK HILL SKI AREA, 15400 Buck Hill Rd., Burnsville. ►6 435-7187

Nine runs, four chairs, three tow ropes, one J-bar. Longest run, 200 feet; vertical drop, 304 feet. Snowmaking. Rental equipment, lessons. Prices not set at this writing. AE, MC, V accepted.

COMO PARK SKI AREA, 1306 W. Arlington St., St. Paul. ►8 489-1804

Three runs, two tow ropes. Night skiing, snowmaking. Rental equipment, lessons, snacks. Prices not set at this writing.

HYLAND HILLS SKI AREA, 8800 Chalet Rd., Bloomington. 835-4604 ►6

Twelve runs, one chair lift, five rope tows. Longest run, 2,000 feet; vertical drop, 176 feet. Snowmaking, instruction, rentals. Prices not set at this writing.

WELCH VILLAGE SKI AREA, off U.S. 61 south of Hastings. 222-7079 ►12

Thirty runs, five chairs, one rope tow, two T-bars, one "mighty mite." Night skiing, snowmaking. Longest run, 4,000 feet; vertical drop, 350 feet. Rental equipment, ski school, two cafeterias, sandwich bar. Prices not set at this writing.

WILD MOUNTAIN, Taylors Falls. ►10 291-7980

Fourteen runs, three chair lifts, two rope tows. Longest run, 5,000 feet; vertical drop, 300 feet. Snowmaking facilities, equipment rentals, instruction, night skiing,

cafeteria. Prices not set at this writing.

THEODORE WIRTH SKI AREA AND JUMP, Glenwood and Plymouth Avs., Minneapolis. 522-4584 ►2

Six runs, three tow ropes. Longest run, 300 feet; vertical drop, 200 feet. Night skiing, snowmaking. Rental equipment, lessons, snacks. $2 adults, $1.75 juniors weekdays; $3.25 and $2.75 weekends.

CURLING

ST. PAUL CURLING CLUB, 470 Selby Av., St. Paul. ►8 224-7408

Curling has been a popular sport in St. Paul for more than a century. The St. Paul Curling Club keeps this venerable sport alive, sponsoring men's, women's, and mixed leagues.

FISHING

MINNESOTA DEPARTMENT OF NATURAL RESOURCES, Section of Fisheries, Centennial Office Bldg., 658 Cedar St., St. Paul. ►7 296-3325 general information 296-5406 license information

Minnesota law requires persons between the ages of 16 and 65 to obtain a valid fishing license before fishing in the state. Persons over age 65 need only carry some form of identification that indicates their birth date. Minnesota fishing licenses can be obtained at county offices and at many bait, tackle, and sporting goods stores. 1981 license fees were $5.50 for resident individuals, and $8.50 for a combination (family) license. Non-resident fees were $10.50 for individuals, $15.50 for a combination. A short-term (three-day) non-resident license was $5.50. Fees are expected to change in 1982. Approximately 1.5-million fishing licenses were sold in Minnesota in 1980.

Where To Fish

MISSISSIPPI RIVER

Often overlooked as a fishing resource, the Mississippi runs through the heart of the metropolitan area and yields a wider variety of fish than any other local fishing spot. A 40-pound muskie has been taken from the Mississippi where it runs through Anoka, and catfish, northerns, and bass are caught close to downtown St. Paul.

MINNEAPOLIS CHAIN OF LAKES ▶2

Minneapolis is said to have the best in-town fishing lakes in the nation. Lake of the Isles and Lake Calhoun are both surrounded by city parkland, and shore and non-motorized boat fishing is open to anyone. Portions of Lake Calhoun go as deep as 100 feet. Both of these lakes, and a third, Cedar Lake, are connected by lagoons. Good-size large-mouth bass, northerns, and crappies are often caught in all three lakes. Lake Harriet and Lake Nokomis are also open to public fishing.

GERVAIS, KELLER, PHALEN LAKES ▶8, 9

Lake Phalen, the southernmost link in this chain of lakes, is within the St. Paul city limits. It is surrounded by public parkland and open to shore fishing. Phalen is home to some large northerns, as well as a variety of other fish. Lake Gervais is known as a good spot for large-mouth bass.

LAKE MINNETONKA ▶5

Located in the western suburbs, Minnetonka is one of the largest lakes in the state. Walleyes and northern pike can be counted on here, as well as bass and crappies as big as two pounds.

In addition to these spots, there are more than 200 other lakes in the metro area that support fish, and approximately 500 miles of good fishing river. For detailed information on 88 of these sites where public access is permitted, write for the *Twin Cities Metropolitan Area Public Boat Launch Guide,* Department of Natural Resources Regional Office, 1200 Warner Rd., St. Paul 55106. The guide is also available by calling 296-8853, and at all county libraries. The guide is free and gives location, hours, parking, and permit information for each access site, as well as notes on what types of fish may be found at each location.

Ice Fishing

Fishing isn't limited to summer weather in the Twin Cities. As soon as the ice is safe, a whole new breed of fishermen appears, complete with tip-ups, fishing shacks, and hand-warmers. Call 296-3325 for information on local lakes where ice fishing is permitted.

GOLF

MINNESOTA GOLF ASSOCIATION, 6550 York Av. S., Suite 301, Edina 55435.
927-4643

Sponsors tournaments for members of affiliated clubs and publishes a free calendar of golfing events.

Golf Courses

The following Twin Cities area golf courses are open to the public. Greens fees are those charged in 1981 and are subject to change. Length and par are for men's (white) tees.

BAKER GOLF COURSE, 3025 Parkview Dr., Medina. ►4
473-7418

Two nine-hole courses. One 1,757 yards, par 30; the other 3,111 yards, par 36. $4.50 for nine, $3 for juniors and seniors. Additional nines $2.

BELLWOOD OAKS, 13239 E. 210th St., Hastings. ►12
437-9944

Eighteen holes, 6,591 yards, par 73. $3.25 for nine, $5.50 for 18, $1 more weekends.

BIRNAMWOOD GOLF COURSE, 12424 Parkwood Dr., Burnsville. ►6
890-7964

Nine holes, 1,385 yards, par 27. $3.50; $3.75 weekends.

BLUFF CREEK GOLF CLUB, 1025 Fourth St., Chaska. ►5
445-5685

Three miles south of Chanhassen on Hwy. 101. Eighteen holes, 6,321 yards, par 70. $4.75 for nine; $6.75 for 18; $5.50 and $7.50 weekends.

BRAEMAR GOLF COURSE, 6364 Dewey Hill Rd., Edina. ►5
941-2072

Eighteen holes, 6,300 yards, par 71, plus nine-hole par-three course. $4.75 for nine, $7.50 for 18; $3.25 for par-three. Edina residents may buy cards allowing them to make reservations and reducing their greens fees.

BRIGHTWOOD HILLS GOLF COURSE, 1975 Silver Lake Rd., New Brighton. ►9
633-7776

Nine holes, 1,556 yards, par 30. $3.50, $1.75 for second nine. Seniors $2, juniors $2 weekdays only.

BROOKLAND PAR-THREE GOLF COURSE, 8232 Regent Av. N., Brooklyn Park. ►4
561-3850

Nine holes, 1,031 yards, par 27. $2.75; $1.75 students and seniors.

BROOKLYN PARK GOLF COURSE, 77th Av. N. and Hwy. 52, Brooklyn Park. ►4
425-9978

Nine holes, 2,700 yards, par 32. $4.80; $2.40 for juniors before noon; $4.35 for seniors at restricted times.

BROOKVIEW GOLF COURSE, 8200 Wayzata Blvd., Golden Valley. ►4
544-8446

Eighteen holes, 6,300 yards, par 72, plus nine-hole par-three course. $5 for nine, $7.50 for 18,

$3.50 for nine (par-three), $7 for 18 (par-three). Golden Valley residents can buy cards reducing their greens fees.

CASTLE GREEN COUNTRY CLUB, 5399 Geneva Av., North St. Paul. ►9
777-1381

Nine holes, 1,440 yards, par 27. $3.50 until 4 p.m. weekdays; $3.75 after 4 and all day weekends.

CASTLEWOOD GOLF COURSE, 21850 N. Harrow Av., Forest Lake Twp. ►10
464-6233

Nine holes, 3,000 yards, par 36. $5 nine, $6 all day; $3 seniors and children for nine, weekdays, $6 nine, $8 for 18 on weekends.

CEDAR HILLS GOLF AND SKI, 9735 Eden Prairie Rd., Eden Prairie. ►5
934-9822

Nine holes, par 28. $3.50; $2.75 for seniors; $4 weekends.

CIMARRON PUBLIC GOLF COURSE, 664 Cimarron St., Lake Elmo. ►10
739-9010

Nine holes, 1,521 yards, par 27. $2.25 before 7 a.m. $3.25 7 a.m. to 4 p.m., $3.50 after 4; $4 all day weekends.

COLUMBIA GOLF MANOR, 3300 Central Av., Minneapolis. ►2
789-2627

Eighteen holes, 6,131 yards, par 71. $5.40 for nine, $7.40 for 18, $3.40 after 6 p.m.

COMO PARK GOLF COURSE, 1306 W. Arlington St., St. Paul. ►8
489-1804

Eighteen holes, 5,500 yards, par 69. $7.

COON RAPIDS BUNKER HILLS MUNICIPAL GOLF COURSE, 12800 Bunker Prairie Park Dr., Coon Rapids. ►3
755-4140

Eighteen holes, 6,670 yards, par 72; plus nine holes, 2,300 yards, par 32. Long course $4.75 for nine, $7.50 for 18; $8 weekends. Short course $4, $4.50 weekends.

COUNTRY VIEW GOLF COURSE, 2926 N. Hwy. 61, Maplewood. ►9
484-9809

Eighteen holes, 2,668 yards, par 54. $3.75 for nine; $2.25 seniors; $4 after 4 p.m. and weekends. $2 second nine.

DAHLGREN GOLF CLUB, Dahlgren Twp. ►5
445-4393

West of Chaska on County Rd. 43, off Hwy. 212. Eighteen holes, 6,465 yards, par 72. $5 for nine, $7 for 18; $9 weekends.

DAYTONA GOLF CLUB, 14740 Lawndale Lane, Dayton. ►4
427-6110

Northwest of Champlin-Anoka Bridge on County Rd. 12 (Dayton Rd). Eighteen holes, 6,741 yards, par 72. $5.50 for nine, $6 for 18; $6 and $7 weekends.

DWAN GOLF COURSE, 3301 W. 110th St., Bloomington. ►6
887-9602

Eighteen holes, 5,470 yards, par 68. $4.50 for nine, $7 for 18. Membership (open to anyone) reduces greens fees.

EDENVALE GOLF COURSE, 14500 Valley View Rd., Eden Prairie. ►5
937-9347

Eighteen holes, 5,700 yards, par 70. $5 for nine, $7.35 for 18, $5.25 after 3 p.m.; $8.40 weekends.

EKO-BACKEN GOLF AND SKI, 22560 N. Manning Trail, Scandia. ►10
433-2601

Nine holes, 4,620 yards, par 34. $4 for nine, $6 for 18; $5 and $7 weekends.

ELM CREEK GOLF COURSE, 18940 Hwy. 55 (Olson Memorial Hwy.), Plymouth. ►4
478-6716

Two nine-hole courses. One 2,921 yards, par 35; the other 1,693 yards, par 29. Long course $4.50, $5 weekends. Short course $3.50. Combination 18 $6.25; $7 weekends.

FORT SNELLING GOLF COURSE, Fort Snelling. ►2, 8
726-9331

Nine holes, 2,760 yards, par 35. $4.50; $2 additional nines. Season tickets available.

GEM LAKE PUBLIC GOLF COURSE, 4039 Scheuneman Rd., Gem Lake. ►9
429-9873

Eighteen holes, 3,393 yards, par 54. $3.50 for nine, $5.50 for 18.

The ubiquitous joggers around Twin Cities lakes.

GOODRICH GOLF COURSE,
1820 N. Van Dyke Av., Maplewood. ►9
777-7355
Eighteen holes, 5,805 yards, par 70. $7; $5.50 after 5 p.m.

GREENHAVEN GOLF COURSE,
W. Main St., Anoka. ►3
427-3180
Eighteen holes, 5,900 yards, par 71. $5.25 for nine, $7.50 for 18.

FRANCIS A. GROSS GOLF COURSE, 2201 St. Anthony Blvd., Minneapolis. ►2
789-2542
Eighteen holes, 6,343 yards, par 71. $7.40 before 4 p.m., $5.40 4 to 6 p.m., $3.40 after 6.

HAMPTON HILLS GOLF COURSE, 5313 Juneau Lane, Plymouth. ►4
559-9800
Eighteen holes, 6,249 yards, par 72. $4.50 for nine, $6 for 18; $5 and $7 weekends; $4 after 5 p.m. weekends only.

HIAWATHA GOLF COURSE,
4553 Longfellow Av. S., Minneapolis. ►2
724-7715
Eighteen holes, 6,630 yards, par 73. $5.40 for nine, $7.40 for 18; $5.40 4 to 6 p.m., $3.40 after 6.

HIGHLAND PARK GOLF COURSE, 1403 Montreal Av., St. Paul. ►8
699-3650
Eighteen holes, 6,265 yards, par 72. $5 for nine, $7 for 18. St. Paul residents can buy tickets reducing their greens fees.

HIGHLAND PARK NINE-HOLE COURSE, 2051 Edgecumbe Rd., St. Paul. ►8
699-6082
Nine holes, 2,912 yards, par 35. $4.50 for nine, $2 additional nines. St. Paul residents can buy tickets reducing their greens fees.

HOLLYDALE GOLF COURSE,
4710 Holly Lane N., Plymouth. 559-9847 ►4
Eighteen holes, 5,922 yards, par 71. $4.50 for nine, $6.50 for 18; $5 and $7 weekends.

HYLAND GREENS GOLF COURSE, W. 102nd St. and Normandale Rd., Bloomington. ►6
887-9668
Two nine-hole, par-three courses. One 1,560 yards, the other 1,260. $3.68 for long nine, $3.15 for short nine. Juniors and seniors can buy cards reducing greens fees M-F.

ISLAND VIEW COUNTRY CLUB, Waconia. ►5
448-5335
One mile northeast of Waconia on old Hwy. 5. Eighteen holes, 6,137 yards, par 72. $5.25 for nine, $6.75 for 18; $5.75 and $8 weekends. Nine-hole rate available only after 3 p.m. weekends.

KELLER PARK GOLF COURSE,
2166 Maplewood Dr., Maplewood. ►9
484-3011
Eighteen holes, 6,190 yards, par 71. $7; $5.50 after 5 p.m. Special rates for juniors and seniors at restricted times.

LAKEVIEW GOLF COURSE,
4520 W. Branch Rd., Mound. ►5
472-3459

Eighteen holes, 5,100 yards, par
69. $3.75 for nine, $6.25 for 18;
$4.25 and $6.25 weekends.

**MAJESTIC OAKS COUNTRY
CLUB,** 701 N.E. Bunker Lake
Blvd., Ham Lake. ►9
755-2142

Eighteen holes, 6,300 yards, par
72, and nine holes, 1,800 yards,
par 29. $7.50 for 18, $8 for weekends, $4.75 for nine on long
course after 4:30 p.m. weekends
only; $4.25 for short nine, $2.25
for additional nines.

**MANITOU RIDGE GOLF
COURSE,** 3200 N. McKnight
Rd., White Bear Lake. ►10
777-2987

Eighteen holes, 5,817 yards, par
70. $7.50 for 18, $5.50 after 4:30
p.m.

**MEADOWBROOK GOLF
COURSE,** 201 Meadowbrook Rd.
(at Excelsior Blvd.), Hopkins. ►5
929-2077

Eighteen holes, par 72. $5.40
for nine, $7.40 for 18.

**MENDOTA HEIGHTS PAR-
THREE COURSE,** 1695 Dodd
Rd., Mendota Heights. ►12
454-9822

Nine holes, 1,277 yards, par 27.
$4.30 for nine, $2.75 additional
nines; $3.30 for juniors and sen-
iors.

NEW HOPE GOLF COURSE,
8130 Bass Lake Rd., New Hope.
537-1149 ►4

Nine holes, 1,375 yards, par 27.

$3.25; $2.25 for juniors and seniors M-F.

NORMANDALE GOLF, 4800
W. 77th St., Edina. ►5
835-4653

Nine holes, 1,575 yards, par 27.
$3.25 for nine, $4.50 all day; $6
weekends. $2.50 for nine for jun-
iors and seniors.

**ORCHARD GARDENS GOLF
CLUB,** 155th St. and County Rd.
5, Burnsville. ►6
435-5771

Nine holes, 1,527 yards, par 27.
$3.65; $3.90 weekends; additional
nines $2.10.

**ORONO PUBLIC GOLF
COURSE,** 265 Orono Orchard
Rd., Orono. ►5
473-9904

Nine holes, 2,139 yards, par 33.
$4.30 for nine, $6.85 for 18; $2.80
for seniors, weekday mornings.

PARKVIEW GOLF CLUB, 1310
Cliff Rd.,Eagan. ►12
454-9884

Eighteen holes, 4,502 yards, par
62. $4 for nine, $7 for 18; 50 cents
off for juniors M-F before 3 p.m.;
$5 for 18 for seniors M-F before 3.

RED OAK GOLF COURSE, 855
Red Oak Lane, Mound. ►5
472-3999

Nine holes, 1,188 yards, par 27.
$2.75, $3 weekends; $2 for juniors
and seniors between noon and 3
p.m. M-F only.

ROSEVILLE GOLF COURSE,
232 Hamline Av. N., Roseville.
633-5817 ►9

Nine holes, 1,412 yards, par 27.

$3.25, $2.25 for juniors noon to 3:30 p.m. M, W, F only; $1.75 for seniors living in Roseville noon to 3:30 M-F, $2.25 for seniors not living in Roseville at those times.

SCOTTDALE GOLF CLUB, Credit River Twp. ►6
435-7182

Nine holes, 3,145 yards, par 36. $3.90 for nine mornings, $4.50 afternoons, $6.50 for 18; $5.50 for nine weekends, $7.50 for 18.

SCOTT-TEE'S GOLF CENTER, 8000 N. Lakeland Av., Brooklyn Park. ►4
425-9391

Nine holes, 705 yards, par 27. Scott-Tee's was closed for most of the 1981 golf season. Call for 1982 greens fees.

SUNDANCE GOLF COURSE, Dayton. ►4
425-5757

Eighteen holes, 5,675 yards, par 71. $5 for nine, $7.25 for 18. $4 and $6 after 3 weekends.

THEODORE WIRTH GOLF COURSE, Plymouth and Glenwood Avs., Minneapolis. ►2
522-2818 (par three)
522-4584 (long course)

Eighteen holes, 6,200 yards, par 72; plus nine holes, 1,240 yards, par 27. $5.40 for nine on long course, $7.40 for 18; $3.65 for nine on par-three course, $2.35 for additional nines. Juniors and seniors can buy cards reducing their greens fees.

UNIVERSITY OF MINNESOTA GOLF COURSE, Larpenteur and Fulham Avs., Falcon Heights. ►9
373-1646 (par three)
373-1645 (long course)

Eighteen holes, 6,123 yards, par 71; plus nine holes, 1,440 yards, par 27. Long course: $7.95 for 18 for the public, $6.90 for U of M Alumni Association members, $5.65 for staff, and $4.25 for students; $4.90 for public and alumni after 5:30 p.m.; $3.90 for students and staff after 5:30. Short course: $3.45 for the public, $2.95 for staff, $2.30 for students.

HANG-GLIDING

NORTHERN SKY GLIDERS, P.O. Box 364, Minneapolis 55440.

Information- and safety-oriented club for Twin Cities hang-glider enthusiasts. Meetings held first Tue of every month at 7 p.m. at the Southdale Hennepin County Library, 7001 York Av. S., Edina.

MINNESOTA GLIDERS, 2530 Nicollet Av., Minneapolis. ►2
870-0096

Information, equipment, and hang-gliding instruction.

NORTHERN SUN HANGLIDERS, 628 Larpenteur Av. W., St. Paul. ►8
489-8300

Information, equipment, and hang-gliding instruction.

HUNTING

Hunting is prohibited in Minneapolis and St. Paul, and by municipal ordinance in many suburban communities. Call municipal authorities before venturing out to hunt anywhere in the seven-county metropolitan area.

Anyone wishing to hunt in the state who is over the age of 16 must have a valid Minnesota hunting license. Hunters between the ages of 13 and 15 are required to obtain a firearms safety certificate. Participation in an adult hunter education program is advised but not required for all adult hunters. For licensing and hunting-season information, call the Department of Natural Resources at 296-4506.

Hunting on private lands is allowed in some of the more rural communities in the metro area. It is up to the hunter to obtain the landowner's permission before hunting on private property. Check local papers and Yellow Pages listings for private game farms that allow hunting for a fee.

ICE SKATING

Lighted outdoor rinks with warming houses are maintained in almost every neighborhood in Minneapolis and St. Paul during the winter. Many suburban communities also have outdoor rinks. Call your local parks department for detailed information. Year-round indoor skating is available at the following arenas:

COTTAGE GROVE ARENA, 8020 S. 80th St., Cottage Grove. 458-2345 ►11

ICE CENTER SKATING RINK, 5800 Wayzata Blvd., Golden Valley. ►4
545-1614

MINNETONKA ICE ARENA, 3401 Williston Rd., Minnetonka. 933-1545 ►5

ROSEVILLE ICE ARENA, 1200 Woodhill Dr., Roseville. ►9 484-0268

VICTORY MEMORIAL ICE ARENA, 1900 42nd Av. N., Minneapolis. ►2
521-2208

OUTINGS

MINNESOTA ROVERS OUTING CLUB, P.O. Box 14133, Dinkytown Station, Minneapolis 55414.
522-2461—Tripline

The Minnesota Rovers sponsor hiking, canoeing, backpacking, and a variety of other outings. Regular Tue evening trips or "happenings." Call the Tripline for up-to-the-moment details on outings. Club membership is $7 per year.

RACQUET CLUBS

The following metro area racquetball and/or indoor tennis facilities are open to the general public. Facilities charging membership fees are listed in the Minneapolis and St. Paul Yellow Pages under "Racquetball Courts—Private" and "Tennis Courts—Private." For information on outdoor tennis facilities, contact your local parks and recreation department (Minneapolis 348-2121, St. Paul 292-7400).

BROOKPARK TENNIS & RAC-

QUET CLUB INC., 6801 Winnetka Av. N., Brooklyn Park. ►4
533-9261

Four indoor tennis and five racquetball courts open to the public every day of the year 6 a.m. to midnight. Shorter weekend hours in the summer. Other facilities include a one-eighth-mile track, whirlpool, and sauna.

COACH RACQUET CLUB, 3020 N. Harbor Lane, Plymouth. 559-0430 ►4

Two racquetball courts open to the public M-F 7 a.m. to 11 p.m.; Sat 9 to 5; Sun 10 to 5. Closed weekends July and August. Membership available.

DAYTONA GOLF AND TENNIS CLUB, Dayton. ►4
427-6110

Four indoor tennis and four racquetball courts open to the public seven days a week 7:30 a.m. to 11 p.m. Summer hours 8 a.m. to 10 p.m.

MINNEAPOLIS TENNIS CENTER, 600 Kenwood Pkwy., Minneapolis. ►2
377-7440

Ten tennis courts, covered during the winter, open to the public seven days a week. Winter hours 7 a.m. to midnight; summer 9 a.m. to 9 p.m.

NICOLLET INDOOR TENNIS, 4005 Nicollet Av., Minneapolis. ►2
825-6844

Eleven tennis courts, six of them covered during the winter, open to the public seven days a week. Winter hours 7 a.m. to midnight; summer 8 a.m. to 9 p.m.

ST. PAUL INDOOR TENNIS CLUB, 600 De Soto St., St. Paul. 774-2121 ►8

Five indoor tennis courts open to the public seven days a week, 8 a.m. to 11 p.m. Summer open M-F only.

WEST SIDE RACQUET CLUB, 924 S. Robert St., West St. Paul. 451-8154 ►12

Six racquetball courts open to the public W, F 7 a.m. to 10:30 p.m.; M, Tue, Thu, Sat 8:30 to 10:30; Sun 10 a.m. to 10 p.m. Summer hours M-F 9 to 9; Sat 9 to 6; Sun 10 to 1 and 5 to 9. Other facilities include sauna and exercise room.

RIDES AND AMUSEMENTS

CIRCUS, 7577 Brooklyn Blvd., Brooklyn Park. ►4
560-4422

Bumper cars, miniature golf, some 100 electronic games. All indoors, open year-round. Free admission. Open M-Thu 10 a.m. to 10 p.m.; F-Sat 10 to midnight; Sun noon to 9.

SPRING LAKE PARK AMUSEMENT, Hwys. 10 and 65, Spring Lake Park. ►3
786-4994

Water slide, two 18-hole miniature golf courses, game room. Open seven days a week, April-October. Hours Sun-Thu 9:30 a.m. to 11 p.m.; F, Sat 9:30 a.m. to 12:30 a.m. Free admission.

VALLEYFAIR, 1 Valley Fair Dr. (off Hwy. 101), Shakopee. ►6
445-6500

The Twin Cities' major amusement park has more than 45 manicured acres of rides and shows, including one of the largest rollercoasters in the Midwest and the Corkscrew. Entertainment includes a Great American high-diving show. All rides and shows are included in the price of admission, which in 1981 was $9 for adults, $8 for children, $6 for seniors, and $6 after 5 p.m. for everyone. Open seven days a week 10 a.m. to 10 p.m. summer, weekends only in September.

WILD MOUNTAIN ALPINE SLIDE, County Rd. 16, north of Taylors Falls. ►10
291-7980

Fast, scenic ride on 1,700-foot-long alpine slide. Open June-August seven days; weekends only in spring and fall. Hours 10 a.m. to 8 p.m. Tickets $2.50 per ride for adults, $1.50 for children; five-ride book $10. Wed night all-you-can-ride $5.

ROWING

MINNESOTA BOAT CLUB, Navy Island, St. Paul. ►7
222-9014

Located on Navy Island just under the Wabasha Bridge on the Mississippi River, downtown St. Paul. Membership in the Minnesota Boat Club is open to the public. 1981 dues were $50 per year. Club supplies boats and instruction. No previous rowing experience necessary and no age limit. Club season usually begins in April and goes through October, depending on the weather. Regular competitions are held, and spectators are welcome.

RUNNING

MINNESOTA DISTANCE RUNNERS ASSOCIATION, P.O. Box 14064, University Station, Minneapolis 55414.
822-5007—Raceline

Raceline provides free up-to-date information on registration and starting times for most races in the Twin Cities, and for important races throughout Minnesota. The association sponsors several races a year and publishes a quarterly magazine containing race calendars and finishing times. Membership $7.50 for adults, $3 for persons 18 and under. Family memberships $10.

SKYDIVING

MINNESOTA SKYDIVERS CLUB, 866 W. County Rd. I, St. Paul 55112.
(507) 645-8608

Provide training and drops. Clubhouse open Sat, Sun 8 a.m. to 6 p.m. Drop zone is at the Carlton airport in Stanton, Minn. Write to the address above for information.

SPELUNKING

RAMSEY COUNTY PARKS AND OPEN SPACE
771-3413

Limestone caves are common along the shores of the Mississippi River south of St. Paul. Caves on the Ramsey County parkland are located in Lilydale (south of Harriet Island) near what used to be a brickyard. To reach the caves, take Plato Blvd. from St. Paul to Water St., then take Jay Av. to the brickyard. There are no facilities on the site, and the road is not maintained. Call the number listed above for a permit application. Along with the application, Ramsey County will send an information sheet on caves and fossils.

STABLES, HAY RIDES, SLEIGH RIDES

Hennepin County is said to have more horses per acre than any place east of California. Most of them are concentrated in the western portion of the county, around rural communities like Medina, although trails and horse enthusiasts can be found throughout the metropolitan area.

There are about 75 Western saddle clubs in and around the Twin Cities. Contact the nearest local stable for information on clubs in your area. The only polo club in the Twin Cities is based in Maple Plain and open to any interested person with a horse.

The following is a list of stables that offer rentals, lessons, hay rides, or other services. For information on public horse trails, see the Parks section of this book (page 278).

BUNKER HILL STABLES, Bunker Hills County Park, Coon Rapids. ►3
757-7010
Hay rides, English trail rides, pony rides, rentals. Open year-round. Reservations required.

DIAMOND-T RANCH, 4889 Pilot Knob Rd., Eagan. ►12
454-1464
Located near the Minnesota Zoo. Trail rides, rentals, hay rides, sleigh rides, winter riding.

HANSON'S RANCH, County Rd. 89, Shakopee. ►6
445-9970
Hay rides, trail rides, sleigh rides.

HOLLOW HAVEN FARM, 8411 Great Plains Blvd., Chanhassen. ►5
934-5525
Riding lessons by appointment. No rentals.

JONATHAN STABLES, Chaska. ►5
443-2686
Dressage and riding lessons. Work with show and hunting horses a specialty. Fox hunting in the fall. No rentals.

KING'S X RANCH, INC., 10924 N. Arcola Trail, Stillwater Twp.
439-6680 ►10
Horses bought and sold, hay rides, horses for parades and weddings.

NORTH OAKS RIDING STABLES, 8540 Kimbro Av. N., Stillwater. ►10
439-6878
Boarding, training, lessons, practice rides, rentals, hay and sleigh rides.

WAGON WHEEL RIDING STABLES, R.R. 2 (off County Rd. 70), Lakeville. ►6
461-3175
Hay rides, sleigh rides, trail rides, boarding.

SWIMMING— SUPERVISED BEACHES

In the St. Paul area, Ramsey County maintains seven supervised beaches and a number of public pools. There are seven supervised beaches in Minneapolis. Call the park offices (St. Paul 777-1361, Minneapolis 348-2121) for hours and locations. For locations of swimming beaches in the suburbs, see the Parks section of this book (page 278).

TUBING

APPLE RIVER FLOATERS ASSOCIATION, Box 24, Somerset, WI 54025.

The Twin Cities is less than 30 minutes from the self-proclaimed "tubing capital of the world" —Somerset, Wisconsin. Floaters rent inner tubes for themselves, their friends, and their beer coolers, and spend three hours floating effortlessly down the Apple River. There are several tube-rental outfits in Somerset, all of them easy to find. Rates for large tubes in 1981 were running about $4. The rental fee includes shuttle bus rides to the drop-in point on the river and parking.

Floaters are advised to wear tennis shoes to protect their feet, as well as sun screen and hats if they are sensitive to heavy sun exposure.

Somerset is located 25 miles east of St. Paul on Hwys. 35 and 64. Write the above address for more information.

SNOW TUBING

EKO-BACKEN GOLF COURSE, 22560 N. Manning Trail, Scandia. 433-2601 ▶10

Tube sliding on snow. Open F 5 to 7:30 p.m. and 8 to 10:30 p.m.; Sat, Sun for three 2½-hour sessions beginning at 2, 5, and 8 p.m. Each session is $5 for adults, $4 for children under 13. Group parties can be arranged for other nights of the week.

GREEN ACRES RECREATION, Demontreville Rd. and 55th St. N., Lake Elmo. ▶10 770-6060

Open M-Thu 2 to 5 p.m. and 6 to 9 p.m.; F-Sun four 2½-hour sessions beginning at 11 a.m., 2, 5, 8 p.m. Each session is $5 for adults, $4 for children 12 and under.

SPORTS FOR THE HANDICAPPED

COURAGE CENTER, 3915 Golden Valley Rd., Golden Valley 55422. ▶4 588-0811

Sponsors a variety of athletic and camping programs for children, adolescents, and adults with physical disabilities. Programs include the St. Croix Valley Deaf Athletic Association, two summer camps, and the Rolling Gophers teams that compete in men's and women's wheelchair basketball nationally and in several other sports. Contact the center for information and applications.

Pro soccer action with the Minnesota Kicks.

Chapter Seventeen

SPECTATOR SPORTS

Fans of professional and big-time college athletics have plenty to cheer about in Minnesota. The Twin Cities area hosts teams in every major professional sport except basketball, and the University of Minnesota competes in men's and women's sports in the Big Ten.

There will be, however, a major change in the Twin Cities sports landscape when the Hubert H. Humphrey Metrodome, a domed stadium that will seat more than 60,000 people, opens in downtown Minneapolis in the spring of 1982. The Minnesota Twins will christen the dome with their home opener April 6. The Twins, Vikings, and Kicks will play in the dome, and it is likely that the University of Minnesota football team will also move its home games to the dome in the near future. Administrative and ticket offices for the professional football, baseball, and soccer franchises will be moved to the dome when it opens.

In addition to pro and collegiate sports, a wide variety of community athletic programs are offered throughout the metro area, providing ample competitive activity for participants and spectators alike.

PROFESSIONAL SPORTS

MINNESOTA KICKS, 7200 France Av. S., Edina. ►5
831-5425

The North American Soccer League's Minnesota Kicks will play nine indoor home games November 1981 through February

---

(See Locator Key Map, pages 8-9)

►1 Mpls. Downtown
►2 Mpls. Excluding Downtown
►3 Mpls. North Suburbs
►4 Mpls. Northwest Suburbs
►5 Mpls. Southwest Suburbs
►6 Mpls. South Suburbs

►7 St. Paul Downtown
►8 St. Paul Excluding Downtown
►9 St. Paul North Suburbs
►10 St. Paul Northeast Suburbs
►11 St. Paul Southeast Suburbs
►12 St. Paul South Suburbs

1982 at the Met Center, 7901 Cedar Av., Bloomington. Tickets $5 and $3 at the box office. The Kicks will play 16 home games at the Hubert H. Humphrey Metrodome, downtown Minneapolis, April through August 1982. Tickets $7, $5, $3.75 at the box office. AE, MC, V, S accepted for all tickets. Season tickets available at about a 10 percent discount off single-game prices.

Kicks games are broadcast live over WAYL 980 AM radio.

MINNESOTA NORTH STARS,
7901 Cedar Av. (Met Sports Center), Bloomington. ▶6
853-9310

The National Hockey League North Stars will play 40 home games at the Met Center in 1981-82. Some pre- and post-season games will also be played at the Met. Tickets $15, $12, $8 can be charged on MC, V, S by calling 853-9300. Season tickets are available, at about a 15 percent discount off single-game ticket prices.

North Star hockey games are broadcast live by KSTP radio.

MINNESOTA TWINS, 8001 Cedar Av., Bloomington. ▶6
854-4040

The 1982 American League season will be the Twins' first under glass—Teflon-coated fiberglass to be exact. The Twins' opening day in 1982 will inaugurate the downtown Minneapolis Metrodome. Many fans are mourning the loss of outdoor baseball, but the Twins' management hopes the new facility will attract larger crowds. Tickets $7, $6, and $3 (general admission) can be charged on MC, V by calling 854-8601. Tickets also available at Donaldsons in downtown Minneapolis and the St. Paul offices of Midwest Federal Savings and Loan.

Twins games are broadcast live by WCCO 830 AM radio.

MINNESOTA VIKINGS, 9520 Viking Dr., Eden Prairie. ▶5
941-9060

The National Football League's Minnesota Vikings will play their last season outdoors at Met Sta-

Roy Smalley (left) and Hosken Powell of the Twins.

dium (8001 Cedar Av., Bloomington) in 1981-82 before they move to the downtown Minneapolis dome in the fall of 1982. The 1981-82 season will also be the last opportunity for Vikings fans to engage in the refined activity of pre- and post-game tailgating. Parking lot tailgating has become an elaborate ritual for many Minnesota fans. The new dome has no central parking area and hence no tailgate gathering spot.

Season tickets for the Vikings have always been notoriously difficult to obtain, and the move to the dome is not expected to alleviate this problem. Some single-game tickets can usually be purchased at the Vikings' ticket office before the season begins, and some single-game tickets are also available on the day of the game. Tickets $18 and $12; no credit cards accepted.

Vikings games are broadcast live by WCCO 830 AM radio.

BIG TEN SPORTS

UNIVERSITY OF MINNESOTA MEN'S ATHLETICS, 205 Bierman Athletic Bldg., 516 15th Av. S.E., Minneapolis. ►2
373-3181

The Golden Gophers field Big Ten teams in every major sport. Tickets are required for football, basketball, hockey, baseball, and some other events. Ticket prices vary by sport; student discounts available. Credit cards accepted.

Gopher football and basketball games are broadcast live by WCCO 830 AM radio. Gopher hockey is broadcast live by WWTC 1280 AM radio.

UNIVERSITY OF MINNESOTA WOMEN'S ATHLETICS, 238 Bierman Bldg., 516 15th Av. S.E., Minneapolis. ►2
373-2255

Tickets $3 ($2 for students) required for volleyball (fall season), basketball, gymnastics, softball, swimming and diving, and track and field. Tickets usually available at the door. No credit cards. Checks accepted.

HIGH SCHOOL SPORTS

MINNESOTA STATE HIGH SCHOOL LEAGUE, 2621 Fairoaks Av., Anoka. ►3
427-5250

The Minnesota State High School League coordinates league sports for Minnesota high schools and organizes state championship playoff events. Call for annual state tournament schedule. State high school tournament games for hockey and boys' and girls' basketball are usually played in Minneapolis and St. Paul in March and attract large numbers of spectators. The tournaments are generally covered live by local television and radio.

COMMUNITY TEAMS AND LEAGUES

Local parks and community groups sponsor well-organized sports activities for both adults and children throughout the metropolitan area. Adult and junior programs for hockey, soccer, and softball are particularly popular. Contact your local park office for details on team sports activity in your area.

MET CENTER

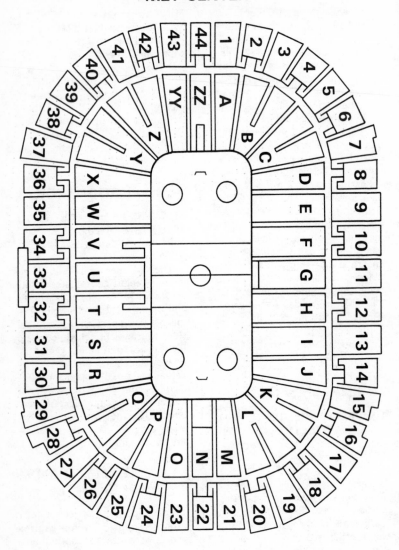

Met Center, 7901 Cedar Av., Bloomington. Tickets: 853-9300. Home ice for the Minnesota North Stars. Paid parking in adjacent lot.

314

U OF M WILLIAMS ARENA
BASKETBALL

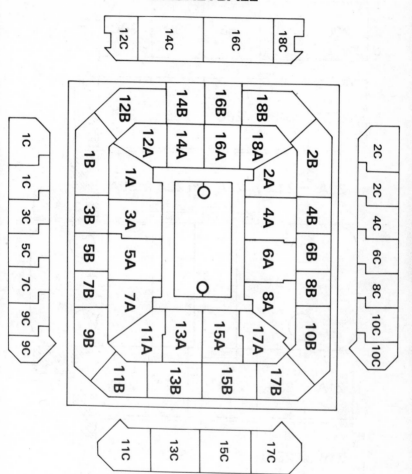

Williams Arena, Oak St. and University Av. S.E., Minneapolis. Tickets: 373-3181. Home court for U of M men's basketball. All seats reserved. Some restricted views in C sections 13, 14, 15, and 16. Wheelchair seating on request. Parking in paid lots and ramps in university area.

315

U OF M WILLIAMS ARENA
HOCKEY

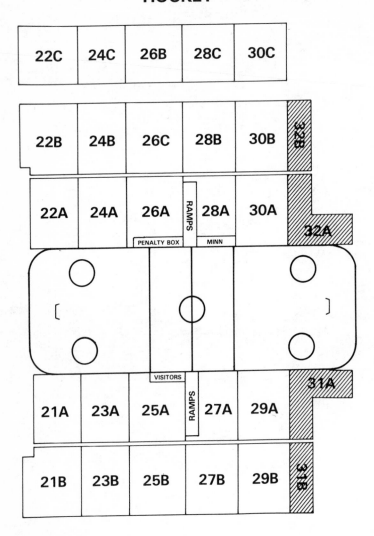

Williams Arena, Oak St. and University Av. S.E., Minneapolis. Tickets: 373-3181. Home ice for U of M hockey. Seats in sections 31 and 32 A and B general admission; all other seats reserved. Some restricted views on B and C decks. Wheelchair seating on request. Parking in paid lots and ramps in university area.

Chapter Eighteen

SHOPPING AREAS

Minneapolis and St. Paul offer one of the premier shopping experiences in the country. Skyway systems, pedestrian malls, excellent public transportation, adequate parking, and a fine selection of specialty shops and department stores make the Twin Cities' downtown areas both interesting and convenient. Beyond the two cities, the metropolitan area is ringed by eight major regional shopping malls and more than 100 other shopping centers. The nation's first enclosed, climate-controlled mall, Southdale, was built in Edina 26 years ago.

In addition to the downtowns and the malls, the Twin Cities has a number of neighborhood shopping areas. These areas attract shoppers looking for small specialty shops, restaurants, and a real neighborhood flavor. Neighborhood shopping areas are usually found along old streetcar routes and at busy intersections.

The newest—and, to many Twin Citians, the most exciting—shopping spots in the metro area are the collections of specialty stores and boutiques housed in converted warehouses and factories. Miniature, more elegant versions of Boston's Faneuil Market, Minneapolis' St. Anthony Main and Butler Square and St. Paul's Park Square Court, for example, offer shops whose settings are as intriguing as their merchandise.

The next several pages contain descriptions of a sampling of popular Twin Cities shopping areas. An extensive listing of a variety of local stores follows the descriptions.

(See Locator Key Map, pages 8-9)

►1 Mpls. Downtown
►2 Mpls. Excluding Downtown
►3 Mpls. North Suburbs
►4 Mpls. Northwest Suburbs
►5 Mpls. Southwest Suburbs
►6 Mpls. South Suburbs

►7 St. Paul Downtown
►8 St. Paul Excluding Downtown
►9 St. Paul North Suburbs
►10 St. Paul Northeast Suburbs
►11 St. Paul Southeast Suburbs
►12 St. Paul South Suburbs

DOWNTOWN MINNEAPOLIS

Nicollet Mall is the best-known element of Minneapolis' downtown (►1). Recently extended, the mall runs along Nicollet Av. for 13 blocks, from First St. all the way to the Loring Green area. The entire length of the mall is decorated with banners, fountains, and weather sculptures, and is open only to pedestrian and bus traffic. Bus shelters along the mall play classical music, and in the winter they're furnished with heaters. The mall is the major street for women's fashion stores, bridal shops, and design centers, and passes branches of the Twin Cities' four preeminent department stores. It is also the site of many city celebrations and festivities, so that shoppers may encounter an outdoor concert, art show, or parade when visiting the mall.

The skyway system, which connects the second-story levels of downtown buildings with pedestrian walkways, also presents a variety of shopping opportunities. The skyways are lined with specialty shops and restaurants, and open onto the sales floors of the largest department stores. The hub of the skyway system is the IDS Center's Crystal Court, a dramatic open gallery whose roof is formed by a cascade of transparent cubes.

The Minneapolis City Center project, scheduled for completion in 1983, will be a significant addition to an already vibrant downtown. City Center is expected to house at least 100 stores, several restaurants, a large hotel, and many offices. It will be located on Nicollet Mall between Sixth and Seventh Sts.

DOWNTOWN ST. PAUL

Downtown St. Paul's shopping streets (►7) have undergone enormous changes in the last few years. The biggest addition has been the new Town Square complex, which includes the largest store in the Donaldsons department store chain, as well as a number of other shops, restaurants, and an unusual four-level, glass-enclosed public park.

St. Paul's extensive skyway system links Town Square to many older commercial establishments. Some of these older buildings have been renovated in the last several years and now offer fresh shopping opportunities. Dayton's downtown St. Paul store was completely refurbished in 1981.

A few blocks southwest of Town Square, near the intersection of W. Fifth and St. Peter Sts., is one of the most prestigious shopping areas in the Twin Cities. Frank Murphy's, an exclusive women's clothier; Gokey's, the oldest department store in the state; and Bockstruck's, a distinguished jeweler, are just a few of the establishments located here. New shops were added in the W. Fifth St. area when the Carriage Hill renovation (at 14 W. Fifth St.) opened in 1980.

St. Paul's downtown offers a comfortable mix of old and new. Landmark Center, the elegantly renovated Old Federal Courts

Building, gives a major emphasis to downtown cultural activity as the site of noon lectures, afternoon concerts, and various gallery exhibits. Another popular downtown attraction is the Science Museum of Minnesota, with its Omnitheater extravaganzas and a variety of science and natural history exhibits. One of the flashiest new features downtown is the news banner that wraps around the top of the Minnesota Public Radio Building at the corner of Eighth and Cedar Sts.

MAJOR REGIONAL SHOPPING MALLS

BROOKDALE, Hwys. 100 and 152, Brooklyn Center. ►4
BURNSVILLE CENTER, I-35W and County Rd. 42, Burnsville. ►6
EDEN PRAIRIE CENTER, 8301 Flying Cloud Dr., Eden Prairie. ►5
MAPLEWOOD MALL, I-694 and White Bear Av., Maplewood. ►9
NORTHTOWN SHOPPING CENTER, Hwy. 10 and University Av. N.E., Blaine. ►9
RIDGEDALE, Hwy. 12 and County Rds. 18 and 73, Minnetonka. ►5
ROSEDALE, Hwy. 36 between Snelling and Fairview Avs. N., Roseville. ►9
SOUTHDALE, W. 66th St. and France Av. S., Edina. ►5

Eight major malls, each having more than 700,000 square feet of retail space, dot the Twin Cities suburban area. Each has at least two major department stores (most have four), dozens of specialty shops, and many branches of popular clothing store chains. While the malls seem to have many of the same stores, each tries to cater to the tastes of the particular area in which it's located.

The granddaddy of Twin Cities malls—and the first enclosed suburban mall in the country—is Southdale, in Edina. Southdale was built in the middle of a cornfield 26 years ago and was a catalyst to the development of Minneapolis' southern suburbs. The suburban shopping-mall concept was so successful it was copied nationally. Here in the Twin Cities, Southdale's developers (the owners of the Dayton's department store chain), repeated their success three times, creating a "Dale" empire that now includes Rosedale, Ridgedale, and Brookdale as well as Southdale. Southdale is as popular today as the day it opened, and on busy shopping days it becomes, in effect, the third-largest "city" in the state.

Look for a vast array of holiday programming and community activities in Twin Cities malls. Programs range from special Christmas presentations, to warm-weather fashion and flower shows, to all-season craft and antique fairs. One Twin Cities mall, Brookdale, sponsors a "Leg It" program, which allows people in need of exercise to walk or jog in the mall before the stores open.

SPECIALTY MALLS

GALLERIA, 3500 W. 70th St., Edina. ►5

BONAVENTURE, 1501 S. Plymouth Rd., Minnetonka. ►5

Operating on the principle that "small is beautiful," Galleria and Bonaventure offer an aura of style and elegance the larger malls often lack. There are no department stores in either one—just dozens of pricey specialty shops whose merchandise glitters in soft lighting and rich surroundings.

Bonaventure has two tiers of shops, a courtyard with plants and fountains, and a circular glass elevator that allows shoppers to see and be seen. Galleria's cobblestone "main street" has recently been extended and is anchored at each end with a restaurant that offers both meals and fresh baked goods. The two malls have some of the same shops, and shoppers can find the best of everything in them, from brass doorknobs, to Belgian chocolates, to designer dresses.

Bonaventure is located next to Ridgedale in Minnetonka; Galleria is a block south of Southdale in Edina. Both are open M-F 10 a.m. to 9 p.m.; Sat 9:30 to 6; Sun noon to 5.

MAJOR TWIN CITIES AREA SHOPPING CENTERS

The following list, based on information compiled by the Metropolitan Council in 1980, includes shopping centers of 150,000 square feet or more. Centers are listed by the city or suburb in which they are located.

Major regional centers are those of more than 700,000 square feet; *secondary regional centers* are those of 400,000 to 700,000 square feet; *district centers* are those of 150,000 to 400,000 square feet.

BLAINE ►9
Northtown Shopping Center (major regional), Hwy. 10 and University Av. N.E.
786-9704.

BLOOMINGTON ►6
Normandale Plaza Shopping Center (district), 5101 W. 98th St. (at Normandale Blvd.).

Southtown (secondary regional), I-494 and Penn Av. S.
881-2800.

Valley West Shopping Center (district), France Av. S. and Old Shakopee Rd.

BROOKLYN CENTER ►4
Brookdale Center (major regional), Hwys. 100 and 152.
922-2888.

BROOKLYN PARK ►4
Village North Shopping Center (district), Brooklyn Blvd. and Zane Av. N.

BURNSVILLE ►6
Burnsville Center (major regional), I-35W and County Rd. 42.
435-8181.

Diamondhead Mall (district), 100 W. Burnsville Pkwy.

COON RAPIDS ►3
Coon Rapids Shopping Center (district), East River Rd. and Hwy. 10.

Red Owl Family Center (district), Coon Rapids and Crooked Lake Blvds.

Village Ten Shopping Center (district), 2040 Northdale Blvd.

COTTAGE GROVE ►11
Grove Plaza (district), 80th St. and Point Douglas Rd.

CRYSTAL ►4
Crystal Shopping Center (district), 56th Av. N. and W. Broadway.

EDEN PRAIRIE ►5
Eden Prairie Shopping Center (major regional), 8301 Flying Cloud Dr.
941-8704.

EDINA ►5
Galleria (district), 3500 W. 70th St.

Southdale Center (major regional), W. 66th St. and France Av. S.
922-4400.

Yorktown Fashion Mall (district), 3300-3600 Hazelton Rd. (between France and York Avs. S.).

GOLDEN VALLEY ►4
North Star Shopping Center (district), 36th Av. N. and Hwy. 100.

MAPLEWOOD ►9
Maplewood Mall (major regional), I-694 and White Bear Av.
770-5020.

MINNETONKA ►5
Ridgedale Center (major regional), Hwy. 12 and County Rds. 18 and 73.
922-1938.

Ridgehaven Mall (district), Hwy. 12 and Plymouth Rd.

7 Hi Shopping Center (district), Hwys. 7 and 101.

RICHFIELD ►6
Richfield Hub Shopping Center (district), 66th St. and Nicollet Av.

ROBBINSDALE ►4
Ward's Terrace Mall (district), France Av. and 36th St.

ROSEVILLE ►9
Har Mar Mall (secondary regional), 2100 Snelling Av. N.
631-0340.

Rosedale Center (major regional), Hwy. 36 between Snelling and Fairview Avs. N.
922-4445.

ST. ANTHONY ►2
Apache Plaza (secondary regional), 37th Av. N.E. and Silver Lake Rd.
788-1666.

ST. LOUIS PARK ►5
Knollwood Plaza Shopping Center (district), Hwy. 7 and Texas Av. S.
933-8041.

ST. PAUL ►8
Hillcrest Shopping Center (district), White Bear and E. Larpenteur Avs.

Midway Center (district), University and Snelling Avs.
645-8191 (merchants' association).

Phalen Shopping Center (district), Prosperity and Magnolia Avs.

Sun Ray Shopping Center (district), Hwy. 12 and McKnight Rd.

SHAKOPEE ►6
Minnesota Valley Mall (district), Hwys. 169 and 300.

WEST ST. PAUL ►12
Signal Hills Shopping Center (district), S. Robert and Orme Sts. 457-0589.

NEIGHBORHOOD SHOPPING AREAS

CEDAR-RIVERSIDE, Minneapolis. ►2

Cedar-Riverside is a collection of shops, bars, and restaurants that serves as a support system for students on the West Bank of the University of Minnesota's Minneapolis campus. Some of the shops along Cedar Av. and Riverside have retained an aura of the 1960s' counter-culture. There are import shops, coffee houses that still have an occasional folk singer, and a cinema that screens mostly foreign films. There are also several music shops, bookstores, and camping-equipment stores. Rising above the shops and restaurants is a high-rise housing experiment that provides a home for thousands of students, elderly persons, and low-income families.

Although Cedar-Riverside has become rather tired-looking in recent years, new establishments, particularly restaurants, are being added to the scene in anticipation of the increased traffic generated by the nearby domed sports stadium that will open in 1982.

Another south Minneapolis college shopping area can be found in Dinkytown, on the University of

Shopping at St. Anthony Main.

Minnesota's East Bank. Dinkytown has its own array of bookstores, boutiques, and restaurants, though it lacks some of Cedar-Riverside's color and eccentricity.

UPTOWN, Minneapolis. ▶2

The intersection of Lake St. and Hennepin Av. in south Minneapolis is one of the busiest four corners in the Twin Cities. Located just a couple miles south of downtown, not far from the Guthrie Theater and Walker Art Center and only a few blocks from Lake Calhoun and Lake of the Isles, shops here range from venerable establishments like Schlampps (a furrier and clothier) to trendy new art galleries and design shops.

The entire area along Hennepin Av. from about 26th St. past the Lake St. intersection is considered part of the Uptown district. Uptown is thus a city within a city, boasting its own post office, the original store in the Lund's grocery chain, several antique shops, bookstores, bakeries, restaurants, and popular night spots. Two movie houses near the Lake and Hennepin intersection specialize in classic double-feature movies.

The city has begun a major—and controversial—refurbishing of this vital area, which will eventually include a mini-shopping mall called Calhoun Square. Other improvements that have been completed include a new streetscape and a modern, underground branch of the Minneapolis Public Library.

GRAND AV., St. Paul. ▶8

Grand Av. in its heyday was an important streetcar line, serving some of the most tasteful residential neighborhoods in the city. Then it succumbed to the commercial tackiness of a string of auto dealerships in the late 1950s. Happily, in the '70s, Grand experienced a renaissance, when a number of specialty merchants turned the street into a 10-block bazaar of interesting and unusual shops. Today, a meander down Grand between Dale St. and Snelling Av. will yield a variety of treasures.

Dozens of shops are grouped in and around restored buildings like Crocus Commons and Victoria Crossing, and some stand alone in Victorian frame houses. Antiques, crafts, candies, books, and clothing are for sale on the avenue, as are toys, artwork, and many other items. In addition, there are several fine restaurants along Grand, and their numbers are growing. In the summer they offer weary browsers a place to stop for a cool drink on an open patio. Year-round they offer a wide selection of standard American food and ethnic specialties.

Grand Av. merchants sponsor two major street festivals each year, usually in early June and again near the Christmas holidays.

Hours for Grand Av. shops vary. Many are open weekdays 10 a.m. to 5:30 p.m., and until 4 on Sat. Some stay open M, Thu evenings.

50TH AND FRANCE, Edina. ▶5

Edina spruced up and ran a mall through its downtown (at the intersection of 50th St. and France Av.) in an attempt to maintain the area's vitality in the face of the mass attraction of Edina's other major shopping area, Southdale. The city needn't have worried. Edina's downtown shops enjoy a large and faithful clientele who are drawn by the stylish mixture of elegant and preppy clothing, jewelry, books, and a variety of gift items. The area also has art galleries, movie theaters, a supermarket, and several restaurants.

Less than a mile east of France at 50th and Xerxes is a concentration of antique shops that offer browsers a quantity and variety not found elsewhere in the Twin Cities. The antique dealers began to congregate here several years ago and seem to have found strength in numbers.

A shopper traveling north on France Av. from 50th St. will find a strip of new food-specialty shops called Morningside Plaza. This small plaza includes a health-food store, a discount bakery, a fish market, a Chinese restaurant, and deep-dish pizza to eat in or take out. Just down 44th St. from France alert shoppers will find Reindeer Square, a specialty gift shop that draws customers from all over the metropolitan area.

RESTORATIONS

ST. ANTHONY MAIN, 201 S.E. Main St., Minneapolis. ►1

Located just across the Mississippi from downtown Minneapolis, St. Anthony is on the *original* Minneapolis main street. Until recently this historic area was dominated by warehouses and put to mostly industrial uses. That changed rapidly when the idea of in-town revival caught on.

St. Anthony Main itself is a renovated mattress factory that now houses a pleasant mix of specialty shops and restaurants. Last year the original market was expanded to include a second building, the Salisbury Market, that is modeled loosely after Faneuil Hall in Boston. It has a variety of food-specialty shops, including a wine store and a meat market. The two buildings are connected by walkways, allowing shoppers to browse their way through both without being exposed to the weather.

The buildings on Main have an elegant yet casual atmosphere. Shops are done up in brick, exposed beams, and glass. In the walkways of the buildings, carts sell jelly beans, popcorn, and souvenirs. Restaurants and wine bars open onto the corridors.

Across the cobbled street from St. Anthony Main is a developing park that overlooks the Mississippi River. Free open-air concerts are given in the park in the summertime.

BUTLER SQUARE, 100 N. Sixth St., Minneapolis. ►1

Butler Square is a onetime warehouse and officially designated historic site whose gutted interior has become an eight-story atrium surrounded by shops and offices. The building is enhanced by exposed beams and an airy glass-and-greenery environment that's especially welcome during the winter.

Butler Square West, an expansion into the back half of the original warehouse, was opened in 1981. It closely resembles the initial renovation, and shoppers are free to stroll from one half of the building to the other. Suspended in the atrium of the newer section is a life-size George Segal body sculpture of flying acrobats, complete with safety net.

Restaurants in Butler Square spill into the gallery of the building's atriums and provide a patio dining experience year-round.

PARK SQUARE COURT, 225 E. Sixth St., St. Paul. ►7

Park Square Court is a fine example of building renovation in St. Paul's Lowertown area. It is the first of what will be a major revitalization of the nine-block area between Fourth Pl. and Seventh St., and Wall and Jackson Sts., on the east edge of St. Paul's downtown. Park Square Court now houses a number of arty pottery and plant shops, as well as specialty stores and restaurants.

WAYZATA

One of the Twin Cities' more prestigious suburbs, Wayzata (►5) used to be considered the last outpost of civilization for travelers setting out for the West. Wayzata sits on the shore of Lake Minnetonka, and the big lake's proximity gives the town the air of a New England village. There's a pretty, old railroad station, a few select shops, and a fine French restaurant, the Chouette. A trip to Wayzata is more of an outing than a shopping trip, but it's enjoyable all the same.

Not far from Wayzata is Excelsior, a former resort town that's now favored by growing numbers of shoppers and antique hunters. Antique stores are located in town and on approaching roadways. Local stores can supply maps that detail the locations of most of the area's shops.

Both Wayzata and Excelsior are served by excursion boats in the summertime. Visitors can arrange to take a one- or two-hour cruise around Lake Minnetonka that includes a guided tour of attractions along the shoreline.

STILLWATER

Stillwater (►10) is an historic lumber town on the east bank of the beautiful St. Croix River. In recent years, the community has undergone careful restoration and now offers a pleasant shopping experience in a country setting, only 30 minutes from St. Paul. The town's old riverfront warehouses are packed with specialty shops; a former post office houses gift, antique, and pastry shops; and another major renovation project, the Grand Garage, provides an elegant setting for clothing, accessory, and gift boutiques.

Stillwater also has a number of fine Victorian homes that are periodically opened for tours, and there are several restaurants worth visiting, including those of the famous Lowell Inn. During the summer, shoppers can stroll along the riverbank or take a paddleboat excursion down the St. Croix. A tour book that explains Stillwater's history and architecture is available in local shops for $1.

Ridgedale, in Minnetonka: a major Twin Cities mall.

Chapter Nineteen

STORES, SHOPS, MARKETS, BOUTIQUES

The following lists of stores and shops provide a sampling of what's available throughout the Twin Cities in downtowns, suburbs, and specialty malls. Inclusion of a particular shop is not necessarily a recommendation, and because of space limitations, many worthy establishments have not been included. Although every effort has been made to provide accurate information, the *Twin Cities Guide* cannot be responsible for changes. If it's important, call first.

Credit card abbreviations used are AE—American Express; CB—Carte Blanche; DC—Diners Club; MC—MasterCard (Master Charge); V—Visa (BankAmericard); and S—Shoppers Charge, a local charge card.

DEPARTMENT STORES

The Twin Cities has branches of the major national full-service and discount department store chains. The following department stores are among the finest department stores that are locally owned and/or operated.

DAYTON'S, 700 Nicollet Mall, Minneapolis. ▶1
375-2200
A full-service department store operation that was established more than 80 years ago in downtown Minneapolis. Its downtown St. Paul store at E. Seventh and Cedar Sts., 375-6800, has just been completely renovated. Both are open M, Thu

---

(See Locator Key Map, pages 8-9)

▶1 Mpls. Downtown
▶2 Mpls. Excluding Downtown
▶3 Mpls. North Suburbs
▶4 Mpls. Northwest Suburbs
▶5 Mpls. Southwest Suburbs
▶6 Mpls. South Suburbs

▶7 St. Paul Downtown
▶8 St. Paul Excluding Downtown
▶9 St. Paul North Suburbs
▶10 St. Paul Northeast Suburbs
▶11 St. Paul Southeast Suburbs
▶12 St. Paul South Suburbs

9:30 a.m. to 9 p.m.; Tue, W, F, Sat 9:30 to 5:45. Check telephone directories for six Twin Cities suburban locations. Dayton's charge accepted at all.

DONALDSONS, 601 Nicollet Mall, Minneapolis. ▶1
332-3113

Another home-grown full-service department store. Brand-new store in downtown St. Paul's Town Square, E. Seventh and Cedar Sts., 222-2811. Both open M, Thu 9:30 a.m. to 8 p.m.; Tue, W, F, Sat 9:30 to 5:45. Check telephone directories for five suburban Donaldsons locations. AE, Donaldsons charge accepted at all.

POWERS, S. Fifth St. and Nicollet Mall, Minneapolis. ▶1
332-2141

Full-service department store with boutique-type shops on its lower floor. Open M, Thu 9:30 a.m. to 7 p.m.; Tue, W, F, Sat 9:30 to 5:45. Check telephone directories for six other Twin Cities locations. Powers charge accepted at all.

VAN ARSDELL'S, 27 Signal Hills (S. Robert and Orme Sts.), West St. Paul. ▶12
457-9261

Complete lines of men's and women's clothes, shoes, and accessories. Open M-Sat 10 a.m. to 9 p.m.; Sun 11 to 5.

Also at:

2100 N. Snelling Av. (Har Mar Mall), Roseville, 631-0531.

37th Av. N.E. and Silver Lake Rd. (Apache Plaza), St. Anthony, 781-4811.

Har Mar Mall and Apache Plaza stores open M-F 10 a.m. to 9 p.m.; Sat 9:30 to 5:30; Sun noon to 5.

MC, V, S, Van Arsdell's charge accepted at all.

YOUNG QUINLAN, 901 Nicollet Mall, Minneapolis. ▶1
332-3266

Men's and women's clothes, shoes, and accessories. Open M, Thu 9:30 a.m. to 7 p.m.; Tue-W, F-Sat 9:30 to 5:30. AE, MC, V, S accepted.

WOMEN'S CLOTHING

ALTA MODA, Galleria, 3620 W. 70th St., Edina. ▶5
920-7204

Women's designer and better clothing imported exclusively from Italy. Sizes 4-16. Open M-F 10 a.m. to 9 p.m.; Sat 10-6; Sun noon to 5. AE, MC, V accepted.

B. NATHAN'S, Galleria, 3545 W. 69th St., Edina. ▶5
927-8676

Designer dresses, sportswear, coats, and accessories. Open M-F 10 a.m. to 9 p.m.; Sat 10 to 6; Sun noon to 5. AE, MC, V, S, Nathan's charge accepted.

BRAUN'S, 516 Nicollet Mall, Minneapolis. ▶1
332-6562

Women's dresses, sportswear, coats, accessories. Open M, Thu 10 a.m. to 7 p.m.; Tue-W, F-Sat 10 to 5:45. AE, MC, V, S, Braun's charge accepted. Check telephone directories for other locations.

CARL NYGREN'S, 911 Excelsior Av. W., Hopkins. ►5
938-9662

Dress boutique also carrying coordinates, coats, lingerie, and accessories. Open M-Thu, Sat 9 a.m. to 5:30 p.m.; F 9 to 6. MC, V, S, Nygren's charge accepted.

CAROLE OF EDINA, 3929 W. 50th St. (at France Av.), Edina. ►5
926-6559

Women's classic sportswear in sizes 2 to 14. Some accessories. Open M, Thu 9:30 a.m. to 9 p.m.; Tue-W, F-Sat 9:30 to 5:30. AE, MC, V, S accepted.

CASUAL CORNER, Brookdale Center, Brooklyn Center. ►4
566-2400

Just sportswear in sizes 3 to 13 and accessories. Open M-F 10 a.m. to 9:30 p.m.; Sat 10 to 6; Sun noon to 5. MC, V, S accepted. Check telephone directories for other locations.

CEDRIC'S, Galleria, 3534 W. 70th St., Edina. ►5
925-3424

Clothes for men and women. Women's clothes include better separates, sportswear, accessories, and jewelry. Open M-F 10 a.m. to 9 p.m.; Sat 10 to 6; Sun noon to 5.
Also at:
Burnsville Center, Burnsville, 435-8871; open M-F 9:30 a.m. to 9:30 p.m.; Sat 9:30 to 6; Sun noon to 5:30.
Ridgedale Center, Minnetonka, 546-5595; open M-F 8:30 a.m. to 9:30 p.m.; Sat 8:30 to 6; Sun 1 to 5.
AE, MC, V, S, Cedric's charge

accepted at all. DC accepted at Ridgedale.

CHRISTEN B, Yorktown Fashion Mall, 3441 Hazelton Rd., Edina. ►5
831-5950

Traditional women's clothes. Resort wear shop. Open M, Thu 10 a.m. to 9 p.m.; Tue-W, F-Sat 10 to 5:30. AE, MC, V accepted.

R. S. CONRAD, 310 Banning, White Bear Lake. ►10
426-8006

Classic tailored designs in better sportswear. Accessories, lingerie, Pappagallo shoes. Open M, W, Thu 9:30 a.m. to 9 p.m.; Tue, F 9:30 to 6; Sat 9 to 5. AE, MC, V accepted.

DAVID EDWINS FASHIONS, Har Mar Mall, 2100 Snelling Av. N., Roseville. ►9
633-1029

Misses' dresses, coats, accessories. Open M-F 10 a.m. to 9 p.m.; Sat 10 to 5:30. V, MC, S accepted.

EAST ROOM, 3940 W. 50th St. (at France Av.), Edina. ►5
927-6430

Dresses, sportswear, lingerie, coats, and shoes. Open M-W, F-Sat 9:30 a.m. to 5:30 p.m.; Thu 9:30 to 9. MC, V, S accepted.

EDWARD HOLMBERG, 100 N. Sixth St. (Butler Square West), Minneapolis. ►1
375-9030

Chic new women's store that sells only designer fashions. Women's sizes 4 to 16. Open M-F 10 a.m. to 9 p.m. Sat 10 to 6. AE, MC, V, S accepted.

EPITOME, Galleria, 3585 W. 69th St., Edina. ►5
920-2978

Dresses, suits, sportswear, accessories, and stationery. Open M-F 10 a.m. to 9 p.m.; Sat 10 to 6; Sun noon to 5. AE, MC, V, S accepted.

FEMINIQUE, 811 LaSalle Court, Minneapolis. ►1
332-3188

Designer fashions and limited-edition designs from around the world. Women's sizes 4 to 14. Open M, Thu 10 a.m. to 7 p.m.; Tue, W, F, Sat 10 to 5:30. AE, MC, V, S accepted.

FOSTER'S BOOTIER/COTTON GIN, 5009 France Av. S., Edina. 926-7112 ►5

Large selection of women's casual and dress shoes as well as all natural-fiber designer and better dresses, sportswear, and cotton sweaters. Open M, Thu 10 a.m. to 8:30 p.m.; Tue, W, F, Sat 10 to 6. AE, MC, V, S accepted.

FRANK MURPHY, Fifth and St. Peter Sts., St. Paul. ►7
291-8844

Designer and better dresses, suits, sportswear, coats, lingerie, accessories, and shoes. Watch for annual late-winter sale. Open M 9 a.m. to 7 p.m.; Tue-Sat 9 to 5:30. Also at 769 Cleveland Av. S. (Highland), St. Paul, 698-5585; open M-Sat 9:30 a.m. to 5:30 p.m. AE, V, MC, S accepted at both.

E. T. FRENCH LTD., Bonaventure, 1515 Plymouth Rd., Minnetonka. ►5
544-6978

Traditional and classic sportswear for men and women. Men's sizes 30-40 (slacks), 38-44 (sports coats). Women's sizes 1-14. Open M-F 10 a.m. to 9 p.m.; Sat 10 a.m. to 6 p.m.; Sun noon to 5. AE, MC, V, S accepted.

GOSSELIN'S OF COURSE, 1662 Grand Av., St. Paul. ►8
699-7777

Sportswear by Dean's, Emily, Gordon, and Lanz. Accessories, coats, and Christmas ornaments. Open M, Thu 9:30 a.m. to 8 p.m.; Tue-W, F-Sat 9:30 to 5:30. AE, MC, V, S accepted.

HAGER OF EDINA, 3946 W. 50th St. (at France Av.), Edina. 927-7978 ►5

Women's department store carrying dresses, sportswear, coats, jewelry, accessories, and shoes. Lines include dresses by Leslie Faye and sportswear by Bleyle and Haymaker. Open M-W, F-Sat 9:30 a.m. to 5:30 p.m.; Thu 9:30 to 9. MC, V, S accepted.

HAROLD, 818 Nicollet Mall, Minneapolis. ►1
332-8561

Exclusive lines of clothes, coats, and shoes. Beauty shop. Open M-W, F-Sat 9:30 a.m. to 5:30 p.m.; Thu 9:30 to 7. AE, MC, V, S, Harold charge accepted.

R. D. HINQUIST CO., IDS Center, 80 S. Eighth St., Minneapolis. ►1
332-4501

Designer and other fine dresses, suits, sweaters, silk shirts, and accessories. Open M, Thu 9:30 a.m. to 8 p.m.; Tue-W, F-Sat 9:30 to 5:45. AE, MC, V, S accepted.

JACKSON GRAVES, 904 Nicollet Mall, Minneapolis. ►1 333-1563

High-fashion separates, suits, coats, jewelry, and accessories. Also in St. Paul at 2057 Ford Pkwy. (Highland), 698-5555. Minneapolis and Highland stores open M, Thu 9:30 a.m. to 8 p.m.; Tue-W, F-Sat 9:30 to 5:30.

Also at:

Rosedale Center, Roseville, 63l-1600.

Southdale Center, Edina, 927-8668.

Dales stores open M-F 10 a.m. to 9:30 p.m.; Sat 9 to 6; Sun noon to 5.

AE, MC V, S accepted at all.

JOHN W. HELLER, Southdale Center, Edina. ►5 927-5448

Better dresses, sportswear, coats, and accessories. Open M-F 9:30 a.m. to 9:30 p.m.; Sat 9:30 to 6; Sun 1 to 5. AE, MC, V, S, Heller's charge accepted.

JUSTER'S, 500 Nicollet Mall, Minneapolis. ►1 333-1431

Primarily a men's store, Juster's also carries tailored women's suits, blazers, slacks, dresses, jewelry, scarves, and shoes, primarily for the business woman. Open M, Thu 9:30 a.m. to 8 p.m.; Tue-W, F-Sat 9:30 to 5:30.

Also at:

Maplewood Mall, Maplewood, 770-3911; open M-F 10 a.m. to 9 p.m.; Sat 10 to 6; Sun noon to 5.

Brookdale Center, Brooklyn Center, 561-4800

Ridgedale Center, Minnetonka, 544-6600

Southdale Center, Edina, 927-8781.

Dales stores open M-F 10 a.m. to 9:30 p.m.; Sat 9:30 to 6; Sun noon to 5. AE, MC, V, S, Juster's charge accepted at all.

KI CLAYTON, Bonaventure, 1651 S. Plymouth Rd., Minnetonka. ►5 545-9400

Fine traditional suits, sportswear, and accessories. Open M-F 10 a.m. to 9 p.m.; Sat 10 to 6; Sun noon to 5. AE, MC, V, S accepted.

KRAPU'S, Yorktown Fashion Mall, 3413 Hazelton Rd., Edina. ►5 835-1122

Dresses, sportswear, coats, accessories, and jewelry. Open M-F 10 a.m. to 9 p.m.; Sat 10 to 5:30. MC, V, S accepted.

LAMP, 795 E. Lake St., Wayzata. ►5 473-0747

Contemporary designer dresses, sportswear, and handbags. Open M-F 9:30 a.m. to 5:30 p.m.; Sat 10 to 5. AE, MC, V, S accepted.

LANCER (Check telephone directories for locations.)

Brand-name clothing for men and women, including sportswear, tailored and evening clothes, accessories, and unusual gifts. Hours vary. AE, MC, V, S, Lancer's charge accepted at all.

L'ATELIER, Galleria, 3470 W. 70th St., Edina. ►5 920-1312

Dress boutique also carrying

quality sportswear and imported lingerie. Hand-painted silks; dresses designed for customers. Open M-F 10 a.m. to 9 p.m.; Sat 10 to 6; Sun noon to 5. AE, V, S accepted.

LEN DRUSKIN'S, 3925 W. 50th St. (at France Av.), Edina. ►5
927-7923

Better dresses, suits, sportswear, gowns, and accessories. Open M, Thu 9:30 a.m. to 8:30 p.m.; Tue-W, F-Sat 9:30 to 5:30. AE, MC, V, S accepted.

LUCILLE'S, 5105 Vernon Av. S., Edina. ►5
929-8111

Fine clothes in sizes 4 to 16; accessories. Open M-F 9:30 a.m. to 9 p.m.; Sat 9:30 to 5:30. Lucille's charge accepted.

MAGGIE INC., 431 E. Lake St., Wayzata. ►5
473-8853

Designer fashions in dresses, sportswear, and accessories. Open M-F 9:30 a.m. to 5:30 p.m. (9 to 5 summer); Sat 10 to 4. MC, V, S accepted. Also at 201 S.E. Main St. (St. Anthony Main), Minneapolis, 623-1188; open M-Sat 10 a.m. to 9 p.m.; Sun noon to 6. AE, MC, V, S accepted.

MARNALEE, 2914 Hennepin Av. S. (at Lake St.), Minneapolis. 827-3705 ►2

Dresses, suits, separates, coats, and accessories. Open M 9:30 a.m. to 9 p.m.; Tue-Sat 9:30 to 5:30.

Also at:

8020 Olson Memorial Hwy. (Hwy. 55) (Golden Valley Shop-

Edina's Galleria, one of the area's newer specialty malls.

ping Center), Golden Valley, 545-4372; open M, Thu 9:30 a.m. to 9 p.m.; Tue-W 9:30 to 6; Sat 9:30 to 5:30.

MC, V, S accepted at both.

MARVIN ORECK, Southdale Center, Edina. ▶5
927-8661

Dresses, sportswear, shoes, coats, and accessories. Open M-F 9:30 a.m. to 9:30 p.m.; Sat 9:30 to 6; Sun noon to 5. MC, V, S accepted.

R.L. McMUFFEE, 5014 France Av. S., Edina. ▶5
926-2889

Classic separates, blouses, and accessories including hats and ties. Open M, Thu 10 a.m. to 8:30 p.m.; Tue, W, F, Sat 10 to 5:30. MC, V, S accepted.

MES AMIES, 818 W. 46th St. (at Bryant Av.), Minneapolis. ▶2
824-9776

Name brand classic and fashion sportswear, suits, blazers, blouses, and shirts. Open M-Sat 10 a.m. to 6 p.m. Also at 4941 France Av. S., Edina, 920-0547; open M-W, F-Sat 9:30 a.m. to 5:30 p.m.; Thu 9:30 to 9. MC, V, S accepted at both.

MILTON'S, Brookdale Center, Brooklyn Center. ▶4
561-3450

Evening dresses, fur and wool coats, bridal shop, and some sportswear. Open M-F 10 a.m. to 9:30 p.m.; Sat 9 to 6; Sun 1 to 5 (closed Sun summer). Second location in Rosedale Center, Roseville, 636-0405. MC, V, S accepted.

MR. G'S, IDS Center, 80 S. Eighth St., Minneapolis. ▶1
339-5914

Junior size fashions for women 25 and older. Dresses, skirts, blazers, coats, swimsuits, and accessories. Open M-F 10 a.m. to 5:45 p.m.; Sat 10 to 5:15.

Also at:

Ridgedale Center, Minnetonka, 546-3883.

Southdale Center, Edina, 926-1444.

Ridgedale and Southdale stores open M-F 10 a.m. to 9:30 p.m.; Sat 9:30 to 6; Sun 12:30 to 5:30.

Rosedale Center, Roseville; open M-F 10 a.m. to 9:30 p.m.; Sat 10 to 6; Sun noon to 5:30.

AE, MC, V, S accepted at all.

NINA B, Burnsville Center, Burnsville. ▶6
435-6186

Junior sportswear, including some dressy coordinates and accessories. Open M, Thu 9:30 a.m. to 8 p.m.; Tue, W, F, Sat 9:30 a.m. to 5:30 p.m. Check telephone directories for five other Twin Cities locations. MC, V, S, Nina B's charge accepted.

NYGREN'S AT THE LAKE, 409 Second St., Excelsior. ▶5
474-6164

Popular-priced and better dresses, suits, sportswear, coats, lingerie, jewelry, and accessories. Open M-Sat 9:30 a.m. to 5:30 p.m. AE, MC, V, S accepted.

PANACHE, Burnsville Center, Burnsville. ▶6
435-6273

Outerwear only—coats, jackets, blazers, down vests. Open

M-F 10 a.m. to 9:30 p.m.; Sat 9:30 to 6; Sun noon to 5:30.

Also at:

Ridgedale Center, Minnetonka, 546-7371.

Rosedale Center, Roseville, 636-9449.

Southdale Center, Edina, 926-1208.

Dales stores open M-F 10 a.m. to 9:30 p.m.; Sat 9:30 to 6; Sun noon to 5. AE, MC, V, S accepted at all.

THE PARLOUR, Rosedale Center, Roseville. ►4
636-5840

Better clothing in classic styles including sportswear, dresses, and evening wear. Designer lines. Accessories. Open M-F 10 a.m. to 9:30 p.m.; Sat 9:30 to 6; Sun 1 to 5. AE, MC V, S accepted.

PECK & PECK, 932 Nicollet Mall, Minneapolis. ►1
339-7969

Better women's dresses, suits, sportswear, coats, and accessories including camel-hair coats, Larry Lavine blazers, and apparel by Liz Claiborne and Evan Picone. Open M, W, F-Sat 9:30 a.m. to 5:30 p.m.; Tue, Thu 9:30 to 7:30. Check telephone directories for five other Twin Cities locations. AE, MC, V, S accepted.

RODIER PARIS, Bonaventure, 1687 S. Plymouth Rd., Minnetonka. ►5
544-6770

Tailored classic French designs by Rodier in suits, separates, dresses, coats, blouses, and accessories. Quality fabrics, mostly knits. Open M-F 10 a.m. to 9 p.m.; Sat 10 to 6; Sun noon to 5. AE, MC, V accepted.

SHE, Southdale Center, Edina. ►5
926-1557

Classic women's fashions by Austin Hill, J. G. Hook, Sero, and others. Sizes 4 to 14. Open M-F 10 a.m. to 9:30 p.m.; Sat 9:30 to 6; Sun noon to 5. Also located in Ridgedale, 546-1513; Rosedale, 636-0685; and Town Square in downtown St. Paul, 292-8643. AE, MC, V, S accepted at all stores.

M.C. SMITH & CO., 811 LaSalle Av., Minneapolis. ►1
339-1931

Young designer sportswear and accessories. Open M, Thu 10 a.m. to 8 p.m.; Tue, W, F, Sat 10 to 6. AE, MC, V, S accepted.

ST. CLAIR DRESS SHOP, 243 Snelling Av. S. (at St. Clair Av.), St. Paul. ►8
699-9387

Career clothes for mature women. Dresses, separates, pantsuits, accessories. Open M-W, F-Sat 9:30 a.m. to 5:30 p.m.; Thu 9:30 to 8:30. MC, V, S accepted.

THE STABLE (Check telephone directories for locations.)

Brand-name, reasonably priced dresses, suits, sportswear, outerwear, accessories, and gifts. Hours vary. AE, MC, V, S, Stable charge accepted at all.

THEODORE'S, 29 W. Sixth St., St. Paul. ►7
227-7676

Designer dresses, suits, sportswear, coats, lingerie, accessories, and gifts. Open M-F 9:30 a.m. to 5:15 p.m.; Sat 9:30 to 5 (2 summer). Also at Rosedale Center, Roseville, 636-1050; open M-Sat 9:30 a.m. to 9:30 p.m.; Sun 1 to 5; and 3565 W. 69th St. (Galleria), Edina, 929-4615; open M-F 10 a.m. to 9 p.m.; Sat 10 to 6; Sun noon to 5. AE, MC, V, S accepted at all.

VILLAGE SHOP, 326 Washington Av., White Bear Lake. ▶10
429-4330

Name-brand misses and junior sportswear; some dresses, accessories. Open M-F 9 a.m. to 9 p.m.; Sat 9 to 6. Other locations at 229 S. Main St., Stillwater, 430-1682, and 6606 Cahill Av. E., Inver Grove Heights, 455-5595. AE, MC, V, S accepted.

WATER STREET CLOTHING CO., 287 Water St., Excelsior. 474-0474. ▶5
Contemporary women's clothing. Open M-F 9:30 a.m. to 6 p.m.; Sat 9:30 to 5:30. AE, MC, V, S accepted.

Furs

ALBRECHT'S, 829 Nicollet Mall, Minneapolis. ▶1
333-8104
Furs made, sold, remade, repaired, stored, and cleaned. Fine women's dresses, sportswear, and accessories. Also at 3930 W. 50th St. (at France Av.), Edina, 927-8808. Both open M-Sat 9:30 a.m. to 5:30 p.m. In St. Paul at 680 Cleveland Av. S. (Highland), 690-1567; open M-Sat 10 a.m. to

5:30 p.m. AE, MC, V, S accepted at all.

BJORKMAN'S, 931 Nicollet Mall, Minneapolis. ▶1
333-6255
Furs and complete fur service as well as women's fashions, mostly sportswear separates. Open M 10 a.m. to 7:30 p.m.; Tue-Sat 10 to 5:30. AE, CB, DC, MC, V, S accepted. Also at 3401 Hazelton Rd. (Yorktown Fashion Mall), Edina, 831-5610; open M-F 9:30 a.m. to 9 p.m.; Sat 9:30 to 5. AE, MC, V, S accepted. Women's designer clothing, coats, and accessories only at Edina—no furs.

RIBNICK FUR, 224 N. First St., Minneapolis. ▶1
332-4321
New and used fur coats for both men and women. Unusual selection of used furs. Summer hours M-F 9:30 a.m. to 4:30 p.m.; winter hours M, Thu 9:30 to 8; Tue, W, F, Sat 9:30 to 6; Sun noon to 5. MC, V accepted.

SCHLAMPP'S, 2919 Hennepin Av. S., Minneapolis. ▶1
823-7272
Large selection of better dresses, coats, furs, and accessories. Delivery and pick-up service for furs. Open M 9 a.m. to 9 p.m.; Tue-Sat 9 to 5:30.

Lingerie

HOUSE OF FORRESTER, Galleria, 3689 W. 69th St., Edina. 929-2205 ▶5

Designer and better lingerie, robes, and loungewear; cosmetics, hosiery and gloves, mastectomy forms. Open M-F 10 a.m. to 9 p.m.; Sat 10 to 6; Sun noon to 5.

KATHY GELAO'S, Carriage Hill Plaza, 14 W. Fifth St., St. Paul. 227-5760 ►7

Designer lingerie, robes, and loungewear, plus a selection of custom bedding, bath accessories, and linens. Open M-Sat 9 a.m. to 5:30 p.m. AE, MC, V, S accepted.

PEACOCK BRA BAR, 4942 France Av. S., Edina. ►5 920-0610

Lingerie, robes, summer dresses, models' coats, pantyhose as well as bras. Open M-Sat 10 a.m. to 5:30 p.m. MC, V, S accepted.

POLLY BERG, Galleria, 3555 W. 69th St., Edina. ►5 920-0183

Lingerie, nightwear, bath and bedroom accessories. Open M-F 10 a.m. to 9 p.m.; Sat 10 to 6; Sun noon to 5. AE, MC, V, S accepted.

SATIN & LACE, 3922 W. 50th St., Edina. ►5 922-1172

Designer lingerie by Prima, Lori Caufield, and others. Open M-W, F 10 a.m. to 5:30 p.m.; Thu 10 to 9; Sat 11 to 5. AE, MC, V.

Women's Shoes

D. C. MAGNUSON/FAMO-LARE, Bonaventure, 1615 Plymouth Rd., Minnetonka. ►5 545-4811

Designer shoes by D. C. Magnuson, Famolare, Charles Jourdan, Amalfi, and others. Open M-F 10 a.m. to 9 p.m.; Sat 10 to 6; Sun noon to 5. New location in the Galleria, Edina.

FIFTH ST. BOOTERY, 359 Wabasha St., St. Paul. ►7 222-4449

Fashion shoes, formal and casual, and boots for women only. Open M-F 9:30 a.m. to 5:30 p.m.; Sat 9:30 to 5. Also at Rosedale Center, Roseville, 631-9350; and Southdale Center, Edina, 927-8465; open M-F 10 a.m. to 9:30 p.m.; Sat 9:30 to 6; Sun noon to 5. AE, MC, V, S accepted at both.

NAPIERS FINE FEMININE FOOTWEAR, 831 Nicollet Mall, Minneapolis. ►1 335-7691

Specializing in narrow widths. Also handbags. Open M 9:30 a.m. to 7 p.m.; Tue-Sat 9:30 to 5:30. Also at Ridgedale Center, Minnetonka, 546-5501; open M-F 10 a.m. to 9:30 p.m.; Sat 9:30 to 6; Sun noon to 5. AE, MC, V, S accepted at both.

PAPPAGALLO, Galleria, 3561 W. 69th St., Edina. ►5 925-3388

Pappagallo shoes in classical, feminine styles and accessories including hats, handbags, ribbons, socks, and gifts. Open M-F 10 a.m. to 9 p.m.; Sat 10 to 6; Sun noon to 5. AE, MC, V, S accepted.

SHOE ALLEE, 3940 W. 50th St. (at France Av.), Edina. ►5 926-9922

Fashion shoes and accessories. Open M-W, F-Sat 9:30 a.m. to

5:30 p.m.; Thu 9:30 to 8:30. MC, V, S accepted.

SOLDATI SHOES, LaSalle Court, 811 LaSalle Av., Minneapolis. ►1
332-4597

Designer shoes by Charles Jourdan, Givenchy, Mignani, Joan and David, Anne Klein, Rossi, and others. Accessories. Open M, Thu 10 a.m. to 9 p.m.; Tue-W, F-Sat 10 to 5:45. Also at Southdale Center, Edina, 929-6741, and Rosedale Center, 488-2541; open M-F 9:30 a.m. to 9:30 p.m.; Sat 9:30 to 6; Sun noon to 5. AE, MC, V, S accepted at both.

Women's Special Sizes

ELEGANT X, Wayzata Bay Shopping Center, County Rds. 15 and 16, Wayzata. ►5
473-1393

Full line of women's clothes and lingerie in sizes 12 to 20, 12½ to 26½, and 34 to 46. Open M-Thu 10 a.m. to 6 p.m.; F 9:30 to 9; Sat 9:30 to 5. Also at 66th St. and Nicollet Av. (Hub Shopping Center), Richfield; Miracle Mile Shopping Center, St. Louis Park; and Apache Plaza, New Brighton. MC, V, S accepted.

LANE BRYANT, Ridgedale Center, Minnetonka. ►5
544-3500

Sizes 10 to 24 for tall women, and 38 to 52 for big women. Suits, jackets, sportswear, bras, girdles, and shoes. Open M-F 10 a.m. to 9:30 p.m.; Sat 10 to 6; Sun noon to 5. Also at Rosedale Center, Roseville, 636-0615; open M-F 10

a.m. to 9:30 p.m.; Sat 9:30 to 6; Sun noon to 5. MC, V, Lane Bryant's charge accepted at both.

MORE WOMAN, Maplewood Mall, Maplewood. ►9
770-5522

Dresses, sportswear, coats, swimsuits, bras, girdles, nylons, lingerie, and jewelry; sizes 12½ to 52. Open M-F 10 a.m. to 9 p.m.; Sat 10 to 6; Sun noon to 5. MC, V, S accepted.

SHELLY'S TALL GIRL SHOPS, Brookdale Center, Brooklyn Center. ►4
566-4884

Sportswear, dresses, and coats for tall women in junior and misses sizes 5 to 20. Also at Rosedale Center, Roseville, 636-1268, and Southdale Center, Edina, 920-2668. All open M-F 10 a.m. to 9:30 p.m.; Sat 9:30 to 6; Sun noon to 5. MC, V, Shelly's charge accepted at all.

SIZE 5-7-9 SHOP, Ridgedale Center, Minnetonka. ►5
544-3579

Casual wear, some coordinates, coats, and accessories. Open M-F 10 a.m. to 9:30 p.m.; Sat 9:30 to 6; Sun noon to 4. MC, V accepted.

Maternity Fashions

LADY MADONNA MATERNITY BOUTIQUE, 3466 W. 70th St., Edina. ►5
927-4527

Fashionable maternity clothes, lingerie. Open M-F 10 a.m. to 9 p.m.; Sat 10 to 6; Sun noon to 5. Second location in St. Anthony

Main, 201 S.E. Main St., Minneapolis, 379-9477. MC, V, S accepted.

OVER THE RAINBOW MATERNITY FASHIONS, 1426 W. Lake St., Minneapolis. ►2
825-2437

Stylish maternity fashions by leading manufacturers. Second location at 1051 Grand Av., St. Paul. Both open M, Thu 10 a.m. to 7:30 p.m.; Tue, W, F, Sat 10 to 5. Outlet store at 119 N. Fourth St. (332-0446) sells seconds of the same merchandise. Outlet store open Tue-F 9 a.m. to noon.

SHIRLEY'S MATERNITY FASHIONS, Brookdale Center, Brooklyn Center. ►4
561-4250

Maternity fashions only. Also at Southdale Center, Edina, 926-3515. Both open M-F 10 a.m. to 9:30 p.m.; Sat 9:30 to 6; Sun noon to 5. Also at Rosedale Center, Roseville, 636-0146; open M-F 10 a.m. to 9:30 p.m.; Sat 10 to 6; Sun noon to 5. MC, V, S accepted at all.

Women's Fashion Bargains

THE CLOTHES HORSE, 1614 W. Lake St., Minneapolis. ►2
822-6600

Women's clothes in sizes 4 to 18 sold at about half off retail prices. Large section of recycled clothing. Open M, F 10 a.m. to 8 p.m.; Tue, W, Thu, Sat 10 to 5. MC, V accepted.

DOUG'S OUTLET STORE, Golden Hills Center, 5400 Wayzata Blvd., Golden Valley. 545-2488 ►4

Sleepwear samples in junior sizes 7-13 sold at half off retail prices. Open M-F noon to 4:15.

THE FACTORY STORE, 1015 S. Sixth St., Room 105, Minneapolis. ►1
332-2724

Outlet store for Sharpe Manufacturing Co. Car, pant, and dress coats, designer samples, fabric and notions sold 30 to 40 percent off regular retail prices. Open M-F 9:30 to 3:30; Sat 9 to 1.

HOUSE OF LARGE SIZES OUTLET STORE, Phalen Shopping Center, 1369 E. Magnolia St., St. Paul. ►8
771-4097

First-quality merchandise in sizes 14½ to 32½ and 38 to 52 sold at 30 to 50 percent off retail prices. Open M-F 9:30 a.m. to 9 p.m.; Sat 9:30 to 5:30; Sun noon to 5. MC, V, S accepted. Also at Sixth and St. Peter Sts., St. Paul, 225-0805; open M, Thu 9:30 a.m. to 8 p.m.; Tue, W, F, Sat 9:30 to 5:30. MC, V, S accepted.

HOUSE OF SAMPLES, INC., 3615 White Bear Av., White Bear Lake. ►10
777-6606

Name-brand women's clothing in sizes 7 to 10 sold at one-third to half off retail prices. Open M-Sat 10 a.m. to 5 p.m. Closes 1 p.m. Sat June 1 to Sept. 1. S accepted.

LE SHOP, 926 Nicollet Mall, Minneapolis. ►1
332-5700

American designer fashions—including dresses, suits, jeans, sweaters, and coats—sold at 20 to

40 percent off retail prices. Open M-Sat 9:30 a.m. 5:30 p.m. AE, MC, V accepted.

LOEHMANN'S, Loehmann's Plaza, 5141 W. 98th St., Bloomington. ►6
835-2510

Designer dresses, gowns, suits, jackets, blouses, furs, swimsuits, and accessories at 30 to 50 percent off retail prices. Sizes 2 to 18 (no half sizes). Open M-Tue, Thu-Sat 10 a.m. to 5:30 p.m.; W 10 to 9:30.

MARY T.'S SAMPLE SHOP, 1326 N. Rice St., St. Paul. ►8
488-9136

Infants', children's and women's clothes, 75 percent of which are samples, sold at 30 percent off retail prices. Open M-F 10 a.m. to 5:30 p.m.; Sat 9:30 to 4. MC, V, S accepted.

MINNEAPOLIS RAG STOCK & EXPORT CO., 909 S. Second St., Minneapolis. ►1
333-6576

All kinds of used clothes for men and women. Second location at 315 14th Av. S.E., Minneapolis, 331-6064. Second Av. store hours M, Thu 9 to 9; Tue, W, F 9 to 6; Sat 9:30 to 5. MC, V accepted.

RECIE'S SAMPLE SHOP, 1702 Grand Av., St. Paul. ►8
698-8841

Women's clothes in sizes 7 to 10 (some 12s and 14s) sold at about one-third off retail prices. Open M, Thu 10 a.m. to 9 p.m.; Tue, W, F, Sat 10 to 5:30. Also at 1975 Seneca Rd., Eagan, 454-7720.

MC, V, S accepted at both.

SAMPLE MART, 5406 Florida Av. N. (downstairs), Crystal. ►4
533-0077

Name-brand women's clothes, mostly in sizes 7, 8, 9, and 10, sold at one-third or more off retail prices. Open M-Thu 10 a.m. to 6 p.m.; F 10 to 9, Sat 9:30 to 5:30.

THE SAMPLE RACK, 4313 Upton Av. S., Minneapolis. ►2
922-3828

Women's samples in sizes 8 to 12 sold at one-third off retail prices. Open M-F 10 a.m. to 6 p.m.; Sat 9:30 to 5:30. MC, V, S accepted.

SAMPLES, 2715 N. Fernbrook Lane, Plymouth. ►4
559-2863

Women's dresses and sportswear, mostly in sizes 9 and 10, sold at one-third off retail prices. Open Tue-F 10 a.m. to 5:30 p.m.; Sat 10 to 4.

THE WEAR HOUSE by Braun's, 1224 Eden Prairie Center, Eden Prairie. ►5
944-6747

Name-brand accessories and sportswear, dresses, and coats in junior sizes 5 to 13 and misses sizes 8 to 14 sold at one-third off retail prices. Open M-F 10 a.m. to 9 p.m.; Sat 9:30 to 6; Sun noon to 5. AE, MC, S and Braun's/Gigi charge accepted.

WOOL-N-SHOP (North Central Wool Marketing Corp.), 101 27th Av. S.E., Minneapolis. ►2
331-1813

Brand-name, top-quality

woolen clothes, blankets, and fabrics sold at 15 to 20 percent off retail prices. Open M-F 9 a.m. to 5 p.m.; Sat 10 to 4. MC, V accepted.

MEN'S CLOTHING

AL JOHNSON CLOTHING INC., Dinkytown, 318 14th Av. S.E., Minneapolis. ►2
378-1442

Specializing in traditional men's suits, sportcoats, shirts, ties, and imported sweaters. Open M-F 9:30 a.m. to 6 p.m.; Sat 9:30 to 5. AE, MC, V, S accepted.

ANTHONIE'S, 801 E. 78th St. (off I-494), Bloomington. ►6
854-3370

Imported and domestic clothes for men and women. Men's clothes include suits, casual wear, and shoes. Second location at the Grand Garage in Stillwater. Bloomington hours M, Thu 10 to 9; Tue-W, Fri-Sat 10 to 6. AE, DC, MC, V, Anthonie's charge accepted.

ARTHUR KORITZ, Northstar Center, 120 S. Seventh St., Minneapolis. ►1
332-5484

Top-of-the-line suits, sportcoats, furnishings, and sportswear. Open M-F 9:30 a.m. to 5:30 p.m. Sat during winter 9 to 1. AE, MC, V accepted.

BELLESON'S, 3908 W. 50th St. (at France Av.), Edina. ►5
927-4694

American-made clothes by Daks, Austin Leeds, Donald Brooks, etc. Outerwear and shoes.

Selected stock of traditional women's clothing. Open M, Thu 9 a.m. to 9 p.m.; Tue-W, F-Sat 9 to 6. AE, MC, V accepted.

BROWN CLOTHING CO., 522 Nicollet Mall, Minneapolis. ►1
333-7711

Brand-name clothes for men, young men, and boys. Big and tall men's shop. Open M, Thu 9:30 a.m. to 8 p.m.; Tue-W, F-Sat 9:30 to 5:30. AE, CB, DC, MC, V, S accepted.

CEDRIC'S, Galleria, 3534 W. 70th St., Edina. ►5
925-3424

Fashionable suits, sportcoats, shirts, and shoes. Open M-F 10 a.m. to 9 p.m.; Sat 10 to 6; Sun noon to 5. Also at Burnsville Center, Burnsville, 435-8873; open M-F 9:30 a.m. to 9:30 p.m.; Sat 9:30 to 6; Sun noon to 5:30; and Ridgedale Center, Minnetonka, 546-5595; open M-F 8:30 a.m. to 9:30 p.m.; Sat 8:30 to 6; Sun 1 to 5. AE, MC, V, S, Cedric's charge accepted at all; DC accepted at Ridgedale only.

CHAIX, Roanoke Bldg., 109 S. Seventh St., Minneapolis. ►1
333-0606

Fine suits, sportcoats, trousers, and accessories for the businessman. Suits by Petrocelli, Givenchy, and C.H. Oliver. Suits also custom-made. Open M-F 9 a.m. to 5:30 p.m.; Sat by appointment. AE, MC, V accepted.

CYRUS, LaSalle Court, 35 S. Eighth St., Minneapolis. ►1
339-3779

European designer clothes. Sportswear, sweaters, shirts, furnishings. Open M, Thu 9:30 a.m. to 8 p.m.; Tue-W, F-Sat 9:30 to 6. AE, MC, V accepted.

CY'S MEN'S WEAR, 507 W. Broadway (between Washington and Lyndale Avs.), Minneapolis. 521-2275 ▶1

Brand-name suits, sportcoats, shirts, casual wear, shoes, furnishings, and outerwear. Names include Saxony Hall, Palm Beach, Wright, Arrow, London Fog, Bass. Open M, F 9 a.m. to 9 p.m.; Tue-Thu, Sat 9 to 6. AE, DC, MC, V, S, Cy's charge accepted.

EKLUND CLOTHING CO., 403 Hennepin Av. E., Minneapolis. 379-2234 ▶1

Full line of men's, young men's, and boys' clothes including suits by Hart, Schaffner & Marx, outerwear by Zero King, and shoes by Florsheim. Big and tall sizes. Work clothes, bowling shirts, and lettering. Open M, Thu 9:30 a.m. to 9 p.m.; Tue-W, F-Sat 9:30 to 5:30. V, S, Eklund's charge accepted.

FOREMAN & CLARK, 503 Hennepin Av. (second floor), Minneapolis. ▶1 333-0685

Suits, sportcoats, topcoats, slacks, ties, and belts. All clothes made especially for Foreman & Clark and carry the store's label. Large selection. Good values. Open M, Thu 9 a.m. to 9 p.m.; Tue-W, F-Sat 9 to 5:30. Check telephone directory for four other Twin Cities locations.

HUNTLEY'S LTD., 2922 Hennepin Av. S., Minneapolis. ▶2 827-2933

Traditional men's suits, sportcoats, slacks, casual wear, furnishings. New women's department carries classic suits and sportswear. Open M-Sat 10 a.m. to 6 p.m.; evening hours may vary. AE, MC, V accepted.

JUSTER'S, 500 Nicollet Mall, Minneapolis. ▶1 333-1431

Men's and women's clothes. Complete line of men's suits, sportcoats, slacks, accessories, casual wear, and shoes. Open M, Thu 9:30 a.m. to 8 p.m.; Tue-W, F-Sat 9:30 to 5:30. Check telephone directory for other Twin Cities locations. AE, MC, V, Juster's charge accepted.

K-G MEN'S STORE, Northtown Shopping Center, 158 N.E. Northtown Dr., Blaine. ▶9 786-8930

Complete line of men's clothing from jeans to suits, including accessories, outerwear, and shoes. Open M-F 10 a.m. to 9 p.m.; Sat 9:30 to 6; Sun noon to 5. Also at Eden Prairie Center, Eden Prairie, 944-1573; open M-F 10 a.m. to 9 p.m.; Sat 9:30 to 6; Sun noon to 5; Maplewood Mall, Maplewood, 770-3903; and Burnsville Center, Burnsville, 435-8691; open M-F 10 a.m. to 9 p.m.; Sat 10 to 6; Sun noon to 5. AE, MC, V, S, K-G charge accepted at all.

LANCER (Check telephone directories for locations.)

Men's and women's clothes. Men's clothes include casual wear, sportcoats, slacks, and suits. Brand names at reasonable prices. Hours vary by store. AE, MC, V, S, Lancer's charge accepted at all.

LIEMANDT'S, 900 Nicollet Mall, Minneapolis. ►1
332-8473

Complete line of men's clothing including suits by Hart, Schaffner & Marx and Hickey Freeman, shirts by Arrow and Hathaway, casual wear by Jack Nicklaus, and shoes by Florsheim and Bass. Open M, Thu 9:30 a.m. to 8 p.m.; Tue-W, F-Sat 9:30 to 5:30. Check telephone directories for five other Twin Cities locations. AE, MC, V, S, Liemandt's charge accepted.

MERLE'S FOR MEN, IDS Center, 80 S. Eighth St., Minneapolis. 341-4141 ►1

Updated classics in European and American clothes. European lines include Zanella trousers, Daniel Schagen shirts, and Fiorucci accessories. Open M, Thu 9:30 a.m. to 8 p.m.; Tue-W, F-Sat 9:30 to 5:45. AE, MC, V accepted.

RICHMAN BROS., Northtown Shopping Center, 141 N.E. Northtown Dr., Blaine. ►9
786-6140

Suits, sportcoats, slacks, outerwear, shirts, and furnishings, most made for Richman Bros. and carrying the store's label. Styles range from traditional to contemporary. Also at Maplewood Mall, Maplewood, 777-5150; open M-F 10 a.m. to 9 p.m.; Sat 10 to 6; Sun noon to 5. AE, MC, V, S accepted at both.

SIMS LTD., LaSalle Court, 43 S. Eighth St., Minneapolis. ►1
333-5275

Traditional clothing by Southwick, Norman Hilton, Polo, etc. Suits to casual wear, plus outerwear, accessories, and shoes. Open M 9:30 a.m. to 8 p.m.; Tue-Sat 9:30 to 5:30. Also at 727 Lake St., Wayzata, 473-4633; open M 9:30 a.m. to 8 p.m.; Tue-Sat 9:30 to 6. Traditional women's clothes downtown only. AE, DC, MC, V, Sims' charge accepted at both.

UNICO, IDS Center, 80 S. Eighth St., Minneapolis. ►1
338-3427

European fashions for men in suits, sportcoats, slacks, shirts, ties, and briefcases. Open M, Thu 10 a.m. to 8 p.m.; Tue-W, F-Sat 10 to 6. AE, MC, V, S accepted.

HUBERT W. WHITE, First National Bank Arcade, E. Fourth and Minnesota Sts., St. Paul. ►7
222-7458

Quality traditional clothing by H. Freeman, Oxford, Walter Morton, etc. Silk ties, oxford-cloth shirts. Allen Edmonds shoes. Open M-F 9 a.m. to 5:30 p.m.; Sat 9 to 3. Also at 611 Marquette Av., Minneapolis, 339-8236; open M-F 9 a.m. to 5:30 p.m.; Sat 9 to 1; and Ridgedale Center, Minnetonka, 546-8735; open M-F 10 a.m. to 9:30 p.m.; Sat 9 to 6; Sun noon to 5. AE, MC, V, S accepted at all.

Men's Special Sizes

ARDEN'S FOR MEN UNDER 5′9″, Westbrook Mall, 5717 Xerxes Av. N., Brooklyn Center. ►4
566-8180

Moderately priced suits and sportcoats in sizes 35 extra small to 50 portly short, slacks in waist sizes 28 to 50. Shirts. Open M-F

10 a.m. to 9 p.m.; Sat 10 to 6. MC, V accepted.

FOURSOME, 841 E. Lake St., Wayzata. ►5
473-4667

Men's and women's clothing. Big and tall men's shop, shoes, large jean department, outdoor store. Open M, Thu 8:30 a.m. to 9 p.m.; Tue-W, F-Sat 8:30 to 6. AE, MC, V, S, Foursome's charge accepted.

JERRY LEONARD BIG AND TALL MEN'S SHOPS, Westbrook Mall, 5605 Xerxes Av. N., Brooklyn Center. ►4
566-1340

Work clothes to formal wear for big men sizes 44 to 66, tall men 6'2" to 7'2". Suits by Palm Beach and Phoenix. Shoes by Nunn Bush. Shirts and furnishings. Call for catalog. Open M-F 10 a.m. to 9 p.m.; Sat 10 to 6; Sun noon to 5.

Also at:
2110 Burnsville Center, Burnsville, 435-5525; open M-F 10 a.m. to 9:30 p.m.; Sat 9:30 to 6; Sun noon to 5:30.

2875 Snelling Av. N., Roseville, 633-7110; open M-F 9 a.m. to 8:30 p.m.; Sat 9 to 5; Sun noon to 5.

5000 Normandale Rd. (Hwy. 100 at 50th St.), Edina, 920-7877; open M, Thu 9 a.m. to 8:30 p.m.; Tue-W, F 9 to 5:30; Sat 9 to 5.

AE, DC, MC, V, S accepted at all.

D.W. STEWART'S, Galleria, 3676 W. 70th St., Edina. ►5
920-5757

Fine apparel for big and tall men. Better and designer suits, coats, shirts, slacks, and other clothing in regular sizes 46-54;

long sizes 44-54; and extra-long sizes 40-54. Open M-F 9 a.m. to 9 p.m.; Sat 10 to 6; Sun noon to 5. AE, MC, V, S accepted.

Men's Fashion Bargains

KAPLAN BROS., 1435 Franklin Av. E., Minneapolis. ►2
871-1233

Work clothes, casual wear, outerwear, underwear, etc., sold at discounts. Open M-F 9 a.m. to 9 p.m.; Sat 9 to 6.

NATE'S, 25 N. Fourth St., Minneapolis. ►1
331-1401

Suits, sportcoats, slacks, overcoats, raincoats, shirts, and accessories sold at 25 to 30 percent off retail prices. Open M, Thu 8:15 a.m. to 8:45 p.m.; Tue-W, F-Sat 8:15 to 5:45.

NEW YORK CLOTHING, 850 W. County Rd. 42, Burnsville. 435-8187 ►6

Designer suits, sportcoats, slacks, and overcoats sold at a third to a half off regular retail prices. Oleg Cassini, Adolfo, Danieli, other name designers. Second location at Burnhaven Mall, Burnsville, 884-9104. Open M-F 10 a.m. to 9:30 p.m; Sat 9:30 to 6; Sun noon to 5:30. AE, DC, MC, V, S accepted.

ROBB'S CLOTHING, INC., 3650 Hazelton Rd., Edina. ►5
927-6100

Brand-name and designer clothes for men and women sold at discount. Men's clothes include suits, sportcoats, slacks, shirts, ties, and shoes. Open M-F 10 a.m.

to 9 p.m.; Sat 10 to 5. MC, V, S accepted.

CHILDREN'S CLOTHES

CHILDREN'S BOOTERY, 66th St. and Xerxes Av. S., Edina. ►5 869-8676

Shoes and stockings in sizes infant to 3. Open M-W, F 9:30 a.m. to 5:30 p.m.; Thu 9:30 to 8. Children's Bootery charge only.

CHILDREN'S GENERAL STORE, 3933 W. 50th St. (at France Av.), Edina. ►5 925-2841

Mostly clothes for boys and girls in sizes infant to 14; blocks, stuffed animals, and games also sold. Open M, Thu 9:30 a.m. to 9 p.m.; Tue-W, F-Sat 9:30 to 5:30. AE, MC, V, S accepted.

CHILDREN'S WORLD, 812 E. Lake St., Minneapolis. ►2 825-6673

Clothes in sizes for infants through teens. Open M, Thu-F 9 a.m. to 8 p.m.; Tue-W, Sat 9:30 to 5:30. MC, V, S accepted.

DISCO BABY, LaSalle Court, 811 LaSalle Av., Minneapolis. ►1 332-7726

Boys' and girls' clothes in sizes infant to 14 and children's jewelry. Open M-F 9:30 a.m. to 5:30 p.m.; Sat 9:30 to 5. AE, MC, V accepted.

FANTASIA FOR CHILDREN, 8014 Hwy. 55, Golden Valley. ►4 544-6141

Boys' and girls' clothing in sizes infant to 14. Open M-F 10 a.m. to

9 p.m.; Sat 10 to 5:30. Also at 2053 Ford Pkwy. (Highland), St. Paul, 698-4411; and Knollwood Plaza, St. Louis Park, 933-2871. MC, V, S accepted.

HAUGLAND'S FOR THE YOUNG, Crystal Shopping Center, Crystal. ►4 537-7060

Boys' clothing in sizes infant to 16, girls' in infant to teen sizes. Open M-F 9:30 a.m. to 9 p.m.; Sat 9 to 6. MC, V, S accepted. Also at Burnsville Center, Burnsville, 435-5623; Ridgedale Center, Minnetonka, 544-8900; Rosedale Center, Roseville, 646-3977; 7 Hi Shopping Center, Minnetonka, 474-6624; Southdale Center, Edina, 926-4439; and Sun Ray Shopping Center, St. Paul, 735-4900. Call individual stores for hours.

KID'S CLOTHES, Midland Center, 2703 Winnetka Av. N., New Hope. ►4 544-0000

Clothing in boys' sizes infant to 16, girls' infant to 14. Open M-F 10 a.m. to 9 p.m.; Sat 10 to 6; Sun noon to 5. MC, V, S accepted.

PIED PIPER, 1752 Grand Av., St. Paul. ►8 699-8877

Toys and clothes for boys and girls in sizes infant to 14. Open M, Thu 10 a.m. to 8:30 p.m.; Tue-W, F-Sat 10 to 5:30. AE, MC, V accepted. Second location at 14 W. Fifth St., St. Paul, 293-0175.

PIP & PEGGOTY, Galleria, 3629 W. 69th St., Edina. ►5 929-1446

Traditional, preppie clothes for

children. Girls' sizes 4 to 14, boys' sizes 4 to 20. Open M-F 10 a.m. to 9 p.m.; Sat 10 to 6; Sun noon to 5. AE, MC, V accepted.

WAYZATA CHILDREN'S SHOP, 800 E. Lake St., Wayzata. 473-2575 ►5

Clothes for boys and girls in sizes infant to 14 and toys, some of them stuffed. Open M-F 9 a.m. to 5:30 p.m.; Sat 9 to 5. MC, V and Wayzata Children's Shop charge accepted.

WEE THREADS, Bonaventure, 1523 Plymouth Rd., Minnetonka. 545-0675 ►5

Handmade and better quality children's clothing and accessories. Infants through size 14. Open M-F 10 a.m. to 9 p.m.; Sat 10 to 6; Sun noon to 5. AE, MC, V accepted.

Children's Bargains

BANANAS, 17610 19th Av. N., Plymouth. ►4
473-3383

Brand-name children's clothes and accessories, some salesman's samples, and some recycled clothing, all at significant discounts off regular retail prices. Ongoing 70-percent-off rack. Unusual play area for shoppers' children. Open Tue-Sat 9 a.m. to 5 p.m. MC, V accepted.

CHILDREN'S SAMPLE SHOP, Robin Center, 4064 Hwy. 52, Robbinsdale. ►4
537-3330

Boys' and girls' clothes in sizes infant to 14 sold at 25 to 40 percent off retail prices. Open M-F 10

a.m. to 9 p.m.; Sat 10 to 5; Sun noon to 5. MC, V, S accepted.

MARY T'S KINDERMART SAMPLE SHOP, 1326 N. Rice St., St. Paul. ►8
488-9136

Women's and maternity clothing as well as children's clothing, all sold at significant discounts. Open M-F 10 a.m. to 5:30 p.m.; Sat 9:30 to 4:30. MC, V, S accepted.

OUTDOOR CLOTHING AND EQUIPMENT

ANTARTEX SHEEPSKIN SHOP, 928 Nicollet Mall, Minneapolis. ►1
339-1276

Sheepskin coats, wool sweaters, and other outerwear for men and women. Some rugs. Open M-Sat 9:30 a.m. to 5:30 p.m. (M-F 10 to 5 summer.) V accepted.

THE ARGONAUTES INC., 1040 University Av., St. Paul. ►8
645-0831

Sport and commercial scuba-diving equipment and services including air fill, repairs, local and foreign trips, underwater photography. Open M-F 11 a.m. to 7 p.m.; Sat 10 to 5. MC, V, S accepted.

ASPEN LEAF, 6950 York Av. S., Edina. ►5
927-4671

Downhill and cross-country skis and equipment, tennis equipment and clothing, running shoes, camping equipment, women's casual wear, and racquet stringing. AE, MC, V, S accepted. Three other Twin Cities locations.

BJORKLUND SPORTS, 831
Marquette Av., Minneapolis. ►1
333-4832

Sports footwear and clothing,
including running suits, socks and
sweatbands. Name-brand merchandise. Open M-W, F-Sat 9:30
a.m. to 6 p.m.; Thu 9:30 to 9.
Check telephone directory for
four other Twin Cities locations.

BURGER BROTHERS, 4402
France Av. S., Edina. ►5
927-7365

Everything for hunting, fishing,
camping, and cross-country skiing. Kits for fly- and jig-tying.
Also at 9833 Lyndale Av. S.,
Bloomington, 884-8842; and 5927
John Martin Dr., Brooklyn Center, 560-6310. Archery equipment
at Bloomington store. Open M-F
9 a.m. to 9 p.m.; Sat 9 to 6; Sun
11 to 5. AE, MC, V, S accepted.

**EASTERN   MOUNTAIN
SPORTS,** 1627 W. County Rd.
B., St. Paul. ►8
631-2900

Camping and backpacking
equipment, cross-country skis,
canoes, climbing equipment, and
casual clothing and footwear.
Mail-order catalog, equipment
rental. Open M-F 10 to 9; Sat 9 to
5:30. MC, V, S accepted.

EATON'S WESTERN WEAR,
12795 Cedar Av. S., Apple Valley.
454-5055 ►12

Boots, jeans, shirts, Western
clothing for the whole family.
Tailoring service available. Open
M-F 9:30 a.m. to 9 p.m.; Sat 9:30
to 6. AE, MC, V accepted.

EDDIE BAUER, Foshay Tower,

821 Marquette Av., Minneapolis.
339-9477 ►1

Famous goose-down outerwear,
camping equipment, boots, and
shoes. Open M-W, F-Sat 9:30
a.m. to 5:45 p.m.; Thu 9:30 to
8:30. AE, MC, V, S accepted.

FOOTLOCKER, Dayton-Radis-
son Arcade, 23 S. Seventh St.,
Minneapolis. ►1
332-5671

Shoes for all sports by Adidas,
Nike, Converse, Puma, etc.
Clothing and accessories for some
sports. Open M, Thu 9:30 a.m. to
9 p.m.; Tue-W, F-Sat 9:30 to
5:45. MC, V, S accepted. Check
telephone directory for nine other
Twin Cities locations.

FREE RIDE, 3336 Hennepin Av.
S., Minneapolis. ►2
823-5526

Wind surfers, skateboards,
roller skates, wetsuits, sunwear.
Rentals. Open M-F 10 a.m. to 8
p.m.; Sat-Sun 9:30 to 6. Hours
may change in winter.

GOKEY'S, 21 W. Fifth St., St.
Paul. ►7
292-3900

Men's and women's sports-
wear, shoes, special sporting
equipment. Started by a French
bootmaker in 1850 and still
known for made-to-measure
snakeproof boots. Also at 785 E.
Lake St., Wayzata, 475-2475; and
the Galleria, Edina, 926-6644. St.
Paul hours are M 9:30 a.m. to 8
p.m.; Tue-F 9:30 to 5:30; Sat 10 to
5. AE, MC, V, S accepted.

HOIGAARD'S, 3350 S. Hwy.
100, St. Louis Park. ►5
929-1351

Skiing, camping, backpacking and climbing equipment, sportswear, casual furniture, and awnings. Open M-F 9 a.m. to 9 p.m.; Sat 9 to 5:30. AE, MC, V, S accepted.

LE SKI HUT, Colonial Square Shopping Center, 1175 E. Wayzata Blvd., Wayzata. ▶5
473-8843

Skiing equipment and clothing, some sporting goods sold during the winter; tennis clothing, swimwear, and equipment for all sports sold during the summer. Ski school, windsurfing lessons. Open M-F 10 a.m. to 6 p.m.; Sat 9 to 5; longer hours in winter. MC, V, S accepted.

MAIN STREET OUTFITTERS, 3680 W. 70th St., Edina. ▶5
922-4783

Casual sporting clothes and shoes for men and women. Second location at St. Anthony Main, Minneapolis. Open M-F 10 a.m. to 9 p.m.; Sat 10 to 6; Sun noon to 5. AE, MC, V accepted.

MIDWEST MOUNTAINEERING, 309 Cedar Av. S., Minneapolis. ▶2
339-3433

Quality tents, packs, boots, climbing equipment, cross-country skiing and canoeing gear. Equipment repair service. Mail-order service. Free advice. Second location in Town Square, downtown St. Paul. Minneapolis location hours M-F 10 a.m. to 9 p.m.; Sat 10 to 6. AE, MC, V accepted.

SCUBA CENTER, 5015 Penn Av. S., Minneapolis. ▶2
925-4818

Equipment and services including air fills, repairs, instruction, photography, and local and overseas charters. Windsurfing lessons and equipment. Open summer M-F 10 a.m. to 9 p.m.; Sat 10 to 6; winter M-Sat 10 to 6. MC, V accepted.

SITZMARK'S SKI SHOP, 1160 W. County Rd. E (at Lexington Av.), Arden Hills. ▶9
484-8555

Clothing and equipment for downhill and cross-country skiing. Open winter M-F 10 a.m. to 9 p.m.; Sat 9 to 5:30; Sun noon to 5; summer Tue-Sat 9 to 5. Closed for about a month in the summer. AE, MC, V, S accepted.

THE SPORT SET, Southdale Center, Edina. ▶5
926-6060

Quality sportswear for men and women, including the Fila line. Second location in Bonaventure, Minnetonka. Open M-F 10 a.m. to 9:30 p.m.; Sat 9:30 to 6; Sun noon to 5. AE, MC, V accepted.

WYOMING OUTFITTERS, 6803 York Av. S., Edina. ▶5
926-8444

Outdoor clothing and traditional clothes for men and women as well as boots, brand-name tents, canoes, and other equipment. Open M-W 10 a.m. to 7 p.m.; Thu-F 10 to 9; Sat 10 to 6; Sun noon to 5. AE, MC, V accepted.

Outdoor Clothing and Equipment Bargains

HAGEN IMPORTS, 510 First

Av. N. (next to Butler Square), Minneapolis. ▶1
333-5913

Men's and women's down-filled vests and jackets, gloves, etc., sold at 30 percent off retail prices. Usually open M-F 9 a.m. to 4:30 p.m. Call first.

KURYSH MFG. CO. OUTLET STORE, 508 Fourth St., White Bear Lake. ▶10
429-7719

Men's, women's, and children's snowmobile suits, vests, ski jackets, and insulated underwear sold at about half off retail prices. Open M-F 7:30 a.m. to 4 p.m.

MARCEAU SPORTS, 3740 Williston Rd., Minnetonka. ▶5
933-6144

Manufacturer of 100 percent wool ski sweaters, hats, and mittens sells samples and last year's items in children's size 4 to adult men's and women's at about half off retail prices. Open M-F 9 a.m. to 5 p.m. Longer hours in the summer.

ACCESSORIES

BERMAN BUCKSKIN, 26 Hennepin Av., Minneapolis. ▶1
339-4000

Men's and women's leather coats, jackets, and accessories. Open M-Sat 9 a.m. to 5:30 p.m. Check telephone directories for about 10 other Twin Cities locations. Hours vary. AE, CB, DC, MC, V, S accepted at all.

GUCCI, 917 Nicollet Mall, Minneapolis. ▶1
339-5555

Leather accessories and shoes. Also scarves, ties, luggage, attaché cases, and desk accessories. Open M-W, F-Sat 10 a.m. to 5:30 p.m.; Thu 10 to 7:30. AE, CB, DC, MC, V, S accepted.

HUSSEY'S EXCLUSIVE HATTERS, 20 Glenwood Av., Minneapolis. ▶1
332-3717

Just men's hats, including custom-made varieties. Cleaning, refinishing, blocking available. Open M-F 8 a.m. to 5 p.m.; Sat 8 to 1.

J. STANLEY LTD., INC., Bonaventure, 1543 Plymouth Rd., Minnetonka. ▶5
546-6636

Men's and women's leather accessories, including handbags, briefcases, and gift items. Open M-F 10 a.m. to 9 p.m.; Sat 10 to 6; Sun noon to 5.

Bargain Accessories

COLLECTIONS BOUTIQUE, Westwood Center, 2312 Louisiana Av. S., St. Louis Park. ▶5
542-8336

Handbags, belts, and other accessories sold at 20 to 25 percent off retail prices. One of the largest handbag selections in the area. Open 10 a.m. to 6 p.m.; Sat 10 to 5.

JEWELRY

AMERINJECO INDIAN ARTS, Southdale Center, Edina. ▶5
920-1133

Southwestern American Indian jewelry, Navajo rugs, Pueblo art,

Stores, Shops, Markets, Boutiques 349

Black Hills gold. Open M-F 10 a.m. to 9:30 p.m.; Sat 9:30 to 6; sometimes open Sundays. AE, DC, MC, V, S accepted.

BADINER JEWELERS AND GEMOLOGISTS, IDS Center, 80 S. Eighth St., Minneapolis. ►1
338-6929
A line of unusual crafted jewelry complements a variety of name-brand merchandise. Open M, Thu 9:30 a.m. to 7:30 p.m.; Tue-W, F-Sat 9:30 to 5:30. AE, MC, V, S accepted.

FREDRICK BETLACH JEWELERS, 539 E. Lake St., Wayzata. 473-8833 ►5
Jewelry designed and manufactured. Open Tue-Sat 10 a.m. to 5 p.m. AE, MC, V accepted.

H. BOCKSTRUCK CO., 27 W. Fifth St., St. Paul. ►7
222-1858
A full-service jewelry store also carrying silver, china, crystal, pewter, stainless, and figurines. Jewelry repair, manufacturing, and silversmith services available. Open M 9 a.m. to 8:15 p.m.; Tue-F 9 to 5:15; Sat 9 to 4:45. AE, MC, V, Bockstruck's charge accepted.

CHARLEMAGNE FINE JEWELRY & GIFTS, St. Anthony Main, 201 S.E. Main St., Minneapolis. ►1
378-0441
Fine contemporary jewelry, crystal, gifts, and unique handblown crystal candles. Open M-Sat 10 a.m. to 9 p.m.; Sun noon to 6. Also at 1276 Grand Av., St. Paul, 699-1431; open Tue-Sat 10:30 a.m. to 5:30 p.m.

AE, CB, DC, MC, V, S accepted at both.

ERICA'S JEWELRY, 2805 W. 43rd St., Minneapolis. ►2
920-5575
Hand-designed, handmade jewelry in gold and silver. Open Thu-Sat 11 a.m. to 5 p.m. MC, V, S accepted.

GOODMAN JEWELERS, 86 E. Seventh St., St. Paul. ►7
227-7557
Specializing in Star Brite diamonds. Open M, Thu 9:30 a.m. to 7:45 p.m.; Tue-W, F-Sat 9:30 to 5:15. AE, MC, V, S, Goodman's charge accepted at all stores. Check telephone directories for other locations.

GREFFIN JEWELERS, 3009½ Hennepin Av. S. (at Lake St.), Minneapolis. ►2
825-9898
Custom settings in 14 and 18K gold. Colored gems and diamonds. Open M-Sat 10 a.m. to 5:30 p.m. AE, MC, V accepted.

J.B. HUDSON JEWELERS, 700 Nicollet Mall (in Dayton's), Minneapolis. ►1
375-2847
Fine jewelry, silver, china; repairs. Open M, Thu 9:30 a.m. to 9 p.m.; Tue-W, F-Sat 9:30 to 5:45. Hudson's, Dayton's charge accepted. Check telephone directory for other locations.

JACOBS' JEWELERS, 804 Nicollet Mall, Minneapolis. ►1
332-0484
Watches, diamonds, colored stones, crystal, porcelain giftware, sterling flatwear, gold-filled jewel-

ry, repairs, custom work. Open M
9:30 a.m. to 6:30 p.m.; Tue-Sat
9:30 to 5:30. Check telephone directory for other locations. AE,
CB, DC, MC, V, S, Jacobs'
charge accepted.

KORST & SONS, 3901 W. 50th
St. (at France Av.), Edina. ►5
926-0303

Jewelers, gemologists, and designers. Pewter holloware and
serving pieces and silver, in addition to jewelry. Open M-F 9 a.m.
to 5:30 p.m.; Sat 9 to 5. AE, CB,
DC, MC, V, S accepted.

R.L. McPECK GOLDSMITH,
Butler Square, 100 N. Sixth St.,
Minneapolis. ►1
338-1089

Custom-made jewelry of solid
gold. Open M-W, F 10 a.m. to 6
p.m.; Thu 10 to 8; Sat 10 to 5.
AE, MC, V, S accepted.

MOREL JEWELERS, IDS Center, 80 S. Eighth St., Minneapolis.
338-6766 ►1

Fine jewelry, diamonds,
watches, and fine gifts. Open
M-Sat 9 a.m. to 5:30 p.m. Second
location in the Galleria, Edina,
926-1818.

MORGAN'S, Midwest Plaza
Bldg., Suite 1740, 801 Nicollet
Mall, Minneapolis. ►1
332-0453

Jewelry of 14 and 18K gold,
diamonds and colored stones,
watches. Open M-F 9 a.m. to 5:30
p.m.; Sat 9 to 5. AE, MC, V, S accepted.

SCHEHERAZADE, Galleria,
3525 W. 69th St., Edina. ►5
926-2455

Designer jewelry and one-of-a-
kind pieces, mostly in gold and
silver. Wedding ring sets. Open
M-F 10 a.m. to 9 p.m.; Sat 10 to
6; Sun noon to 5. AE, MC, V, S
accepted.

S. VINCENT JEWELERS, 867
Grand Av., St. Paul. ►8
222-4559

Custom-designed wedding rings
and other handcrafted gold jewelry. Open M-Tue, Sat 10 a.m. to
5:30 p.m.; W-Thu, F 10 to 8; Sun
noon to 4. AE, MC, V, S accepted.

Jewelry Bargains

SWEEN-LUNDEEN, INC., 322
S. Fourth St., Minneapolis. ►1
332-1333

Watches, clocks, gold chains,
assorted gifts, and appliances at
discount prices. Open M-F 9 a.m.
to 5:15 p.m.; Sat 9 to noon. MC,
V accepted.

SUPERMARKETS

The Twin Cities has its share of
regional and national chain supermarkets. Most offer good service
and a reasonable selection of standard supermarket fare. The following stores, however, are home-
grown establishments that Twin
Citians mention most often when
they're speaking of exceptional
service and selection.

BYERLY FOODS, 3777 Park
Center Blvd. (Hwy. 100 and W.
36th St.), St. Louis Park. ►5
929-2100

Wide, carpeted aisles, luxury
appointments, and foods from

around the world make Byerly's the Rolls Royce of supermarkets. Fresh flowers, fresh fish, unusual and expensive gifts, and a post office desk that is open late hours are features at Byerly stores.

Also at:

7171 France Av. S., Edina, 831-3601.

5725 Duluth St., Golden Valley, 544-8846.

1959 Suburban Av., St. Paul, 735-6340.

All open 24 hours, seven days a week.

JERRY'S FOODS, 5125 Vernon Av. S., Edina. ►5
929-2685

Supermarket offering prime meats, fresh seafood, and gourmet foods. Nine Twin Cities locations.

LUND'S, 1450 W. Lake St. (block west of Hennepin Av.), Minneapolis. ►2
825-2446

Supermarket featuring wide variety of produce, ethnic specialties, and gourmet foods. Also fresh flowers, fish, live lobsters, and Minnesota wild rice.

Also at:

3945 W. 50th St. (at France Av.), Edina, 926-2536.

6228 Penn Av. S. (off Crosstown Hwy. 62), Richfield, 861-1883.

4471 Winnetka Av. N., New Hope, 536-8557.

All open seven days a week 8 a.m. to midnight.

DELICATESSENS

AL'S KENWOOD DELI, 2115 W. 21st St., Minneapolis. ►2
377-7150

Free delivery, or eat at Al's. Tables outside summer. Open M-Sat 10 a.m. to 5 p.m.

BEGAM'S DELICATESSEN, 1332 Grand Av., St. Paul. ►8
698-2212

New York-style deli. Open M-Sat 9 a.m. to 6 p.m.; Sun 9 to 2.

THE BROTHERS, 19 S. Seventh St., Minneapolis. ►1
339-2705

Popular deli restaurant. Kosher foods available. Open M, Thu 7:30 a.m. to 9:30 p.m.; Tue-W, F-Sat 7:30 to 8:30. MC, V accepted. Check telephone directories for other locations.

CECIL'S KOSHER DELICATESSEN, Highland, 651 Cleveland Av. S., St. Paul. ►8
698-9792

Restaurant and take-out deli featuring kosher foods. Open M-Thu 9:30 a.m. to 9 p.m.; F-Sun 9 to 6:30.

EMILY'S LEBANESE DELICATESSEN, 641 University Av. N.E., Minneapolis. ►2
379-4069

Lebanese breads and foods to take out or eat in. Open M, W, Thu 9 a.m. to 9:30 p.m.; F-Sun 9 a.m. to 10:30 p.m.

LE PETIT CHEF, 5932 Excelsior Blvd., St. Louis Park. ►5
926-9331

Topnotch French food—meats, vegetables, pastries, and breads—to take out. Call for hours.

LINCOLN DEL, 4100 W. Lake St., St. Louis Park. ►5
927-9738

Meats, salads, baked goods, and kosher foods available at extensive take-out section of deli restaurant. Open Sun-Thu 7 a.m. to midnight; F 7 to 1 a.m.; Sat 7 to 2 a.m. Also at 5201 Wayzata Blvd., St. Louis Park, 544-3616, and 4401 W. 80th St., Bloomington, 831-0780. Both open M-Thu 7 to 1 a.m.; F 7 to 2 a.m.; Sat 8 to 2 a.m.; Sun 8 to midnight.

MAKIESKY'S DEL, 7204 Minnetonka Blvd., St. Louis Park. ►5
929-1621

Restaurant service and kosher foods available. Open seven days a week 7 a.m. to 11 p.m.

MOTHER'S DELICATESSEN, 1826 Como Av. S.E., Minneapolis. ►2
331-8450

Restaurant service and kosher foods available. Open M-F 10 a.m. to 8 p.m. (to 10 summer).

PEOPLE'S NUTRITIONAL BAKERY, 918 University Av., St. Paul. ►8
224-3484

Take-out sandwiches, breads, and baked goods. M-F 7:30 a.m. to 2 p.m.; Sat 9 to 3:30.

POT BELLI DELI, Midland Plaza, 3592 Owasso St., Shoreview. ►9
484-4404

Homemade stew, soups, salads, and traditional deli fare. Eat in or

Good food from around the world.

take out. Open M-F 6 a.m. to 8 p.m.; Sat 9 to 6.

WESTWOOD DELICATESSEN AND SUPERETTE, 7115 S. Cedar Lake Rd., St. Louis Park. ►5
544-3864

Kosher deli; lox a specialty. Open seven days a week 9 a.m. to 10 p.m.

ZORKA AND OLLIE'S, 819 W. 50th St., Minneapolis. ►2
823-7713

Natural-food deli with a juice bar in the summer. Open summers M-F 10 a.m. to 9 p.m.; Sat 10 to 5; Sun noon to 6. Winter hours M-F 10 to 7; Sat 10 to 8; Sun noon to 6.

BAKERIES

BUNGALOW BAKE SHOP, 1080 Grand Av., St. Paul. ►8
225-1101

Wedding cakes a specialty. Open Tue-Sat 7 a.m. to 5:30 p.m.

GELPE'S OLD WORLD BAKERY, 2443 Hennepin Av. S., Minneapolis. ►2
377-1870

Specialties include croissants, French bread, and tortes. Kosher and non-kosher foods. Sunday *New York Times* always available. Open M-Thu 7 a.m. to 7 p.m.; F 7 to sundown; Sun 8 a.m. to 1 p.m. New location in March 4th, at Eighth and LaSalle, downtown Minneapolis, 332-9190. Open M-F 9 a.m. to 5 p.m.

GEORGE'S CAMPUS BAKERY, 409 14th Av. S.E., Minneapolis. ►2
378-1898

A Dinkytown institution famous for its variety of freshly baked cookies. Open M-Sat 6:30 a.m. to 6 p.m.

JERABEK'S BAKERY, 61 W. Winifred St., St. Paul. ►8
225-6523

Specialty wedding cakes and delivery service. Open M-F 7 a.m. to 5:30 p.m.; Sat 7 to 2:30. Also in Skyway Bldg., 378 Wabasha St., St. Paul, 222-1044; open M-F 7 a.m. to 5:30 p.m.

JOYCE'S BAKERY, 4406 France Av. S., Edina. ►5
922-7172

Specializing in Danish rolls, Joyce's has been in business 60 years. Open M-F 7 a.m. to 5:30 p.m.; Sat 7 to 5.

KESSEL BAKERY, 258 Snelling Av. S. (at St. Clair Av.), St. Paul. 698-3838 ►8

Old World pumpernickel, sourdough rye, French bread, and other specialties sold M-Sat 7 a.m. to 6 p.m.; Sun 7 to 1.

MIDDLE EAST BAKERY, 555 Snelling Av. N., St. Paul. ►8
644-4409

Pocket bread. Open M-F 9 a.m. to 6 p.m.; Sat 9 to 4.

NAPOLEON'S, 1932 St. Clair Av., St. Paul. ►8
690-0178

Croissants, brioche, and other French specialties are made fresh every day at this new bakery. Open W-Sat 8 a.m. to 5 p.m.; Sun 8 to 2.

NICOLLET BAKERY, 3749

Nicollet Av., Minneapolis. ►2
823-1741

Specializing in wedding cakes. Salt-free and dietetic baked goods. Open M-Sat 6 a.m. to 6 p.m. Food stamps accepted.

NEW YORK BAKERY & BAGELS, 8128 Minnetonka Blvd., St. Louis Park. ►5
933-3535

New York-style water bagels and bread sticks. Open seven days a week 8 a.m. to 8 p.m.

PEOPLE'S COMPANY BAKERY, 1534 E. Lake St., Minneapolis. ►2
721-7205

Whole-wheat French bread, special-order cakes, whole-grain cookies, carrot cake. Open M-F 9 a.m. to 6 p.m.; Sat 9 to 5.

PEOPLE'S CO-OP BAKERY, 918 University Av., St. Paul. ►8
224-3484

Nutritional baked goods, salads, and sandwiches. Open M-F 7:30 a.m. to 2 p.m.; Sat 9 to 3:30.

SCANDIA BAKERY AND KONDITORI, 2713 E. Lake St., Minneapolis. ►2
724-5411

Fresh Scandinavian baked goods and other foods. Visit the Konditori (coffee shop) and try one of Scandia's open-face sandwiches. Open M-F 6 a.m. to 5:30 p.m. Second location at 1005 Nicollet Mall, downtown Minneapolis, 333-8363, called Mrs. Scandia Kaffestue.

SHERMAN'S BAKERY, 7987

Southtown Center, Bloomington. 888-4614 ►6

Fine French breads and croissants from this bakery are used in many area restaurants. Open M-F 7 a.m. to 7 p.m.; Sat 7 to 6. Second location at 2236 Carter Av., St. Paul, 645-7578, open M-Sat 8 a.m. to 6 p.m.

WUOLLET BAKERY, 2308 W. 50th St., Minneapolis. ►2
922-4341

Souffle cakes are an unusual feature at this bakery, which also specializes in custom orders. Open Tue-Sat 7 a.m. to 5:30 p.m.

Bakery Bargains

CATHERINE CLARK'S BROWNBERRY OVENS, INC., 9412 Lyndale Av. S., Bloomington. ►6
884-6836

Thrift store offering many varieties of bread at 30 to 40 percent off retail prices, 10 percent more off Tue and Sun. Open M-F 9 a.m. to 6 p.m.; Sat 9 to 5:30. Food stamps accepted.

EMRICH BAKING CO. ECONOMY STORE, 922 E. 24th St., Minneapolis. ►2
871-2961

Thrift store selling at half off retail prices the first day, two-thirds off the second day. Additional 10 percent off for senior citizens and on purchase of $3.50 or more. Open M-F 9 a.m. to 5 p.m.; Sat 9 to 4.

METZ OLD HOME THRIFT STORE, 2900 Park Av., Minneapolis. ►2
823-6244

Day-old bread and cakes sold at

10 to 20 percent off retail prices, 10 percent more off on Wed. "Super savings day" is Sat. Open M-Sat 9 a.m. to 6 p.m.

Also at: 15704 Wayzata Blvd., Wayzata, 473-7671; open M-F 9 a.m. to 8 p.m.; Sat 9 to 6; Sun 11 to 5.

97 Sherburne Av., St. Paul, 293-0688; open M-F 9 a.m. to 6 p.m.; Sat 8 to 5.

3207 Sibley Memorial Hwy., Eagan, 454-7998; open M-F 9 a.m. to 6 p.m.; Sat 8 to 5; Sun 11 to 5.

1190 Prosperity Av. (Phalen Shopping Center), St. Paul, 771-4137; open M-F 9 a.m. to 6 p.m.; Sat 8 to 5.

PEPPERIDGE FARM THRIFT STORE, 4505 France Av. S., Minneapolis. ►2
927-9111

Breads, cookies, baked goods and other items from the Pepperidge Farm product line, sold at a discount. Open M-F 10 a.m. to 6 p.m.; Sat 9 to 5.

WONDER BREAD & HOSTESS CAKES THRIFT SHOP, 1200 Third Av. S., Minneapolis. ►1
332-3326

Thirty to 50 percent savings on day-old route returns. "Super bargain days" are Wed and Sat. Also at:

1213 E. Cliff Rd., Burnsville, 890-7335.

5130 Winnetka Av. N., New Hope, 533-2268.

2404 N. Rice St., Roseville.

MEATS AND FISH

CAPITAL CITY FISH CO., 511 E. Seventh St., St. Paul. ►7
224-3645

Fresh fish and seafood from around the world. Large selection. Open M-Wed 8 a.m. to 4:30 p.m.; Thu-F 8 a.m. to 5:30 p.m.; Sat 9 to 2.

CROCUS HILL MEAT MARKET, 674-676 Grand Av., St. Paul. ►8
225-6521

Choice meats cut to order. Telephone ordering and delivery. Open Tue-Sat 8 a.m. to 5:30 p.m.

FESTE FARMS MEAT MARKET, 4919 Central Av. N.E., Minneapolis. ►2
571-7530

Open M-F 10 a.m. to 6 p.m.; Sat 9 to 5.

FIDELMAN KOSHER MEAT MARKET, 540 Winnetka Av. N., Minneapolis. ►2
544-5215

Kosher meats and poultry cut to order. Open M-F 8 a.m. to 5:30 p.m.; Sun 8 to noon.

INGEBRETSEN GROCERY, 1601 E. Lake St., Minneapolis. ►2
729-9331

Scandinavian butcher shop and grocery featuring lefse (potato bread), lutefisk (fish soaked in lye, a Christmas favorite), herring, Swedish sausage, and home-smoked ham. Open M-F 9 a.m. to 6 p.m.; Sat 9 to 5.

KRAWCZYK SAUSAGE CO., 125 Lowry Av. N.E., Minneapolis. ►2
781-9856

Polish sausage and other Polish

specialties. Open M-Thu, Sat 9 a.m. to 6 p.m.; F 9 a.m. to 7 p.m.

MASSACHUSETTS BAY SEA-FOOD, 4507 France Av. S., Minneapolis. ►2
922-8900

Fresh seafood flown in daily from both coasts. Open Tue-F 10 a.m. to 6 p.m.; Sat 10 to 5.

PIONEER SAUSAGE CO., 616 Rice St., St. Paul. ►8
224-0484

Retail smoked meats and sausages. Open M 11 a.m. to 5:30 p.m.; Tue-Thu 9 to 5:30; F-Sat 8 to 5:30.

SOMETHING'S FISHY, 977 E. Lake St., Wayzata. ►5
475-1767

Live lobster and fresh seafood. Open Tue-Sat 10 a.m. to 6 p.m.

TEL-AVIV KOSHER MEATS, 655 Snelling Av. S., St. Paul. ►8
690-4367

Kosher meats and poultry. Open M-Wed 9:30 a.m. to 5 p.m.; Thu 9:30 to 7; F 9:30 to 3; Sun 9:30 to 1.

RUBIN'S KOSHER MEAT MARKET, 1887 Randolph Av., St. Paul. ►8
690-5837

Open M-F 8 a.m. to 5:30 p.m.; Sun 8 to 2.

FRUITS AND VEGETABLES

For complete information on farm stands selling seasonal fruits and vegetables grown in Minnesota, as well as pick-your-own farm locations and a list of large and small in-town farmers' markets, write for the *Directory of Minnesota-Grown Fruits and Vegetables,* published annually by the Minnesota Department of Agriculture, Marketing Services Division, 90 West Plato Blvd., St. Paul 55107. The booklet is free.

AAMODT'S STILLWATER OR-CHARDS, 6428 Manning Av. N., Stillwater. ►10
439-3127

Apples, apple pie, and cider seven days a week from 8 a.m. to 9 p.m. August through Christmas.

APPLESIDE MARKET, 8501 Lyndale Av. S., Bloomington. ►6
884-5820

Fruits and vegetables in and out of season. Open M-F 9 a.m. to 8 p.m.; Sat 9 to 6; Sun 11 to 6.

MINNEAPOLIS FARMERS' MARKET, 312 Lakeside Av. (east of Lyndale Av., between Glenwood Av. and Hwy. 55), Minneapolis. ►2
333-1718

Fresh produce, shipped-in fruit, and starter plants sold at lower prices than at most supermarkets. Merchandise changes seasonally. Open M-Sat 5:30 a.m. to 1 p.m.; Sun 8 to 2.

ST. PAUL FARMERS' MARKET
227-8101

Long a feature at 10th and Jackson Sts., the St. Paul Farmers' Market was about to move as this was being written. Call for details on new location. Open Sat 5 a.m. to 1 p.m. Seven other St.

Paul locations hold farmers' markets on weekdays. Call the main number for information. For a recorded message describing the types of produce available in a particular week, dial 227-1181.

FOOD COOPERATIVES

There are more than 40 food cooperatives operating in Minneapolis, St. Paul, and the surrounding suburbs. Most of them offer grains, nuts, dried fruits, pasta, oils, and other non- or semi-perishable groceries at low cost. For a complete list of addresses and phone numbers of Twin Cities area co-ops, write the All Cooperating Assembly, P.O. Box 14440, Minneapolis 55414, or call 376-8357, M-F 1 to 5 p.m.

FOOD SPECIALTIES

CARBONE BROTHERS GROCERY, 335 University Av. E., St. Paul. ►8
224-1816

Italian specialties. Open M-Sat 9 a.m. to 6 p.m.

CENTRAL ORIENTAL GROCERY AND GIFTS, 4864 Central Av. N.E., Minneapolis. ►2
572-0079

Japanese, Korean, Chinese, and Vietnamese food specialties. Open M-F 10 a.m. to 7 p.m.; Sat 10 to 6; Sun 1 to 5.

COSSETA'S, 226 Ryan Av., St. Paul. ►8
222-3476

Imported Italian and Greek foods. Cheese, oils, salami, pasta,

candies, and ice cream. Complete Italian deli. Open M-Sat 8:30 a.m. to 5:30 p.m.

CROCUS HILL FOOD MARKET, 674-676 Grand Av., St. Paul. ►8
225-7818

Unusual and hard-to-find groceries from all over the world in an old-fashioned, full-service store. Charge accounts, meats cut to order, telephone ordering, and delivery. Open Tue-Sat 8 a.m. to 5:30 p.m.

DELMONICO'S, 1112 N.E. Sumner St., Minneapolis. ►2
331-5466

Italian specialties. Open Tue-Sat 8 a.m. to 7 p.m.; Sun 11 to 1.

EL BURRITO, 196 Concord St., St. Paul. ►8
227-2192

Mexican foods. Open M-F 9:30 a.m. to 8 p.m.; Sat 9 to 7; Sun 9 to 3.

FIRST ORIENTAL FOOD, 3225 E. Hennepin Av., Minneapolis. ►2
488-4296

Chinese, Japanese, Korean, Thai, and Vietnamese groceries. Open M-F 10 a.m. to 7 p.m.; Sat 9 to 7; Sun noon to 5.

FOUR SEASONS CHEESE & FRUITS, 2232 Carter Av. (at Como Av.), St. Paul. ►8
644-7144

Cheese, fruit, bulk nuts, bulk coffee, coffee beans. Open M-Thu 10 a.m. to 6 p.m.; F 10 to 8; Sat 9 to 6; Sun 11 to 5. Other locations at 867 Grand Av., St.

Paul, and 1200 Nicollet Mall, downtown Minneapolis.

JOSEPH'S FOOD MARKET, 736 Oakdale Av., St. Paul. ▶8
225-7400

Mexican foods including home-made Mexican sausage. Open M-Sat 9 a.m. to 6 p.m.

KIM'S ORIENTAL GROCERY, 689 Snelling Av. N., St. Paul. ▶8
646-0428

Chinese, Japanese, Laotian, Vietnamese, and other Oriental groceries. Open M-Sat 10 a.m. to 7 p.m.; Sun noon to 5.

KWONG TUNG FOODS INC., 326 Cedar Av., Minneapolis. ▶2
338-1533

Oriental groceries. Open M-Sat 10 a.m. to 6 p.m.

MIDWEST NORTHERN NUT CO., 3105 Columbia Av., Minneapolis. ▶2
781-6596

Fresh-roasted nuts of all kinds sold at discounts in display room. Nuts can be bought unroasted or roasted without salt. Open M-F 8 a.m. to 5 p.m.

MILL CITY FOODS, 2552 Bloomington Av., Minneapolis. ▶2
721-2072

General grocery with Oriental section. Open M-Sat 10 a.m. to 8 p.m.; Sun noon to 6.

MORGAN'S MEXICAN-LEBANESE FOODS, 736 S. Robert St., St. Paul. ▶8
291-2955

Open M-Sat 9 a.m. to 6 p.m.

Take-out food available.

MORRIS & CHRISTIE'S, 3048 Hennepin Av. S. (at Lake St.), Minneapolis. ▶2
825-2477

Complete line of Greek foods. Open M-Sat 9 a.m. to 9 p.m.; Sun 11 to 6.

ORIENTAL PLAZA, INC., 607 Cedar Av., Minneapolis. ▶2
338-2064

Canned and dried foods from the Orient, as well as gift items and fresh Oriental vegetables and some seafood. Open M-Sat 10 a.m. to 6 p.m.

PASTA AND CHEESE, Bonaventure, 1605 Plymouth Rd., Minnetonka. ▶5
545-1818

Fresh pasta, imported and domestic cheeses and meats, imported tinned foods, homemade ice cream. Open M-F 10 a.m. to 9 p.m.; Sat 10 to 6, Sun noon to 5.

PAVO'S, 57 S. Ninth St., Minneapolis. ▶1
339-6397

Health foods. Open M-F 8:30 a.m. to 5:30 p.m.; Sat 9 to 5:30. AE, MC, V, S accepted.

RAESS QUALITY STORE, 1783 St. Clair Av., St. Paul. ▶8
699-1358

French, Swiss, and Austrian specialties. Open M 1 to 6 p.m.; Tue-Sat 9 a.m. to 6 p.m.

UNITED NOODLE CO., 2015 E. 24th St., Minneapolis. ▶2
721-6677

Oriental specialties. Open

M-Sat 9 a.m. to 6 p.m.; Sun 10 to 4.

HERBS AND SPICES

MARCO POLO HERBS AND SPICES, 3031 Hennepin Av. S., Minneapolis. ►2
824-5140

Selections of herbs, spices, and teas. Open M-Sat 10:30 a.m. to 5:30 p.m.

RED STAR HERBS, 3005 16th Av. S., Minneapolis. ►2
724-8414

Supplies area co-ops with herbs, spices, and teas. Sells small and large quantities to retail customers at significant discounts off regular retail prices. Open M-F 1 p.m. to 4 p.m.; Sat 10 a.m. to 4 p.m.

CANDY

DARVEAUX CONFECTION-NAIRE, St. Anthony Main, 201 S.E. Main St., Minneapolis. ►1
378-1216

Fudge in unusual flavors such as rum raisin, brandy alexander and pina colada. Second location in Butler Square, 100 S. Sixth St., Minneapolis, 333-0658. Open M-Thu 10 a.m. to 10 p.m.; F-Sat 10 to 11; Sun noon to 10.

FANNY FARMER CANDY SHOPS, INC., IDS Crystal Court, 80 S. Eighth St., Minneapolis. ►1
338-4873

IDS Center store open M-Sat 9:15 a.m. to 5:30 p.m. Check telephone directories for numerous other locations.

GODIVA CHOCOLATIER, Bonaventure, 1645 S. Plymouth Rd., Minnetonka. ►5
545-6226

Elegant Belgian chocolates. Open M-F 10 a.m. to 9 p.m.; Sat 10 to 6; Sun noon to 5. AE, MC, V, S accepted.

GOGGIN CANDY CO., 902 S. Fourth St., Stillwater. ►10
439-1516

Chocolates, candy bars, hard candies, and gifts. Open M-F 8:30 a.m. to 5 p.m.; Sat 10:15 to 5.

LA BONBONNIERE, 7600 Parklawn Av., Edina. ►5
831-2101

Open M-F 9 a.m. to 5 p.m.

MAUD BORUP CANDIES, 14 W. Fifth St., St. Paul. ►7
293-0530

Nuts and homemade chocolate. Nut toffee a specialty. Also at 53 S. Eighth St., Minneapolis, 339-7161. Both stores open Sun-F 8:30 a.m. to 5:30 p.m.; Sat 8:30 to 6. MC, V accepted at both.

MME. LARCELE, St. Anthony Main, 201 S.E. Main St., Minneapolis. ►1
378-0222

Variety of French, Swiss, and Belgian chocolates. Open M-Sat 10 a.m. to 9 p.m.; Sun noon to 6. MC, V accepted.

REGINA'S CANDY SHOPS, 1088 Grand Av., St. Paul. ►8
225-6385

All candy handmade. Specialties are fudge and English toffee. Open M-Sat 9 a.m. to 5:30 p.m.

Also at:

248 Cleveland Av. S., St. Paul,

698-8603, open M-Sat 9 to 5:30.

1905 S. Robert St., West St. Paul, 455-8864, open M-F 10 a.m. to 6 p.m., Sat 10 to 6.

14150 Nicollet Av. (Cobblestone Court), Burnsville, 435-3433; open M-F 11 a.m. to 7 p.m.; Sat 11 to 6.

TRUFFLES, Galleria, 3688 W. 70th St., Edina. ►5
922-1411

Chocolates, candies, and gifts from all over the world. Open M-F 10 a.m. to 9 p.m.; Sat 10 to 6; Sun noon to 5.

WOOD'S CHOCOLATE SHOP, 225 E. Sixth St., St. Paul. ►7
227-7800

Chocolates and Victoria brittle are specialties. Open M-Sat 9 a.m. to 5 p.m. Also at 3777 Park Center Blvd. (Byerly's), St. Louis Park, 929-2100, open Sun-Thu 8 a.m. to midnight, F-Sat 8 a.m. to 2 a.m. MC, V accepted at both.

Candy Bargains

ABDALLAH CANDIES, 12220 12th Av. S., Burnsville. ►6
890-4770

Imperfect candies, raisins, walnuts, and other nuts sold at discounts. All candy is handmade, much of it dipped. Open M-F 8 a.m. to 5 p.m.; Sat 9 to 1. Second location at 3805 Cedar Av., Minneapolis, 722-1312, open Tue-F 10 a.m. to 4:30 p.m.; Sat 10 to 2.

ANTIQUES

AMERICAN CLASSICS, 4944 Xerxes Av. S., Minneapolis. ►2
926-2509

Primitive American country antiques. Refinishing, reupholstering, chair caning, and other furniture restoration services available. Open M-Sat 10:30 a.m. to 5 p.m.; Sun noon to 4. MC, V accepted.

ANTIQUES MINNESOTA, 1516 E. Lake St., Minneapolis. ►2
722-6000

A large building housing more than 75 antique dealers who display a variety of merchandise, from fine glass to roll-top desks. No entrance fee. Open M, Wed-Sat 10 a.m. to 5 p.m.; Sun noon to 5.

ANTIQUITY ROSE, 429 Second St., Excelsior. ►5
474-2661

Antiques of all kinds. Tea room open M-F 11 a.m. to 2:30 p.m. Store open M-Sat 10:30 to 4:30. MC, V, S accepted.

ARCHITECTURAL ANTIQUES, 401 N. Third St., Minneapolis. ►1
378-2844

Stained-glass windows, fireplace mantles, pillars, railings, doors, fixtures, and some furniture displayed on the second floor of a large warehouse. Open M-F 9 a.m. to 5 p.m.; Sat 10 to 2.

BLACK SWAN COUNTRY STORE, 3020 W. 50th St. (at Xerxes Av.), Minneapolis. ►2
926-9134

Primitives, kitchenware, gifts, and books on antiques. Open Tue-Sat 10:30 a.m. to 5 p.m. MC, V accepted.

CHARISMA PLACE, 3011 W.

50th St. (at Xerxes Av.), Minneapolis. ►2
926-5400

Specializes in oak furniture. Refinishing available. Open W-Sat 10:30 a.m. to 4:30 p.m.

CHIMNEY HOUSE ANTIQUES, 1472 Grand Av., St. Paul. ►8
698-3036

Sells and rents antique clothing. Antique furniture. Open Tue-Sat 11 a.m. to 5 p.m.

FJELDE & CO. ANTIQUES, 3022 W. 50th St. (at Xerxes Av.), Minneapolis. ►2
922-7022

Specialists in woodwork and furniture refinishing. Open Tue-Sat 10 a.m. to 5 p.m. V accepted.

GRAND HOUSE, 889 Grand Av., St. Paul. ►8
222-6520

Victorian furniture and light fixtures. Open M-Sat 10 a.m. to 5 p.m. MC, V accepted.

MAGGIE'S CORNER, 1112 Grand Av., St. Paul. ►8
298-0913

Furniture, accessories, and a variety of other antiques. Open M-Sat 10 a.m. to 4:30 p.m. MC, V accepted.

MAYFAIR ANTIQUES, 1128 Harmon Pl., Minneapolis. ►1
338-1802

Architectural and fine antiques. Light fixtures, brass, copper, and wooden accessories. Open M-F 9 a.m. to 5 p.m.; Sat 10 to 4.

NAKASHIAN-O'NEIL, INC., 23

W. Sixth St., St. Paul. ►7
224-5465

This design studio carries fine antiques as well as other home furnishings and accessories. Open M-Sat 9 a.m. to 5:30 p.m. (closed most Sat in the summer).

REMAINS TO BE SEEN, 2306 W. 50th St. (at Penn Av.), Minneapolis. ►2
926-6001

Specializing in baskets, miniatures, and cards. Open Tue-Sat 10 a.m. to 5 p.m. MC, V accepted.

STUDIO, 3016 W. 50th St. (at Xerxes Av.), Minneapolis. ►2
922-6120

Antique jewelry. Open Tue-Sat 10:30 a.m. to 4:30 p.m. MC, V accepted.

YANKEE PEDDLER, 5008 Xerxes Av. S., Minneapolis. ►2
926-1732

Open Tue-Sat 10:30 a.m. to 4:30 p.m.

HOME FURNISHINGS

THE BOXSHOP, 1413 Washington Av. S., Minneapolis. ►2
338-7092

Box-frame furniture in natural finishes with cushions made-to-order. Open M-F 11:30 a.m. to 5:30 p.m.; Sat 10 to 5.

R.J. BRANDON GALLERIES, Brandon Square, 3535 W. 70th St., Edina. ►5
920-7150

Fine traditional furniture by Drexel and Heritage. Open M-F 10 a.m. to 9 p.m.; Sat 10 to 6; Sun 1 to 5. MC, V, S accepted.

BUCK'S UNPAINTED FURNITURE STORES, 2005 E. Lake St., Minneapolis. ►2
724-9405

Open M-F 10 a.m. to 7 p.m.; Sat 9:30 to 5.

Also at:

1023 Excelsior Av. W., Hopkins, 935-7457; open M-F 10 a.m. to 8 p.m.; Sat 9:30 to 5:30.

8806 Lyndale Av. S., Bloomington, 884-0901; open M-F 10 a.m. to 8:30 p.m.; Sat 9:30 to 5; Sun noon to 4.

1639 Larpenteur Av. W. (west of Snelling Av.), Falcon Heights, 646-9647; open M-F 10 a.m. to 9 p.m.; Sat 9:30 to 5:30; Sun noon to 4:30.

Custom finishing available at all stores. MC, V, S accepted at all stores.

BUTCHER BLOCK SHOPPE, 1250 E. Wayzata Blvd., Wayzata. 473-3206 ►5

Butcher block tables and chairs for casual dining. Open M-W, F-Sat 10 a.m. to 5 p.m.; Thu 10 to 8:30. MC, V accepted.

CARROLL'S FINE FURNITURE, 1203 W. County Rd. E, Arden Hills. ►9
484-8533

Specializing in traditional furniture by Drexel, Henredon, Heritage. Some antiques and contemporary pieces. Design service. Open M, Thu-F 9:30 a.m. to 9 p.m.; Tue-W, Sat 9:30 to 5:30. AE, MC, V, S accepted.

CASUAL LIVING, INC., Leisure Lane, 7101 France Av. S., Edina. 925-4900 ►5

Rattan, wicker, and cane furniture and accessories for indoors and outdoors. Gourmet kitchenware. Open M-F 10 a.m. to 8:30 p.m.; Sat 10 to 5:30; Sun 12:30 to 4:30. MC, V, S accepted for kitchenware only.

CONCORD HOUSE, 13820 Wayzata Blvd. (Hwy. 12 and I-494), Minnetonka. ►5
544-9546

Ethan Allen furniture—early American in maple and pine, English reproductions in cherry. Design service available. Also at 7101 France Av. S. (Leisure Lane), Edina, 926-6551. Both stores open M-F 10 a.m. to 9 p.m.; Sat 10 to 5; Sun 1 to 5. MC, V accepted at both.

CREATIVE FURNITURE, 23 S. Eighth St., Minneapolis. ►1
339-2297

Modern furniture and accessories by Barzilay, Billingham, Classic, Gallery, etc. Open M, Thu 9:30 a.m. to 9 p.m.; Tue-W 9:30 to 5:45; Sat 9:30 to 5. AE, MC, V, S accepted.

DAYTON'S FURNITURE DEPARTMENT AND HOME STORE, 700 Nicollet Mall, Minneapolis. ►1
375-2491

Variety of furniture and accessories. Design service available.

Also at:

E. Seventh and Cedar Sts., St. Paul, 375-6874.

Brookdale Home Store, 5701 Xerxes Av. N., Brooklyn Center, 375-5376.

Ridgedale Center, Minnetonka, 375-5665.

Rosedale Home Store, 1375 Commerce St. (Hwy. 36 and

Hamline Av.), Roseville, 375-6381.

Southdale Home Store, 7235 France Av. S., Edina, 375-4345.

Downtown stores open Tue-W, F-Sat 9:30 a.m. to 5:45 p.m.; M, Thu 9:30 to 9. Suburban stores open M-F 10 a.m. to 9:30 p.m.; Sat 9:30 to 6; Sun noon to 6. Dayton's charge accepted at all stores.

DESIGN MODERN INTERIORS, 1709 Snelling Av. N. (at Larpenteur), Falcon Heights. ►9
645-0800

Scandinavian furniture, fabrics, and accessories. Moderate prices. Design service available. Open M-W, Sat 10 a.m. to 6 p.m.; Thu-F 10 to 9. MC, V, S accepted.

DIRECTIONS, 174 Southdale Center, Edina. ►5
920-2401

Chrome, brass, wood, and wicker furniture and accessories. Open M-F 10 a.m. to 9:30 p.m.; Sat 9:30 to 6; Sun noon to 5. AE, MC, V accepted.

EDINBORO GALLERIES, Yorktown Fashion Mall, 3409 Hazelton Rd., Edina. ►5
835-0740

Handcrafted upholstered furniture, and picture and mirror galleries. Open M-F 10 a.m. to 9 p.m.; Sat 10 to 6; Sun noon to 4. MC, V, S accepted.

FREEMAN'S LIGHTING CONCEPTS, Galleria, 3465 W. 69th St., Edina. ►5
925-4252

Wide variety of lighting fixtures, lamps, doorbells. Open M-F 10 a.m. to 9 p.m.; Sat 10 to

6; Sun noon to 5. Other locations in Brighton Village, New Brighton, 636-7111; Bonaventure, Minnetonka, 544-4020; and Maplewood Plaza, 770-6411.

GABBERT'S FURNITURE, Galleria, 3501 W. 69th St., Edina. ►5
927-1500

Two-hundred-fifty room settings of quality furniture and accessories. Design service available. Open M-F 10 a.m. to 9 p.m.; Sat 10 to 6; Sun noon to 5. MC, V, S accepted.

GUILD, INC., 401 N. Third St., Minneapolis. ►1
333-4345

Quality traditional and contemporary furniture for homes and offices. Sales made through interior decorators only. Carpeting and accessories. Open M-F 8:30 a.m. to 5 p.m.; Sat 8:30 to noon.

GUNKELMAN'S, 1116 Nicollet Mall, Minneapolis. ►1
333-0526

Unusual home accessories, from baskets to antiques. Design studio. Open M-F 10 a.m. to 5 p.m.

INTERNATIONAL DESIGN CENTER, 100 Second Av. N., Minneapolis. ►1
341-3441

Specializing in Scandinavian furniture and accessories. Huge showroom in an old warehouse. Open M-W, F-Sat 9:30 a.m. to 5:30 p.m.; Thu 9:30 to 9. No credit cards.

MILLBRIDGE COUNTRY STORE, Bonaventure, 1675 S.

Plymouth Rd., Minnetonka. ►5
544-5404

Primitive reproductions, quilts. Design advice available. Open M-F 10 a.m. to 9 p.m.; Sat 10 to 6; Sun noon to 5. MC, V, S accepted.

MODERN CENTER, INC., 1100 Nicollet Mall, Minneapolis. ►1
335-0644

Contemporary furniture and accessories, including Scandinavian furniture imported directly. Residential and commercial design service available. Open M, Thu 9:30 a.m. to 7 p.m.; Tue, W, F 9:30 to 6; Sat 9:30 to 5. MC, V accepted.

NEWTIQUES, 201 W. Lake St., Minneapolis. ►2
870-9328

New furniture in the old style—round oak tables, rolltop desks, brass items, butcher block tables. Open M-Sat 10 a.m. to 5 p.m.

OXMAN'S, 648 Second Av. N., Minneapolis. ►2
338-3777

Custom-made contemporary furniture. Lighting and accessories. Design service available. Open M-W, F 9 a.m. to 5:30 p.m.; Thu 9 to 8; Sat 9 to 4. AE, MC, V accepted.

PARTNERS 4 DESIGN, Galleria, 3601 W. 69th St., Edina. ►5
927-4444

Allmilmo, Boffi, and other designer kitchen and bathroom cabinetry. Design and construction services. Open M-Sat 10 a.m. to 6 p.m.

PIER ONE IMPORTS, 5220 Central Av. (off I-694), Columbia Heights. ►3
571-9417

Baskets, rattan, and a variety of other types of home accessories and giftware. Open M-Sat 10 a.m. to 9 p.m.; Sun noon to 5. MC, V accepted. Check telephone directories for five other Twin Cities locations.

ROCHE-BOBOIS, Galleria, 3675 W. 69th St., Edina. ►5
929-0471

Fine European contemporary designs in furniture and accessories. Open M-F 10 a.m. to 9 p.m.; Sat 10 to 6; Sun noon to 5. AE, MC, V, S accepted.

ROOM & BOARD, 3350 W. 70th St. (at York Av.), Edina. ►5
927-8835

Casual furniture and accessories, storage systems, kitchen equipment. Also at 14314 Burnhaven Dr. (Burnside Plaza), Burnsville, 435-8818; and Ridgehaven Mall, Minnetonka, 546-2075. Open M-F 10 a.m. to 9 p.m.; Sat 10 to 6; Sun noon to 5. AE, MC, V, S accepted at both.

SAWHILL FURNITURE, 89 S. 10th St., Minneapolis. ►1
339-8910

Solid hardwood butcher block furniture and kitchen cabinets. Also juvenile furniture. Open M-Sat 9 a.m. to 5 p.m. Also at 3519 W. 70th St. (Brandon Square), Edina, 925-2611; open M-F 10 a.m. to 9 p.m.; Sat 10 to 6; Sun noon to 5. MC, V accepted at both.

SCANDINAVIAN DESIGN,

Ridgedale Center, Minnetonka. 545-2802 ►5

Scandinavian furniture and accessories including lamps, rugs, and Finnish crystal. Open M-F 10 a.m. to 9:30 p.m.; Sat 9:30 to 6; Sun noon to 5. Also at Maplewood Mall, Maplewood, 770-2330; open M-F 10 a.m. to 9 p.m.; Sat 10 to 6; Sun noon to 5; and at 1001 Nicollet Mall, downtown Minneapolis. MC, V, S accepted at all stores.

SLUMBERLAND, Southdale Square, 2936 W. 66th St., Richfield. ►6
866-8452

Mattresses (the four largest brands), name-brand sleeper sofas, brass beds, and waterbeds. Check the telephone directory for other locations. All stores open M-F 10 a.m. to 9 p.m.; Sat 10 to 5:30; Sun 1 to 5. MC, V, S accepted at all stores.

SWENSON'S CARRIAGE HOUSE, 1044 W. Hwy. 110, Mendota Heights. ►12
452-1160

Traditional Ethan Allen furniture. Design service available. Also at 1111 E. Hwy. 36, Maplewood, 483-2624. Both open M-F 10 a.m. to 9 p.m.; Sat 10 to 5:30. MC, V accepted at both.

THE TICK TALK SHOP, Bonaventure, 1681 Plymouth Rd., Minnetonka. ►5
546-3375

Large selections of floor, wall, and mantel clocks and designer telephones. Open M-F 10 a.m. to 9 p.m.; Sat 10 to 6; Sun noon to 5.

Mayfair Antiques, Harmon Court, downtown Minneapolis.

AE, MC, V accepted.

TREASURE'S ISLAND, 4200 W. Lake St., St. Louis Park. ►5 927-7913

Baby furniture including cribs, playpens, high chairs, and dressers. Open M-F 9 a.m. to 6 p.m.; Sat 9 to 5:30; Sun noon to 5. MC, V, S accepted.

UNPAINTED PLACE, 1601 Hennepin Av. S., Minneapolis. 339-1500 ►1

Manufacturer and retailer of unpainted furniture. Open M, Thu 9 a.m. to 8 p.m.; Tue-W, F 9 to 6; Sat 9 to 4.

VENUS WATERBEDS & FURNISHINGS, 6900 York Av. S., Edina. ►5 925-2822

Waterbeds, sheets, dressers, and other furnishings. Also at 5717 Xerxes Av. N. (Westbrook Mall), Brooklyn Center, 566-0850; Har Mar Mall, Roseville, 631-9226; and Ridgehaven Mall, Minnetonka, 541-9077. Open M-F 10 a.m. to 9 p.m.; Sat 10 to 6; Sun noon to 5. MC, V accepted.

VICTORIAN REPRODUCTIONS INC., 1601 Park Av., Minneapolis. ►2 338-3636

Victorian furniture in solid handcrafted mahogany. Tables with genuine Italian marble tops. Open M-Tue 10 a.m. to 4 p.m.; W-Thu 10 to 8; F-Sat 10 to 4. MC, V accepted.

WICKER WORKS, 3054 Excelsior Blvd., Minneapolis. ►5 922-3032

Large selection of new and antique furniture of wicker and rattan. Window blinds and fabrics also available. Open M-F 9 a.m. to 8 p.m.; Sat 9 to 6; Sun 1 to 5. AE, MC, V accepted.

THE WICKER WORLD, 823 Excelsior Av. W., Hopkins. ►5 935-8814

Wicker and rattan furniture, accessories, baskets, roll-up blinds, and fabrics. Custom cushions available. Open Tue, W, Fri, Sat 10 a.m. to 5 p.m.; Thu 10 to 8. MC, V accepted.

WICKES FURNITURE, 6725 York Av. S. (across from Southdale), Edina. ►5 920-1330

Large selection of brand-name furniture and accessories. Also at I-694 and E. River Rd., Fridley, 571-2800. Both open M-F 10 a.m. to 9 p.m.; Sat 10 to 6; Sun 11 to 6. MC, V accepted at both.

WIESSNER'S CREATIVE DESIGN, 1670 Grand Av., St. Paul. 698-6666 ►8

Formerly Nelson's Interiors. Primarily a design studio offering special-order furniture, carpet, draperies, fabrics, and accessories from dozens of catalogs. Open M-F 9 a.m. to 5:30 p.m.; Sat 9 to 1 (winters only). MC, V, S accepted.

Kitchen Specialties

ANDERSON'S CHINA SHOP, 912 Nicollet Mall, Minneapolis. 336-6671 ►1

Kitchen and dining gifts and accessories, as well as a wide selection of fine crystal and china. Open M-Sat 9:30 a.m. to 5:30 p.m. MC, V accepted.

CINNAMON TOAST, 3940 W. 50th St., Edina. ►5
920-4070

Pots, pans, paraphernalia for gourmet cooks. Also coffees and teas. Open M-W, F-Sat 9:30 a.m. to 5:30 p.m.; Thu 9:30 to 8:30. Also at 1603 S. Plymouth Rd. (Bonaventure), 545-2130; open M-F 10 a.m. to 9 p.m.; Sat 11 to 6; Sun noon to 5. Cooking school at Bonaventure. AE, MC, V, S accepted at both stores.

ELEMENTS, St. Anthony Main, 201 S.E. Main St., Minneapolis. 378-9371 ►1

Butcher block tables, storage systems, fabric stretchings, kitchen equipment, and accessories. Open M-F 10 a.m. to 9 p.m.; Sat 10 to 10; Sun noon to 6. MC, V accepted. Also at 1142 Burnsville Center, Burnsville, 435-6146; open M-F 10 a.m. to 9:30 p.m.; Sat 10 to 6; Sun noon to 5:30; and at 2941 Hennepin Av., Minneapolis. AE, MC, V, S accepted.

FIVE SWANS, 309 E. Lake St., Wayzata. ►5
473-4685

Scandinavian home accessories including china, glassware, and cookware. Open M-Sat 9 a.m. to 6 p.m.

THE KITCHEN WINDOW, Yorktown Fashion Mall, 3421 Hazelton Rd., Edina. ►5
831-4252

Large selection of kitchen gadgets, cookware, and serving accessories. Complete cooking school as well as store. Open M-F 10 a.m. to 9 p.m.; Sat 10 to 5:30; Sun noon to 4. AE, MC, V accepted.

MAID OF SCANDINAVIA, S.E. corner of Hwys. 7 and 100, St. Louis Park. ►5
927-7996

Gifts from Scandinavia, cookware, wedding decorations, and party supplies. Open M-W, F 9 a.m. to 5 p.m.; Thu 9 to 8:30; Sat 9 to 1:30.

Also at:

3523 W. 70th St. (Brandon Square), Edina, 920-9646; open M-Thu 10 a.m. to 9 p.m.; F 10 to 6; Sat 10 to 5.

5717 Xerxes Av. N (Westbrook Mall), Brooklyn Center, 566-9360; open M-F 10 a.m. to 9 p.m.; Sat 10 to 6.

2335 Fairview Av. N. (across from Rosedale), Roseville, 633-2592; open M-F 10 a.m. to 9 p.m.; Sat 10 to 5. MC, V accepted.

MAINPLACE, St. Anthony Main, 201 S.E. Main St., Minneapolis. ►1
378-1218

Home accessories and Marimekko fabrics. Open M-Sat 10 a.m. to 9 p.m.; Sun noon to 6. AE, MC, V accepted.

118 EAST, 924 Nicollet Mall, Minneapolis. ►1
338-5592

Gourmet cookware, kitchen and dining accessories, home furnishings. Open M-Sat 9:30 a.m. to 5:30 p.m. Also at Ridgedale Center, Minnetonka, 546-1234; open M-F 10 a.m. to 9:30 p.m.; Sat 9:30 to 6; Sun noon to 5. AE, MC, V, S accepted at both.

TD 2, 2945 Hennepin Av. S. (at Lake St.), Minneapolis. ▶2
827-1707

Contemporary cookware and gifts including china, glassware, flatware, gourmet cooking utensils, and jewelry. Open M-Sat 9 a.m. to 5:30 p.m. AE, MC, V, S accepted.

TH'RICE, 1086½ Grand Av., St. Paul. ▶8
225-0513

Cooking equipment, cookbooks, a few teas, and giftware as well as a complete cooking school. Open M-Sat 10 a.m. to 5:30 p.m. AE, MC, V accepted.

Home Furnishing Bargains

BROADWAY SALES, 1000 W. Broadway, Minneapolis. ▶2
529-9577

Furniture, appliances, hardware, and other merchandise sold at varying discounts. Open M-F 9 a.m. to 8 p.m.; Sat 9 to 5; Sun 1 to 5 (not open every Sun). MC, V accepted.

CHET CODY UNCLAIMED FREIGHT, 605 W. Broadway, Minneapolis. ▶2
522-6539

Furniture sold at 25 percent off retail prices. Open M-Sat 8 a.m. to 5:30 p.m. MC, V accepted.

DAYTON'S OUTLET STORE, 701 Industrial Blvd. (south of I-35W), Minneapolis. ▶2
375-2553

New overstocks and slightly damaged or one-of-a-kind items of furniture, appliances, televisions, stereos, etc., sold at varying discounts. Open M-F 9 a.m. to 9 p.m.; Sat 9 to 6; Sun noon to 6. Dayton's charge accepted.

GABBERT'S ODDS 'N ENDS ROOM, Galleria, 3501 W. 69th St., Edina. ▶5
927-1500

A small assortment of odd pieces, some damaged, discontinued, or returned, is sold at varying discounts. Open M-F 10 a.m. to 9 p.m.; Sat 10 to 6; Sun noon to 5. MC, V, S accepted.

LONDON SALES, 10726 France Av. S., Bloomington. ▶6
884-3900

Home and office furniture, accessories, and stereo equipment including discontinued, freight-damaged, and liquidated merchandise and close-outs sold at about half off retail prices. Open M-F 9 a.m. to 9 p.m.; Sat 9 to 5. MC, V accepted.

MONTGOMERY WARD'S BARGAIN OUTLET STORE, 1700 Wynne Av. (at warehouse), St. Paul. ▶8
647-2275

Surplus and damaged furniture and major appliances sold at varying discounts. Open M-F 9 a.m. to 9 p.m.; Sat 9 to 5:30. MC, V, Ward's charge accepted.

NORTHLAND ALUMINUM PRODUCTS, 5120 County Rd. 16 (Cedar Lake Rd.), St. Louis Park. 920-2720 ▶5

Seconds of discontinued lines of Nordicware (cookware and bakeware) and microwave accessories sold. Open the first weekend of each month, F noon to 9 p.m.; Sat

9 a.m. to 5 p.m.; Sun 10 to 5. AE, MC, V accepted.

SEARS RETAIL OUTLET STORE, 2700 N.E. Winter St., Minneapolis. ►2
874-3636

Mostly furniture and major appliances sold at varying discounts. Open M-F 9 a.m. to 9 p.m.; Sat 9 to 5. Sears charge accepted.

GIFTS AND SPECIALTIES

BASKET SHOPPE, 1652 Grand Av., St. Paul. ►8
699-1888

Baskets, candles, cards, gifts, and a large selection of mugs. Open M-Sat 9 a.m. to 5 p.m.

BLUE BIRD GIFTS, Ridgedale Center, Minnetonka. ►5
546-2550

Collectibles, figurines, pottery, and other gifts. Also at Rosedale Center, Roseville, 631-2559. Both open M-F 10 a.m. to 9:30 p.m.; Sat 9:30 to 6; Sun 1 to 5. AE, MC, V, S accepted at both.

BLUE WATER INDIAN ARTS, American National Bank Bldg., E. Fifth and Minnesota Sts., St. Paul. ►7
298-0799

Silver and turquoise jewelry from the American Southwest. Open M-F 9:30 a.m. to 5:30 p.m.; Sat 11 to 4. AE, MC, V, S accepted.

THE CAT HOUSE, Bonaventure, 1621 Plymouth Rd., Minnetonka. ►5
544-4143

All kinds of gifts for cat lovers. Open M-F 10 a.m. to 9 p.m.; Sat 10 to 6; Sun noon to 5. AE, MC, V, S accepted.

THE CHIMNEY CORNER, 111 Multifoods Bldg., 733 Marquette Av., Minneapolis. ►1
338-4017

Toys, quilts, linens, and other gift and household items, all handcrafted by senior citizens. Open M-F 10 a.m. to 4 p.m. Other locations at 1505 Park Av., Minneapolis, 339-7581, and 3614 Bryant Av. S., Minneapolis, 822-3194.

CLOTH AND CLAY, Butler Square, 100 N. Sixth St., Minneapolis. ►1
332-0097

Minnesota handcrafted pottery, fine glassware. Open M-Thu 10 a.m. to 9 p.m.; F-Sat 10 to 10; Sun noon to 5. MC, V accepted.

COURAGE CENTER HOME-CRAFTERS GIFT SHOP, 3915 Golden Valley Rd., Golden Valley. ►4
588-0811

Wooden toys, ornaments, sewn items, and other gifts made by handicapped artisans. Open M-F 10 a.m. to 4:15 p.m. Other locations in the skyways at 200 Bremer Tower, Seventh and Minnesota Sts., downtown St. Paul, 227-1221; and 243 Multifoods Bldg., Seventh and Marquette, downtown Minneapolis, 332-5758.

CRAFT CONNECTION, Butler

Square, 100 N. Sixth St., Minneapolis. ►1
333-1313

Jewelry, candles, fibers, cards, graphics, baskets, and hand-blown glass. Open M-F 10 a.m. to 10 p.m.; Sat 10 to 6. House subject to change. AE, MC, V accepted.

DENEEN POTTERY, 230 E. Fifth St., St. Paul. ►7
226-8682

Handcrafted pottery. Potters can be watched while working. Open M-F 10 a.m. to 4 p.m. MC, V accepted.

DIFFERENT DRUMMER, 12907 Ridgedale Dr., Ridge Square S., Minnetonka. ►5
546-4806

Gifts, greeting cards, and books. Open M-F 10 a.m. to 9 p.m.; Sat 10 to 5; Sun noon to 5. MC, V, S accepted.

FIRST DAISY, First National Bank Skyway, 332 Minnesota St., St. Paul. ►7
222-8917

Hummels, fresh flowers, books, collectibles, and gifts. Open M-F 9 a.m. to 5:30 p.m.; Sat (December only) 9 to 5:30.

GALLERY OF BURL, 350 Robert St., St. Paul. ►7
224-2107

Tables, desks, and other items crafted from redwood burl. Crafts, jewelry, and prints. Open M-F 9 a.m. to 5 p.m. AE, MC, V, S accepted.

THE LEFT CENTER, 4400 Excelsior Blvd., St. Louis Park. ►5
926-6033

Left-handed scissors, sport gloves, school supplies, and other items designed exclusively for left-handed people. M-F noon to 5:30 p.m.; Sat 10 to 3. S accepted.

LeROY'S, 2054 Burnsville Center, Burnsville. ►6
435-5461

Fine gifts and collectibles. Open M-F 10 a.m. to 9:30 p.m.; Sat 9:30 to 6; Sun noon to 5:30. AE, MC, V accepted.

MARCH 4TH, LaSalle Court, 811 LaSalle Av., Minneapolis. ►1
338-4404

This unusual avant-garde gift and clothing store now houses a branch of Gelpe's bakery. Open M, Thu 9:30 a.m. to 8 p.m.; Tue, W, F, Sat 10 to 5:30. MC, V accepted.

MOLE HOLE, 3907 W. 50th St. (at France Av.), Edina. ►5
922-2700

China, cookware, jewelry, and lamps. Open M-Sat 9:30 a.m. to 5:30 p.m. MC, V, S accepted.

OFF THE WALL, 4316 Upton Av. S., Minneapolis. ►2
926-1273

Pottery, weavings, jewelry, and artwork by regional artists. Open M-Sat 10 a.m. to 5 p.m. MC, V accepted.

PARKER-HANLEY, Galleria, 3474 W. 70th St., Edina. ►5
920-4222

Elegant gifts in porcelain, china, and crystal. Open M-F 10 a.m. to 9 p.m.; Sat 10 to 6; Sun noon to 5. AE, MC, V, S accepted.

PINK PONY, 3940 W. 50th St. (at France Av.), Edina. ►5
925-1200

Gifts and accessories. Open M-Sat 9:30 a.m. to 5:30 p.m.

PLYMOUTH BUILDING GIFTS AND CARDS, 14 S. Sixth St., Minneapolis. ►1
339-1130

Soft sculptures, collectible dolls, glassware, other unusual gifts. Open M-F 9 a.m. to 5 p.m.; Sat 10 to 4. AE, MC, V accepted.

POTTERY WORKSHOP (SANSEI POTTERY), 1129 Grand Av., St. Paul. ►8
224-7159

Stoneware and pottery handcrafted on the premises. Open F 10 a.m. to 5:30 p.m.; Sat 10 to 4.

QUIRK OF FATE, 521 Third St., White Bear Lake. ►10
426-2887

Crystal, brass, jewelry, and other fine gifts. Open M-F 10 a.m. to 6 p.m.; Sat 10 to 5:30. MC, V, S accepted.

RAINBOW BALLOON, 5004 France Av. S., Edina. ►5
926-3430

Unusual cards, soft toys, mobiles, and other gifts, many in a heart or rainbow motif. Will deliver balloon bouquets. Open M-Sat 10 a.m. to 6 p.m. MC, V accepted.

REINDEER HOUSE, 3419 W. 44th St., Minneapolis. ►2
920-6950

Large selection of handcrafts, ribbons, and Anita Beck cards. Open M-Sat 9:30 a.m. to 5:30

p.m.; Sun 1 to 5. Second location at 773 Cleveland Av. S., St. Paul, 699-4593.

SHAPERO'S, 1300 Nicollet Mall, Minneapolis. ►1
375-9309

Gift shop in the Hyatt Regency Hotel. Tobacco, cards, gifts, and a fine line of fragrances and cosmetics. Open M-Sat 7 a.m. to 11 p.m.; Sun 8 a.m. to 10 p.m. AE, MC, V accepted.

THE SOFT COLLECTION, Galleria, 3639 W. 69th St., Edina. 920-4450 ►5

Unusual clothing and soft sculptures, gifts and collectibles. Open M-F 10 a.m. to 9 p.m.; Sat 10 to 6; Sun noon to 5. AE, MC, V accepted.

THREE ROOMS UP, Galleria, 3515 W. 69th St., Edina. ►5
926-1774

Porcelain, pottery, and other works by Minnesota artisans. Open M-F 10 a.m. to 9 p.m.; Sat 10 to 6; Sun noon to 5. MC, V accepted.

TIDEPOOL GALLERY, 3907 W. 50th St. (at France Av.), Edina. ►5
926-1351

Gifts from the sea including rare and collector seashells, coral, and jewelry. Open M-Sat 10 a.m. to 5:30 p.m. MC, V, S accepted.

T. WILLIAMS, Hwy. 5 and County Rd. 4, Eden Prairie. ►5
937-1527

Wildlife gifts, woodcarvings, pewter and crystal. Open M-F 10 a.m. to 9 p.m.; Sat 10 to 5:30. MC, V, S accepted.

WEST BANK TRADING CO., 419 Cedar Av., Minneapolis. ►2 338-4477

Clothes, pottery, jewelry, cookware, cards, toys, games, furnishings, etc. Open M-F 10 a.m. to 8 p.m.; Sat 10 to 6. MC, V accepted.

Bargain Gifts

PRACTICAL WEDDING GIFTS, 4104 42nd Av. S., Minneapolis. ►2 722-6447

This store will exchange unneeded wedding gifts as well as sell gifts for cash, trading stamps, or cigarette coupons. Open Tue-F noon to 5 p.m.; Sat 10 to 4.

Minnesota Specialties

HELLO MINNESOTA, Butler Square, 100 N. Sixth St., Minneapolis. ►1 332-1755

Almost anything pertaining to Minnesota can be found here: wild rice, native crafts, stuffed and carved loons, pipestone, art. Large selection of books about Minnesota and books by Minnesota authors. Maps, postcards, souvenirs. Open M-Sat 10 a.m. to 10 p.m.; Sun noon to 5. AE, MC, V, S accepted.

MINNEAPPLE CART, St. Anthony Main, 201 S.E. Main St., Minneapolis. ►1 379-8504

Look for this free-standing cart inside St. Anthony Main near Anthony's Wharf. T-shirts, mugs, totes, bibs, and other specialties, all carrying the chilly "Minneap-ple" emblem. Open M-Sat 10 a.m. to 9 p.m.; Sun noon to 6.

Museum Shops

AMERICAN SWEDISH INSTITUTE SHOP, 2600 Park Av., Minneapolis. ►2 871-3004

Swedish glass, jewelry, linen, pewter, etc. Open Tue-Sat 1 to 4 p.m.; Sun 1 to 5.

THE EXPLORE STORE, 30 E. 10th St., St. Paul. ►7 221-9414

Gift store in the Science Museum of Minnesota. Books, posters, weather instruments, maps, optical instruments, and other science and natural-history gifts. Open M-Sat 9:30 a.m. to 8:30 p.m.; Sun 11:30 to 8; closed M during the winter. Second location in the Minneapolis Public Library, 300 Nicollet Mall, 372-6680. Open Tue-Sat 10 a.m. to 5 p.m.; Sun 1 to 4:30. AE, MC, V accepted at both.

MINNEAPOLIS INSTITUTE OF ARTS MUSEUM SHOP, 2400 Third Av. S., Minneapolis. ►2 870-3100

Sculpture, silver, stained glass, porcelain, jewelry, wall hangings, calendars, and cards. Open Tue-W, F-Sat 10 a.m. to 4:30 p.m.; Thu 10 to 8; Sun noon to 4:30. MC, V accepted.

WALKER ART CENTER BOOK SHOP, Vineland Pl., Minneapolis. ►2 375-7633

Books, posters, jewelry, toys, and gifts. Open Tue-Sat 10 a.m.

to 5 p.m. (to 8 during Guthrie Theater season); Sun 11 to 5. AE, MC, V, S accepted.

Import Shops

ASIA MART, 908 Marquette Av., Minneapolis. ▶1
338-1058

Oriental vases, knickknacks, and dolls. Open M-Sat 10 a.m. to 6 p.m.

DUBLIN WALK, Sheraton-Ritz Hotel, 315 Nicollet Mall, Minneapolis. ▶1
338-5203

Waterford crystal, Beleek china, Connemara marble jewelry, Irish linen, wool sweaters and blankets. Open M-Sat 9:30 a.m. to 6 p.m. AE, MC, V, S accepted.

HERITAGE II, 2230 Carter Av. (at Como Av.), St. Paul. ▶8
646-6296

Imports from the British Isles and Scandinavia including woolens, porcelain, china, rosemaling, pewter, and needlepoint kits. Open M-F 10:30 a.m. to 5:30 p.m.; Sat 10 to 5. MC, V, S accepted.

IMPORT HOUSE, Dinkytown, 427 14th Av. S.E., Minneapolis. ▶2
378-1310

Cotton clothes and handcrafted gifts, mostly from India. Open M-Sat 10:30 a.m. to 7 p.m.

INDIGO, 10 S. Fifth St., Minneapolis. ▶1
333-2151

Folk arts, textiles, and fine collectibles from Asia, Africa, and the Pacific. Open M-W, F, Sat 10 a.m. to 6 p.m.; Thu 10 to 8. AE, MC, V accepted.

NORD HUS SCANDINAVIAN GIFTS, 1102 Grand Av., St. Paul. 226-3650 ▶8

Danish crystal, Norwegian Porsprund, Swedish clogs, linens, and other Scandinavian gifts. Open M-F 10 a.m. to 5:30 p.m; Sat 10 to 5. AE, V, S accepted.

OLD MEXICO SHOP, Summit Hills Mall, 1053 Grand Av., St. Paul. ▶8
222-3273

Mexican and Guatemalan clothes, folk art, tiles, and rugs. Open M-Sat 10 a.m. to 5 p.m. AE, MC, V, S accepted.

SCANDIA IMPORTS, 33 S. Eighth St., Minneapolis. ▶1
339-6339

Scandinavian jewelry, ceramics, glass, pewter, clogs, and Norwegian hand-knit sweaters. Open M, Thu 9:30 a.m. to 8 p.m.; Tue-W, F-Sat 9:30 to 5:45. MC, V accepted.

UKRANIAN GIFT SHOP, 2422 Central Av. N.E., Minneapolis. ▶2
788-2545

Easter eggs, cookbooks, sweaters, and ceramics. Open M-Sat 9 a.m. to 5 p.m. Open from Memorial Day to Labor Day M-F 9 a.m. to 5 p.m.; Sat 9 to 3.

UNITED NATIONS GIFT SHOP, 1026 Nicollet Mall, Minneapolis. ▶1
333-2824

UNICEF cards and a variety of gifts from around the world.

Open M-Sat 10 a.m. to 5 p.m.

YAMATO IMPORTS, 320 Marquette Av., Minneapolis. ►1
332-2828

Oriental clothes, jewelry, china, pottery, prints, and teak furniture. Open M-F 10 a.m. to 6 p.m.; Sat 10 to 4. AE, DC, MC, V accepted.

Scents and Soaps

CASWELL-MASSEY OF MINNEAPOLIS, Galleria, 3630 W. 70th St., Edina. ►5
926-3908

Elegant fragrance shop that also sells shaving brushes and other toiletries. Open M-F 10 a.m. to 9 p.m.; Sat 10 to 6; Sun noon to 5. MC, V accepted.

GARDEN OF EDEN, Butler Square, 100 N. Sixth St., Minneapolis. ►1
339-6909

Biodegradable soaps, shampoos, lotions, creams, and perfumes. Open M-F 10 a.m. to 9 p.m.; Sat 10 to 6; Sun noon to 5. Also at 3015 Hennepin Av. S. (at Lake St.), 823-6949; open M, Thu 9:30 a.m. to 8 p.m.; Tue-W, F-Sat 9:30 to 6; and 867 Grand Av. (Victoria Crossing), St. Paul, 225-1144; open M-F 10 a.m. to 8 p.m.; Sat 10 to 5:30; Sun noon to 5. MC, V, S accepted at all.

BOOKSTORES

General Interest

B. DALTON BOOKSELLER,

Once a warehouse, Butler Square now stands for shopping.

815 Nicollet Mall, Minneapolis. 333-2428 ▶1

General-interest chain bookstore carrying an enormous variety of paperback and hardcover titles, including best-sellers and publishers' remainders. Open M, Thu 9:30 a.m. to 9 p.m.; Tue-W, F-Sat 9:30 to 5:45. AE, MC, V, S, Dayton's charge accepted. Check telephone directories for 14 other Twin Cities locations.

BOOKCASE, 633 E. Lake St., Wayzata. ▶5
473-8341

General-interest bookstore carrying fine stationery and children's and picture books. Open M-Sat 9:30 a.m. to 5:30 p.m. Bookcase charge accepted.

BOOKFAIR, IDS Center, 80 S. Eighth St., Minneapolis. ▶1
333-1403

General-interest bookstore. Special orders. Postcards, greeting cards, bookmarks. On skyway level. Open M, Thu 9:30 a.m. to 8 p.m.; Tue-W, F 9:30 to 5:30; Sat 10 to 5. MC, V, S accepted.

BOOKS GALORE, Minnehaha Mall, 2510 E. Lake St., Minneapolis. ▶2
722-8940

General-interest bookstore with large selection of periodicals. Open M-F 10 a.m. to 9 p.m.; Sat 10 to 6; Sun noon to 5. MC, V accepted.

THE BOOK MILL, 3940 W. 50th St., Edina. ▶5
927-6455

General-interest bookstore. Will special order for 50-cent fee. Also carries calendars, bookbags,

related gifts. Open M-W, F-Sat 9:30 a.m. to 6 p.m.; Thu 9:30 to 8:30. MC, V, S accepted.

BROWSER'S BOOKSHOP, 7 Hi Shopping Center, 4858 Hwy. 101, Minnetonka. ▶5
474-2523

Family bookstore. No extra charge for special orders. Open M-F 9:30 a.m. to 9 p.m.; Sat 9:30 to 6; Sun 12:30 to 5. MC, V, S accepted.

CALHOUN BOOK STORE, 3946 Lyndale Av. S., Minneapolis. ▶2 Minneapolis. ▶2
823-1882

Specializing in non-fiction hardcovers, most of them new. Open M-Sat 9 a.m. to 5 p.m.

CORNER BOOKSHOP, 7927 Southtown Center, Penn Av. and I-494, Bloomington. ▶6
888-4300

General-interest bookstore featuring a good selection of children's books. Open M-F 10 a.m. to 9 p.m.; Sat 10 to 5:30; Sun, Labor Day to Memorial Day only, noon to 5. MC, V, S accepted.

DONEGAL BAY BOOKSTORE, 4055 Hwy. 7, St. Louis Park. ▶5
925-0591

General-interest bookstore located across the highway from the original Lincoln Del. Special section on chemical dependency. Monthly mystery readers' group. Free special orders. Open M-F 9:30 a.m. to 9 p.m; Sat 9:30 to 6; Sun 11 to 4. MC, V, S accepted.

GRINGOLET BOOKS AND

CAFE, St. Anthony Main, 201 S.E. Main St., Minneapolis. ▶1
378-2000

General-interest books, foreign periodicals, ongoing remainder sale. Cafe serves fine meals, espresso, wine, and beer. Bookstore open Sun-Thu 10 to 10; Fri 10 to 11; Sat 10 to midnight. Cafe has slightly shorter hours. AE, MC, V, S accepted.

HUNGRY MIND, Mac Market, 1648 Grand Av., St. Paul. ▶8
699-0587

Mostly paperbacks including poetry, small-press books, psychology, and children's books. Sofa for customers' reading pleasure. Discount on most books. Open M-F 9 a.m. to 8 p.m.; Sat 10 to 6; Sun noon to 5.

LAKEWOOD BOOKSTORE, 3401 Century Av. N., White Bear Lake. ▶10
770-1835

Lakewood Community College bookstore featuring mostly texts; some mass-market and science fiction books. Open M-F 8:30 a.m. to 3:30 p.m. (9 to 1 during the summer.)

LITTLE PROFESSOR BOOK CENTER, Apache Plaza, 37th Av. N.E. and Silver Lake Rd., St. Anthony. ▶2
789-7760

General-interest books and magazines, rental library, used-book exchange, and cassette copy service. Open M-F 10 to 9; Sat 9:30 to 5:30; Sun noon to 5. MC, V, S accepted.

MICAWBER'S BOOKS, 2238

Carter Av. (at Como Av.), St. Paul. ▶8
646-5506

Specializing in children's books (many of them autographed), picture books, publishers' overstock, and Penguin paperbacks. Open M-F 10 a.m. to 6 p.m.; Sat 10 to 5:30; Sun noon to 5.

ODEGARD BOOKS, Victoria Crossing, 857 and 867 Grand Av., St. Paul. ▶8
222-2711

Well-stocked general-interest bookstore. Espresso cafe; comfortable seating for browsers. Sale books (publishers' remainders) at 867 Grand Av. Strong on fiction and literature. Open M-Thu 10 a.m. to 10 p.m.; F-Sat 10 to 11; Sun noon to 5. MC, V accepted.

ORR BOOKS, 3043 Hennepin Av. S. (at Lake St.), Minneapolis. 823-2408 ▶2

New and used books, mostly paperbacks. Open M-F 10 a.m. to 8 p.m.; Sat 10 to 6; Sun noon to 5. Open M-F to 9 summer.

RUSOFF & CO. BOOK DEALERS, Dinkytown, 1302 S.E. Fourth St., Minneapolis. ▶2
378-2242

General-interest bookstore specializing in literature and carrying literary and critical journals. Open M-Sat noon to 5. AE, V accepted.

SAVRAN'S PAPERBACK SHOP, 301 Cedar Av. (near West Bank campus), Minneapolis. ▶2
333-0098

Large paperback selection plus publishers' remainders (hardcovers and paperbacks) and unusual periodicals. Open M-F 10 a.m. to 9 p.m.; Sat 10 to 6.

ST. PAUL BOOK & STATIONERY, Town Square, Sixth St. and Cedar Av., St. Paul. ►7
227-9156

General-interest books, office and school supplies, and gifts. Open M, Thu 9 to 9; Tue-W, F-Sat 9 to 6. AE, MC, V, S, SPBS charge accepted. Check telephone directories for other locations.

THE UNICORN BOOKSTORE, 4314 Upton Av. S., Minneapolis. 920-0220 ►2

General-interest bookstore specializing in travel and children's books and special orders. Open M-Sat 10 a.m. to 5:30 p.m. Unicorn charge accepted.

WALDENBOOKS, INC., 3005 Hennepin Av. S. (at Lake St.), Minneapolis. ►2
824-9890

Part of large, national general-interest bookstore chain. Open M-F 10 a.m. to 8 p.m.; Sat 10 to 5:30. AE, MC, V, S accepted. Check telephone directory for several other Twin Cities locations.

THE WORDSMITH, 310 S. Main St., Stillwater. ►10
439-3527

General-interest books; also cards, gifts, music. Open M-Sat 9:30 a.m. to 5:30 p.m.

Specialty Bookstores

AMAZON BOOKSTORE, 2607 Hennepin Av. S., Minneapolis. 374-5507 ►2

Books, periodicals, and crafts by women. Book-lending service. Open M-F noon to 8 p.m.; Sat 10 a.m. to 6 p.m.

AMERICAN OPINION BOOKSTORE, 8550 Bryant Av. S., Bloomington. ►6
881-8227

John Birch Society sales. Hours vary because store is in a private home. Call first.

ARCHITECTURE STORE, Northwest Crossing, 402 Wabasha St., St. Paul. ►7
227-0761

Bookstore of the Minnesota Society, American Institute of Architects. Architectural books, children's books, and AIA documents. Open M-F 9 a.m. to 5 p.m.; Sat 10 to 3. MC, V accepted. A new Architecture Store is now open at 910 Nicollet Mall, downtown Minneapolis. Check the telephone directory for the new number.

BOOKS ABROAD, 25 University Av. S.E., Minneapolis. ►2
378-0961

Foreign-language books, special orders. Open M-F 10 a.m. to 5 p.m.; Sat 9 to 5.

COMIC CITY, 3149½ Hennepin Av. S., Minneapolis. ►2
823-4445

New and used comics and related materials. Mail-order service available. Open M-F 11 a.m. to 7 p.m.; Sat 11 to 6.

ENRICA FISH MEDICAL BOOKS, 814 Washington Av. S.E., Minneapolis. ►2
623-0707

Medical books and equipment.

Special orders. Open M-F 9 a.m. to 6 p.m.; Sat 11 to 3.

GNOSTICA BOOK STORE, 213 E. Fourth St., St. Paul. ►7
291-1970

Astrology, palmistry, occult books. Tarot cards. Open M-Sat 9 a.m. to 4:30 p.m. MC, V accepted.

UNCLE EDGAR'S MYSTERY BOOKSTORE, 1930 Fourth Av. S. (at Franklin Av.), Minneapolis. 874-7575 ►2

New and used mystery books are the specialty of this store. Open M-F noon to 8 p.m.; Sat noon to 6.

UNCLE HUGO'S SCIENCE FICTION BOOK STORE, 1934 Fourth Av. S. (at Franklin Av.), Minneapolis. ►2
874-9118

New and used science fiction and fantasy books. Used books bought and sold. Open M-F noon to 8 p.m.; Sat noon to 6.

WALKER ART CENTER BOOK SHOP, Vineland Pl., Minneapolis. ►2
375-7633

Books on art, architecture, film, dance; plus children's books, jewelry, and toys. Open Tue-Sat 10 a.m. to 5 p.m. (to 8 during Guthrie Theater season); Sun 11 to 5. AE, MC, V, S accepted.

WORKING WOMAN & MAN BOOKSTORE, 613 W. 24th St., Minneapolis. ►2
871-5657

Socialist, women's, labor, Third World, and history books.

Open M-F 5 to 8 p.m.; Sat 10 to 6; Sun noon to 4.

Periodicals and News

COURTESY NEWS, 473 St. Peter St., St. Paul. ►7
222-3155

Out-of-town papers, foreign papers, hardcover and paperback books. Open seven days a week early morning to 5:30 p.m. Fifty years in business.

DINKYTOWN NEWS, 301 14th Av. S.E. (at University Av.), Minneapolis. ►2
331-7741

Claims to have the largest selections of foreign newspapers and periodicals and political journals in the Twin Cities. Also carries underground comics. Six-hundred newspaper and magazine titles. Open M-F 9 a.m. to 5:30 p.m.; Sat 10 to 5; Sun 9 to 5.

S & S NEWS AND GREETINGS, Skyway, American National Bank Bldg., Sixth and Minnesota Sts., St. Paul. ►7
224-8227

Full line of cards and gifts as well as periodicals and books. Magazine subscription service, party supplies. Open M-F 8 a.m. to 5 p.m.; Sat 9 to 4. AE, MC, V, S accepted.

SHINDERS BOOK & NEWS, 431 Wabasha St., St. Paul. ►7
227-0899

Out-of-town newspapers, magazines, comics, science fiction and fantasy, and some books. Open M-Sat 7 a.m. to 9 p.m.; Sun 9 to

9. Second store at 628 Hennepin Av., Minneapolis.

TOBAK NEWS, 2140 Ford Pkwy., St. Paul. ►8
698-3835

Magazines, newspapers, trade journals, paperbacks, and some hardcover books. Open M-Thu 9:30 a.m. to 9:30 p.m.; F 9:30 a.m. to 10 p.m.; Sat 9:30 to midnight; Sun 9 to 6. AE, MC, V, S accepted.

Religious Books

AUGSBURG PUBLISHING HOUSE, 426 S. Fourth St., Minneapolis. ►1
330-3300

Religious books, curriculum materials, and supplies. Open M-F 8:30 a.m. to 5 p.m.; Sat 8:30 to 1 between Thanksgiving and Christmas only.

BROCHIN'S BOOK AND GIFT SHOP, 4813 Minnetonka Blvd., St. Louis Park. ►5
926-2011

Jewish gift and book shop. Yiddish, Hebrew, and English books. Open M-Thu 9:30 a.m. to 5:30 p.m.; F, Sun 9:30 to 3. Brochin's charge accepted.

EVANGELISM BOOK CENTER, 833 Second Av. S., Minneapolis. ►1
333-6241

Bibles, religious books, cards, curriculum materials, and gifts. Open M 9 a.m. to 7 p.m.; Tue-F 9 to 5:30; Sat 9 to 3 (to 1 Sat July and August, to 5:30 Sat December).

HIGHWAY BOOK NOOK, 404 Penn Av. S., Minneapolis. ►2
374-5458

Bibles and Christian books. Some language books and others. Hours vary; usually Tue-Sat 10 to 1 and 3 to 6. Call first.

MACALESTER PARK BOOK STORE, 1571 Grand Av., St. Paul. ►8
698-8877

Ecumenical religious books, best-sellers, cards, stationery. Open M-F 8:30 a.m. to 5 p.m.; Sat 9 to 1 (closed Sat summer).

MARANATHA BOOK STORE, 13712 Nicollet Av., Burnsville. 893-3434 ►6

Christian books, records, Bibles, posters, t-shirts, and cards. Open M-Thu 10 a.m. to 9 p.m.; F-Sat 10 to 6.

ST. FRANCIS GIFT AND BOOK SHOP, IDS Center, 80 S. Eighth St., Minneapolis. ►1
332-1866

Books, Bibles, statues, jewelry, and candles. Open M-F 10 a.m. to 5 p.m.; Sat 10 to 4. Also at 5717 Xerxes Av. N. (Westbrook Mall), Brooklyn Center, 561-4700; open M-F 10 a.m. to 9 p.m.; Sat 10 to 6; and Southdale Center, Edina, 922-8485; open M-F 10 a.m. to 9:30 p.m.; Sat 9:30 to 6; Sun 1 to 5. MC, V, S accepted at all.

Paperback Books

PAPERBACK EXCHANGE, 2227 W. 50th St. (at Penn Av.), Minneapolis. ►2
929-8801

Used paperbacks for sale and trades. Open M-F 10 a.m. to 5:30 p.m.; Sat 10 to 4.

SETHEL'S PAPERBACK EXCHANGE, Marquette Bldg., 400 Marquette Av., Minneapolis. ►1
375-9504

Used paperbacks for sale at 60 percent of face value. Trades taken at 75 percent of face value. Open M-F 9 a.m. to 5:15 p.m.

Used and Rare Books

BIERMAIER'S B. H. BOOKS, 809 S.E. Fourth St., Minneapolis. 378-0129 ►2

Used and rare books bought and sold. Also maps, posters, printed materials of all kinds. Search service; will special-order new books. Open Tue 11 a.m. to 9 p.m.; W-Sat 11 to 5:30.

THE BOOK HOUSE, Dinkytown, 429 14th Av. S.E., Minneapolis. ►2
331-1430

Some 65,000 used and scholarly books (no textbooks). Open M-Sat 11 a.m. to 11 p.m.; Sun noon to 6:30.

DINKYTOWN ANTIQUARIAN BOOKSTORE, 1316 S.E. Fourth St., Minneapolis. ►2
378-1286

Large selection of collectable modern first editions. Open M-F 10:30 a.m. to 5:30 p.m.; Sat 11 a.m. to 5:30. MC, V accepted.

JAMES AND MARY LAURIE BOOKSELLERS, 251 Snelling Av. S., St. Paul. ►8
699-1114

Used and rare books, mostly in the fields of literature, bookmaking, literary criticism. Prints and maps. Free search service. Open W-F 11 a.m. to 8 p.m.; Sat 9

to 5; Sun noon to 5.

LELAND N. LIEN, ANTIQUARIAN BOOKSELLER, 413 S. Fourth St., Minneapolis. ►1
332-7081

Old, rare, and out-of-print books bought and sold. Bookbinding and appraisal services. Search service. Open M-Sat 10 a.m. to 5:30 p.m. MC, V accepted.

OUDAL BOOK SHOP, 315 S. Ninth St., Minneapolis. ►1
332-7037

Used books, mostly hardcovers. Open M-Sat 10:30 a.m. to 5 p.m.

ROSS & HAINES OLD BOOKS CO., 639 E. Lake St., Wayzata. 473-7551 ►5

Used, rare, and out-of-print books. Reprints of books about Western Americana, American Indian history, and regional history. Open M-Sat 11 a.m. to 5 p.m.

FABRICS

AMLUXEN'S FABRICS, 913 Nicollet Mall, Minneapolis. ►1
333-6393

Fine fabrics from New York and Europe, including wools, cottons, silks, and bridal fabrics. Open M, Thu 9:30 a.m. to 7 p.m.; Tue, W, F, Sat 9:30 to 5:30. AE, MC, V accepted.

COUNTRY PEDDLERS, 2242 Carter Av. (at Como Av.), St. Paul. ►8
646-1756

Handmade quilts, patchwork items, fabrics, templates, patterns. Quilting classes available. Open M 10 a.m. to 7 p.m.; Tue-Sat 10 to 6. MC, V, S accepted.

DELL FABRICS, Miracle Mile Center, 5101 Excelsior Blvd., St. Louis Park. ►5
922-1566

Dress, upholstery, and drapery fabric; patterns and notions. Open M-F 9:30 a.m. to 9 p.m.; Sat 9 to 6; Sun noon to 5. MC, V, S accepted. Check telephone directories for six other Twin Cities locations.

DEPTH OF FIELD, 405 Cedar Av., Minneapolis. ►2
339-6061

Designer fabrics for the home. Specialties are window coverings and stretched fabric wallhangings. Free classes offered in roller shade and drapery construction, other home decorating projects. Open M-F 9:30 a.m. to 8 p.m.; Sat 10 to 6. Check telephone directories for four other Twin Cities locations. MC, V accepted.

MINNESOTA FABRICS, 7991 Southtown Center, Bloomington. 884-7463 ►6

Large selection of dress fabrics as well as drapery and upholstery fabrics. Drapery hardware and made-to-measure drapery service. Open M-F 9:30 a.m. to 9 p.m.; Sat 9:30 to 5:30. MC, V, S accepted. Check telephone directories for 11 other Twin Cities locations.

Fabric Bargains

CALICO CORNERS, 7101 France Av. S., Edina. ►5
925-5600

Contemporary drapery and up-holstery fabrics, some designer fabrics, at up to 40 percent off regular retail prices. Open M, Thu 10 a.m. to 9 p.m.; Tue, W, F 10 to 6; Sat 10 to 5; Sun 1 to 5. MC, V accepted.

DO-IT-YOURSELF UPHOLSTERY SUPPLY, 1558 Larpenteur Av. W. (at Snelling Av.), Falcon Heights. ►9
645-7211

Mostly close-out and remnant fabrics sold at half off retail prices. Upholstery supplies also sold. Open M, Thu 9:30 a.m. to 7:30 p.m.; Tue, W, F 9:30 to 5:30; Sat 9:30 to 4.

FABRIC OUTLET, 5100 County Rd. 18, New Hope. ►4
535-3050

Mill ends and factory surplus, mostly dress fabrics, sold at discounts. Thread and notions also sold at reduced rates. Open M-F 8 a.m. to 6 p.m.; Sat 8:30 to 5.

FABRIC TOWN, 800 Hampden Rd., St. Paul. ►8
645-5721

Fabric outlet store selling remnants by the pound; some irregulars of bath towels and mats; cottons and cotton blends at about 40 percent off retail prices. Embroidery floss, transfers, other notions. Open M-F 9 a.m. to 4 p.m.; Sat 9 to 3. S accepted.

S. R. HARRIS INDUSTRIES, 5100 County Rd. 18, Hopkins. 535-3050. ►5

Warehouse selection of knit and woven yard goods, mostly mill overruns and close-outs, sold at half off retail prices. Sewing notions sold at large savings. Open

M-F 8:30 a.m. to 6 p.m.; Sat 8:30 to 5.

KIEFFER'S LINGERIE FABRICS AND SUPPLIES, 1625 Hennepin Av., Minneapolis. ►1
332-3395

All the materials and trimmings needed to construct ladies' lingerie, including hard-to-find patterns. Mail-order service available. Open M-F 9 a.m. to 4:30 p.m.; Sat 9 to 1.

MILL END FABRICS, Robin Center, 4066 Hwy. 52 N., Robbinsdale. ►4
533-4090

Wide assortment of overstocks from name-brand fabric manufacturers. Open M-F 10 a.m. to 8 p.m.; Sat 10 to 5; Sun noon to 5. Check telephone directories for four other Twin Cities locations. MC, V, S accepted.

NEEDLEWORK AND CRAFT SUPPLIES

BONITA MARIE'S NEEDLEPOINT SHOP, 841 Grand Av., St. Paul. ►8
224-9529

Custom-designed and hand-painted canvases for needlepoint. Materials for counted cross-stitch, other needle crafts. Open M-F 10 a.m. to 5:30 p.m.; Sat 10 to 5. MC, V accepted.

HOUSE OF MACRAME, 5416 Penn Av. S., Minneapolis. ►2
927-8307

Macrame and weaving supplies. Classes offered fall through spring. Open Tue-F 10 a.m. to 5:30 p.m.; Sat 10 to 5 (to 4 summer). Closed M summer.

KNIT AND PURL, 5027 France Av. S., Edina. ►5
926-8710

Needlepoint and crewel supplies, rugs, and counted thread. Open M-Sat 10 a.m. to 5 p.m. (closed M May through September). MC, V accepted.

NEEDLE NEST, 729 E. Lake St., Wayzata. ►5
473-2626

Needlepoint, cross-stitch, and knitting supplies. Open M-F 9:30 a.m. to 4 p.m.; Sat 10 to 4. V accepted.

NEEDLEPOINT ALLIE, 1110 Grand Av., St. Paul. ►8
226-9236

Needlepoint and rug-hooking supplies, footstools, and luggage racks. Open M-F 10 a.m. to 4:30 p.m.; Sat 10 to noon. Closed Sat summer.

NEEDLEWORK UNLIMITED, 3939 W. 50th St., Suite 210, Edina. ►5
925-2454

Needlepoint and counted-thread supplies, including thread, fabrics, and books. Classes and finishing services offered. Open M-F 9:30 a.m. to 4:30 p.m.

PICKET FENCE, 3907 W. 54th St., Minneapolis. ►2
920-7888

Needlepoint canvases and yarn. Open M-F 10 a.m. to 4 p.m; Sat 10 to 3.

STITCHVILLE & FRAME SHOP, 7 Hi Shopping Center,

Hwys. 7 and 101, Minnetonka. 474-1700 ►5

Retail needlecraft supplies and custom framing. Open M, Thu 10 a.m. to 8 p.m.; Tue-W, F-Sat 10 to 5. MC, V, S, Town and Country charge accepted.

THE YARNERY, Mac Market, 1648 Grand Av., St. Paul. ►8 690-0211

Yarn, weaving supplies, looms, etc. Classes offered throughout the year. Open M-Thu 9 a.m. to 8 p.m.; F-Sat 10 to 6.

TOYS AND GAMES

GAMES BY JAMES, Galleria, 3610 W. 70th St., Edina. ►5 925-9656

Games of every sort and variety, in a wide range of prices. Everything from Monopoly sets to electronic games to expensive, handmade backgammon and chess sets. Open M-F 10 a.m. to 9 p.m.; Sat 10 to 6; Sun noon to 5. Second location in Bonaventure, Minnetonka, 546-5446. AE, MC, V accepted.

HOBBITAT, Westbrook Mall, 5717 Xerxes Av. N., Brooklyn Center. ►4 560-8188

Educational toys, games, books, and rhythm instruments. Open M-F 10 a.m. to 9 p.m.; Sat 10 to 6; Sun (mid-Oct. to May only) noon to 5. MC, V, S accepted.

LEARN ME, 642 Grand Av., St. Paul. ►8 291-7888

Books and toys, especially those with educational value. Open M-F

10 a.m. to 6 p.m.; Sat 10 to 5. MC, V accepted.

MUGGINS DOLL HOUSE, Galleria, 3469 W. 69th St., Edina. ►5 922-8044

Handmade dollhouses and dolls and accessories. Open M-F 10 a.m. to 9 p.m.; Sat 10 to 6; Sun noon to 5. MC, V, S accepted.

ROSE AND THORN TOY-STORE, 4756 Chicago Av., Minneapolis. ►2 822-9525

Puppets, handcrafted and folk toys, some commercial name-brand items. Open Tue-F 10 a.m. to 6 p.m.; Sat 10 to 5.

TOYS 'N THINGS, 906 N. Dale St., St. Paul. ►8 488-7284

Children's books and toys, and books about childcare and parenting. Workshops on early childhood education. Open W 9 a.m. to 5 p.m.; Thu 5 p.m. to 8 p.m.; Sat 9 to noon. MC, V accepted.

TOYWORKS, Butler Square, 100 N. Sixth St., Minneapolis. ►1 332-4830

Imported and domestic handmade toys, dolls, kites, and a selection of children's books. Open M-F 10 a.m. to 9 p.m.; Sat 10 to 6; Sun noon to 5. Other stores at Galleria, Edina, 922-7505, and Bonaventure, Minnetonka, 545-2753.

THE TINKER BELL, INC., Wayzata Bay Center, Wayzata. 473-1650 ►5

Dolls, dollhouse miniatures, quality toys, as well as a complete hobby selection. Marklin miniature railway sets. Open M, F 9:30 a.m. to 9 p.m.; Tue-Thu, Sat 9:30 a.m. to 6 p.m. MC, V accepted.

FLORISTS

BACHMAN'S, 6010 Lyndale Av. S., Minneapolis. ▶2
861-7600

One of the largest florist-nursery operations in the country. Green plants, fresh-cut flowers, silk flowers, gifts, and garden supplies, as well as nursery stock are sold at the main store on Lyndale Av. Delivery, plant rentals available. Open M-F 9 a.m. to 8:30 p.m.; Sat 9 to 5:30; Sun 11 to 5. Check telephone directories for 14 other Twin Cities locations.

FIGS AND FERNS, 2405 Hennepin Av. S., Minneapolis. ▶2
377-2246

Green and flowering plants. Free advice on plant problems. Open M-F 11 a.m. to 6 p.m.; Sat 10 to 6.

HOLM AND OLSON, 159 Duke St., St. Paul. ▶8
222-7335

Twenty-four-hour answering service. Open M-Sat 8 a.m. to 5 p.m. Also at 20 W. Fifth St., St. Paul, 224-9641; open M-Sat 8 a.m. to 5 p.m.; and 2100 Snelling Av. N. (Har Mar Mall), Roseville, 631-1445; open M-F 9 a.m. to 9 p.m.; Sat 9:30 to 5:30; Sun 1 to 5 p.m. AE, MC, V, S accepted at all.

LINDSKOOG LATHAM FLOWERS, Northstar Center, 116 S.

Seventh St., Minneapolis. ▶1
333-5357

Fresh and silk flowers, green plants, gifts. Delivery and plant rentals available. Open M-F 8:30 a.m. to 5:30 p.m.; Sat 8:30 to 2. AE, MC, V, S accepted.

LYNDALE GARDEN CENTER, 6412 Lyndale Av. S., Richfield. 861-2221 ▶6

Huge array of lawn and garden supplies, plants and shrubs. Home-grown fruits and vegetables in season. Open M-Sat 8 a.m. to 10 p.m.; Sun 8 to 8.

MINNEAPOLIS FLORAL, 2420 Hennepin Av. S., Minneapolis. 377-8080 ▶2

Home-grown roses, plants, cut flowers, and gifts. Delivery available. Open M-Sat 8 a.m. to 6 p.m.; Sun 8 to 10:30 a.m.

PLANTS, INC., 10906 Wayzata Blvd., Minnetonka. ▶5
545-0898

Houseplants. Delivery available. Open M-F 9 a.m. to 9 p.m.; Sat 9 to 6; Sun noon to 6. AE, MC, V accepted.

TOBACCO

BILLY AND MARTY TOBACCONISTS, 829 Marquette Av., Minneapolis. ▶1
336-6653

Twenty-five house blends of pipe tobacco. Free delivery in downtown Minneapolis. Open M-F 9 a.m. to 5:30 p.m.; Sat 9:30 to 3. AE, MC, V, S accepted.

ST. MARIE TOBACCONISTS,

345 Wabasha St., St. Paul. ►7
291-8063

Fresh-cut gourmet blends of burley, cavendish, or Virginia are specialties. Mail orders. Also at American National Bank Building, E. Fifth and Minnesota Sts., St. Paul, 292-0983, and Peavey Bldg., 730 Second Av. S., Minneapolis, 339-2616. All open M-F 7 a.m. to 5 p.m. AE, MC, V, S accepted at all.

S. SUTTER TOBACCONIST, Leisure Lane, 7101 France Av. S., Edina. ►5
922-1561

Complete line of pipes, cigars, custom-blended tobaccos, and smoking accessories. Open M-F 9 a.m. to 8 p.m.; Sat-Sun 10 to 4. AE, V accepted.

TOBACCO ROAD, LaSalle Court, 41 S. Eighth St., Minneapolis. ►1
335-1315

Imported cigars and pipes, fast pipe repairs, and men's gift items. Open M, Thu 8:30 a.m. to 8 p.m.; Tue-W, F-Sat 8:30 to 6. Also at 201 S.E. Main St. (St. Anthony Main), Minneapolis, 379-4777; open M-Thu 10 a.m. to 9 p.m.; F-Sat 10 to 10; Sun noon to 6; and Southdale Center, Edina, 927-5550; open M-F 9:30 a.m. to 9:30 p.m.; Sat 9:30 to 6; Sun noon to 5. AE, MC, V accepted at all.

TOBAK SHOP, Highland, 2140 Ford Pkwy., St. Paul. ►8
698-3835

Tobacco and smoking supplies. Open M-Thu 9:30 a.m. to 9:30 p.m.; F-Sat 9:30 to midnight; Sun 9 to 6. AE, MC, V accepted.

BARGAIN STORES

The following stores offer a variety of merchandise at bargain prices. For an extensive listing of all types of bargains available in the Twin Cities, pick up a copy of *The Twin Cities Great Buy Guide*, Dorn Books, Edina, 1981, at your local bookstore, or write Dorn Books directly at 7101 York Av. S., Edina, MN 55435.

AX-MAN SURPLUS, 1639 University Av., St. Paul. ►8
646-8653

Hardware, electrical equipment, and miscellaneous bankruptcy merchandise sold at half or more off retail prices. Ax-Man has been in business for 30 years. Open M-F 9 a.m. to 6 p.m.; Sat 9 to 5.

M. F. BANK AND CO., 615 First Av. N.E., Minneapolis. ►2
379-2810

A wide variety of merchandise sold for the accounts of insurance companies at about one-half retail prices. Stock changes every week, but usually includes clothing. Open M-F 8:30 a.m. to 8:30 p.m.; Sat 8:30 to 5; Sun noon to 5.

B. & B. CLOSEOUTS, 525 W. Broadway, Minneapolis. ►2
588-1705

A variety of surplus and trucking salvage merchandise sold at varying discounts. Open M-Sat 11 a.m. to 5 p.m.

BROADWAY SALES, 1000 W. Broadway, Minneapolis. ►2
529-9577

Furniture, appliances, hardware, and other merchandise sold at varying discounts. Open M-F 9 a.m. to 8 p.m.; Sat 9 to 5; Sun 1 to 5 (not open every Sun). MC, V accepted.

BUDGET PAINT & WALL-PAPER, 4009 Minnehaha Av., Minneapolis. ►2
724-7676

Discontinued patterns of first-quality, major-brand wallpaper are sold at 60 to 80 percent off retail prices. About 100,000 rolls are in stock, 1,500 patterns on display. Open M, Thu 9 a.m. to 8 p.m.; Tue, W, F 9 to 5:30; Sat 9 to 5. MC, V accepted.

C.O.M.B. CO., 6850 Wayzata Blvd., Golden Valley. ►4
541-9700

Tools, sporting goods, and a variety of other merchandise sold at an average of half off retail prices. Open M-F 9 a.m. to 9 p.m.; Sat 9 to 5; Sun 10 to 6. AE, MC, V accepted.

CRAZY LOUIE'S SURPLUS CITY, 839 University Av., St. Paul. ►8
291-8035

Tools, household items, health and beauty aids, and a variety of other items sold at an average of half off retail prices. Open M, Thu 9 a.m. to 9 p.m.; Tue, W, F 9 to 6; Sat 9 to 5; Sun 11 to 5. MC, V, S accepted.

DIAMOND VOGEL PAINT CENTERS, 2020 N. Second St., Minneapolis. ►2
521-4707

Factory retail salesroom sells paints, stains, and varnishes at 10

to 40 percent off retail prices. Open M-F 8 a.m. to 5 p.m.; Sat 8:30 to noon. Also at 6315 Cedar Av., Richfield, 869-7581; open M-F 7:30 a.m. to 4:30 p.m.; Sat 8:30 to noon. MC, V accepted.

MONTGOMERY WARD'S BARGAIN OUTLET STORE, 1700 Wynne Av. (at warehouse), St. Paul. ►8
647-2275

Surplus and damaged furniture and major appliances sold at varying discounts. Open M-F 9 a.m. to 9 p.m.; Sat 9 to 5:30. MC, V, Ward's charge accepted.

MONTGOMERY WARD'S CATALOG SURPLUS STORE, 1400 University Av., St. Paul. ►8
647-2100

Overstocks and surplus catalog items, mostly clothing and other soft lines, sold at varying discounts. Also at 1425 S. Robert St., West St. Paul, 647-2595. Both open M-F 9:30 a.m. to 9 p.m.; Sat 9:30 to 5:30; Sun noon to 5. MC, V, Ward's charge accepted at both.

NORTH ST. PAUL OUTLET, 2535 E. Seventh Av., North St. Paul. ►9
777-6765

Liquidation and discontinued merchandise of every description sold at 10 to 50 percent off retail prices. Open M-F 9 a.m. to 6 p.m.; Sat 9-5. S accepted.

J.C. PENNEY OUTLET STORE, Phalen Shopping Center, 1441 E. Magnolia St., St. Paul. ►8
774-0371

Catalog overstocks of clothing,

furniture, small appliances, toys, and other merchandise sold at 30 percent off retail prices. Open M-F 9:30 a.m. to 9 p.m.; Sat 9:30 to 5:30; Sun noon to 5. V, Penney's charge accepted.

SEARS RETAIL OUTLET STORE, 2700 N.E. Winter St., Minneapolis. ►2
874-3636

Mostly furniture and major appliances sold at varying discounts. Open M-F 9 a.m. to 9 p.m.; Sat 9 to 5. Sears charge accepted.

SEARS SURPLUS STORE, 1907 Suburban Av., St. Paul. ►8
739-4330

Catalog surplus clothing, toys, and household goods sold at varying discounts. Also at 9056 Penn Av. S., Bloomington, 884-5317; 6199 N.E. Hwy. 65, Fridley, 571-8010. Stores open M-F 9 a.m. to 9 p.m.; Sat 9 to 6; Sun noon to 5.

STANGEL'S FACTORY DISCOUNT & VARIETY STORES, 9955 W. 69th St., Eden Prairie. 941-0650 ►5

More than 1,000 categories of brand-name, first-quality general household merchandise liquidated at 30 to 70 percent off regular retail prices. Open M-Sat 10 a.m. to 6 p.m. Second location at 212 Water St., Excelsior, open M-Sat 9 a.m. to 7 p.m.; Sun noon to 5. MC, V, S accepted.

SYLVESTER SALES CO., Hwy. 65 and 219th Av. N.E., East Bethel. ►9
434-9571

Household goods and clothing, including factory irregulars of Oshkosh jeans and work clothes, sold at varying savings. Open M-Tue, Thu-Sat 9 a.m. to 5:30 p.m.; W 9 to 9; Sun noon to 5:30. MC, V, S accepted.

TRADER JACK'S FACTORY OUTLET STORE, 615 N. Third St., Minneapolis. ►1
339-1998

Housewares, sporting goods, toys, and other items sold at 30 to 60 percent off retail prices. Open M-F 9 a.m. to 5 p.m.; Sat 9 to 3. Hours vary; call ahead. MC, V accepted.

Nokomis Community Library in south Minneapolis.

Chapter Twenty

COMMUNITY SERVICES

KEY NUMBER
For information on services and referral for all kinds of problems, 24 hours a day, call First Call for Help: 340-7431.

The state of Minnesota is a nationally recognized leader in the delivery of social services. In the Twin Cities alone there are more than 2,000 government, private, and volunteer organizations providing a variety of services to meet human needs.

This listing is necessarily incomplete. It is intended as a handy reference for frequently requested services. Many services have not been included. For more information, call one of the referral services listed below, or check your telephone book under the listings for the county in which you reside. The following listings are arranged by category. An alphabetical index to services is provided at the back of this book.

INFORMATION SERVICES

FIRST CALL FOR HELP, 404 S. Eighth St., Minneapolis. ►1
340-7431

Provides information and referrals from a computerized file of 2,000 community resouces dealing with all kinds of problems. Open 24 hours.

(See Locator Key Map, pages 8-9)

►1 Mpls. Downtown
►2 Mpls. Excluding Downtown
►3 Mpls. North Suburbs
►4 Mpls. Northwest Suburbs
►5 Mpls. Southwest Suburbs
►6 Mpls. South Suburbs

►7 St. Paul Downtown
►8 St. Paul Excluding Downtown
►9 St. Paul North Suburbs
►10 St. Paul Northeast Suburbs
►11 St. Paul Southeast Suburbs
►12 St. Paul South Suburbs

HENNEPIN COUNTY LIBRARY SYSTEM, 7001 York Av. S., Edina. ►5
830-4900

Operates main library (Southdale-Hennepin Area Library) at the above address and 23 branches (check telephone directory locations). Main library open M-Thu 10 a.m. to 9:30 p.m.; F-Sat 10 to 5; Sun noon to 5 (closed Sun summer). Call 830-4933 for information on almost any subject.

MINNEAPOLIS PUBLIC LIBRARY AND INFORMATION CENTER, 300 Nicollet Mall, Minneapolis. ►1
372-6500

In addition to the central library at the above address, there are 14 community libraries (listed under "Public Libraries" in the phone book) throughout the city. Pocket areas are served by a bookmobile, which makes weekly stops. For those who can't get out to a library due to age or illness, the Friends of the Minneapolis Public Library provide Service to the Homebound. Besides books, the library lends magazines, records, tapes, cassettes, films, pictures, filmstrips, slides, and videocassettes. Answers to most any question are provided both over the phone and in person. Call the central library (open M-Thu 9 to 9; F, Sat 9 to 5:30; closed Sat summer) at the above number to find out your nearest library or for general information.

RAMSEY COUNTY PUBLIC LIBRARY, 2180 Hamline Av. N., Roseville. ►9
631-0494

Operates main library at the above address and four branch libraries (check telephone directory for locations). Main library open M-Thu 9:30 a.m. to 9 p.m.; F, Sat 9:30 to 5 (Sat 9:30 to noon summer); Sun 1 to 5. Call the above number for information on almost any subject.

ST. PAUL PUBLIC LIBRARY, 90 W. Fourth St., St. Paul. ►7
292-6311

Operates main library at the above address, 10 branch libraries, and a bookmobile. Special summer activities for children; monthly program calendar available at all libraries. Main library open M, Thu 9 a.m. to 9 p.m.; Tue-W, F, Sat 9 to 5:30 (closed Sat summer). Call 292-6307 for information on almost any subject.

CRISIS SERVICES (HOT LINES AND COUNSELING)

CONTACT TWIN CITIES
341-2896

Provides 24-hour telephone counseling and information and referral. No fee.

CRISIS INTERVENTION
347-3161

Provides 24-hour emergency telephone and walk-in service at Hennepin County Medical Center, 701 Park Av. S., Minneapolis. Provides referrals for additional help. Suicide-prevention services. No fee.

EMERGENCY SOCIAL SERVICE
291-6795

Telephone service available 5

p.m. to 8 a.m. providing emergency shelter, food, counseling referral, and sometimes transportation. No fee.

N.I.P. RAPE COUNSELING CENTER
825-4357

Provides counseling for any rape-related problem. Office open M-F 9 a.m. to 8 p.m.; telephone answered 24 hours. No fee.

WALK-IN COUNSELING CENTER, 2421 Chicago Av., Minneapolis. ►2
870-0565

Provides free,short-term counseling, crisis intervention, and referrals to individuals, couples, and families. Services provided by volunteer mental health professionals. No appointment necessary. Open M, W 1 to 3 p.m., 7 to 9 p.m.; Tue, Thu 7 to 9 p.m. Donations accepted.

YOUTH EMERGENCY SERVICE (YES), 608 20th Av. S., Minneapolis. ►2
339-7033

Provides 24-hour emergency counseling and referral service concerning drug abuse, suicide prevention, venereal disease, and other problems. For those of all ages—not just youth. TTY facilities available. No fee.

GENERAL SOCIAL SERVICES

HALLIE Q. BROWN-MARTIN LUTHER KING CENTER, 270 N. Kent St., St. Paul. ►8
224-4601

Provides family, employment, and senior citizens' services; medical and dental clinic; recreational activities, day care, and summer day-camp; cultural arts programs. Open M-F 8 a.m. to 10 p.m.; some weekend hours. Fees vary with program. Clinic hours M, F 8 a.m. to 5 p.m.; Tue 8 a.m.-9 p.m.; W 8 a.m. to 6 p.m.; Thu 8 a.m. to 4:30 p.m.; Sat 8 to noon.

HENNEPIN COUNTY BUREAU OF SOCIAL SERVICES, 300 S. Sixth St., Minneapolis. ►1
348-8125, 348-4357

Provides aid to needy persons in the form of counseling, financial assistance, chemical-dependency services and medical assistance, foster care, aid for dependent children, food stamps, and emergency assistance. Open M-F 8 a.m. to 4:30 p.m.; telephone answered 24 hours a day. No fee.

JEWISH COMMUNITY CENTER, 1375 St. Paul Av., St. Paul.
698-0751 ►8

Provides social and educational services for pre-schoolers to the elderly. Membership fee, but some services do not require membership. Religious affiliation not required. Hours vary, but include evenings.

LORING-NICOLLET-BETHLEHEM COMMUNITY CENTER, 2539 Pleasant Av., Minneapolis. ►2
872-8811

Provides a variety of community and social services. Programs include a pre-school nursery, employment services, alternative high school programs, a senior program, and cultural arts programs. Also located at 1920 Pillsbury Av. and W. 26th St. and Grand Av. Office open M-F 7 a.m. to 4 p.m. (closed during lunch hour). Fees vary by program.

MINNEAPOLIS URBAN LEAGUE, 1121 12th Av. N., Minneapolis. ►2
377-0011

Provides social work and equal-opportunity services to minority groups to help promote positive interracial relations. Open M-F 9 a.m. to 5 p.m. No fee.

PILLSBURY-WAITE NEIGH-BORHOOD SERVICES, INC., 3501 Chicago Av. S., Minneapolis. ►2
827-5814

Four neighborhood centers and two camps provide a variety of social services and camping experiences for all ages. Other locations at 2529 13th Av. S. (721-1681), 2318 29th Av. S. (721-6691), and 1507 S. Fifth St. (338-5282).

PILOT CITY REGIONAL CENTER, 1315 Penn Av. N., Minneapolis. ►2
348-4700

Provides emergency food assistance, housing counseling, transportation, tool and equipment lending, home maintenance, and information and referral services. Open M-F 8:30 a.m. to 5 p.m. No fee.

RAMSEY COUNTY COMMUNITY HUMAN SERVICES DEPARTMENT, 160 E. Kellogg Blvd., St. Paul. ►7
298-5351

Provides aid to needy persons who meet the eligibility requirements for the federally and state funded public assistance and medical assistance programs. Open 8 a.m. to 6 p.m. Telephones answered 8 to 4:30. No fee.

SABATHANI COMMUNITY CENTER, 3737 Third Av. S., Minneapolis. ►2
827-5981

Provides food and clothing shelves, counseling, recreation programs, elderly services, and emergency housing. Open M-F 8 a.m. to 9 p.m.; summer 8 to 7. Calls answered after hours by tape giving emergency numbers. No fee.

ST. PAUL URBAN LEAGUE, 401 Selby Av., St. Paul. ►8
224-5771

Provides community services in cooperation with the Ramsey County Welfare Department, including housing and economic-development programs. Open M-F 9 a.m. to 5 p.m. No fee.

URBAN COALITION OF MINNEAPOLIS, 89 S. 10th St., Minneapolis. ►1
348-8550

Provides social services primarily to low-income people and people of color. Programs cover weatherization, employment, housing, education, and criminal justice. Open M-F 8 a.m to 5 p.m. No fee.

PHYLLIS WHEATLEY COMMUNITY CENTER, 919 Fremont Av. N., Minneapolis. ►2
374-4342

Provides recreation program,

counseling, day care, social services, summer day-camp, and latch-key program. Red Cross office in building. A special family violence project is offered to men who batter and women involved in those relationships. Office open M-F 9 a.m. to 5 p.m. Fees based on ability to pay and vary with program.

GENERAL FAMILY SERVICES

CATHOLIC CHARITIES OF THE ARCHDIOCESE OF ST. PAUL AND MINNEAPOLIS, 404 S. Eighth St., Minneapolis. ►1
340-7500
Provides information, referral, and placement services for children in adoptive homes or boarding houses; pre- and post-adoption counseling to adoptive parents; individual, couple, group, family, and pre-marriage counseling; chemical-dependency program, refugee resettlement services, teen shelters, and services for the elderly. Open M, F 8:30 a.m. to 4:30 p.m.; Tue 8:30 to 6; W 8:30 to 9. No religious affiliation necessary. Fees based on ability to pay. St. Paul location at Old Sixth and Main Sts. (222-3001).

CENTER FOR RATIONAL LIVING, 2130 Fairways Lane, Roseville. ►9
631-2046
For-profit service provides individual, family, and marriage counseling, sponsors seminars and discussion groups on assertiveness, child rearing, rational living,

and behavior therapy. Sessions by appointment. Telephone answered 24 hours a day. Fees based on ability to pay.

CHILDREN'S HOME SOCIETY OF MINNESOTA, 2230 Como Av., St. Paul. ►8
646-6393
A statewide, voluntary, child and family social service agency established in 1889. Provides pre-adoption counseling, placement and post-placement services for Minnesota residents interested in local and inter-country adoption; post-legal adoption services; counseling to unwed, expectant parents; arrangement of temporary foster care for children; day care and parenting support services at seven locations; and support and guidance for single mothers and their children at two residential treatment centers. Open M-F 8:30 a.m. to 5 p.m.; telephone answered 24 hours for emergencies. No fee for pregnancy counseling. Other fees vary with service and ability to pay.

FAMILY AND CHILDREN SERVICE, 414 S. Eighth St., Minneapolis. ►1
340-7444
Provides counseling and information on marriage and divorce, parent-child relationships; family life education and family advocacy programs. Fees based on ability to pay.

FAMILY SERVICE OF GREATER ST. PAUL, INC., 333 Sibley St., St. Paul. ►7
222-0311
Provides counseling and educa-

tional services relating to marriage, pre-marital relationships, parent-child relationships, personal growth, and emotional stress. Programs include crisis intervention, travelers aid, and services to seniors. Open M, Thu 8:30 a.m. to 9 p.m.; Tue, W 8:30 a.m. to 6 p.m.; F 8:30 a.m. to 5 p.m.

JEWISH FAMILY AND CHIL-DREN'S SERVICE, La Salle Court, 811 La Salle Av., Minneapolis. ▶1
338-8771

Provides individual, family, educational, and vocational counseling; job placement, foster family care, and rehabilitation services. Special services to the elderly and family life education. Volunteer opportunities. Open M-W, F 8:30 a.m. to 5:30 p.m.; Thu 8:30 a.m. to 9 p.m. Tape recording provides emergency telephone numbers to after-hours callers. Fees based on ability to pay.

JEWISH FAMILY SERVICE, 1546 St. Clair Av., St. Paul. ▶8
698-0767

Provides personal, marital, and family counseling on short-term or continuing basis. Religious affiliation not required. Open M-F 9 a.m. to 5:30 p.m. and W evenings by appointment. Fees based on ability to pay.

LUTHERAN SOCIAL SERVICES OF MINNESOTA, Metro/West: 2414 Park Ave., Minneapolis ▶2 (871-0221); Metro/East: 1201 Payne Av., St. Paul ▶8 (774-9507).

Provides individual and family counseling; group counseling by interest or need; services to unwed parents; residential programs for retarded children and adults, emotionally troubled teenage girls, young adult male felons. Serves people of all faiths. Adoption program limited to couples who are members of a Christian church.

A community that cares about its elderly.

Offices open M-F 8:30 a.m. to 5 p.m. Evening appointments and groups available. Fees based on ability to pay. Counselors also available in some suburban locations.

PARENTS WITHOUT PARTNERS, 1095 Jenks Av., St. Paul 55106. ►8
771-6647

Sponsors activities, programs, and counseling for single parents and their children. Part of international organization. Write or call for locations of Twin Cities area branches. Membership fee.

YOUTH SERVICES

BOYS CLUBS OF MINNEAPOLIS, 2410 Irving Av. N., Minneapolis. ►2
522-3636

Provides organized sports, music, arts, crafts, and other activities for boys and girls 7 to 18. Facilities include gymnasium and pool. Affiliated club at 3835 Fifth Av. S., Minneapolis, 822-3191. Clubs open Tue-F 3 to 9 p.m. and Sat 10 a.m. to 5 p.m. during the school year; M-F 11 a.m. to 7 p.m. summers. Membership $2 for children 12 to 18, $1 for children 7 to 11.

BOYS CLUB OF ST. PAUL, 375 St. Anthony Av., St. Paul. ►8
224-7515

Open to boys and girls 6 to 18. Call for details on recreational programs. Hours vary, usually Tue-F 4 to 9 during the school year; M-F 9 to 5 summers. A second location is at 287 E. Winifred St., St. Paul, 224-5116.

BRIDGE FOR RUNAWAY YOUTH
377-8800

Twenty-four-hour telephone service for crisis intervention and referral. Provides temporary emergency shelter, food, counseling, medical attention, and recreational program for runaway youth. No fee.

FACE TO FACE HEALTH AND COUNSELING SERVICE, 730 Mendota St. (East Seventh & Minnehaha), St. Paul. ►8
772-2557

Provides pregnancy and venereal-disease testing, short-term counseling (personal, family, drug, sex), and services for abused adolescents. Pregnancy/parenting support services and employment program. Operates community outreach education program. Telephone answered M, W, F 9 a.m. to 5 p.m.; Tue, Thu 9 to 9. Fees based on ability to pay.

MINNEAPOLIS YOUTH DIVERSION PROGRAM (MYDP), 111 E. Franklin Av., Suite 206, Minneapolis. ►2
871-3613

Provides counseling, advocacy, and support for troubled youth. Office hours M-F 8:30 to 4:30; counseling hours are flexible.

ST. PAUL YOUTH SERVICE BUREAU, 1021 Marion St., St. Paul. ►8
292-7191

Provides outreach counseling and referral services for youth and families. Open M-F 8:30 a.m. to 5 p.m. No fee.

TEEN-AGE MEDICAL SERVICE, 2425 Chicago Av. S., Minneapolis. ►2
874-6125, 874-6126

Provides confidential, out-patient, general medical care including dermatology, nutrition, and pregnancy- and venereal disease-testing by appointment (call at least two days in advance). Also provides classes on and examinations for birth control. Open M, F 9 a.m. to noon, 1:30 to 5; Tue, W 1:30 to 5 and 6 to 8 p.m.; Thu 1:30 to 5. Yearly fee of $10, or $4 for each appointment. No one turned away.

WASHBURN CHILD GUIDANCE CENTER, 2430 Nicollet Av. S., Minneapolis. ►2
871-1454

A mental-health agency for children. Offers diagnostic and counseling services to troubled children under 14. Cooperates with other Twin Cities agencies on children's mental-health problems. Open M-F 8:15 a.m. to 5 p.m.

WILDER CHILD GUIDANCE CLINIC, 919 Lafond Av., St. Paul. ►8
642-4000

Provides psychiatric services including diagnosis, treatment, and consultation for those 18 and younger with emotional, behavioral, educational, or personality problems. Open M, W, F 8:30 a.m. to 5 p.m.; Tue, Thu 8:30 to 8. Fees based on ability to pay. Other locations at 13760 Nicollet Av., Burnsville (894-6800) and 2696 Hazelwood Av., Maplewood (770-1222).

YOUNG WOMEN'S CHRISTIAN ASSOCIATION (YWCA), 1130 Nicollet Av., Minneapolis. ►1
332-0501

Provides a variety of services and activities. Open M-F 6:30 a.m. to 10 p.m.; Sat 8 to 6; Sun noon to 6. Check telephone directories for other locations. Membership fee.

YOUTH ACTION, 5005 Valley View Rd., Edina. ►5
926-1851

Provides counseling for youth with psychological, emotional, drug, or behavioral problems. Also provides community education and outreach programs and a temporary crisis home. Open M-F 9 a.m. to 5 p.m. and by appointment. Recording gives emergency telephone numbers after hours. No fee.

SERVICES FOR THE ELDERLY

LITTLE BROTHERS OF THE POOR, 1845 E. Lake St., Minneapolis. ►2
721-6215

Serves elderly shut-ins in Minneapolis and St. Paul. Provides transportation, meals, home visits, advocacy, and a variety of other services to help elderly persons remain independent. Open M-F 9:30 a.m. to 5:30 p.m. Also 24-hour telephone service. No fee.

METROPOLITAN SENIOR FEDERATION, 1951 University Av., St. Paul. ►8
645-0261

Offers discount buying through

a coalition of seniors' groups; supports legislative change aimed at improving the quality of life for seniors; offers a comprehensive health-care program. Open M-F 8:30 a.m. to 5 p.m. Membership fee.

MINNEAPOLIS AGE AND OP-PORTUNITY CENTER, 1801 Nicollet Av., Minneapolis. ▶2 874-5525

Provides assistance, information, and referral services to seniors with medical, dental, and transportation problems. Operates "meals-on-wheels" and health-care programs. Open M-F 8:30 a.m. to 5 p.m. Fees based on ability to pay and program. Some programs available in limited geographical area.

MINNESOTA BOARD ON AG-ING, 204 Metro Square, St. Paul 55101. ▶7 296-2770

Provides information on and referral to a number of services available to senior citizens. Write for a free copy of its booklet, entitled *Minnesota's Services for Seniors.* It contains brief descriptions of more than 300 programs that the board funds. For telephone referrals, seniors in Hennepin County can call 340-7431; in Anoka County, 421-4760; in Carver County, 488-3661; in Dakota County, 894-2424.

SOCIAL SECURITY ADMINIS-TRATION DISTRICT OFFICE, 1811 Chicago Av., Minneapolis. ▶2 378-1151

Provides information and benefits to qualified individuals 62 and older, survivors of covered workers and disabled persons. Also provides Medicare information. Open M-F 9 a.m. to 4:30 p.m. No fee.

UNITED SENIORS, INC., 2507 N. Fremont Av., Minneapolis. ▶2 529-9267

Provides advocacy and referrals for seniors and others with health, housing, food, employment, legal, Social Security, and other problems. Chore service, located at 2100 Emerson Av. N., provides home-maintenance services for Northside seniors. Open M-F 9 a.m. to 5 p.m. No fee.

WOMEN'S SERVICES

ELIZABETH BLACKWELL WOMEN'S HEALTH CENTER, 730 Hennepin Av., Minneapolis. ▶1 872-1492

Provides a nine-session health class, speakers bureau, patient advocacy, referral and counseling on women's issues.

CHRYSALIS CENTER FOR WOMEN, 2104 Stevens Av., Minneapolis. ▶2 871-2603

Multi-service women's center with chemical-dependency outpatient treatment program, diagnosis and referral, crisis intervention, counseling, information and referral, and support groups. Treatment program for children of women in CD treatment. Legal Assistance for Women (L.A.W.) Clinic provides free legal advice, divorce seminars, and legal information seminars. Fees for some services; sliding fee scale. Crisis intervention, information and referral M-F 9 a.m. to 8 p.m.

MINNESOTA WOMEN'S CENTER, 306 Walter Library, 117 Pleasant St. S.E., University of Minnesota, Minneapolis. ►2
373-3850

Provides academic, employment, and financial-aid information, mostly to women. Open to the general public and includes an excellent resource library. Open M-F 8 a.m. to 4:30 p.m. No fee.

NATIONAL ORGANIZATION FOR WOMEN (Twin Cities Chapter), P.O. Box 9629, Minneapolis 55440.
776-7195

The oldest and largest of seven Twin Cities area NOW chapters holds meetings the second Sunday of every month. Fifteen committees work on issues of concern to women. At this writing, their top priority is working against "pro-life" bills and amendments. For information on other chapters, contact Minnesota NOW, Box 3365, St. Paul 55165, 298-0999. Membership open to men and women. Membership fee.

SAGARIS, 2619 Garfield Av., Minneapolis. ►2
872-8866

Provides group and individual counseling in a mental-health collective for women. Sessions by appointment only. Fees based on ability to pay.

WOMEN'S ADVOCATES CEN-

TER, 584, 588 Grand Av., St. Paul. ►8
227-8284

Provides information, referrals, and shelter for battered women. Open 24 hours, seven days a week. No fee.

WORKING OPPORTUNITIES FOR WOMEN, 2233 University Av., St. Paul. ►8
647-9961

Provides help to women who are unemployed, underemployed, or financially disadvantaged. Services include counseling on the job market, personal change, and problems on the job. Open M, W 8:30 a.m. to 9 p.m.; Tue, Thu-F 8:30 to 5. Fees vary with program. Scholarships available. Second location at 2344 Nicollet, Suite 240, Minneapolis (874-6636).

AMERICAN INDIAN RESOURCES

BUREAU OF INDIAN AFFAIRS, 15 S. Fifth St., Minneapolis. ►1
349-5040

Provides social and employment services, education information, credit help, and tribal operations services. Open M-F 8 a.m. to 4:30 p.m. No fee.

MINNEAPOLIS AMERICAN INDIAN CENTER, 1530 Franklin Av. E., Minneapolis. ►2
871-4555

Provides a variety of social services for native Americans, including social and cultural programs. Open M-F 8 a.m. to 4:30 p.m. No fee.

ST. PAUL AMERICAN INDI-AN CENTER, 1001 Payne Av., St. Paul. ►8
776-8592

Provides human services (including advocacy for welfare problems, emergency food needs, and counseling), employment training and assistance, and legal services. Open M-F, 8 a.m. to 5 p.m. No fee.

ST. PAUL AMERICAN INDI-AN MOVEMENT, 643 Virginia Av., St. Paul. ►8
488-7267

Provides emergency social services such as transit, housing, and food, as well as employment services, job referral and placement, legal services, short-term counseling, and advocacy with the Ramsey County Welfare Dept. Open M-F 8:30 a.m. to 5 p.m. No fee.

UPPER MIDWEST AMERI-CAN INDIAN CENTER, 113 W. Broadway, Minneapolis. ►2
522-4463

Multi-service coordinator of American Indian activities. Sponsors Minnesota American Indian Historical Society, senior and child welfare programs, community classes, and other activities. Also sponsors a Sunday morning television program called *Madagimo.* Serves non-Indians as well. Open M-F 8 a.m. to 5 p.m.

HISPANIC RESOURCES

CENTRO CULTURAL CHI-CANO, 1800 Olson Memorial Hwy., Minneapolis. ►2
374-2996

Provides welfare, housing, and senior advocacy programs for Spanish-speaking people. Employment, counseling, and translation services available. Open M-F 8:30 a.m. to 5 p.m.

HISPANOS EN MINNESOTA, 551 State St., St. Paul.
291-7403 ►8

Housing counseling and advocacy; financial, employment, and chemical dependency counseling; health outreach and referral; veteran's service program. Open M-F 8:30 a.m. to 5 p.m. No fees.

INTERNATIONAL LIAISON

INTERNATIONAL INSTITUTE OF MINNESOTA, 1694 Como Av., St. Paul. ►8
647-0191

Provides English classes for refugees, foreign-language classes, and coordinates refugee sponsor programs. Classes at reduced rates to members. Open M-F 8:45 a.m. to 5 p.m.

MINNESOTA INTERNATION-AL CENTER, 711 E. River Rd., Minneapolis. ►2
373-3200

Community volunteer organization that provides liaison between international visitors and students and the people in Minnesota communities, by arranging professional appointments, home stays, hospitality, tours, seminars, discussion groups, speakers bureau, language bank, English classes, and a variety of social and cultural programs. Participation is free and open to all. Office hours M-F 9 a.m. to 5 p.m.

SERVICES FOR GAYS

CHRISTOPHER STREET, 2344 Nicollet Av. S., Minneapolis. ►2 874-7877

Provides counseling and support services for lesbians with sexual or chemical abuse problems. Open M-F 10 a.m. to 10 p.m.

GAY COMMUNITY SERVICES, 2855 Park Av. S., Minneapolis. ►2 827-2821

A counseling, information, and referral service for the Twin Cities gay community. Open M, W 9 a.m. to 10 p.m.; Thu 9 a.m. to 7 p.m.; F 9 a.m. to 5 p.m.; Sat 10 a.m. to 1 p.m.

LESBIAN RESOURCE CENTER, 2104 Stevens Av. S., Minneapolis. ►2 871-2601

Drop-in center for lesbians offers library, support groups, and workshops. Open M, W, F 10 a.m. to 4 p.m.; Tue, Thu 10 a.m. to 8 p.m.

SERVICES FOR PEOPLE WITH PHYSICAL DISABILITIES

COURAGE CENTER, 3915 Golden Valley Rd., Golden Valley. 588-0811 ►4

Provides comprehensive rehabilitation services for children and adults with physical disabilities and speech, hearing, and vision impairments. Services include physical and occupational therapy; vocational rehabilitation (including counseling, placement, and evaluation for computer-related work); transitional residence for disabled young adults (Courage Residence); speech, language, and hearing therapy; hearing-aid loan; adult activity program; communication resource center for non-vocal persons; therapeutic preschool and children's services; home health services; equipment loan; rehabilitation engineering; independent living services (including model Courage Independent Living Home); library services; Handi-Ham amateur radio system; driver education; sports; recreation; camping; and public awareness and education programs. Courage Center services are available regardless of a person's ability to pay.

HEALTH SERVICES

AMERICAN CANCER SOCIETY, 2750 Park Av., Minneapolis. ►2 871-2111

Provides education programs relating to early cancer detection and treatment. Also offers information and services to cancer patients and their families. Call M-F 8:30 a.m. to 4:30 p.m. Second location at 2233 University Av., St. Paul.

HENNEPIN COUNTY MEDI-CAL SOCIETY, Suite 423, Health Associations Center, 2221 University Av. S.E., Minneapolis. ►2
623-3030

Provides physician-referral service (623-9555) M-F 9:30 to 11:30 a.m., 1 to 3 p.m. No fee.

MINNEAPOLIS DISTRICT DENTAL SOCIETY, INC., Metropolitan Medical Office, Suite M08, 825 S. Eighth St., Minneapolis. ►2
332-0443

Provides dentist-referral service. Telephone answered M-F 8 a.m. to 4:30 p.m. with answering service after hours. Call 333-5052 for emergency 24 hours a day.

MINNEAPOLIS PUBLIC HEALTH DEPARTMENT, 250 S. Fourth St., Minneapolis. ►1
348-2301

Provides a variety of health services to city residents, including maternity, family planning, child health and immunization clinics, health and drug education, communicable disease control, foreign travel certificates, and home nursing services. Also handles complaints about unsanitary conditions in restaurants and lack of compliance with the Clean Indoor Air Act. Open M-F 8 a.m. to 4:30 p.m. No fee for most services.

RAMSEY COUNTY MEDICAL SOCIETY, 215 Lowry Medical Arts Bldg., St. Peter St. between Fourth and Fifth Sts., St. Paul. 291-1209 ►7

Provides information, aid, complaint review, and doctor referrals (291-1981). Also maintains Boeckmann Medical Library (224-3346). No fee.

RED DOOR CLINIC, 527 Park Av., Minneapolis. ►1
347-3300

Provides diagnosis and treatment of venereal disease. Walk-in service only; no appointments. Hours vary; call for schedule. Donations accepted.

ST. PAUL DENTAL SOCIETY, 649 Lowry Medical Arts Bldg., St. Peter St. between Fourth and Fifth Sts., St. Paul. ►7
222-7817

Provides information, referrals, and mediation in patient-dentist problems. Open M-F 8:30 a.m. to 4 p.m. No fee.

ST. PAUL-RAMSEY COMMUNITY MENTAL HEALTH CLINIC, 529 Jackson St., St. Paul. ►7
298-4737

Provides clinical treatment, training, and consultation for those suffering from emotional, mental, and related disorders. Open M-F 8 a.m. to 4:30 p.m.; referral service after hours. Fee based on ability to pay.

TEL-MED, 721-7575

Provides three-to-five-minute tape recordings on some 250 health-related topics, plus referrals to sources of additional information and help when appropriate. Tel-Med will send a list of available topics on request. M-F 10 a.m. to 7 p.m. No fee.

WEIGHT WATCHERS, 309 Parkdale III, 5354 Cedar Lake

Rd., St. Louis Park. ▶5
546-3546

For-profit organization providing lectures, counseling, diets, and special group sessions for anyone with a weight problem. Meetings held throughout the Twin Cities area; call for locations and times. Office open M-F 9 a.m. to 5 p.m. Membership fee.

HUMAN REPRODUCTION

ABORTION EDUCATION AND REFERRAL SERVICE, 3255 Hennepin Av., Minneapolis. ▶2
825-4147

Provides educational materials and information on abortion and alternatives. Open M-F 9 a.m. to 4:30 p.m.; telephone messages taken after hours. No fee.

BIRTHRIGHT, INC., 512 Nicollet Mall, Room 633, Minneapolis. ▶1
338-2353

Provides pregnancy testing, counseling, and referral services to any woman with a troubled pregnancy. A "pro-life" organization. Also at 1549 University Av., St. Paul 646-7033. Hours vary; generally by appointment. 24-hour telephone service. No fee.

CHILDBIRTH EDUCATION ASSOCIATION, 2101 Hennepin Av. S., Minneapolis. ▶2
874-1362

Provides 2½-hour class covering nutrition, exercises, and pre-natal care, plus a one-evening class on Caesarean-section births. Classes on various methods of

prepared childbirth offered at several locations. Fees for most classes. Outreach services available.

LA LECHE LEAGUE, 4908 Quail Av. N., Crystal. ▶4
535-3962

Provides moral support and technical knowledge about breast-feeding through monthly meetings and telephone counseling.

MEADOWBROOK WOMEN'S CLINIC, 6490 Excelsior Blvd., St. Louis Park. ▶5
925-4640

Private organization provides abortions by physicians on an outpatient basis, abortion counseling, contraception information, and referrals to other community resources. Open M-F and alternate Sat and Tue evenings. Telephone answered 8 a.m. to 5 p.m. Fees.

PLANNED PARENTHOOD OF MINNESOTA, 1965 Ford Pkwy., St. Paul. ▶8
698-2401

Provides pregnancy tests, sex education, contraception supplies and medical exams, and abortion counseling and clinics, and referrals for infertility problems. Clinics at Inland Bldg., 127 S. 10th St., Minneapolis, 336-8931, and 110 Hamm Bldg., 408 St. Peter St., St. Paul, 224-1361. Open M-F 9 a.m. to 4:30 p.m. Call for Sat and evening hours. Fees based on ability to pay.

ST. PAUL DIVISION OF HEALTH, FAMILY PLANNING PROGRAM, 555 Cedar St., St. Paul. ▶7
292-7735

Provides all medically accepted

methods of birth control, as well as sterilization services, pregnancy testing and counseling, infertility counseling, nutrition services, and physical exams. Open M-F 8 a.m. to 4 p.m. No residency requirement for services. Other clinics located in White Bear Lake and New Brighton. Fees based on ability to pay.

CHEMICAL DEPENDENCY

ALCOHOLICS ANONYMOUS, 1925 Nicollet Av., Room 203, Minneapolis. ►2
874-1447

Provides information and referral service for any alcoholic, family, and friends 24 hours a day. No fee.

ALCOHOLISM AND DRUG ABUSE COUNSELING AND

REFERRAL SERVICE (Family Service of Greater St. Paul), Nalpak Bldg., Suite 500, 333 Sibley St., St. Paul.
222-0311 ►7

Provides alcohol- and drug-use assessment, referral, education, and intervention. Individual, family, and group counseling for alcohol and drug concerns. Aftercare counseling also available. Fees based on sliding scale. Day and evening appointments.

EDEN HOUSE, 1025 Portland Av., Minneapolis. ►1
338-0723

Residential therapeutic drug-abuse treatment center for those with a long history of addiction who have had treatment elsewhere that has failed. Fees often can be paid by government welfare agencies.

HENNEPIN COUNTY CHEMICAL DEPENDENCY DEPART-

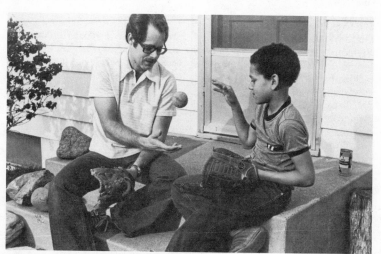

The Big Brother program at work in the Twin Cities.

MENT, 1800 Chicago Av., Minneapolis. ►2
348-7994

Services provided to anyone who is chemically dependent. Staffed 24 hours. No fee.

HENNEPIN COUNTY DETOX-IFICATION CENTER, 1800 Chicago Av., Minneapolis. ►2
347-6111

Provides 24-hour service as a detoxification center and entry point for care of persons who are intoxicated or in withdrawal. Fees based on ability to pay.

HENNEPIN COUNTY METHA-DONE REHABILITATION PROGRAM, 1800 Chicago Av., Minneapolis. ►2
347-6051

Provides rehabilitation, therapy, referral services, and education for candidates with a two-year history of opiate addiction. Open 6 a.m. to 4:30 p.m. No fee.

JOHNSON INSTITUTE, 10700 Olson Memorial Hwy. (Hwy. 55), Plymouth. ►4
544-4165

Non-profit center provides counseling and referral services for treatment of alcoholism, chemical addiction, and related personal and social problems. Downtown office for Employee Assistance Programs located in Suite 4421, IDS Tower, Minneapolis. Open M-F 8 a.m. to 5 p.m. and evenings by appointment. Fees vary.

NEW CONNECTION PRO-GRAMS, 73 Leech St., St. Paul. 224-4384 ►8

Provides primary inpatient, outpatient, and long-term residential treatment and counseling for adolescents and families with drug-related problems. Open M-F 8 a.m. to 4:30 p.m.

PHARM HOUSE CRISIS CEN-TER, 1911 Pleasant Av. S., Minneapolis. ►2
870-7088

Provides clinical treatment, counseling, referral, and resource services for any youth or family needing drug-abuse help. Open seven days a week 9 a.m. to midnight. Fees based on ability to pay.

RAMSEY COUNTY RECEIV-ING CENTER FOR INEBRI-ATES, 155 Second St. (Jackson Annex), St. Paul. ►7

Provides detoxification, evaluation, and referral on a 24-hour emergency basis. Fee of $71 per day is usually covered by insurance or medical-assistance programs.

ST. MARY'S HOSPITAL AL-COHOLISM TREATMENT CENTER, 2414 S. Seventh St., Minneapolis. ►2
338-2229

Provides intensive treatment and counseling for those with alcohol and chemical-dependency problems. Aftercare and family involvement an important part of program. Open seven days a week 8 a.m. to 8:30 p.m. Fee.

ST. PAUL INTERGROUP AL-COHOLICS ANONYMOUS, 951 E. Fifth St., St. Paul. ►7
776-6566

Provides 24-hour telephone information on all area AA branches. No fee.

ST. PAUL-RAMSEY MEDICAL CENTER CHEMICAL DEPENDENCY SERVICE, 640 Jackson St., St. Paul. ►7
221-8802

Provides emergency detoxification, medical services, residential treatment, outpatient services, family counseling, and probate court evaluations for anyone seeking chemical-dependency rehabilitation. Open M-F 8 a.m. to 4:30 p.m. After hours call 221-2121 for emergencies and ask for social worker.

TWIN TOWN TREATMENT CENTER, 1706 University Av., St. Paul. ►8
645-3661

For-profit organization providing residential and outpatient therapy for chemically dependent persons and their families on a 24-hour-a-day basis. Fees.

CHILD CARE SERVICES

CHILD CARE RESOURCE CENTER—SOUTHSIDE, 3602 Fourth Av. S., Minneapolis. ►2
823-5261

Provides workshops, a newsletter, and referrals to child-care centers in south Minneapolis. Open M-F 9:30 a.m. to 5 p.m.

GREATER MINNEAPOLIS DAY CARE ASSOCIATION, Ramar Bldg., Room 104, 111 E. Franklin Av., Minneapolis. ►2
371-3103

Coordinating agency for child care throughout Hennepin County provides services to centers and parents, including computerized information and referrals, public education, and information on the state's sliding-fee program. Open M-F 8 a.m. to 5 p.m.

HENNEPIN COUNTY DAY CARE INFORMATION AND REFERRAL SERVICE, Community Services-Community Resources Division, 1300 Government Center, 300 S. Sixth St., Minneapolis. ►1
348-6688

Provides telephone and mail referrals to licensed day care centers and homes in Hennepin County. Open M-F 8 a.m. to 4:30 p.m. No fee.

RAMSEY COUNTY REFERRAL SERVICE, 160 E. Kellogg Blvd., St. Paul. ►7
298-4260

Provides referrals to day care centers and homes in Ramsey County. Open M-F 7:45 a.m. to 6 p.m. No fee.

LEGAL SERVICES

DIVORCE REFORM, INC., 11702 Cartier Av., Burnsville. ►6
894-7200

Provides assistance to people before, during, and after divorce. Helps members with "do-it-yourself" divorce, or provides referral to an attorney. Telephone messages taken 24 hours; consultations by appointment only. Membership fee.

LAWYER REFERRAL INFOR-

MATION SERVICE
339-8777

Non-profit telephone referral service. Open M-F 9 a.m. to 5 p.m. $15 fee for half-hour conference with a lawyer.

LEGAL RIGHTS CENTER, INC.
871-4886

Court defense program that provides legal assistance for low-income persons involved in criminal cases. Telephone answered 24 hours a day. No fee.

TEL-LAW
227-5297

Telephone tape service that operates 24 hours a day. Provides short tapes on 125 different common legal problems, including estate settlement, adoption, divorce, and civil law. No fee.

VETERANS SERVICES

MINNESOTA DEPARTMENT OF VETERANS AFFAIRS, Veterans Service Bldg., St. Paul. 296-2562 ►8

Administers veterans service programs for the state of Minnesota. Open M-F 8 a.m. to 4:30 p.m.

VETERANS RESOURCE CENTER, 2610 University Av., St. Paul. ►8
376-5084

At this writing, federal funding cuts were forcing the Veterans Resource Center to severely limit its programs. The center is open to all veterans regardless of discharge, and provides help with

V.A. problems and discharge review. Some educational and employment programs are offered. Open M-F 8 a.m. to 4:30 p.m.

CIVIL RIGHTS

MINNEAPOLIS DEPARTMENT OF CIVIL RIGHTS, 2649 Park Av., Minneapolis. ►2
348-7736

Handles complaints about acts of discrimination in employment, real estate, lending, public accommodations, public services, or education on the basis of race, color, creed, religion, ancestry, national origin, sex, affectional preference, disability, age, marital status, or status with regard to public assistance. Open M-F 8 a.m. to 4:30 p.m.

MINNESOTA CIVIL LIBERTIES UNION, 628 Central Av., Minneapolis 55414

Contact the MCLU by mail concerning membership and problems relating to civil liberties.

MINNESOTA DEPARTMENT OF HUMAN RIGHTS, Bremer Tower, Fifth Floor, E. Seventh and Minnesota Sts., St. Paul. ►7
296-5667

Enforcement agency that handles complaints of illegal discrimination in Minnesota. Bilingual (Spanish-English) staff services available. Open M-F 8 a.m. to 4:30 p.m.

ST. PAUL DEPARTMENT OF HUMAN RIGHTS, 515 City Hall, W. Kellogg Blvd. at Waba-

sha St., St. Paul. ►7
298-4288

Handles complaints of discrimination in employment, housing, education, public accommodations, and public services in St. Paul. Open M-F 8 a.m. to 4:30 p.m. No fee.

DRAFT COUNSELING

FRIENDS FOR A NON-VIOLENT WORLD, 1925 Nicollet Av., Suite 101, Minneapolis. ►2
870-1501

Provides counseling and information on the draft and registration. Also concerned with nuclear energy, disarmament, and related topics. Open M-F 9 a.m. to 5 p.m.

CIVIC CONCERNS

CENTER FOR URBAN ENCOUNTER, 3416 University Av. S.E., Minneapolis. ►2
331-6210

Provides consultation, community organizing, seminars, training courses, and information and referrals on metropolitan issues. Open M-F 9 a.m. to 5 p.m. Fees vary.

CITIZENS LEAGUE, 84 S. Sixth St., Minneapolis. ►1
338-0791

Provides research and education on public affairs issues affecting the metropolitan area. Publishes public affairs directory for the Twin Cities. Membership fee. Office open M-F 8 a.m. to 5 p.m.

LEAGUE OF WOMEN VOTERS

OF MINNESOTA, 555 Wabasha St. Paul. ►7
224-5445

The League of Women Voters gathers and distributes material on issues of concern to citizens; it also provides information on voting rights and procedures. Most information is provided free. Open M-F 9 a.m. to 4 p.m. Call the Minnesota chapter for the location of your nearest League office. Membership is open to both men and women.

CONSUMER INFORMATION

BETTER BUSINESS BUREAU OF MINNESOTA, INC., 1745 University Av., St. Paul. ►8
646-4633 (inquiry)
646-4631 (complaint)

Promotes honesty and dependability in advertising and selling, furnishes information and reports on businesses to aid consumers, and helps customers and businesses settle complaints. Open M-F 8:15 a.m. to 4 p.m.; telephone answered 9 to 4. No fee.

CONSUMER-HOME ECONOMICS INFORMATION, University of Minnesota Extension Service
373-0912

Answers questions on housekeeping, furnishings, food and nutrition, food preservation, and clothing. Open M-F 8:30 a.m. to noon and 1 to 4 p.m. No fee.

GENERAL MILLS, INC.—BET-

TY CROCKER CONSUMER CENTER
540-2187

Answers telephone questions on cooking and baking, menu-planning, recipes, and General Mills products. Available M-F 9:30 a.m. to 3:30 p.m. No fee.

INTERNATIONAL MULTI-FOODS CONSUMER KITCHEN
340-3493

Provides telephone answers to questions on baking. Open M-F 7:50 a.m. to 4:35 p.m. No fee.

MINNESOTA INSURANCE IN-FORMATION CENTER, Soo Line Bldg., S. Fifth St. at Marquette Av., Minneapolis. ►1
339-9273

Provides information and answers questions on insurance. Open M-F 8 a.m. to 4 p.m. May to October; 8:30 to 4:30 winter. No fee.

MINNESOTA FUNERAL IN-FORMATION BUREAU, 943 Plymouth Bldg., 12 S. Sixth St., Minneapolis. ►1
332-4058

Provides information on funerals, death and dying, and related subjects. Also acts as a referral service for funeral directors. Open 9 a.m. to 4:30 p.m. No fee.

MINNESOTA GAS CO. CON-SUMER SERVICES, 372-4670

Answers food and household-related questions and provides energy information. Open M-F 8 a.m. to 5 p.m. No fee.

NORTHERN STATES POWER CO. CONSUMER INFORMA-TION SERVICES
330-6000

"Ask NSP" about appliances, insulation, or just about any other home energy-related topic. If more information is needed, call 330-6789. Open M-F 8 a.m. to 5 p.m. No fee.

OFFICE OF CONSUMER SERVICES, STATE OF MINNE-SOTA, Metro Square Bldg., Room 128, E. Seventh and Robert Sts., St. Paul. ►7
296-2331

Mediates individual consumer complaints, conducts in-depth studies of selected consumer problems, and enforces consumer-fraud and toy-safety laws. Many complaints can be taken over the telephone. Open M-F 8 a.m. to 4:30 p.m. No fee.

PILLSBURY CO. CONSUMER SERVICES, 840 Pillsbury Bldg., 608 Second Av. S., Minneapolis 55402. ►1
330-4728

Answers questions by telephone or mail about Pillsbury, Green Giant, and American Beauty food products, and about recipes in Pillsbury cookbooks. Open M-F 8 a.m. to 4:30 p.m. No fee.

ST. PAUL MAYOR AND COUNCIL INFORMATION AND COMPLAINT OFFICE, City Hall, Room 179, Wabasha and Kellogg, St. Paul. ►7
298-4747

Provides information and complaint resolution for St. Paul citizens regarding city services, programs, and policies. General clearing house for information on city government. Open M-F 8 a.m. to 4:30 p.m.

FOR MORE INFORMATION

First Call for Help, 1981 Directory of Community Services, Department of United Way of Minneapolis, MN 55404. Comprehensive alphabetical listing of community services, cross-listed by subject. Provides information on services, eligibility, funding, hours, and fees for each organization listed. Also includes a register of volunteer opportunities listed by area of interest. Two-page listing of reduced-priced goods and services available to senior citizens. 344 pages; $7.50 plus postage and handling.

Index

411

Restaurant Index